LIONEL
A Collector's Guide and History

Volume II: Postwar

Other Books and Videos
by Tom McComas and James Tuohy

Volumes in the Lionel Collector's Guide Series

Volume I: Prewar O Gauge
Volume II: Postwar
Volume III: Standard Gauge
Volume IV: 1970–1980
Volume V: The Archives
Volume VI: Advertising & Art

Lionel Price & Rarity Guides

Postwar 1945–1969, No. 1
Postwar 1945–1969, No. 2
Prewar 1900–1945
1970–1989
1970–1992

Books

Great Toy Train Layouts of America
Collecting Toy Trains

Videos

Lionel: The Movie
Great Layouts of America Series, Parts 1–6
Toy Train Revue Video Quarterly
The History of Lionel Trains
The Making of the Scale Hudson
Fun and Thrills with American Flyer
I Love Toy Trains
The New Lionel Showroom Layout
How to Build a Layout
Lionel Postwar
1991 Lionel Video Catalog
1992 Lionel Video Catalog

LIONEL

A Collector's Guide and History

Volume II:
Postwar

Second Edition

By Tom McComas & James Tuohy

PHOTOGRAPHY BY JACK LANE & TOM McCOMAS

Chilton Book Company
Radnor, Pennsylvania

For Judge John Marshall Tuohy,
Tom and Christopher Mack

Library of Congress Catalog Card Number: 76-13314
ISBN 0-8019-8508-0
Manufactured in the United States of America

CONTENTS

INTRODUCTION

The purpose of this book, of course, is to provide the collector with a useful guide for collecting Lionel trains, and in this regard, the authors believe, the book has been successful. There is a tremendous amount of technical information in the book, covering almost every piece Lionel made between 1945 and 1969.

But there is also much of casual interest in the book, we believe, and this is important, too. Collecting is not some sort of solemn struggle, but something that should be fun, and something that can be enjoyed on several different levels by people with varying degrees of knowledge. The authors would like to think that their books satisfy the needs of the various kinds of collectors — and perhaps some non-collectors whose interest in the hobby might be piqued enough to climb aboard.

As always, the authors had a great deal of help from collectors all over. Not all of them can be singled out but all of them are remembered by us with appreciation. But we would like to mention a few people who have been of special help to us and foremost among these is John Palm, whose knowledge of Lionel trains could easily fill two volumes of this size — perhaps even 10 volumes; his expertise seems unlimited. Thanks, too, to Dave Garrigues for his important contributions and proof-reading. A special thanks should also be given, for a wide variety of support, advice or information, to Richard Baibak, Ed Barbret, Bill Burke of the Santa Fe, Lennie Dean, Harriet Heyman of the *New York Times,* Chet Holley, Leonard Jagelski, Dr. Bob Jones, Jane Ann Piercy, LaRue Shempp, Bob Stein of the Lionel Corporation, Bob Spangler, Bill Vagell and Bill Vezzosi.

One of the hardest problems in making a book like this is getting all the trains that have to be photographed at one place at one time. There are photos in the book made up of trains that belong to as many as eight different collectors. Assembling these items, items that in most cases were extremely rare and valuable, required extraordinary cooperation on the part of the collectors. It was a terrible imposition on them, but the collectors we called on cooperated beautifully. We would like to thank them. They include Dave Garrigues, Fred and Bert Ott, John Palm, Frank Petruzzo, Rick Pozsgay, Earl Rath, Chuck Roehm, Rich Sherry, Matt Volpe, and Hunter von Unshuld.

HISTORY

Joshua Lionel Cowen, who founded the Lionel Manufacturing Company in a second-story loft in New York City in 1900, seemed an unlikely prospect, in the early years of his life, to become a business tycoon.

The young Cowen was, as his parents remarked rather uncomfortably, a "tinkerer." He was constantly fooling with things around the house, idling away hours on strange experiments. He built his first train at the age of seven. He carved a reproduction of a locomotive out of wood, then installed a tiny steam engine of his own design. Unfortunately, it exploded and nearly blew up the kitchen.

Joshua Lionel Cowen.

He also tinkered with electricity, which was then, in the late 1800s, a relatively unharnessed and frightening phenomenon. His experiments with electricity made his parents no more comfortable than his experiments with steam engines in the kitchen.

Apparently concluding that Joshua's creative energies should be channeled into something useful, his parents eventually sent him to Columbia University to study engineering. But Joshua Cowen had a mind too restless to be constrained by formal education. He dropped out of school after a year and went to work as an assembler at the Acme Electric Light Company in New York City, one of the few businesses in the country manufacturing electrical goods at that time.

He kept tinkering at night, though, conducting experiments in the basement of the house. He developed a fuse to ignite the magnesium powder used by photographers for their early flash bulbs. This invention brought him to the attention of the U.S. Navy Department. The Spanish - American War was on and the Navy was searching for a dependable mine detonator. Joshua received a contract for 24,000 of his fuses.

At the age of 18, he opened a small shop on the lower east side of Manhattan to produce the detonators. However, when the contract was completed and the war over, Joshua Cowen found himself with a shop and some capital, but nothing to produce.

Back to tinkering, searching for a marketable product. He developed and discarded a number of devices. Then he developed a slender dry-cell battery, placed it in a metal tube and attached a small light bulb to the end. Joshua Cowen thought he had a terrific use for this invention. He would put it in a flower pot so when the light was turned on it would illuminate the plants.

A man named Conrad Hubert was so excited about Cowen's electrified flower pot that he went on the road to sell them. Cowen and Hubert did all right, but Cowen's enthusiasm for the pots diminished and he sold the business to Hubert. Hubert, too, saw the limitations of electric flower pots, but he did see another use for the portable light tube. He started the Eveready Flashlight Company.

Joshua Cowen was back tinkering again.

Soon he perfected a tiny electric motor. It was a fine motor, he had to admit, but what could he do with it? He considered and rejected a few ideas and then decided to manufacture electric trains. He gave the company his middle name and Joshua Lionel Cowen was in business again.

Cowen's first toy model was a crude, wooden gondola with the motor and a battery concealed underneath. The car, plus 30 feet of track, sold for $6. The same car, without the motor, sold for $2.25.

The appeal of Lionel's train was immediate, but sales were restricted because of limited manufacturing capabilities and the fact that few homes had electricity in 1900. But the use of electricity increased and so did business. Lionel produced its first catalog in 1903 and its first locomotive the following year. It was a model of the electrics used in the Baltimore tunnels by the Baltimore & Ohio. The B&O was the only American railroad using electric locomotives at that time.

The very early Lionel trains were built to run on two-rail tracks that were 2-7/8" gauge, but in 1906 Cowen decided to come out with a three-rail track that was 2-1/8" gauge. Lionel was the first company in America to use this track. Cowen called it Lionel Standard and had the name patented. The track, made of tin plate, was an important contributor to the growth of Lionel and other electric toy train manufacturers who soon adopted it. The Ives Company, for instance, converted to the three-rail track in 1910.

One company that never did convert to the three-rail track was the Knapp Electric & Novelty Company, an early train manufacturer. Knapp eventually quit making electric trains around 1913. Years later, Louis Hertz, the erudite writer and authority on model railroading, asked David W. Knapp, the firm's founder, why he stopped train production.

"Well, for two reasons," replied the elderly Knapp. "First, I felt that they were only a passing fad. And secondly, a couple of fellows named Cowen and Ives came along with their new, improved track."

And that tin-plate track is still being used today.

From the words tin plate, comes the single word "tinplate, and the name sometimes causes confusion. Tin plate is iron or steel covered by a thin coat of tin. Very old trains used to have some tin plate in their construction, but none do now. Only the tracks are made of tin plate. But the name "tinplate" has come to mean a type of mass-produced toy train — like Lionel's — as opposed to hand-made scale model trains. People who collect and operate these mass-produced toy trains are therefore called "tinplaters."

The 1906 Lionel catalog — the first featuring the new Standard gauge track — displayed an electric trolley car, the No. 1 Trolley that all prewar collectors covet. In later years even Joshua Cowen was to wish he had a No. 1 Trolley. He found out that one of the country's premier collectors, LaRue Shempp of Williamsport, Pennsylvania, had a No. 1 Trolley in almost mint condition.

"What would you take for that No. 1 Trolley you've got?" Cowen asked Shempp one day. "That is, provided you ever want to get rid of it."

"I would like a nickel-plated GG-1 to dress up the Congressional Set in my collection," answered Shempp.

Cowen then surprised Shempp by having a nickel-plated GG-1 with copper and brass trim specially made up. He gave it to Shempp.

"Keep me in mind if you ever want to trade that No. 1 Trolley,'" said Cowen. So Shempp now has the only nickel-plated, copper and brass trimmed GG-1 in existence.

The Lionel Company began mass production in 1910 and five years later started manufacturing O gauge along with their popular Standard gauge. They did not foresee then that O gauge, ⅞″ narrower than Standard, would eventually become the more popular track, as the average-size home became smaller and finding room for the big Standard gauge became a problem. Within 25 years after it started making O gauge, Lionel would cease the manufacture of Lionel Standard entirely.

Lionel's first catalog appeared in 1903 and it grew with business. Cowen showed an early flair for promotion and advertising. He was not content to publish a catalog which merely listed the items for sale, their pictures and their prices. He included little feature stories about the company and feverish sales pitches towards his potential customers.

"Come On Boys! I'll Show You Why Lionel Trains Are Better," reads a headline at the beginning of the 1915 catalog. Next to the headline is a photograph of 35-year-old J. Lionel Cowen (his hair starting to recede) and he is telling the boys he is going to take them on a photographic journey through the Lionel factory — "Fun Factory" — to show them how the trains are put together.

After showing how solid Lionel cars are, the catalog has a picture of a competitor's model. The car looks awful. The top is off, and the sides, popped out of the ends, lie dented and awry. The whole thing looks as if it had been burnt with a torch. Under the picture is the caption: "Weak insecure car body."

"Now you can see why Lionel locomotives and cars stand the racket for years and years," says J. Lionel Cowen to the boys. "They will last from five to ten times as long as the flimsy, rickety construction shown in Figure 5 (that sad hulk just described). Show this superior construction (Lionel's) to your parents, and when they buy you a gift, they will want to invest in one that will last for many, many years."

After the pictorial tour of Fun Factory is over, Cowen tells the boys to take their Lionel catalog with them to their toy dealer so they can point out exactly what they want — Lionel.

"Don't get stung. Many a boy has been mighty sorry that he got for Christmas a cheap train and track that wouldn't last anywhere as long as the Lionel."

A half-century later, television commercials for Saturday morning cartoons would employ the same technique used by Joshua Lionel Cowen in his early catalogs — getting kids to tell their parents what products they wanted.

Cowen did not restrict his advertising to catalogs, however. As early as 1929 the company was sponsoring a radio program, the star of which was "Uncle Don" Carney, a well-known children's program actor. Uncle Don was the "Chief Engineer" of the newly formed Lionel Engineers Club and he was forever singing a song to the tune of "Casey Jones." It began like this:

> Come all you club members if you want to hear
> A story about a young engineer.
> Lionel is the little fellow's name
> And he always runs a Lionel electric train.

About this time Cowen started *Lionel Magazine*. Then he dreamed up a promotion that would tie in both the radio program and the magazine. Uncle Don had a contest to determine who had the best home Lionel train layout. Contestants were encouraged to send in pictures of their layouts. The winner would receive $250 in gold and have a picture of the layout published in the magazine. There were also some runner-up prizes.

The judges of the contest included Cowen, Don Carney and two railroad executives. Cowen had a dinner for the judges at his Manhattan apartment the night they were to select the winners. There was a Lionel train running around the huge dinner table carrying appetizers and cigars. It could be stopped at any diner's plate by a flick of an individually controlled switch.

It must have been a marvelous scene: Uncle Don, old Josh and the heads of the Lackawanna and Erie railroads sitting around the dinner table, looking at pictures and passing celery and nuts to one another on a Lionel freight. That hors d'oeuvres set would have made a great collectors' item.

By 1917 Lionel had a new factory located in Irvington, New Jersey — accounting for the name of the later, and now valuable, passenger car — but World War I had begun and the company was converting its facilities to accommodate war production.

Although the manufacture of electric trains was not halted entirely, most of the company's output was devoted to war work. Lionel made compasses, compensating binnacles, azimuthal periscopes and Signal Corps apparatus.

Three decades later, at the start of World War II, Lionel again went into war production, this time stopping the manufacture of its miniature trains entirely. Lionel perfected an oil-filled compass to replace the alcohol-filled instrument used since the 18th Century. For the Signal Corps, Lionel produced high-speed telegraph keys and wind-indicating equipment. They also turned out transformers for radar equipment.

Lionel's technicians encountered a problem in painting compass bowls, however. The whites of day-old eggs were required as binder for the paint, but it was difficult to get enough fresh eggs for the job. They solved this problem by raising their own chickens in one area of the plant. Of course, they were stuck with a lot of leftover egg yolks, but they took care of those by serving omelets in the company cafeteria.

The years between the wars were ones of great change for the nation's railroads. The key to the change was the growth of the diesel engine. In 1933 there were only about 100 diesels in operation throughout the United States and they were all in switching and transfer service.

Then, in May of 1934 amid a great deal of publicity, the Burlington ran a stainless steel, diesel-powered, articulated train called the Zephyr from Denver to Chicago in 13 hours and five minutes, an average speed of 77.5 miles per hour. It passed through more than 150 cities and towns along the way and it was estimated that a half-million people watched it streak by. The Zephyr caught the imagination of the public and in November of 1934 it was put into regular service.

The Union Pacific followed the Zephyr with a custom-built diesel of their own, the M-10000 Streamline, but like the Zephyr, the M-10000 was a permanently coupled train and its engine could not be used for normal service.

The railroads had doubts about converting to diesel power because the early engines were not versatile. At the same time, the railroads had seen how the public had taken to the Zephyr and M-10000. So they compromised. They started "streamlining" their steam locomotives, placing special cowlings over the engine body and painting them bright colors.

Some of the railroads employed top industrial designers, such as Raymond Loewy, Henry Dreyfuss and Otto Kuhler, to style their trains. The New York Central had Dreyfuss streamline their J-3 Hudsons with a nose that looked like the helmet worn by ancient Roman sentinels. Loewy came up with sleek coverings for the Pennsylvania's K-4 Pacifics and later designed the S-1 duplex 6-4-4-6 shown at the New York World's Fair of 1939. That S-1 was the largest steam passenger locomotive ever made, but it was not a very good one.

Other examples of streamlining were the much publicized Milwaukee Road line's Hiawatha, the Southern Pacific Daylights, and the Norfolk & Western Js, the most powerful 4-8-4s ever made and the last of the streamlined steamers to operate in the United States.

Lionel kept abreast of the streamlining developments. The 1937 catalog featured their own versions of the New York Central's Commodore Vanderbilt, the Pennsy's Loewy-styled K-4s and the Hiawatha set, which is one of the most valuable of all prewar collectors' items. Lionel also showed a couple of diesels in 1937 — the Flying Yankee, a Budd-built train similar to the Zephyr, and a reproduction of the M-10000.

Overall view of an extensive O gauge railroad that features operation on three levels: a double track main line, a mountain division and a subway system. Many of the devices used on this layout can be purchased commercially, others are built from scraps.

Lionel showroom layout, 1952.

Photo courtesy of Carstens Publications.

There was nothing unusual about Lionel keeping abreast of developments. Cowen, a short (five feet, five inches), explosive man of enormous energy, was once called by the *New Yorker* magazine, "Perhaps the country's most far-sighted railroader." Cowen sat on the board of directors of several corporations and on those same boards were several railroadmen. Cowen, the toy railroad king, was not afraid to admonish big railroad executives.

"If you're a railroader you need to keep your track in shape, put out new engines and car models and work up other modern equipment — in short, step out of the 1890's," he once said at a meeting of the board of an insurance company. He had a favorite saying, which he repeated at that meeting and many others: "Keep moving. Never stand still. You stand still and you're moving backward."

By the time the streamlining era arrived, Lionel dominated the toy train manufacturing field and all the railroads routinely sent Lionel blueprints of their newest locomotives and rolling stock, hoping for Lionel to reproduce them. Cowen liked to look at the blueprints himself and he was always looking for something different. Once the Southern Railroad sent plans for a new cattle car. Cowen studied them.

"Phooey!" he shouted to no one in particular. "Rejected! This number was hauling mules for the Confederate Army and it was antiquated then!"

Cowen would often shout around the office in sudden flashes of anger but most of his employees were used to it. They understood his volatile disposition and were less intimidated by such eruptions of temper than amused by them. From all reports, and from interviews with former Lionel employees it appears Cowen was uniformly respected and liked by his subordinates.

His enthusiasim was infectious and he never seemed to tire of looking at Lionel products in action. Sometimes he would wander into the New York showroom, which had a large operating layout and was open to the public, and pretend he was just one of the visitors. In coat and hat, he would mingle with a group of parents and children, for instance, and begin shilling his own products.

"Marvelous, aren't they?" he might ask, and then point to a locomotive puffing into view. "They tell me the smoke comes from little pellets you insert in the stacks. Some kind of chemical process. Watch her now as she comes around the curve."

Occasionally he would, with feigned trepidation, work a control at the panel at the side of the layout, pointing out some feature he was afraid the other spectators might have missed. But the layout was changed frequently and there were times when a confused Cowen would ensnarl the situation rather than clarify it. He would abruptly drop his role as ordinary citizen and yell at one of the Lionel employees in the room.

"How the devil does this thing work? Why doesn't someone label these confounded buttons, anyway?"

Although Cowen was quick to produce the prewar Union Pacific and Boston & Maine diesels, their sales were not outstanding and the leader of line during the

streamlining era was still a steamer, the scale model 700E Hudson. Cowen loved the Hudson and had the dies made in Italy and took an intense personal interest in the supervision of its construction. The 700E was the finest single piece the company ever made.

"It was the most beautiful thing my eyes ever beheld," Cowen said about it years later.

The quarter-inch scale model sold for $75, a huge sum in those days, which probably accounts for its scarcity today.

The New York Central used the Hudson for a number of years to pull its most prestigious passenger train, the 20th Century Limited. Before Lionel came out with their scale Hudson, the company had made a Standard gauge engine that vaguely resembled the prototype. The 1931 catalog, in fact, had the engineer of the 20th Century Limited, Bob Butterfield, pictured on the cover. Butterfield and his two grandsons were standing in front of a real Hudson and the engineer was holding a Lionel model while saying to the boys: "Just like mine."

The slogan always drew snickers from train collectors, who knew that the loco Butterfield was holding was a 4-4-4, while the real loco was a 4-6-4.

"Well, it wasn't quite 'Just like mine'," Butterfield admitted after his retirement in the late 1930s. "It lacked one axle. But nowadays they have that axle on their models."

Steamers—although not the Hudson—continued to dominate the Lionel line in 1946 and 1947, the first two years of real production after the war. Lionel brought out its version of the Pennsylvania Railroad's S-2 direct-drive steam turbine. By this time diesels were beginning to take over the operations of the railroads and the S-2 was a last ditch effort by the Pennsy to keep the steam locomotive alive on their line. The Lionel model was a good one and, in appreciation, the Pennsylvania gave Lionel a 5-foot-high, 10-foot-long wooden model of the S-2. It greeted visitors to the showroom for years.

Lionel had some difficulty getting the 1946 catalog printed. The World War II paper shortage was not over when it was time to print the book and the company could not get enough paper to meet its demands. To reach more customers, the advertising department decided to take an ad out in *Liberty* magazine. It was one of the largest print ads in history. Lionel bought 16 consecutive color pages in the center of the magazine, which had a circulation of 8½ million. The pages contained the entire catalog minus the cover. The cover of *Liberty* was a picture of a boy and his father playing with a Lionel train.

The year 1948 was really the beginning of the diesel era for Lionel. They brought out the Santa Fe and New York Central F-3s. The colorful red, silver and yellow Santa Fe F-3, shown in some form every year from 1948 through 1966, was to become the most popular engine Lionel ever made. Cowen, although naturally aware of the popularity of the diesels in the Lionel line, never was a big diesel fan himself. His heart was still with the steamers and electrics right up until his retirement in 1958. He liked the action of the driving rods on steamers and when describing it he would simulate the action with his arms.

"I am not an anti-diesel man," he once said. "They make a pretty engine, but they give a dull performance. They lack movement. I like the electrics, though. They sort of slide along like a real pretty snake. I could watch them for hours."

Cowen was an enthusiastic supporter of the trend toward action cars. When the milk car was new in 1947 Cowen was often to be found in the New York showroom, watching the little man flip out cans for an hour at a time. He became just as excited about the operating cattle car.

"Children want to participate," he would say. "They want movement and action. They don't just want to watch a train go around and around. A few minutes of that and the little nippers will wander off and squeeze out some toothpaste or set fire to the curtains. They've got to get in on the action."

The streamlined diesels revolutionized the graphics of railroading. The flat, smoother surfaces of the locomotives lent themselves to splashy designs and toy manufacturers had a wide variety of eye-catching cars to pick as prototypes. The bright Santa Fe markings, for instance, were a natural for Lionel's F-3. And Santa Fe, as pointed out in the F-3 section of this book, was eager to have Lionel use their road name and paid for one-fourth the cost of the dies. The New York Central paid for one-fourth and General Motors paid for one-fourth.

Through the years Lionel and other toy train manufacturers set up special sections responsible for the selection of prototype and road names. At Lionel, the decision was usually reached by a consensus of Joshua Cowen's son, Lawrence, the president of the corporation; Joshua, the chairman of the board, and Arthur Raphael, the executive vice president. Also consulted were Joseph Bonnano, the chief engineer, and Charles Giaimo, the works manager.

The decision to select a particular railroad name for an item depended on several factors, including the area of the country the railroad serviced, the road's familiarity to the public, the appeal of the graphics and colors, and the sales records, if any, of units that carried the railroad's name in the past.

Sometimes Lionel designers looked through thousands of pages of road heralds and car colorings. And, of course, Joshua Cowen and the other executives looked at the blueprints that the eager railroads sent to Lionel. Suggestions by train collectors and other enthusiasts were also considered, but more often, Cowen claimed, the suggestions they received were already under consideration or had been rejected. One suggestion that was apparently followed was the milk car. According to an article in *Town Journal* magazine in 1953, a teenager had submitted drawings and patents of a milk car from which a plastic man unloaded milk cans. Lionel was already working on such a car, but since the youngster had a workable patent, the company entered into a royalty deal with him and used his idea.

The writer of the article in *Town Journal* listed some other suggestions which had been submitted to Lionel, including one the writer clearly considered too farfetched for Lionel to even consider: "drawings of a proposed device for having a brakeman kick a plastic hobo off a freight train."

If new dies were needed for an item, the selected railroad, as mentioned, would often pay for part of their cost. In the case of the Timken 6464 car, for instance, Timken paid for the tools required to stamp "Timken" on the side. Six-hundred thousand miniature billboards were supplied free by one of the nation's largest outdoor advertising firms, together with 3,000,000 tiny panel ads for such firms as DuPont, Wrigley and General Tire.

Lawrence Cowen (left) and Advertising Manager Joseph Hanson in a 1953 coffee ad.

Arthur Raphael, a brilliant merchandiser who had joined the company as a salesman in 1921 and had become Cowen's closest friend, oversaw sales and promotion. Raphael, who wrote children's books on the side, studied government birth statistics. Through those statistics he determined that the decade between 1948 and 1958 would be a good one for Lionel because of the baby boom during and after World War II. Raphael also watched population shifts, sales of electrical appliances, such as toasters and waffle irons, and the rural electrification program.

"Raphael felt that an up-to-date farmer had as much right to have an electric train as he had to have a vacuum cleaner," says one former Lionel supervisor.

Research by Raphael's staff indicated that the sale of a train set established a buyer of accessories and additional rolling stock for about five years. He felt the "initial" train-owning age was six to nine and he concluded that a boy who was still interested in trains at the age of 14 was likely to be a Lionel customer for life. There are many collectors today who will agree with that assessment.

It appears that Cowen turned over much of the financial aspects of Lionel to his son and Raphael, while he, the old inventor and scratch builder, paid most of his

(continued on page 134)

DIESELS
F-3 UNITS

In February of 1948 Lawrence Cowen, president of the Lionel Corporation and the only son of Joshua Lionel Cowen, sent out inquiries to the Electro-Motive Division of General Motors and to the public relations departments of the Santa Fe and New York Central railroads.

Larry Cowen asked them all if they would be interested in putting up one-quarter of the cost of the dies for a new locomotive Lionel was making. The locomotive was a model of EMD's F-3, which was the first diesel Lionel was manufacturing after World War II.

Lionel planned to have markings of two different railroads on their F-3, Cowen explained in a letter to the three companies. The markings from an eastern railroad would be used for sales in the eastern half of the United States and the markings from a western railroad would be used for western sales. Cowen said that in all probability the two railroads would be the New York Central and the Santa Fe.

The dies and tooling-up for production of the engine would cost between $25,000 and $30,000, according to Cowen, who suggested this cost be split four ways among Lionel, EMD and the railroads. They all agreed. It was easy to see why.

At that point in its history, Lionel printed 1,000,000 catalogs a year. In exchange for a $6,000 investment, the Santa Fe and New York Central would have a two-page spread devoted to their F-3s in the 1948 catalog. They would also cash in on ads in Lionel's *Model Builders* magazine, which had a circulation of 40,000. And, of course, there would be the advertisements for the railroads carried on each of the engines Lionel would make. Cowen estimated that the run for 1948 would be not less than 16,000 units apiece for the New York Central and the Santa Fe.

Electro-Motive's enticement was that a General Motors logo would be placed on every Santa Fe and New York Central F-3 the company ever made. The General Motors logo would also be displayed in the 1948 catalog.

There could hardly be a better way for both the railroads and for General Motors to get such exposure at a cost of $6,000, even if the engines ran only one year. The New York Central ran for eight years and the Santa Fe for 18. It turned out to be a fine investment.

It turned out fine for Lionel, too. The bright red, silver and yellow Santa Fe became the largest selling engine in Lionel's history. Its success was a major factor in Lionel's becoming one of the largest toy companies in the world.

The decision to make the F-3 was reached in 1947 by Cowen, Lionel General Sales Manager Arthur M. Raphael, a brilliant merchandiser who was also executive vice president of the company, and Phillip Marfuggi, then Lionel's vice president. Lionel selected the Beacon Tool and Die Company of Clifton, New Jersey, to make the dies.

Beacon was owned by a man named Vincent Esposito, whose brother, Robert, owned an unpretentious but popular Italian restaurant in nearby Garfield, New Jersey. Some of the regular customers at Bob's Neopolitan Restaurant included Jack Benny, Frank Sinatra and Jackie Gleason. Another regular at Bob's was Bill Vagell, a former magician who became the biggest Lionel dealer on the East Coast and who would often lunch at Bob's with Lionel executives. It was over a spaghetti lunch at Bob's one afternoon in December of 1947 that Raphael, Marfuggi and Vince Esposito closed the deal which called for Beacon to make the dies for the F-3.

1948

For some reason Lionel gave both the Santa Fe and New York Central F-3s the same number, 2333, when they came off the assembly line in 1948. The 1948 catalog showed the Santa Fe in red, yellow and black, but it was never produced that way. It was made in the railroad's real colors — red, yellow and silver, with the silver replacing the black of the catalog. The catalog showed the New York Central in its proper markings, two-tone gray with white striping, but nevertheless the drawings in the catalog of both the New York Central and Santa Fe were rather poor likenesses of the locomotives actually produced.

The detailing on the engines was excellent and included simulated turned aluminum horns on the roof, mesh screen intake ventilators and footsteps on all the trucks. There were grab-irons on the front of the loco and, on the side, there were celluloid windows covering the portholes. However, it is hard now to find F-3's with the original celluloid in the portholes.

Another problem was the plastic used in the body. It was soft and smooth and the paint of the early units had a tendency to chip or flake off. These units, as a result, are hard to find in good condition.

The F-3 was the first twin-motored locomotive offered in O gauge after the war and the power unit, except for the reversing unit, was entirely new. The motors were mounted horizontally and featured internal worm drive gear boxes, similar to the double worm drive that was used on the

F-3s
2368 Baltimore & Ohio
2378 Milwaukee Road AB
2373 Canadian Pacific AA
2379 Rio Grande AB
2242 New Haven AB

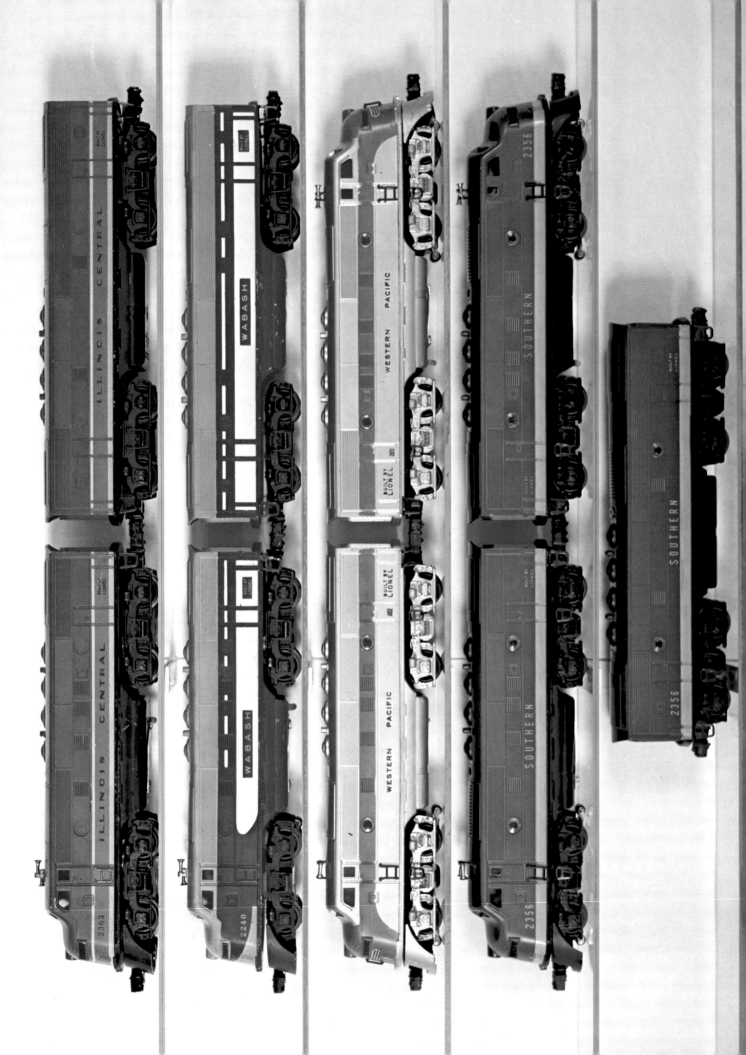

726 and 671 locos in 1946 and explained in detail in the steamer section of this book. The F-3 brush holders were tube-type and made of fibreboard with a metal bracket that was screwed to the motor.

2333 Santa Fe.

The 2333 New York Central and Santa Fe came in AA combinations, one unit with the motors and the other a dummy. Both the power and dummy units had coil-type operating couplers on the front end. The couplers between the units were fixed and could not be uncoupled automatically. The dummy unit had the same truck casting as the power unit but without any gearing.

The F-3s were the first engines Lionel made that had a diesel-sounding horn. The horn, powered by a D-size flashlight battery, was activated by the same DC-powered relay that activated the Lionel whistles. This relay was energized when the whistle controller was pushed on the transformer or whistle control unit.

Lettering 1948.

Lettering 1949 and after.

1949

The Santa Fe and New York Central ran again, both keeping the 2333 number. The only external change was made on the lettering of the New York Central. It was slightly smaller than it had been in 1948. Internally, the only change was on the brush plates. Instead of being metal and fibreboard, they were Bakelite and spring type. The mounting of the horn was entirely different.

Brush plates 1948.   Brush plates 1949 and after.

1950

1950 was Lionel's 50th anniversary year and Magne-Traction was the company's star innovation. It was placed on all engines and the Santa Fe and New York Central finally got their own

numbers. The Santa Fe became 2343 and the New York Central 2344. The appearance of the engines remained the same, except that the GM logo was moved from a point behind the rear access door and placed on the door itself.

Although 1950 was the first year Lionel advertised Magne-Traction, they had actually put it on the 6220 and 622 GM switchers in 1949, without mentioning it in the catalog. The system used on the switchers in 1949 was not too successful, so Lionel tried a couple of different systems in 1950. To make comparisons easier, all the Magne-Traction systems will be explained in this section of the book, even though they were not all used on the F-3s.

Lionel's method of applying magnetic power to the driving wheels of the diesel switchers in 1949 was by magnetizing the axles. The axles in turn transferred the magnetism directly to the wheels. The problem was that the axles had to be made of hard iron, and hard iron begins losing its magnetic power quickly, sometimes within a year. Soft iron, which retains magnetism indefinitely, would have been the perfect material for the axle, except for the fact that soft iron would have bent during the assembly process, a process in which the wheels were machine-pressed against the axles. Hard iron had to be used, but it proved unsuitable for Magne-Traction. The 1949 GM switchers found today show little evidence of magnetic power.

To get a longer magnetic life for the switcher, Lionel in 1950 had two rectangular magnets mounted into the frame of the power truck. One magnet was placed above each of the axles, be-

Magnets between wheels.

tween the wheels but not touching them. The frame was made of cast zinc and the axles were made of stainless steel, both of which were non-magnetic and would not interfere with the transfer of the magnetic force from the magnets to the wheels. The magnets were made of indefinitely energized soft iron.

This system was also used on the Alcos and GG-1s in 1950.

The second magnetic system Lionel tried in 1950 was used on the F-3. This involved placing, on the power truck, non-magnetic stainless steel axles with hollow centers. Inside the hollow axle were placed cylindrical, soft iron magnets. This system proved to be the most effective yet and eventually all Lionel locomotives except the GG-1 and steamers would adopt it.

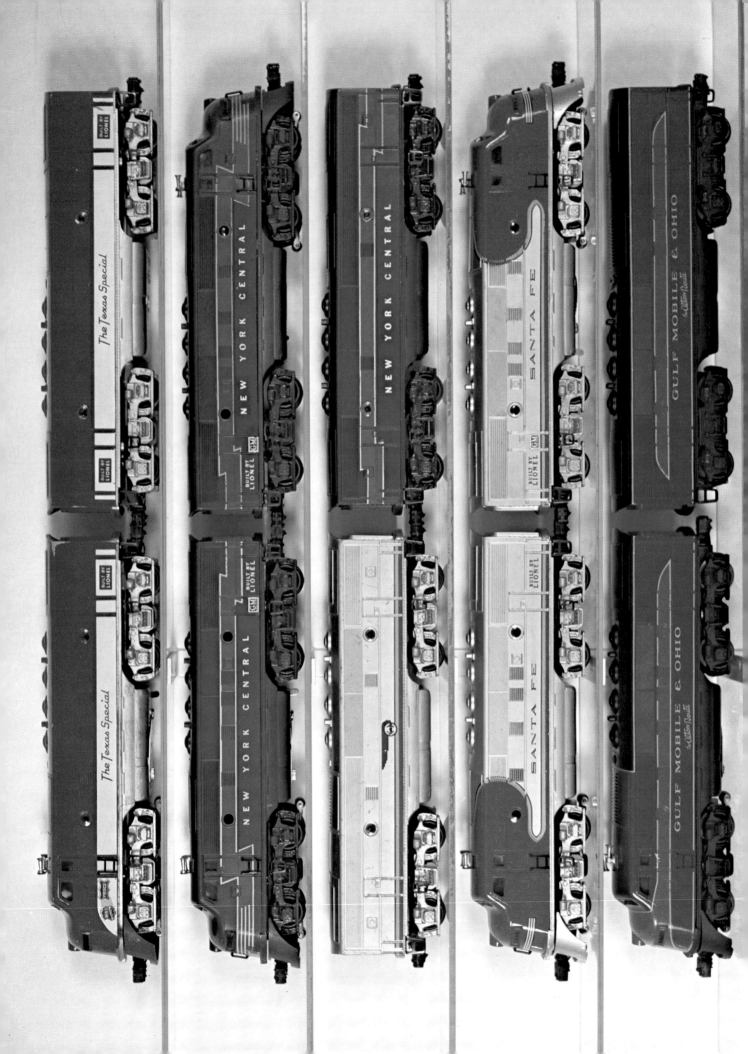

Hollow axle with magnet.

The dummy A unit trucks were changed in 1950 and B units were introduced. The castings of the trucks on the dummy As, as well as on the B units, was lighter and less expensive to make than the castings on the power A units. The B units had non-operating couplers at both ends. The frame of the B unit was made of a combination plastic and sheet metal.

1951

Lionel changed the type of plastic they used for the F-3 bodies. It was now a styrene plastic, which was harder than the type they had been using. It held the paint better and minimized the peeling and chipping prevalent on the earlier models.

The porthole windows, which sometimes came loose the first three years, were improved in 1951. Instead of being made of celluloid the windows were made of a solid clear plastic.

The roller pickup was changed from brass to steel.

1952

The 2343 Santa Fe and the 2344 New York Central continued without change and for the first time were joined by a third F-3, the 2345 Western Pacific. The Western Pacific was painted silver and orange and was identical in construction to the other F-3s except there was no B unit available.

1953

All three road names were offered again but the numbers changed, reflecting several internal and external modifications. The Santa Fe became 2353, the New York Central 2354, and the Western Pacific 2355.

This was the first year it was apparent Lionel had cut down on the amount of handwork required to assemble the locomotives. The wire mesh screening on the roof ventilators was removed and now were cast in plastic with the body itself. The grab-irons on the nose were eliminated. The GM decal was no longer applied by hand. It was heat-stamped.

On the inside, the idler gear was changed. The bronze bearing that had been pressed into the motor casting was removed and a hardened steel pin was pressed into the casting. This was less expensive to produce and install, but it was somewhat noisy, as it had been before.

The horn was improved. It was taken out of the power A unit and placed in the dummy A. Vibrations from the motors in the power unit had

interfered with the sound of the horn. Placing it in the dummy eliminated the vibrations and the horn sounded much better.

Another improvement was in the way the body mounted to the frame. The body had been held on by three screws, two large ones in back and a smaller one in front. The back screws were replaced by a two-prong clip in 1953, eliminating a tendency the back screws had to strip if the body was taken off the frame more than a couple of times.

The frame casting was also changed in 1953. The headlight bracket inside was made a part of the frame. Before, it had been a separate socket that was clipped to the frame. And, on the front edge of the frame, the ridge that ran along the top was shortened, making it easier to place the body on the frame.

1954

The 2353 Santa Fe and the 2354 New York Central continued. The 2355 Western Pacific was dropped. It was replaced by the 2356 Southern, in green, gray and yellow. The Southern was the first F-3 not to have the GM decal. From this point on, all new road names would be without the decal, leaving the Santa Fe and New York Central the only ones with it.

Also introduced in 1954 was the 2245 Texas Special in red, white and silver. It was the first F-3 to be offered in 027. The Texas Special was a single-motored unit, the first for an F-3, and, also for the first time, came in an AB combination. This saved money for Lionel. The B unit was cheaper to make than an unpowered A, since the B did not have a die-cast chassis, roller pickup assembly, headlight bulb and socket, operating coupler, windshield, numberboards, or ornamental horns.

One truck of the Texas Special B unit was altered to receive a self-centering coupler, which was a coupler with a spring under it to make sure it stayed in the center and lined up properly with freight and passenger cars. Previous B units had no self-centering couplers because they only hooked up with A units in ABA combinations and precision coupling wasn't necessary. For the same reason, the rear coupler on the A units was not self-centering, since they usually did not couple with freight or passenger cars. The front end coupler on the A units, however, was self-centering.

The power truck on the 2245 was the rear truck. The horn on the 2245 was placed in the powered A unit. With only one motor, the vibration in the Texas Special was less and it did not interfere with the sound of the horn.

The outward appearance of the F-3s was the same in 1954 as it had been in 1953 but there were some subtle changes. The bottom of the gear boxes on the truck casting was flattened a bit and the lip on the top of the truck was removed.

On the pilot the top bar was cut out and the lip on the bottom was eliminated. This made it

2245 Texas Special AB
2344 New York Central AA
2343C Santa Fe and 2344C
     New York Central B units
2343 Santa Fe AA
Richard Sherry Custom Gulf Mobile & Ohio

11

easier to assemble the pilot and coupler and to run the engine on 027 track. The lip on the F-3 pilot apron had a tendency to catch on 027 uncoupling track and switches.

F-3 pilot (1948-1953).

F-3 pilot (1954-1956).

Lionel attempted to make the F-3s run quieter in 1954 by installing a nylon idler gear. It helped a little but the motor was still somewhat noisy. The nylon gear is found on all F-3s made in 1954 and 1955.

1955

The 2353 Santa Fe, the 2354 New York Central, the 2356 Southern, and the 2345 Texas Special ran again and were unchanged. Another Santa Fe, numbered 2243, was offered in 027. It, like the Texas Special, was single-motored.

Two new road names were available, the 2363 Illinois Central and the 2367 Wabash. Both were twin-motored O gauge models. These engines, along with the 2243, underwent considerable design changes, especially internally.

Externally the 2363 and 2367 had less detailing than the other F-3s, with the porthole windows and the footsteps on all the trucks eliminated. The footsteps on the body were now cast into it rather than being separate pieces. The ornamental horns on the roof were changed from two-piece assemblies to one-piece, press-in mountings.

Original F-3 roof.

F-3 roof in 1955 and after.

The only things mechanically that weren't changed were the reverse unit and the horn relay. The chassis on the power unit was completely altered and the power truck castings used a worm and spur gear drive. The wheel base of the trucks was altered to bring the wheels approximately an eighth of an inch closer together.

The side frames of the trucks were no longer painted. They were a black oxidized casting. In addition, the side frames were no longer screwed on, but staked onto a metal plate. The plate held the coupler pocket assembly, which was made of sheet metal and was cheaper than a casting. These coupler pockets have a tendency to come off.

Each truck on the twin-motored units had its own roller pickup. Before, the front truck had two pickups and the rear truck had none. On the 2243 Santa Fe, the rear truck was the power truck.

The pilot assembly on the new F-3s was no longer screwed on but, like the side frames, was staked to a metal plate. The coil coupler on the pilot was replaced by a magnet-type coupler and the pilot lost some of its detailing. It was also slightly smaller than on the other F-3s.

The motors on the new F-3s were mounted vertically rather than horizontally. This motor was first introduced in 1954 in the twin-motored 2321 Lackawanna FM and from 1955 on was placed across the board in the F-3s, FMs, GPs and electrics. The pivot points of the motors and the trucks beneath them were moved in from the ends, closer to the middle of the engine. This made it possible for the locos to navigate 027 track with less difficulty than the other F-3s, which sometimes brushed their fuel tanks against the 027 switch motors, causing derailments.

The horn returned to the power A unit, the vibration problem being solved in the new engines.

As it had on the Texas Special, Lionel saved money on the three new F-3s by selling them as AB units rather than AA. The B unit trucks changed from cast zinc to stamped sheet metal. The trucks used a sheet metal coupler pocket, but they retained the self-centering springs at one end. They were not interchangeable with B units made before 1955.

Another cost-saving device employed by Lionel in 1955 was in the color of the plastic bodies. Until then Lionel had been rather arbitrary in its choice of colors. Most of the time gray plastic was used. It didn't matter much, because all the road colors would be painted over the plastic, anyway. But in 1955, starting with the Wabash and Illinois Central B units, Lionel used a plastic the same color as the predominant color in the railroad's markings. Then only the striping or less pervasive colors had to be painted on. For instance, the Wabash B unit body was made of blue plastic and the Illinois Central was made of orange.

The changes of 1955 resulted in locomotives that were cheaper for Lionel to make, but they also ran quieter, faster, and pulled a little better. But, of course, they did not look as good.

1956

The 2378 Milwaukee Road and the 2368 Baltimore & Ohio — two units that were to become among the most prized of all the F-3s — were introduced. The 2245 Texas Special and the 2354 New York Central were dropped.

The Milwaukee Road and Baltimore & Ohio came with the cheapened 1955-style chassis and were offered as AB units. Both locos and B units used colored plastic bodies — blue for the B&O and gray for the Milwaukee Road — as the technique of using the predominate road color as the color of the plastic became more widespread.

The 2378 Milwaukee Road was marked two ways. One way had a red stripe running along the bottom of the body and this stripe was bordered by two small yellow stripes. The other way had this same marking, plus another yellow stripe running along the roof line. The top stripe is found on both the A and B units, but more commonly on the B unit.

Collectors sometimes think they have a mismatched set when they have a B unit with the top stripe, and an A unit without it, but that is the way the AB combination often came new. Lionel, somewhere along the line, stopped putting the stripe on the A unit but continued putting it on the B. Versions of the 2378 Milwaukee A with the top stripe are a little harder to find than those without it. Most collectors value the top stripe model more because they think it makes the units look better.

The Wabash F-3 was switched to a single-motored 027 model and its number changed to 2240. The 2240 looked almost the same as the 2367 Wabash had the year before except that the blue paint was slightly darker. It came in an AB combination. The 2240's B unit, as opposed to its O gauge counterpart, was painted blue rather than blue plastic.

The 2243 single-motored Santa Fe was offered again, as were the twin-motored Illinois Central and Southern. There was one small alteration made on the bodies of the new F-3s in 1956. The footstep on the side of the body was reduced in size so it did not protrude as much. This was to eliminate a problem Lionel had with silk screening some of the color schemes.

1957

The 2363 Illinois Central, 2378 Milwaukee Road, 2368 Baltimore & Ohio, 2240 Wabash, and 2356 Southern were all discontinued. Only the 2243 Santa Fe was carried over, but two new road names were added: the 2373 Canadian Pacific and the 2379 Rio Grande. Both were to become choice collectors items.

The 2379 Rio Grande was offered in an AB combination and was the same mechanically as the 2363 Illinois Central and the other F-3s with the 1955-style chassis. The 2373 Canadian Pacific also had the late-style chassis but it was offered as an AA combination, the first of the late-style F-3s to be offered with a dummy A unit. The horn and motors were contained in the power A unit. The chassis of the dummy A unit was designed to accommodate non-power trucks. There was never a B unit built for the 2373 Canadian Pacific.

1958

The 2373 Canadian Pacific was dropped and the Santa Fe returned to O gauge — its number changing to 2383 — and once again featured a twin-motored AA combination.

Although the Santa Fe came with no B unit, the 2243C Santa Fe B unit matched it perfectly. Both had black oxidized trucks with silver frames.

To replace the Santa Fe in 027, Lionel chose the 2242 New Haven, which used the same chassis as the 2243 Santa Fe and came in an AB combination. The pilot on the New Haven was painted black. The 2379 Rio Grande was offered again and was unchanged.

1959

The 2379 Rio Grande was dropped. Only the 2383 Santa Fe remained as a twin-motored F-3. The 2242 New Haven AB ran again. Both the Santa Fe and the New Haven were unchanged.

1960 through 1966

The 2242 New Haven was discontinued, making the 2383 Santa Fe the only F-3 left in the Lionel Line. It ran unchanged through 1966.

Because so many Santa Fes were sold, a great many turn up in poor condition. Restoration and custom paint experts like Richard Sherry of Chicago have saved many scratched and marred locomotives from being cannibalized for parts. Pictured on page 10 with the regular Lionel F-3s is a Sherry-customed Gulf Mobile & Ohio, an example of how custom painting permits collectors to add favorite road names to collections, even if the pieces were never made by Lionel.

The D-size battery used to power the horn in the F-3 units has been a source of some consternation to collectors. Many an otherwise mint item has been severely damaged because the owner neglected to remove the battery when the trains were put in storage. When buying a Lionel item that requires a battery, one should check carefully for battery damage.

RATING

The hardest to find of the F-3s are the Canadian Pacific, New Haven, Milwaukee Road and Baltimore & Ohio. Slightly less difficult to find are the Rio Grande, Illinois Central, Wabash, Western Pacific and Southern.

FM UNITS

The Fairbanks-Morse Company slid rather naturally into the manufacture of railroad locomotives. Long a supplier of railroad supply items, FM, in 1932, developed an opposed piston diesel engine for use in submarines. Based on its success, the company experimented with variations of the engine for yard switcher use, before research was interrupted by World War II.

The original Fairbanks Company, started in the first half of the 19th Century, was not in the railroad business — they made scales — but its founder was. He was Horace Fairbanks of St. Johnsbury, Vermont, and he was president of the St. Johnsbury and Lake Champlain Railroad. He was also governor of Vermont from 1876 to 1878.

Horace Fairbanks was a stern old boy who was fanatically opposed to operating his railroad on Sunday. Not a piece of equipment could be found moving on the railroad on the Sabbath. At least not a piece of equipment was *supposed* to move on Sunday on the St. J. & L.C. — known locally and irreverently as the St. Jesus and Long Coming. The superintendent of the St. J. sometimes found it necessary to send out a work train or a snowplow on Sunday, but knowing Fairbanks' feeling on the matter, the super would have the train or plow eased out of St. Johnsbury as quietly as possible, with neither bell nor whistle sounding.

Eventually Horace Fairbanks went to his reward and the Fairbanks Company became, in time, Fairbanks-Morse and in World War II found itself the manufacturers of the engine that powered half the submarines used by the U.S. Navy. By the end of the war FM was directing a great deal of attention to diesel railroad locomotives. They were building switchers at their Beloit, Wisconsin plant and road units — such as the fancy, 6,000-h.p., three-unit diesel that would power the Olympian Hiawatha — at General Electric's plant at Erie, Pennsylvania.

When FM enlarged their Beloit plant in 1949 all construction was done there, including the 2,400-horsepower Train Master, which came out in 1953. The Train Master was considerably ahead of competing diesels of the time, since it contained all its 2,400 horses in a single unit. The big advantage to railroads having single, high horsepower units was in maintenance. The U.P. conducted a survey about that time which showed the annual cost of maintaining a single-unit diesel was $7,000, regardless of the size or horsepower of the unit. So if a couple of 1,200-h.p. units could be replaced by a 2,400-h.p. unit, the maintenance costs would be cut in half.

There were a few kinks to be ironed out of the Train Master when it first came off the assembly line but after that was done the big diesel became

a reliable performer. Based on its successful design, the FM company had high sales expectations for the Train Master but orders did not come in very fast. Knowing about the Train Master's early bugs, the railroads held back, waiting to observe its performance record. Fairbanks-Morse sold only 105 Train Masters in the United States and 22 in Canada between 1953 and 1956. By that time EMD and Alco had locos of comparable power and FM made no more Train Masters after 1956.

Although the Train Master never sold as much as fairness might indicate it should have, it did force the other diesel builders to develop as good a product. The largest customers for Train Masters were railroads that operated in mountainous terrain.

1954

Lionel's first model of the Train Master, the 2321 Lackawanna, was introduced in 1954, from dies partially financed by Fairbanks-Morse. In exchange for bearing some of the costs of the dies, Lionel placed the Fairbanks-Morse logo on all models of the FM. It should be mentioned here that collectors usually refer to Lonel's Train Master as the "FM," even though the initials refer to the name of the manufacturer and not to the name of the specific locomotive. Since Lionel modeled only one Fairbanks-Morse item, it has caused no confusion.

The Train Master was the first new diesel Lionel had come out with in four years, since the introduction of the Alco FA in 1950. It was an excellent reproduction. The gray, plastic body was well-detailed, with headlights at both ends, nickel-plated wire handrails and running boards on all four sides. The numberboards were backed by clear plastic and lit up, but had no numbers on them. The model was close to true scale, and scale operators often use it on their layouts.

The Lionel model had twin motors, each motor being similar to the one used in the 622 diesel switcher, except the FM motor was a bit smaller.

FM with cab removed.

The FM was the first Lionel diesel to use a stamped, sheet metal frame. Always before the frames had been die-cast. All new types of diesels brought out after 1954 would have sheet metal frames, a much cheaper product for Lionel to make. In fact, the subsequent locomotives would have the frames exposed, but on the FM the plastic shell covered the frame (as opposed, for instance, to the GP-7s and 9s, on which the sheet metal frame is highly visible). There was much less labor involved in stamping than in casting, since there was no waiting for cooling or cleaning of parts required. Although the frame was sheet metal, the simulated fuel tanks, the battery housing, and the truck side panels were die-cast.

Lionel designers came up with an inventive new design for the Train Master's six-wheel trucks. Both trucks, located under the motors, were powered, but only four of the six wheels were powered. The inside set of wheels nearest to the center of the loco on each truck was blind, having no flanges. The reason for this was so these wheels could swing out over the rails on curves and allow the huge engine to negotiate tight O gauge turns. This action is apparent if the FMs are observed closely as they are turning.

FM trucks.

The pilots on the FMs were similar to the F-3s. attached to the trucks and swiveling away from the locomotive on curves. This would enable the coupler, protruding through the pilot, to swing out also and prevent the engine from pulling cars off the track.

The FM coupler was a new type. Before 1954 all diesel locos had electro-magnetic — or coil type — couplers operated by pick-up shoes. The FMs used mechanically operated knuckle couplers, which were activated by a magnet in an uncoupling section of track. The magnet drew down an armature disk, made of a solid piece of steel, and attached to the rear of coupler. The disk, in turn, pulled out a coupler pin and snapped the coupler open.

The new coupling system was much cheaper to produce than the old one because it eliminated the need for each coupler to have its own coil and pick-up shoe. But the FM, a powerful puller designed to haul a lot of cars, put a lot of stress on the coupler while pulling large loads. The action of the train had a tendency to force the coupler open. The coupling system worked better on single-motored locomotives that could not pull as many cars as the FM.

The 2321 Lackawanna which was made in 1954 had a gray body with a maroon stripe that was trimmed in yellow. The 1954 catalog showed the loco with a gray roof, but it was not made that way. It only came with a maroon roof in 1954. The catalog also showed a more complicated color combination at the ends of the Train Master than was actually produced. The ends, as illustrated, were yellow, gray and maroon, but as manufactured were only gray and maroon.

The catalog illustrations were carry-overs from the artist's renderings that appeared in the 1954 advance catalog. These renderings in the advance catalog were made from the handcrafted preproduction model made for the Toy Fair held in New York in February of 1954. The preproduction model, which is now in the collection of LaRue Shempp of Williamsport, Pennsylvania, was substantially different from the production model. In addition to the gray, maroon and yellow coloring, the preproduction model had a black roof, and the screening, which was molded into the body on the production model, was made of wire mesh and separately installed, as on the early F-3s.

Another difference between the prototype model and the production model was the construction of the pilot. It was not attached to the trucks on the prototype, thus restricting the swivel of the coupler. Further experiments showed this to be troublesome on turns and Lionel changed the design.

LaRue Shempp also has in his collection a couple of prototype FM models that Lionel decided not to market: a black and yellow Reading and black, orange and silver Southern Pacific.

"I understand that Lionel made up a dozen of these Southern Pacific FMs for the officials of the railroad," says Shempp. "Lionel kept one for themselves, which they displayed at the San Francisco Toy Fair in 1954. They did not get enough orders from the West Coast to give the green light to its production. I have that one. Rumor has it that there are a dozen others, but I have never authenticated that."

"As for the Reading, I know I have the only one. Eastern orders did not justify its production."

1955

The 2331 Virginian was introduced. It came in yellow and black, with gold lettering. The 2321 Lackawanna was continued but with some slight changes. The most noticeable change was on the roof, which was switched to gray. This was cheaper for Lionel since they saved an extra step. They did not have to mask the roof.

Many collectors think, incorrectly, that gray-roof Lackawannas were made in 1954 and the maroon roofs in 1955 because the '54 catalog showed the Locomotive with a gray roof and the

'55 advance catalog shows it with a maroon roof. In both cases the catalogs were wrong. The 1954 catalog was printed before the maroon roof version was put into production, and the 1955 advance catalog merely showed a picture of the maroon roof Lackawanna from the year before.

Incidentally, Lionel couldn't miss either way they colored the roof, since the Lackawanna Railroad itself painted their Train Masters both ways.

There were a couple of minor changes inside in 1955. The light bracket mounting was switched from a position on top of the motor to a place in front of it. And the magnetic disk on the trucks switched to a two-piece assembly and was sintered iron rather than a solid steel disk.

1956

The 2341 Jersey Central was introduced to the line in 1956. It came in blue and orange with white lettering. The 2321 Lackawanna was unchanged from the year before. The 2331 Virginian underwent a color change — from black and yellow, to blue and yellow. The change in the color might have been due to the fact that the Jersey Central also came in blue and Lionel could have both locos use the same unpainted blue plastic shell. The prototype Virginian also was painted black and yellow first, then blue and yellow.

Some of the very early versions of the blue and yellow Virginian were made with gray plastic shells and the blue was painted on. Very few of these were made and they might have been made starting in late 1955. Whenever they were made, the yellow on the gray shell versions is much lighter than the yellow on the blue plastic shell versions. The yellow on the gray shells is light, like the yellow on the black and yellow Virginians (also made from a gray shell), while the yellow on the blue plastic shell version is darker, almost gold. The difference in the two yellows can be seen on page 14.

The 2341 Jersey Central was made from the same dark blue shell as the Virginian, with the orange painted on. There were two production runs of the Jersey Central in 1956, the only year the locomotive was made. The first run produced a shell that was dark blue, like the Virginian, and the orange was semi-gloss. The second run had a lighter blue shell and the orange was slightly brighter with a high gloss.

The Jersey Central did not sell very well, making it the rarest of the FM units and one of the most prized of all postwar locomotives.

The rarity of the Jersey Central has led to a certain amount of counterfeiting among the more larcenous in the train collecting community. Reproductions are sometimes pawned off as originals. Some of these reproductions are so accurate that even experts have difficulty telling the difference between them and the originals. But there are a couple of ways.

One way is by the lettering, which on most reproductions is silk-screened rather than heat-stamped. Heat-stamping leaves a slight impression in the plastic that silk-screening does not. Another way to tell the difference is by examining the FM decal. Reproduction decals are pressure sensitive, as opposed to the old water release decals. And, in most cases, the decals on the reproductions are brighter than on the original, the white figure in the decal of the originals having yellowed with age. The orange paint is usually different, too. On the reproductions, the orange paint is darker and it has a flat finish. The Lionel orange is lighter with a gloss finish.

1957

The 2341 Jersey Central and the 2321 Lackawanna were dropped in 1957. The 2331 blue and yellow Virginian continued but the shade of blue was slightly lighter, the same color as the blue on the late run Jersey Centrals the year before.

1958 through 1966

The 2331 Virginian remained the same in 1958 and then was discontinued until 1965, when it was reintroduced with a new number, 2322, but otherwise was identical to the 1958 version. The 2322 ran again in 1966 and then was dropped.

RATING

All the FMs are highly prized. The Jersey Central, of course, is the most in demand, but both Virginians are in demand, with the black and yellow version being more difficult to find than the blue and yellow. The Lackawanna with the maroon roof is more sought after than the all-gray version, but both are more common than the Jersey Central or Virginian.

In general, most of Lionel's locomotives that were introduced in 1955 and after were of poorer overall quality than those, like the FM, that were introduced before. However, although the FM is considered an excellent piece of work, it still presaged some of the things that were to come, such as stamped sheet metal frames, magnetic couplers and numberless number boards.

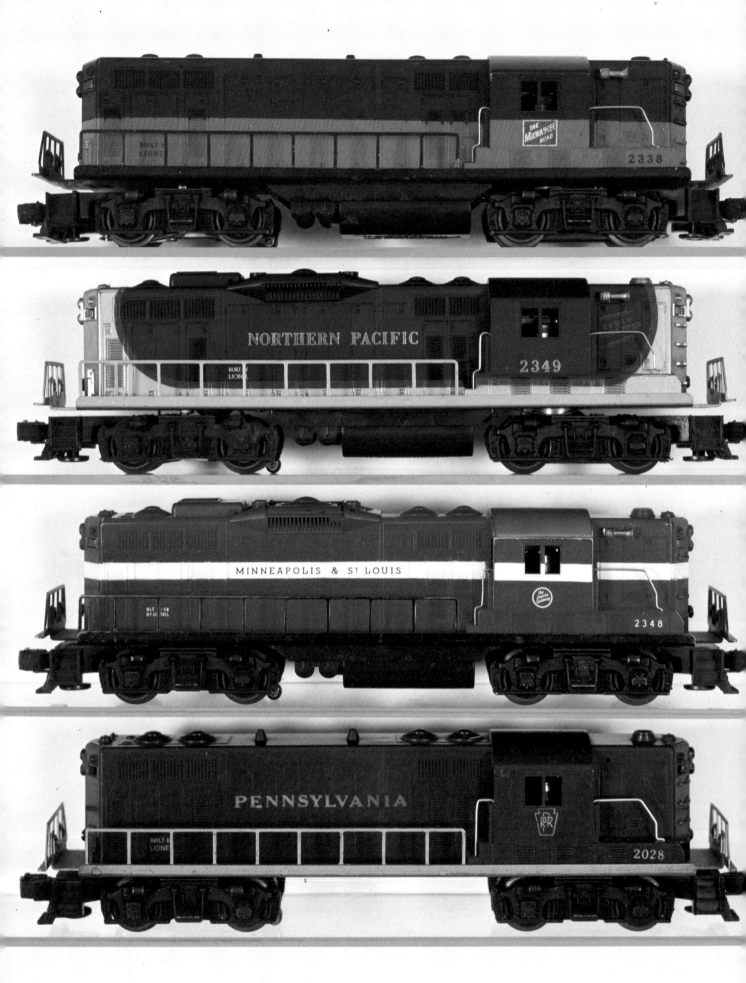

GP-7s & GP-9s

General Motors became involved in the manufacture of train locomotives in 1930, when they acquired as subsidiaries the Electro-Motive Corporation and the Winton Engine Company.

Electro-Motive, a design and sales organization, had had success teaming with Winton in the manufacture of gas-electric rail cars. Electro-Motive would do the design, Winton would install the motors, and they would contract the work for the frames and bodies.

After the acquisition of EMC-Winton, General Motors began marketing diesel switchers and passenger engines, including the engines for the Burlington Zephyr and Union Pacific M-10000. In 1939, GM introduced the EMC F-T, the first mass-produced road freight diesel. Electro-Motive and Winton were merged with GM in 1941, becoming GM's Electro-Motive Division, or EMD.

During this period Alco had also been making diesel switchers, as well as developing the DL 109 passenger diesel. But Alco's main effort was still in the production of steam locomotives. When World War II broke out, the War Production Board decided Alco was best suited to steam production and severely curtailed its diesel activity. General Motors, with a huge new facility in La-Grange, Illinois, was allowed to continue building freight diesels during the war and as a result had quite a technological jump on Alco and other train makers in the development of diesel power after the war.

But while EMD held a position of prominence in the sales of passenger and freight road diesels, Alco had rather quietly been developing the road switcher. Alco made a few of these engines before the war and many afterwards.

Essentially a road switcher was a yard switcher outfitted with road trucks and upgraded power. It could thus be used for almost any task on main line or branch service. The road switchers were practical, but since they lacked the frills of the streamlined diesels, General Motors was reluctant to make one, thinking railroads would not accept them for passenger service. However, Alco's success with the RS series road switcher in the years immediately after the war forced GM to reconsider.

What EMD came up with was something called the BL (-1 and -2), which was a dressed down version of the F-3 with a rear window added to the cab, a beveled engine compartment for visibility, and end platforms. By retaining a semi-streamlined look, GM thought the BL would be attractive to railroads for suburban and local passenger trains, while still being able to perform freight service. They sold only 58 of them.

It was back to the drawing boards for the EMD designers, who finally threw in the towel and decided to let form follow function. The result was the GP-7, a utilitarian-looking engine that was dependable and easy to maintain.

The GP (for "General Purpose," nicknamed, naturally, "Geep") was an immediate success. Between 1949, when it was brought out, and 1954, a total of 74 different railroads bought the GP-7.

The GP-7 was followed by the GP-9, which had 1,750 horse power compared to 1,500 for the GP-7. The only difference in appearance of the two models was that the GP-7 had two vertical rows of louvres under the radiator shutters at the far end of the long hood and three rows under the cab. The GP-9 had no louvers under the radiators shutters and either had one row or none under the cab. The difference between the GP-7 and GP-9 was not, as was largely supposed, the presence or absence of the dynamic brake blister on top of the long hood. Both GP-7s and GP-9s came with or without the brake blisters.

The toy model which Lionel called the GP-9 (the Minneapolis & St. Louis, the Northern Pacific and the Boston & Maine) was not a GP-9 at all, but a GP-7 with a dynamic brake blister.

2349 Northern Pacific.

1955

The Lionel model of the GP-7 came out in 1955 with the introduction of the 2328 Burlington, the 2338 Milwaukee Road, and the 2028 Pennsylvania.

Like the FMs from the year before, the Lionel geep had sheet metal frames, but instead of having nickel-plated wire handrails, the geep handrails were sheet metal. They did not look as good as the FM handrails, but were more durable.

The geeps featured Magne-Traction and operating couplers at both ends. The couplers, pilot steps and trucks were all one unit, as on the FM, but the steps were plastic rather than cast. The plastic pilot steps worked reasonably well, but had a tendency to break.

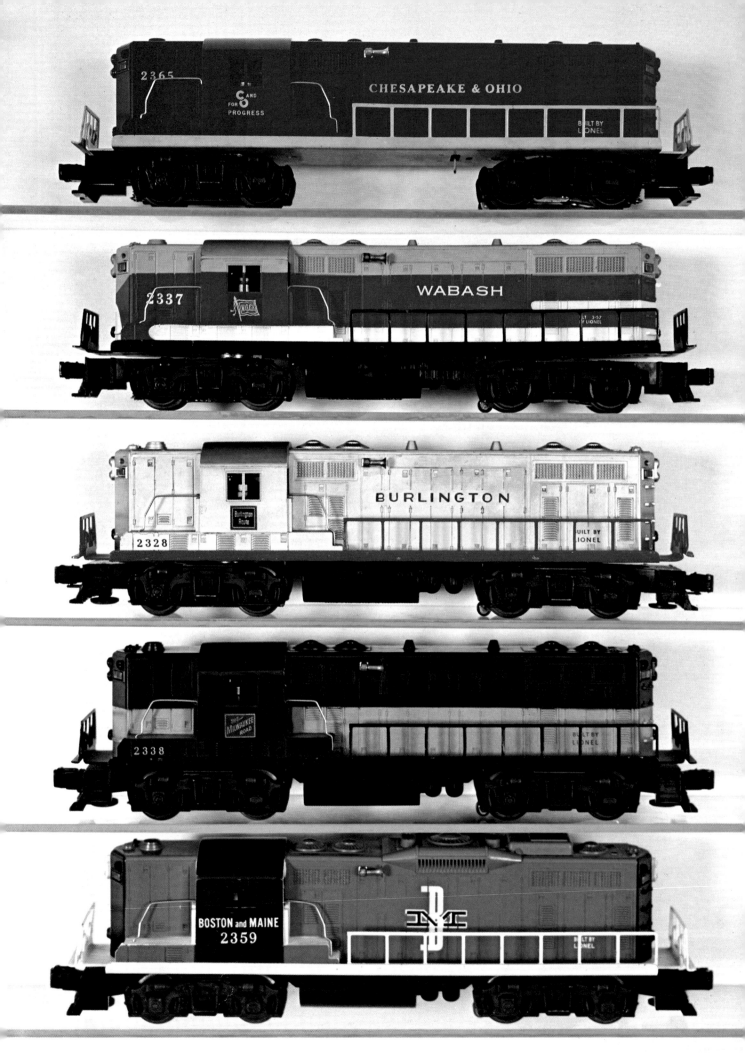

The GP's power truck, under the cab, and motor, attached to the power truck, were the same as those on the Wabash and Illinois Central F-3s, which were newly designed in 1955 (see F-3 section). The geeps had three-position reverse.

2349 with cab removed.

Of the three GP-7s introduced in 1955, the 2328 Burlington and the 2338 Milwaukee Road were identical in construction but for some reason known only to the Lionel sales department the Burlington was designated an 027 item and sold for $23.50, while the Milwaukee Road was designated O gauge and sold for $25.00. Both the 2328 and 2338 had horns, headlights at both ends, headlight lenses and numberboards (without numbers), simulated horns along the long hood, and wire handrails attached to the cab. Both had operating couplers and power trucks at the short hood end and non-powered trucks at the other end.

The Burlington and Milwaukee Road had plastic fuel tanks below the frame. This tank held the battery that powered the horn and was an inventive way to camouflage the battery, although it was hard to remove because the power truck got in the way.

The 2328 Burlington had a red frame, silver body and black lettering. The 2338 Milwaukee Road was black with an orange stripe running around the body. The 1955 catalog displayed the 2338 with the stripe on the cab, but very few were made that way. The most common way the Milwaukee Road was made was with the orange stripe interrupted by an all-black cab. The orange cab variation is thought to have been produced for Sears in 1955 only.

The body of the 2338 Milwaukee Road was made of unpainted orange plastic, with the black painted on. The herald on the orange cab version had a tendency to chip off, since it was silk-screened to the plastic rather than to the paint, and did not adhere as well. The numbering on the orange cab version was black instead of white, as it was on the black cab model.

The 2028 Pennsylvania GP-7 was also an 027 model, but it had less detailing than the Burlington and Milwaukee Road. The Pennsy had a headlight at the short hood end only and had no headlight lens or markerlight lenses. Neither did it have a horn, horn detailing or simulated fuel tank beneath the frame. It sold for $18.50.

The 2028 Pennsylvania came in unpainted maroon plastic with gold lettering and a gold frame. Some of them came with silver or yellow lettering. The gold and silver lettering is usually wiped off the engines, as it did not adhere well to the plastic. Some 2028s have a tan-colored frame rather than gold.

1956

The 2028 Pennsylvania was dropped in 1956, while the 2328 Burlington and the 2338 Milwaukee Road ran again. The Burlington stayed the same. It was offered in a set in 1956 but the catalog illustration had most of it hidden behind another train, probably contributing to poor sales.

The 2338 Milwaukee Road also remained the same in 1956, with the exception of the color of the orange plastic, which was lighter and more washed out than the year before. The year before, when the orange plastic was more translucent, it had been necessary to paint the black sections of the body on the inside as well as on the outside. With the washed out plastic it was only necessary to paint the black on the outside.

1957

1957 saw the 2328 Burlington and the 2338 Milwaukee Road dropped. They were replaced by the 2339 Wabash, offered in an O gauge set. It was the same structurally as the Milwaukee Road and Burlington. It had an unpainted blue plastic shell with gray and white stripes and a black chassis.

1958

In 1958 the number of the Wabash changed to 2337 as it was given non-operating couplers and became an 027 item. The color of the plastic was changed from blue to black or gray, so that the blue was painted on and it was not quite as shiny as the O gauge version had been. In place of the Wabash in O gauge came the 2348 Minneapolis & St. Louis. Everything about this model was the same as the previous O gauge models except it had the dynamic brake blister glued to the top (it fitted over the two exhaust stacks visible on top of the GP-7s). This made it, in the eyes of the Lionel engineers, a GP-9, although, as explained earlier, this blister was not the determining factor in identifying a GP-9. The Minneapolis & St. Louis was gray plastic painted red with a white stripe, blue cab roof and red lettering.

1959

The 2348 Minneapolis & St. Louis remained the same in 1959, while the 2339 Wabash was

2365 *Chesapeake &*
Ohio GP-7
2337 *Wabash GP-7*
2328 *Burlington GP-7*
2338 *Milwaukee Road*
GP-7
2359 *Boston & Maine*
GP-9

discontinued. Replacing it was the 2349 Northern Pacific GP-9. The rather elaborate color scheme of the Northern Pacific consisted of a black plastic body, painted black, with red and gold trim and gold frame.

1960 - 1962

The Northern Pacific ran again in 1960. The Minneapolis & St. Louis was dropped. In 1961 the Northern Pacific was dropped and the blue, black and white 2359 Boston & Maine GP-9 took its place.

The 2359 Boston & Maine was joined in 1962 by the 2365 Chesapeake & Ohio GP-7. The C&O was a stripped-down version without horn or plastic belly tanks or operating couplers. There was another model of the Chesapeake & Ohio made for Sears, which had a horn. It was numbered 2347 and made in 1962 only. It is the rarest item in the GP category.

1963 - 1965

The 2365 Chesapeake & Ohio was continued in 1963, while the 2359 Boston & Maine was dropped. In 1964 there were no GP units offered but in 1965 the Boston & Maine reappeared, this time with the number 2346. There was no apparent reason for the number change. The only difference between the Boston & Maine in 1965 and the earlier one was in the color of the blue, which was slightly darker and of a higher gloss in 1965.

1966

The 2346 Boston & Maine ran again in 1966 without change and then all GPs were dropped from the line.

The 2338 Milwaukee Road with the orange stripe on the cab is the second rarest item in the GP category. It is rare enough that some collectors have never seen one. This includes Percy Rogers, an enthusiastic collector from Lake Forest, Illinois. One day Rogers was riding a train into Union Station in St. Paul, Minnesota, when he spotted a GP-7 pulling a long line of freight cars.

"Look!" Rogers shouted to his wife. "There's the Milwaukee Road with the orange stripe on the cab. That's the variation I need for my collection."

"Oh, no!" his wife responded. "You're not going to start collecting *real* trains, too. We can't afford it. Besides, we don't have the room."

RATING

Following the Sears C&O and the orange cab Milwaukee Road in desirability are the 2349 Northern Pacific, the 2348 Minneapolis & St. Louis, and the 2028 Pennsylvania.

The advance catalog of 1955, the first year the geeps ran, showed a Union Pacific GP-7 with the 2028 number. This UP was never produced, except as a prototype for the New York toy fair. It is yellow, gray and red and is in the collection of LaRue Shempp, who obtained it through the old master, Bill Vagell, a man who got several big time collectors started in the hobby. The Union Pacific preproduction model still has the Lionel tag on it, "Not for sale. Showroom only."

The same 1955 advance catalog showed a GP-7 in what appeared to be Katy markings with the number 2328. The production model of the 2328 was, of course, the Burlington. It is not known whether there ever was a preproduction model of the Katy made.

2347 Sears with horn.

ALCOS

The American Locomotive Company never achieved the success in diesel production as General Motor's Electro-Motive Division, but Alco was actually involved in diesels before EMD. As far back as 1906, Alco and General Electric combined to make diesel-electrics, and then in the 30s Alco-GE got together with Ingersoll-Rand to make some more.

During the 30s Alco made many diesel switchers, although their main activity was still in steam locomotives. Alco's first passenger diesel, the DL-109, came out in 1940. It was a car body diesel, similar to EMD's E passenger series, and was styled by industrial designer Otto Kuhler. But Alco also had its eye on EMD's freight hauling F-Ts, which had been on the market since 1939.

Alco's plans to bring out its own car body freight diesel were interrupted by World War II. War Production Board restrictions delayed Alco's introduction of a road diesel freight hauler until January of 1946, when the FA-1 was introduced. It was Alco's 1,500 horse power answer to EMD's F-3, a successor to the 1,350 h.p. F-T.

The "flatnose" FAs were distinctive, with lines of classic simplicity, and they had guts, too. But they also had weak crankshafts and leaked a lot of oil. All in all, the Alcos never sold as well as their EMD F-series competitors, one reason being that more railroads were geared to maintain the two-cycle EMDs than the four-cycle Alcos. The same was true of the company's 2,000 horse power passenger diesel, the PA, introduced in September of 1946. It was a beautiful locomotive, perhaps the most popular diesel among train lovers ever built, but EMDs E-7s, 8s and 9s outsold the PAs by more than three to one.

Alco and GE had merged their locomotive products in 1940 and sold them under the name of Alco-GE until 1953, when GE decided to go out on its own. American Locomotive Company changed its name to Alco Products in 1956 and then went out of the new train business in 1969.

Lionel's model of the Alco FA was introduced in 1950 in the yellow, gray and red markings of the Union Pacific. It was numbered 2023 and came as an AA combination, one unit powered and the other a dummy. This was the first time Lionel had offered a two-unit diesel in 027.

Although it was a good model as far as detailing and styling, the Lionel Alco was rather undersized. It was quite a bit smaller than Lionel's F-3, while in real life both locos were about the same size. Lionel's Alcos also had the wrong-type trucks. The real FAs used AAR type-B trucks, as did all Alco road power of BB configuration. The Lionel model of the FA had AAR type-A trucks, which Alco used on its switchers. Lionel merely used the same trucks on the Alco as it had used on the GM switcher. The trucks were correct on the switcher but not on the FA.

But mechanically, the Alcos were excellent. They had Magne-Traction and used the same motor and power trucks that were used on the 622 switcher and the same horn system used in the F-3. The motor was smooth and of high quality, making the Alco one of the best running locos Lionel made in the entire postwar period. The trucks were die-cast, as were the frame and gear box, and the front trucks had ladders on them.

The Alco was offered in both passenger and freight sets. The passenger set used three of the streamline cars that were introduced in 1948 with the 671 steam turbine. In the Alco Union Pacific set the cars were numbered 2481 Plainfield, 2482 Westfield, and 2483 Livingston. They were yellow with gray roofs and red striping, matching the loco. The Alcos fit well with these smaller passenger cars and together they made a good looking set, which is commonly called the Anniversary Set (it came out in Lionel's 50th Anniversary year). This is the most desirable 027 set of the postwar period.

The 2023 came with a yellow body, gray roof and gray frame, with red lettering and striping and black trucks. A few, however, came with a gray nose and trucks, similar to the way they were shown in the 1950 catalog. These apparently were from early runs.

Following is the chronological development of the Alcos after 1950.

1951

The same sets were offered as in the year before, but the color scheme was changed. Instead of the authenic yellow and gray of the Union Pacific, the color scheme was silver, with gray roof and black lettering and striping. The numbers of the cars were changed to 2421 Maplewood, 2422 Chatham, and 2423 Hillside.

The number of the locomotive remained 2023 but there were mechanical changes on the Magne-Traction. The axles themselves were now magnetized, rather than having a magnet attached to them. Some Alcos were equipped with leftover magnets from the year before, however, which is why the number was not changed yet.

For some reason the silver Alcos made this year have a tendency to develop mildew stains. They are hard to find without these stains. The reason for the mildewing is hard to determine, but could have been connected with the kind of paint and plastic used.

Lionel dealers reported that sales increased when the color scheme of the Union Pacific was changed, although it is doubtful the Union Pacific ever painted its trains that way. A rare variation of the silver U.P. is a factory repainted version that has a painted yellow body underneath. The color of the plastic of this body is black.

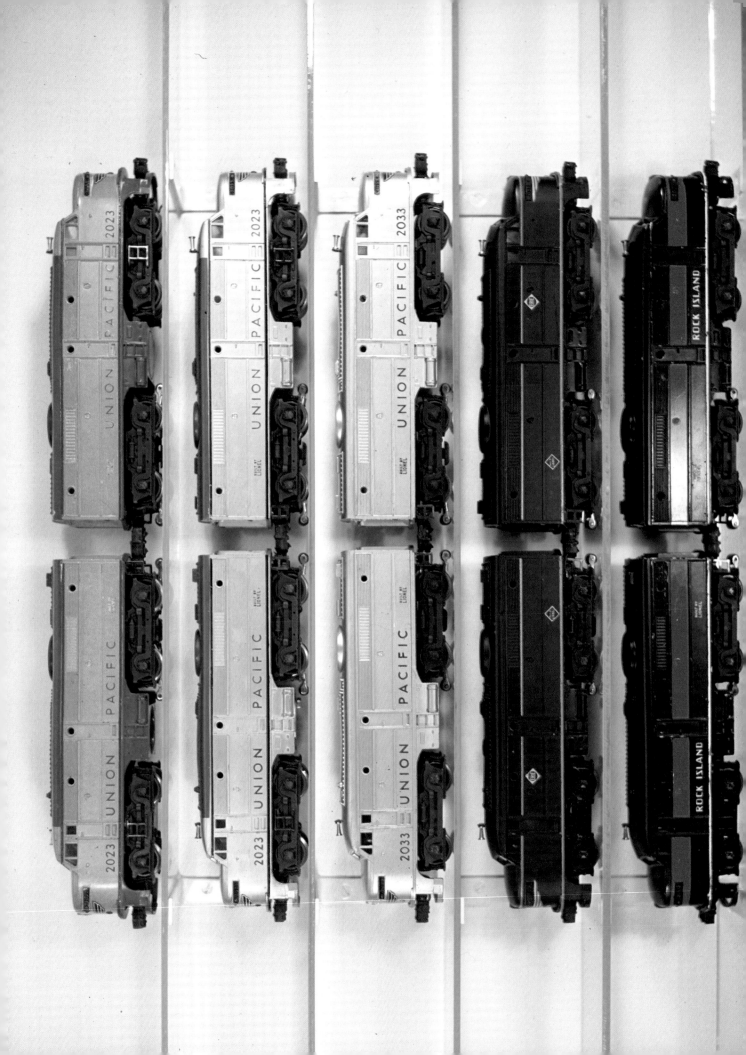

ALCOS
2023 Union Pacific AA
2023 Union Pacific AA (gray roof)
2033 Union Pacific
2032 Erie AA
2031 Rock Island AA

1952

The Union Pacific set was changed again, this time eliminating the gray roof and the black striping. The numbers of the passenger cars remained the same, but the number of the locomotive was changed to 2033. This was because it was the first year all the engines had the new style Magne-Traction. There was one other change on the loco. The step that had been located on the front truck was eliminated.

Two new road names were introduced: the 2032 Erie and the 2031 Rock Island. The Erie was painted all black with yellow striping and heralds. It headed a freight set. The Rock Island, in black and red with white lettering and striping, was offered as a separate item only. Another 2031

1953

There were no changes in the sets or the locomotives, except that a slight, saucer-shaped rise appeared on the roof of the loco near the front. This was a result of a change in the molding to eliminate a warping problem that had been widespread on the Alcos the previous years.

1954

The 2033 Union Pacific, the 2032 Erie and the 2031 Rock Island were all available but not in sets. All the Alcos were dropped from the line in 1955. The GPs replaced them as an 027 diesel.

1957

The Alcos reappeared, but in a much cheapened form. Three were available: the 202 Union Pacific, the 204 Santa Fe, and the 205 Missouri Pacific.

The 202 Union Pacific came in orange with black lettering. It had a headlight and a two-position reverse. It had a sheet metal frame, rather than cast, and the front pilot, which used to be metal and part of the frame, was now plastic and part of the body. The number boards had no numbers. One screw held the entire body to the frame. It used plastic trucks. There was no front coupler.

The Union Pacific came as an A unit only and used the same type of motor that was introduced into the switch engines in 1955, a motor made from fabricated sheet metal stamping rather than a casting. It still had Magne-Traction.

The 204 Santa Fe and the 205 Missouri Pacific were available in AA combination. They had non-operating front couplers, Magne-Traction and a three-position reverse, making them of somewhat higher quality than the Union Pacific. They had no horn. The switcher-type trucks were now made of plastic instead of metal. So while they cheapened the trucks, they still were technically incorrect.

The 204 Santa Fe came in the freight colors of blue and yellow with red striping. Many railroads, including the Santa Fe, used one set of colors for their freight locomotives and another for their passenger locos. The Santa Fe freight colors were blue and yellow, while their passenger colors were silver and red. The 1958 Lionel catalog illustrated the 204 Santa Fe in its freight

colors at the head of a set of passenger cars, something that would never have happened on the real railroad. To compound the error, elsewhere in the 1958 catalog a Santa Fe F-3 in silver and red passenger colors was shown at the head of a freight set.

The 205 Missouri Pacific came in light blue with white lettering.

1958

The 202 Union Pacific was dropped. The 205 Missouri Pacific was available again, as was the blue and yellow Santa Fe, but the number of the Santa Fe was changed to 208 because of the addition of a remote control horn. Both locos came in AA combinations.

Two new two-unit Alcos were introduced: the 210 Texas Special and the 209 New Haven. The 210 Texas Special, in red and white with a black frame, had non-operating couplers on both ends, Magne-Traction and headlight, but no horn. The 209 New Haven, in black, orange and white, had a horn and was mechanically and electrically the same as the 208 Santa Fe.

A single-unit Alco, the 216 Burlington, was introduced in 1958. It came in silver with red lettering, and had a front coupler but no horn.

A bottom-of-the-line 212 U.S. Marine Corps Alco was introduced also. It was blue with white lettering. It had no front coupler or horn. An uncataloged dummy A unit is known to exist.

There was a change on the trucks of the Alcos in 1958. When the non-power trucks were changed to plastic in 1957 it was discovered they would heat up and warp when the loco derailed, so in 1958 Lionel redesigned the truck frame, making it metal. The side panels remained plastic, however, since they did not come in contact with the wheels and axles, the parts that generated the heat.

The redesigned trucks were used on the top-of-the-line Alcos, the ones with the horn and three-position reverse, but the cheaper ones continued to use all plastic truck assemblies.

1959

The 208 Santa Fe ran again, but all the other Alcos from the year before were dropped, except for the 212 U.S. Marines. Introduced this year was the 217 Boston & Maine and the 218 Santa Fe. The 218 came in passenger colors of silver and red, while the Boston & Maine came in blue and black with white lettering. Both had headlights, three-position reverse, and Magne-Traction. The 218 Santa Fe came as an AA combination, but the 217 Boston & Maine was offered in an AB combination. This was the first time any Alco had ever been offered with a B unit. An uncataloged Boston & Maine, numbered 226, was also available with a horn.

There were also 227 & 228 Canadian National Alcos made in 1959. They were uncataloged versions made for Parker Brothers. They were green, with yellow markings and lettering. The 228 came with front coupler and the 227 without front coupler or reverse unit.

1960

The 218 Santa Fe was unchanged, while the 208 Santa Fe, the 217 Boston & Maine and the 212 U.S. Marines were dropped. Two new units were offered: the 224 U.S. Navy and the 225 Chesapeake & Ohio. The 224 had a headlight and was offered in an AB combination. The Chesapeake & Ohio had a headlight, a two-position reverse and a front coupler. It was an A-unit only.

1961

The 218 Santa Fe ran again as an AA combination, but there was also a Santa Fe AB combination. In the AB combination the A unit was numbered 220 and the B unit was numbered 218C. The 218 had a headlight, Magne-Traction, horn and a three-position reverse. The 220 had a headlight and Magne-Traction.

New this year was the 231 Rock Island in red and black with white lettering. This loco had headlight, two-position reverse, Magne-Traction and front coupler. It came in an 027 gift pack box with three operating "space age" cars and a caboose. An all-black version with white lettering is also known to exist.

The 224 U.S. Navy was dropped, while the 229 Minneapolis & St. Louis was introduced. It was an A-unit only, with front coupler, headlight, Magne-Traction, horn and two-position reverse.

The Chesapeake & Ohio ran again, but its number was changed to 230 because it no longer had a front coupler.

1962

The 218 Santa Fe ran again, but only in AA. The 220 and 218C were dropped. The 229 Minneapolis & St. Louis remained the same as the previous year, but came with a B unit. The 231 continued as an A unit only. The 230 Chesapeake & Ohio was dropped.

The Texas Special was reintroduced in 1962, with the number 211. It had front coupler, headlight, Magne-Traction and a two-position reverse. It came in an AA combination.

The 222 Rio Grande was introduced. It had front coupler, a single axle drive and no reverse unit.

Also introduced was the 232 New Haven. It was the bottom-of-the-line unit, with headlight, Magne-Traction and two-position reverse. It had only a single axle drive and no front coupler. It was all-orange with white and black lettering.

1963

The 218 Santa Fe ran again, unchanged from the previous year, and so did the 231 Rock Island, but another Santa Fe was added to the line, the 223. It had the red and silver color scheme and came in an AB combination, with headlight, horn and two-position reverse, but it did not have Magne-Traction. Magne-Traction was also dropped from the 211 Texas Special in 1963.

The 229 Minneapolis & St. Louis and the 232 New Haven were dropped. The Rio Grande had its front coupler removed and its number was changed from 222 to 221. It was the only single-unit Alco in the Lionel line.

1964

The 218 Santa Fe, the 223 Santa Fe, and the 231 Rock Island were dropped. Running in the place of the discontinued Santa Fes was the 212 Santa Fe, in red and silver, without Magne-Traction. It had a horn and headlight. The 221 Rio Grande remained the same as the previous year. The 211 Texas Special was dropped.

The Minneapolis & St. Louis reappeared with a new number — 213. It came as an AA combination with front coupler, headlight and two-position reverse. It had no horn or Magne-Traction.

1965-1969

The 212 Santa Fe continued without change in 1965, while the 213 Minneapolis & St. Louis and the 221 Rio Grande were dropped. The 211 Texas Special was brought back again, with all features being the same as they were on the previous run.

In 1966 the 212 Santa Fe and the 211 Texas Special ran again without change. Both the 212 Santa Fe and the 211 Texas Special were dropped in 1967 and no Alcos were offered in that year or in 1968.

The 2041 Rock Island in black and red with white lettering was introduced in 1969. This model looked very much like the early die-cast frame version from the 50s. It had a headlight, front and rear couplers, and a two-position reverse. Lionel also reintroduced the Chesapeake & Ohio and gave it the number 2024. It was almost featureless, having only a front coupler.

There were so many cheap Alcos made by Lionel through the years that it is hard to keep track of them all, since the company seemed willing to make up uncataloged "department store" specials for almost anyone who asked. During the 1960s the company was disorganized and had no firm sales policies. A few uncataloged Alcos not already mentioned are the 215 Santa Fe unit; 216 M. & St. L. A; 221 Santa Fe A in olive; 221 USMC A in olive; 1055 Texas Special A; 1065 Union Pacific A; 1066 Union Pacific A; and 219 Mo Pac AA.

RATING

In order to establish a scale of availability and desirability, the Alcos have to be divided into groups. The first would be those better Alcos made before 1957. The second would be the cheaper Alcos made in 1957 and after.

Of the first group, the hardest to find is the yellow UP with a gray nose. This can truly be classified as rare. Next in scarcity is the Rock Island, followed by the silver UP with gray roof. Most common would be the all-silver UP and the yellow UP.

The cheaper Alcos have to be subdivided into double units and single units. The hardest to find of the double units is the 209 New Haven AA. Next is the 204 Santa Fe AA in freight colors, followed by the 217 Boston & Maine AB and then the 224 U.S. Navy AB. The most sought after of the A units are the uncataloged 227 and 228 Canadian Nationals and the all-orange 232 New Haven.

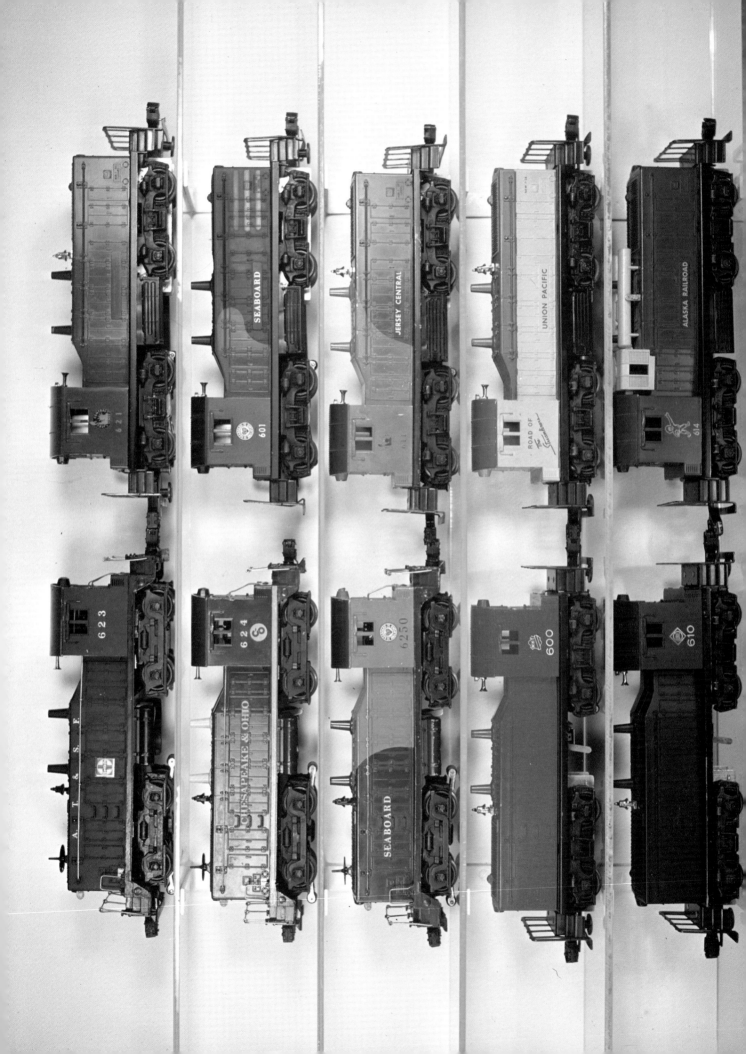

GM SWITCHERS

The prototype for Lionel's diesel switcher was Electro-Motive's NW-2, although Lionel itself did not seem sure of that fact for several years and many collectors are still not sure.

When the switcher came out in 1949, Lionel did not refer to it by a prototype number in the catalog. The catalog merely said the switcher was an accurate model of a "GM switching engine." Lionel continued this general sort of reference until 1955, when the catalog called the switcher a Model of GM's "1,000 horsepower SW-1."

This was a mistake and perhaps accounts for the reason so many collectors call the switcher an "SW" today. The NW-2 was the 1,000 horsepower locomotive, not the SW-1, which was 600 horsepower. There were other differences between the NW-2 and the SW-1.

Although they both had the same frame, the NW-2's hood was longer, coming out to the edge of the front stairwell. The SW-1's hood, two feet shorter, contained in that stairwell area a sandbox. The NW-2 had two exhaust stacks and the SW-1 had only one, while the bell of the NW-2 was located just forward of the front stack and the bell of the SW-1 was located at the front of the hood. Both came with or without that "brakewheel" looking structure on top, which was actually a radio antenna.

In 1956 the Lionel catalog changed its copy and properly identified its diesel switcher as a 1,000 h.p. NW-2.

The "W" in the NW and SW General Motors designation meant the frames of those locomotives were welded. Earlier models in the EMD switcher series, the NC and SC, had cast iron frames, made by the General Steel Casting Corporation of Granite City, Illinois. General Motors eventually dropped all the Cs, preferring the Ws because they could be made in GM's own shops.

The year-by-year development of Lionel's diesel switchers:

1949

The model of the NW-2 had a cast zinc frame, along with cast trucks. It also featured front and rear headlights, automatic couplers, wire handrails, running lights, and Magne-Traction. It was an excellent model and was of a completely new design. None of the parts had ever been used on any previous Lionel model.

Introduced in both O gauge and 027, the switchers were numbered 622 and 6220. This followed the pattern set by the steamers of having three-digit numbers indicate O gauge and four-digit numbers indicate 027.

The power truck and motor used a combination worm and spur drive system (explained in more detail on page 43). The motor was attached to the power truck by only one screw and could be separated easily from the truck for repair work. The truck panels were accurate reproductions of the AAR type-A trucks which EMD used on their diesel switchers. The wheels had bronze bearings.

1949 frame with bell.

The Magne-Traction on the switchers was the first that Lionel placed on any locomotive, but, as explained in the F-3 section of the book, the system had its flaws.

The switchers in 1949 featured a mechanically activated bell for the first time. The bell and hammer were placed on the front truck and the hammer was driven off the front axle and struck the bell continuously as the axle turned. The previous bell system used by Lionel, on the steam switcher, was electrically energized. The only trouble with the new system was that the bell could not be turned off, as the electrical system could, and the incessant ringing was annoying to many operators — especially if they were adults. These locomotives are often found today with the bell system removed.

The 1949 catalog showed the 622 and 6220 coming in all-black with Lionel markings, but none are known to exist that way. They came with the markings of the Santa Fe. On the hood above the handrails is the A.T. & S.F. markings and below that is the Santa Fe herald decal. Some of the early switchers had the General Motors decal below the Lionel number on the cab, but the later and more common way for the GM decal to be found is below the "Built by Lionel" box at the front of the hood.

GM SWITCHERS
623 Santa Fe
624 Chesapeake & Ohio
6250 Seaboard
600 MKT
610 Erie

621 Jersey Central
601 Seaboard
611 Jersey Central
613 Union Pacific
614 Alaska

The 622 had its number on the front end of the locomotive, just below the radiator. The 6220 did not have its number there, although the catalog showed one there.

1950

The catalog showed the 622 with New York Central markings, but it is not known to have been made that way. It is commonly found with A.T. & S.F. markings, as it appeared in late 1949. It has the GM logo below "Built by Lionel" and "622" underneath the radiator. However, at least one train expert recalls seeing a New York Central 622 diesel. He is Dan Moss of Mobile, Alabama, a specialist in prewar Lionel, but quite informed about postwar, too. For many years Moss did repair and assembly work on Lionel trains.

"I once had a 622 lettered N.Y.C.," says Moss. "I cannot remember if the body was purchased unassembled, or if the unit was purchased complete. I think I received the body with the N.Y.C. markings on it from a grab bag and then assembled the engine myself.

"Years ago Lionel would offer grab bags of miscellaneous parts to dealers. There might be a 10-dollar grab bag, or a 15-dollar one, or a 25-dollar one. The 25-dollar one, for instance, might have 100 dollars worth of parts in it. You just took your chances when you ordered. Sometimes you would get things you could use and sometimes not. It was actually better for collectors than for dealers, since the dealers might get stuck with parts that would sit on their shelves forever, but since I was a collector I would often order things through grab bags. They were usually parts and miscellaneous pieces that were sitting in the Lionel bins that they wanted to get rid of — odd ball or discontinued stuff that the inventory was too low on to distribute the normal way.

"That's how I believe I received the 622 N.Y.C., through a grab bag. Anyway, I had it in the latter half of the 50s, when a man came through and saw it. He said he just had to have it because he was such a great N.Y.C. fan. That's not unusual in these parts. I'm a fan of the New York Central myself. I let him have it — for thirty or forty dollars — and it was years later that I realized he had obtained a very rare item. I did not even remember his name by then. But somewhere, there is a lucky collector with a New York Central 622."

As mentioned earlier, Magne-Traction was changed on the diesel switcher in 1950. At the same time, Lionel put a cast weight in the frame

above the power truck to improve the pulling power. In spite of these changes, the 622 still did not pull as well as it should have.

Weighted frame, 1950 and after.

The ball-thrust bearing system was changed in 1950. The year before the ball bearings had no retainer, but now a retainer was added to the power truck. This took up more space and required a larger pocket in the frame for the power truck to fit into. As a result, the way the motor was mounted to the trucks was changed and consequently the 1949 and 1950 motors and power trucks were not interchangeable.

1951

The diesel switchers were dropped.

1952

The black Santa Fe was reintroduced, with the number 623. This time it was shown properly in the catalog. The markings were the same as the 1950 version of the Santa Fe except that the GM decal was dropped from the side of the hood.

The 624 Chesapeake & Ohio in blue with yellow lettering and trim was introduced. Inside and outside it was the same as the 623 Santa Fe.

There was a couple of mechanical changes made. Magne-Traction was again adjusted, this time to the system with the magnet inside the axle of the power truck, the system first used on the 2343 and 2344 F-3 diesels in 1950. With the introduction of the new style Magne-Traction the pulling power of the diesel switchers was greatly increased.

The bothersome mechanical bells were eliminated from the switchers this year.

1953

The 623 Santa Fe and the 624 Chesapeake & Ohio ran again without change.

1954

The 623 Santa Fe and the 624 Chesapeake & Ohio continued unchanged, while the 6250 Seaboard in blue and orange with white lettering was introduced. The four-digit 6250 number indicated the Seaboard was an 027 item, but there was no difference between it and the O gauge

623 and 624. Most times an 027 item was a cheapened version of an O gauge item but there were exceptions. The 6250 Seaboard was an exception. The 6250 was the first switcher to come in a set since 1950.

The lettering on the 6250 was applied by decal.

1955

The 623 Santa Fe and the 624 Chesapeake & Ohio were dropped. The 6250 Seaboard continued without change except that the lettering was rubber-stamped rather than decal. The rubber-stamped version of the 6250 is harder to find than the decaled version, but the decal version had a tendency to flake and is much harder to find in good condition than the rubber-stamped version is.

The 6250 Seaboard was the last of the "scale-detailed" diesel switchers because in 1955 a greatly cheapened version of the switcher was introduced. The first of the cheap models were the 600 M-K-T and the 610 Erie.

The bodies of the 600 and 610 were essentially the same as the other diesel switchers, but without wire handrails, marker lights or radio antenna. The exhaust stacks, which had been attached separately, were now a part of the plastic casting of the body. The bell and horn were changed to die-cast metal. One addition to the body was riveting detail on the cab roof.

The frame was changed from cast to stamped sheet metal, with sheet metal stairs and handrails. The handrails on the front of the diesel had been wire. The stamped handrails were cheaper to assemble and stronger — the old wire rails were easily bent and broken — but did not look as good.

The couplers were no longer electro-magnetic and the headlights were now non-operating.

The fuel tanks that had been located on the underside of the frame between the trucks were eliminated, further detracting from the appearance.

The motor and the power truck were now connected in such a way that they could not be separated. This made repair work on them difficult.

The frame of the power trucks, which had been cast, were changed to stamped aluminum and was inferior to the old model. It was made of aluminum in order not to interfere with the Magne-Traction, but the vibration from the motor caused the power truck frame to shake and eventually the motor loosened and shifted and the frame would interrupt the action of the armature and the engine would quit running.

The non-power trucks were shifted from the front to the rear, and were made of sheet metal starting in 1955. Also starting in 1955 some switchers came with only one of the power axles magnetized. Before, both axles were magnetized on all switchers.

The side panels of both trucks were no longer screwed on, for easy removal, but were staked on. They were also wrong.

The truck panels were changed from models of the AAR type-A trucks to models of the Blomberg truck, the kind used by EMD on road diesels of B-B configuration, but not on yard switchers such as the NW-2. The Blomberg truck was used on the F-3, and Lionel's model was a good one, but it should not have been used on the EMD switcher.

The most prominent feature of the Blomberg truck is the outside spring hanger which protrudes from the side between the wheels. These permitted better cushioning of side-to-side movement, a cushioning necessary on high speed road transportation but not on the slower traveling NW-2s.

The 600 M-K-T came in bright red unpainted plastic body with white lettering. The sheet metal frame was black on most, although some had a gray frame with yellow handrails. The 610 Erie came in black with yellow lettering and a black frame.

The 6250 Seaboard and the diesel switchers that came before it sold for $25. The 600 M-K-T and the 610 Erie sold for $13.95. The prices reflected the qualities of the locomotives.

1956

The 600 M-K-T and the 610 Erie were dropped, as was the 6250 Seaboard. Replacing the 6250 was a 601 Seaboard, with the sheet metal frame and other 1955 alterations, but with an operating headlight, simulated plastic fuel tank, and a horn. This was the first switcher to come with a horn. To make room for it the E-unit was moved forward, and so that the E-unit fit properly, a portion of the power truck frame was cut out. The new plastic fuel tank did not look as good as the old tank, but at least it improved the barren looks of the tankless 1955 version. The 601 had a black and red color scheme with white lettering. It had operating couplers. It sold for $25.

Also introduced was the 621 Jersey Central. It came in unpainted blue plastic with a black frame and orange lettering. It was shown in the 1956 catalog with an orange frame and orange lettering but it is not known to have been produced that way. The 621 was without operating headlights or fuel tanks, like the Katy and Erie from the year before, and it had only one magnetic axle. It had a horn and operating coupler. It sold for $22.50.

1957

The number of the Seaboard was changed to 602 as the operating couplers were dropped. A working headlight was added and the price remained $25. The 621 Jersey Central continued, but with a brighter shade of blue. A new 611

Jersey Central was introduced. It had a blue plastic body, with the rear portion painted orange, making it two-tone blue and orange.

1958

The 602 Seaboard and the 611 Jersey Central ran again without change. The 613 Union Pacific was introduced. It came in yellow and gray with red lettering and a black frame. It had an operating headlight, non-operating couplers, and two magnetic axles.

1959

The 602 Seaboard, 611 Jersey Central and 613 Union Pacific were dropped. The 614 Alaska was introduced. It came in blue with yellow lettering on a black frame. It had an operating headlight and non-operating couplers, and the front coupler was not self-centering. It had a two-position reverse, the first switcher to have that instead of a three-position reverse. The reverse lever stuck out the top of the hood, to the right of the dynamic brake unit, which was the outstanding feature of this loco. The unit was made of yellow plastic and was placed in front of the cab, along with hooded air reservoirs. On real engines these reservoirs would normally be placed on the bottom of the frame, except in special cases, such as when extra-large water tanks on the bottom might take up so much room that the air reservoirs would not fit.

Dynamic brakes were never actually put on NW-2s. They were put on a few of the larger SW-7s, -8s, -9s and -1200s, although never on the Alaska. They were put on EMD switchers serving railroads in rugged regions.

The Lionel model is commonly found with the brake unit and air tanks missing, because they were poorly secured to the body and fell off easily. Most of the 614 Alaskas had the "Built by Lionel" box at the front of the hood in the same blue as the rest of the body, but there is a variation in which the "Built by Lionel" and its rectangle border appear in yellow.

1960

The 614 Alaska was the only switcher available.

1961

The 616 Santa Fe with black body and white lettering and striping was introduced. It featured a horn, headlight, non-operating couplers and Magne-Traction.

1962

The 616 Santa Fe was continued without change and another Santa Fe, numbered 633, was introduced in medium blue with yellow lettering. It featured a headlight, but had only a single-drive axle on its power truck. All other diesel switchers up to this time had double-axle drive. It had a two-position reverse and no front coupler. This was a very cheap model.

1963

The number of the black Santa Fe was changed to 617 as it now came with front and rear self-centering couplers. And for the first time since 1954 it had marker lights and radio antenna. But it only had one magnetic axle, a two-position reverse, and a much cheaper frame, similar to the one used on the 633.

The cheap blue Santa Fe had its number changed, too, from 633 to 634, reflecting the addition of a front coupler.

1964

The 617 and 634 Santa Fes were dropped and no diesel switchers ran.

1965

The 634 Santa Fe was offered again, unchanged from 1963.

1966

The 634 ran again with no change, except that the warning stripes on the front of the loco were eliminated.

1967 and 1968

No diesel switchers offered.

1969

A 645 Union Pacific was offered and it was the cheapest ever made. It had single-axle drive, non-operating couplers, no other features. It came in an all-yellow body with red lettering and striping.

RATING

Like the Alcos, the switchers have to be broken into two groups in determining their desirability. There are the good early ones, and there are the cheaper ones made starting in 1955.

Of the better GM switchers, the 622 black version with NYC markings shown in the 1950 catalog would be the most valued by collectors. Next would come the 6220 and 622 bell-ringing Santa Fes, followed by the 6250 Seaboard. There are fewer rubber-stamped 6250 Seaboards of the 1955 variety than there are decal versions of 1954, but a decal version with the decal in excellent shape is harder to find than any rubber-stamped model. The good switchers that turn up most often are the 623 Santa Fe and the 624 Chesapeake & Ohio.

Of the cheaper switchers, the 613 Union Pacific is the most difficult to find. Then comes the 614 Alaska with brake unit and air tanks intact, followed by the orange and blue 611 Jersey Central. The 617 Santa Fe made in 1963 is also rather scarce. An uncataloged 634 Union Pacific was available around 1966. It was painted yellow and is difficult to find.

This is a group — again like the Alcos — that would be good for new collectors to take an interest in. With the exception of the all-but-phantom 622 with NYC markings, the diesel switchers are available, not economically prohibitive, and there are no significant variations.

44 TONNERS

627 Lehigh Valley
629 Burlington
625 Lehigh Valley

628 Northern Pacific
626 Baltimore & Ohio

Lionel introduced its model of the 44-ton switcher with a splashy display in the 1956 catalog.

"Originally built by the General Electric Company as an industrial switcher," the copy beside a picture of the 628 Northern Pacific said, "this versatile, practical 400 h.p. locomotive proved so successful that today many of the big railroads use her for short-run freight and passenger service."

The Lionel copywriters were off again, not letting the facts stand in the way of a good story.

Although the 44-ton switcher was of industrial size, it was not designed for industry. Just the opposite. It was designed specifically for the railroads as a result of a labor situation.

In 1937 the railroads and the firemen's union reached an agreement that any diesel locomotive over 90,000 pounds would have to have a fireman aboard. This was an effort to protect firemen's jobs. It was then that the 44-ton diesel was developed. At 88,000 pounds it was the largest locomotive that one man could operate under the agreement. The first 44-tonner was made by the Davenport Locomotive Works of Davenport, Iowa, in February of 1939, and delivered to the Rock Island Railroad.

Later General Electric became the leader in the production of the 44-ton diesel. Some of them, through traction modifications, found their way into industrial use, but the great majority of them

were used by common carriers. After 1963 the railroads found little use for the small switchers because the firemen restrictions were relaxed and larger locomotives were permitted to operate with only one man.

625 Lehigh Valley.

The Lionel model of GE's 44-ton switcher was not a particularly good one. It was about twice as large proportionately as it should have been. To be in scale, the Lionel's 44-tonner should have been about the same size as the 41 Army switcher. As it was, it was the same size as the GM switcher which in real life weighed three times as much as a 44-ton diesel. Apparently Lionel wanted another diesel in their 027 line to go along with the GM switcher and to replace the Alco, which was discontinued in 1955.

The 44-ton diesel used the same trucks as the 1955 version of the GM switcher. These trucks were models of the trucks used on road diesels and were incorrect for yard diesels. Also, the Lionel model of the 44-tonner had the catwalks, or porches, at each end, which the real 44-ton diesels did not have.

The frame of the 44-ton diesel was the same as the GM switchers used after 1955. It was sheet metal and had sheet metal railings at each end. The trucks, too, except for the addition of plastic steps at the ends, were the same as were used on the NW-2 switcher, the power truck having the same aluminum stamping.

1956

There were three road names introduced in 1956: the 627 Lehigh Valley in all red with white lettering: the 628 Northern Pacific in black with yellow lettering; and the 629 Burlington in silver with red lettering. The 627 and 629 were poorly illustrated in the catalog, while the 628 Northern Pacific was shown somewhat differently from the model manufactured. The pictured model had only one cab window and ventilators on the side, while the one produced had several cab windows and panels on the side. Also the grill work on the front of the loco was different in the picture from the actual model.

All three versions of the 44-ton switcher had Magne-Traction, but the Lehigh Valley had it on only one power axle. All three models had operating couplers on both ends and one headlight.

1957

In 1957, the 629 Burlington was dropped. The 628 Northern Pacific and the 627 Lehigh Valley ran again without change. A new Lehigh Valley, numbered 625, was offered in red and black. It had dummy couplers. Also new in 1957 was the 626 Baltimore & Ohio in blue with yellow lettering.

1958

In 1958 all the 44-ton diesels were dropped except the 625 Lehigh Valley, which ran without change. After that the 44-ton diesels were dropped from the line.

RATING

The entire 44-ton diesel category is rather unglamorous and is not in great demand by collectors, partly because — for a group that ran only three years and were poorly displayed in the catalog — they sold pretty well. Most difficult to find are the Baltimore & Ohio, and the Burlington, followed by the 625 Lehigh Valley, the Northern Pacific and the 627 Lehigh Valley in red.

ELECTRICS
GG-1s

The Pennsylvania Railroad spent much of the 1930s completing its electrified rail network, going south from New York to Washington and west from Philadelphia to Harrisburg.

As part of the electrification program, various locomotives were being designed, and, as they were completed, they were tested on a special section of track near Claymont, Delaware. In September of 1934 two electric locomotives rolled out of GE's Erie works and immediately began the Claymont trial runs. One of the locomotives, which were somewhat similar in appearance, was called an R-1. The other was called a GG-1.

The R-1 had a center cab like the GG-1, but it had a 4-8-4 wheel arrangement with a rigid frame for its driving axles. The GG-1 had two 4-6-0 frames which were articulated. The GG designation came from the fact that the Pennsylvania gave a class G designation to its ten-wheel locos and the new locomotive was actually two ten wheelers back-to-back.

At the end of the testing — which was started before the GG-1 was completed and covered about two years for all the locomotives in the competition — the GG-1 was chosen to become the prototype for a fleet of electrics that would perform both passenger and freight service. It was a good choice.

That first GG-1, which eventually was given the number designation 4800, was still in service 40 years later. So were most of the 138 others that were built for the Pennsy between 1935 and 1943. In the history of railroading there has never been a locomotive with the performance record of the GG-1.

It is powerful, it is fast — attaining speeds of 100 miles per hour with ease — and it has tremendous acceleration. It is also handsome, managing to look contemporary through a succession of fashion vogues.

The first GG-1 had a body heavy with rivets and rather cumbersome angles. One of the nation's top industrial designers, Raymond Loewy, was called upon to style the locomotive and he smoothed off some of the corners and suggested the body be welded rather than riveted, which looked better and was cheaper. He added a Brunswick green paint job and over that placed the distinguishing five gold stripes.

Since then the GG-1 has had several other markings, including those of Amtrack, for whom, up to the summer of 1976, it was the prime mover between New Haven and Washington.

Since many railroad experts consider the GG-1 the finest all-around locomotive ever built, it is appropriate that when Lionel came out with a reproduction of the loco, it was a good one.

1947
The GG-1 was the first electric Lionel made after the war. They probably would have made a model of it sooner had not the war interrupted production plans. Although the detailing on the model was excellent, it was not in scale, because to be so would have made it about half again as long as it was, and it probably would not have been able to negotiate Lionel's O gauge track.

The 1947 catalog pictured the GG-1 with a Pennsylvania number of 4911, although the Lionel number was 2332 and the Pennsylvania number did not appear on the locomotive. Some early printings of the catalog also called the GG-1 a 6-8-6 for some unknown reason.

The locomotive was, like its prototype, a 4-6-6-4, and it came with four sets of articulated trucks, all of which swiveled independently of each other. The trucks were cast and good reproductions of the real ones. The pilots, as they were on the original, were attached to the end trucks and moved when they did. There were coil-operated couplers on each end, and their pickup shoes mounted to the bottom of each truck. These shoes had a tendency to break off when going through switches and once broken the couplers would not operate.

The GG-1s made in 1947 were single-motored units and used the same motor and motor mounting that were used in the 671 and 726 steamers, except the GG-1 motor was mounted at a 30-degree angle. These single-motored GG-1s were not really contained in a frame. The power truck was secured to the body by means of a pivot screw which went through the roof of the cab. This method was similar to that used in the prewar Flying Yankee and City of Portland. The result was the same, too. The early GG-1s had a tendency to wiggle-waggle as they went down the track.

Another disadvantage of the pivot screw was that it detracted from the appearance of the GG-1, prominently displayed as it was on the top of the cab. Also detracting from the realism of the model was the E-unit lever that protruded from the cab top just ahead of the pivot screw.

There were headlights at both ends of the loco, along with two red marker lights in each of the four corners. The wheels on both the power and dummy trucks had nickel rims.

One of the outstanding features of Lionel's GG-1 was the pantograph. It was quite authentic looking, right down to the insulators. The pantographs were collapsible and could actually be used for overhead cantenary operation if desired. There was a soldering lug inside the cab and wires could be added that ran from this lug to the positive terminal of the E-unit. At the same time the wires leading to the roller pickups were disconnected. Power would then flow from the pantograph to the motor. The insulators were rubber and functional, preventing the metal corners of the pantograph from touching the body.

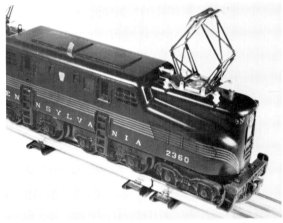

GG-1.

At the time the GG-1 was introduced, Lionel had plans to make a cantenary system of their own available, but they never did, although they had some mock-up poles made. Nevertheless, if rigged up to another type of cantenary system, the GG-1 will run. The advantage of a cantenary system is that two locos can be operated on the same track independent of each other.

The GG-1 was the first locomotive Lionel made that had a horn instead of a steam whistle. To recreate the sound of the real GG-1's horn — which was different from the air horn sound of diesels — Lionel placed a metal rod in a plastic box and when the horn was energized the rod vibrated, creating the harsh, buzz-like drone of the GG-1 horn.

The 2332 came in the glossy Brunswick green and the five gold stripes of the Pennsylvania. The locomotive had the Pennsylvania keystone on the sides and on the ends. The keystone was red and gold. The keystone on the side had the letters "PRR" in the middle, while the keystones on the ends had "2332" in the middle. The keystones were decals. A very few of the "PRR" keystones have turned up through the years rubber-stamped on. These are difficult to find. Many

collectors feel the rubber-stamped keystones were made in late 1947 or in 1948. These rubber-stamped keystones are a little larger than the decal versions.

Some of the first GG-1s off the assembly line resulted in another rare variation. Several hundred were painted semi-gloss black rather than dark green. The exact number cannot be determined for sure, but it is generally believed to be no more than half a day's production. These black GG-1s, with the original lettering, are the most valued of all the GG-1s. Not many collectors have ever seen one. One who has is Dan Moss of Mobile, Alabama.

"I bought a mint one once," says Moss, who repaired Lionel equipment for many years. "I complained about paying $75 for it. I sold it years ago for $150. I can't help but wonder about that today."

Another collector who has seen a black GG-1 is Bill Vagell, the former East Coast Lionel dealer who used to visit the Lionel factory often. But Vagell claims the locomotives were not really black, just an extremely dark shade of green.

"There were so few made on that first day's run that hardly anybody saw them and now the story has gotten around that they were black," says Vagell. "They looked black inside but if you took them out in the sunlight you could see they were very dark green. That Brunswick green is real dark anyway, but this was even darker and that's what they corrected.

"I got so mad at everybody calling them black that in 1963 I took eight GG-1s of my own, painted them black and brought them back to Lionel to put the Pennsylvania striping and markings on."

The Vagell GG-1s were exactly like the production run of 1963, except they were shiny black. The lettering was decaled and the striping was sprayed on. Vagell at the same time had two other GG-1s marked by the Lionel factory. One was gold plated and the other copper. Both are now in the collection of LaRue Shempp of Williamsport, Pennsylvania.

1948 and 1949
The 2332 ran again with no changes.

1950
The number was changed to 2330 as the GG-1 was extensively overhauled. First of all, it had twin motors which were mounted vertically. It was the same type motor used in the Alcos and GE switchers. The trucks were changed to accommodate the vertical motors.

An amazing thing happened in the 1950 catalog. The Lionel copywriters forgot to mention that the 2330 was twin-motored, one of the few times in history that the catalog underplayed anything.

Replica of Milwaukee Road bi-polar.
2332 GG-1 green
2360 GG-1 Tuscan red
2360-25 GG-1 green
2360 GG-1 Tuscan red

Perhaps the copywriters overlooked the extra motor in their excitement over Magne-Traction, which was new in 1950. The GG-1s Magne-Traction system had magnets mounted on the frame of the truck, between the wheels. They would keep this type of Magne-Traction all the way through their production run, even when other locos went to the system of Magne-Traction which put the magnets inside the axle.

The disadvantage of mounting magnets on the frame of the truck was that they rested close to the inside of the wheels and sometimes the wheels and magnets rubbed against each other, causing the locomotive to run improperly.

But with the twin motors and with twin Magne-Traction the 2330 was a powerful piece of equipment, containing almost three times the pulling power of its single-motor predecessor. There is one thing that should be pointed out about repairing the frame-magnet type of Magne-Traction used on the GG-1s (as well as on the steam locos and the early Alcos).

When it is necessary to remove a wheel for some reason, such as repairing a bent axle or replacing a worm gear, it is important to put something magnetic between the magnet and the wheel before taking the wheel off. If this is not done, approximately 50 per cent of the magnetic power will be lost — and then collectors wonder why a newly serviced GG-1 is a poorer puller than it was before. Another factor that causes loss of magnetic strength is strong vibration, like that caused by hammering on the wheels during repair.

When the magnetic power of the GG-1 is not interfered with, it will pull as much, if not more, than any other locomotive Lionel ever made. One of the reasons this is so is because the GG-1 had 12 drive wheels that actually came in contact with the track. Another reason is that its die-cast body made it heavier than most other locos. The FM and the F-3 both had twin motors, and were good pullers, but they only had eight drive wheels that came in contact with the track and they had plastic bodies. They lose most pulling contests to the GG-1.

The horn on the 2330 was different from the 2332. It now made the same air horn sound as the diesels. The new sound was the same as the diesels' but the relay system was spring loaded, which meant it did not depend on gravity to open the contact, as the other horns did. The battery for the horn on the 2330 was housed over the pilot truck at one end. It was difficult to take out, requiring the removal of the truck first. Incidentally, the 1½ volt, D-sized battery that came

with the 2330 was a Ray-O-Vac, a slight irony, since Joshua Lionel Cowen invented the dry cell and started the company that eventually became Eveready.

The wheels were also changed in 1950. They no longer had steel rims and were made of sintered iron rather than zinc. They were made of iron because zinc was non-magnetic and could not be used in connection with Magne-Traction.

The frame of the 2330 was made of aluminum, also because of Magne-Traction. The frame had to be made of a non-magnetic substance. But Lionel found aluminum was too soft and too easily bent, and in late 1950 began using brass frames. Most GG1s from then on had brass frames.

In spite of all the improvements made on the GG-1 in 1950, it sold for the same price it had in 1949 — $37.50 — which was almost as amazing as the fact that the catalog writers forgot to mention that the locomotive had two motors.

1951
The GG-1s were dropped. Several of Lionel's good items were dropped in 1951, including the 773 Hudson and the Irvington cars. The Korean War and uncertainty about the future may have contributed to this.

1955
The GG-1 was reintroduced, this time with the number 2340. Lionel had planned changes in the locomotive which never came about, but they used the new number anyway. This same situation arose again in 1956. The price of the loco was $49.50 in 1955 and the catalog feverishly announced that the GG-1 had TWIN MOTORS. It said it twice in headline-size type, underlined for emphasis.

Mechanically and electrically the 2340 was the same as the 2330, but it came in two color schemes: dark green again, and for the first time, Tuscan red. Both had the five stripe gold markings and red decaled keystones.

The Tuscan red 2340 was available separately or with four passenger cars, the set being called the Congressional. On the real Pennsylvania, only 12 of the 139 GG-1s were painted Tuscan red and these were all used for passenger service, but, coincidentally, none was used on the Congressional Limited run between New York and Washington. For this prestigious train the railroad used Brunswick green locos with five stripes until 1955. Then it had three GG-1s painted silver and these were used on the Congressional.

For purposes of identification Lionel put a suffix on the 2340 number, although it did not appear on the locomotive. The green was 2340-25 and the Tuscan was 2340-1. The color of the green was slightly darker and duller on the 2340 than it had been on the 2330.

Although the 2340 was the same mechanically as the 2330, there was a slight difference on the body of some of the 2340s. There are two portholes towards the top of the side of the cab, on either side of the Pennsylvania herald. On the real GG-1 these portholes are the sand ports. On the Lionel GG-1s made before 1955 these sand ports were merely depressions, there was no actual hole in the metal. But on the 2340 of 1955 there is a small, smooth hole that actually broke through the metal.

1956

There was no change in the GG-1, although the number was changed to 2360. On the Lionel boxes and in the catalog the green was numbered 2360-25 and the Tuscan 2360-1. The Congressional set was still available. The sand port on some 2360s, through a casting flaw, was jagged and smaller than the year before. Not all the flashing was cleared away.

1957

The 2360-25 Brunswick green was still available with five gold stripes, but it was not illustrated in the catalog. The 2360-1 Tuscan red had its gold striping changed from five stripes to one thick stripe. This followed a change that the Pennsylvania Railroad made.

The Pennsy keystone on the side was much larger and was red and white, rather than red and gold. The Pennsylvania lettering on the side was much larger, too.

The Congressional set was dropped and the Tuscan red came with a freight set.

1958

The 2360-25 in Brunswick green and the 2360-1 in Tuscan red ran again without change. No sets. Both dropped the next two years.

1961

The 2360 returns, this time in Tuscan only with solid stripe. The air intake ventilators on the right front of the loco were reduced in size and the pickup shoe on the pilot truck was moved from the front to the back. There were also a few extra holes in the bottom plate. The holes were there because it was the same assembly that was used on the milk car and the holes were for that car.

It is not clear why they reduced the size of the intake ventilators. On the real GG-1s the ventilators were moved up after it was discovered that snow could float into the lower ventilators and clog them. The 2360 came in a $100 freight set and was listed separately for $59.95.

1962

The 2360 remained the same and came in both a freight set and with gold-striped passenger cars. It sold separately for $60.

Decaled 2360.

1963

The 2360 stayed the same except the Pennsylvania lettering was decaled rather than heat stamped, as it had been from the beginning. This was the last year the GG-1 ran.

RATING

The original single motor 2332 is the most available of the group. The black version in excellent condition or better is the rarest. All GG-1s are popular with collectors.

GG-1s are typically found with the center area of the striping and lettering worn, especially the letters N-S-Y-L-V-A, since youngsters usually picked up the loco from the middle. Naturally, original lettering and striping that is clear and unworn is preferred.

Shown with the GG-1s on page 36 is a replica of one of the Milwaukee Road's famous bi-polars. Custom-made by Pierre Maurer of Nutley, New Jersey and Robert Spangler, these limited production models use GG-1 frames, motors, and truck assemblies. Many tinplate trains have been modeled after the giant bi-polars, including the great Lionel 381 Standard gauge model.

The real bi-polars, introduced in 1919, were wonderful engines. They were used in a mountainous stretch of the Milwaukee Road between Othello and Tacoma, Washington. Shortly after the first bi-polar was put in service, the railroad arranged a series of pulling contests between it and some of the mighty steamers of the time, like the Mallet 2-6-6-2. The bi-polars always won.

OTHER ELECTRICS

In addition to the GG-1, Lionel made three types of electrics during the postwar years. They were: General Electric's EP-5 rectifier, built for the New Haven Railroad; GE's E-33, built for the Virginian; and GE's 80-tonner.

During the 1950s and 1960s the double-cabbed EP-5s were common along the New Haven, which, back in 1907, was the first railroad to install Westinghouse's 11,000 volt, 25-cycle, single-phase AC electric system.

A rectifier-type loco converts alternating current into direct current, a process in which a great deal of heat is generated. The box-like structure on the roof of the EP-5s and E-33s was the cooling unit, which dissipated the heat. The advantage of rectifiers was that they could pack more horsepower into a smaller space than motors, such as the GG-1, that ran on alternating current. For instance, the GG-1 was rated at 4600 horsepower and the EP-5 at 4000, but the GG-1 required a body that was much bigger than the EP-5's.

1956

Lionel's model of the EP-5 was the 2350 New Haven and it was introduced in 1956. It was an accurate model except for the trucks. The real EP-5 had six-wheel trucks, while the Lionel model had the Blomburg-style four-wheel trucks, which Lionel had originally made for the F-3.

Although Lionel's model was given the number 2350, the number boards on the loco bore the number 375, which was the actual number of one of the New Haven's EP-5s.

The 2350 New Haven used a new plastic body casting and stamped frame, but its single motor and power trucks were the same as those used in the F-3, and the horn bracket was the same as that used in the FM. The pantograph was the same as those used on the GG-1, except on the New Haven there were no rubber insulators needed, since the body was plastic.

The frame was made of sheet metal, although the battery box on the bottom of the frame was die-cast. The 2350 New Haven had headlights and operating couplers at both ends and had Magne-Traction.

The 2350 came in the familiar New Haven patchwork black, orange and white color scheme, but there were color variations in the lettering. The most common letter coloring had the large "N" on the side in white against a black background, while the large "H" was in orange against a white background. Along with this, the words "New Haven" were in white and the number 2350 was in orange. A rare version, made only during the first run in 1956, had the "N" and "New Haven" in orange against a black background, while the "H" and the "2350" were in black against a white background.

Rare orange "N" New Haven.

1957

The 2350 New Haven ran again, unchanged, and the 2351 Milwaukee Road EP-5 was introduced. In real life, the Milwaukee Road never had an EP-5 on their line. Neither did the Great Northern nor the Pennsylvania. The Milwaukee Road did have a somewhat similar looking "Little Joe" electric at one time.

The 2351 Milwaukee Road was identical to the New Haven except for the color scheme, which was yellow, maroon and black with yellow lettering on a maroon background.

1958

The 2350 New Haven and the 2351 Milwaukee Road were unchanged. The 2352 Pennsylvania was introduced. Its color scheme was Tuscan red with gold lettering and striping. Otherwise exactly the same as the 2350 and 2351.

1959

The 2350 New Haven and 2351 Milwaukee Road were dropped. The 2352 Pennsylvania continued without change. The 2358 Great Northern was introduced and it was the same as the other EP-5s except for its color scheme, which was orange, green and yellow with yellow lettering and striping. For some reason the decals on the 2358 Great Northern were defective and are usually found deteriorated in some manner, even when new in the box. There are reproduction decals available for the Great Northern nowadays.

1960

The 2358 Great Northern was available without change, while the 2352 Pennsylvania was dropped. This was the last year for the EP-5s.

RATING

The most sought after of the group is the 2350 New Haven with the orange "N" and the black "H." Next is the Great Northern, followed by the Pennsylvania, the Milwaukee Road and the white "N" New Haven.

THE VIRGINIA RECTIFIER

Virginian electric.

Lionel introduced their model of the Virginian rectifier in 1958. It was a good model of the E-33, which GE built for the railroad. Once again, the trucks on the model were wrong. Lionel threw on the F-3 trucks, as they had done on so many other diesels and electrics. But the body was especially cast for the Virginian.

The model used the same pantographs as the EP-5s and the GG-1s and the same type frame as the GPs. There was a minor alteration to the frame, however. A handrail was spot-welded to the frame on the short hood end. This was not present on the GP's frame. Also, the front handrail on the E-33 was cut and bent to fit in slots in the plastic body.

The Virginian rectifier was a poor seller. It was rather ugly; it looked as if the designers couldn't figure out what they wanted it to be — an electric, a Geep, or something in between. Although it was offered for two years, 1958 and 1959, the second year Lionel was merely trying to get rid of the stock they had built up the year before.

Because so few Virginian rectifiers were sold, it is now the most valued of the rectifiers, more so than any of the EP-5s except the orange "N" New Haven.

520

The cheapest electric Lionel made was the 520. It was a model of an 80-ton box-type loco. A bottom-of-the-line item, the 520 had a stamped sheet metal frame and unpainted red plastic body. It had a 2-4-0 wheel arrangement with an operating coupler and a two-wheel pilot truck at one end and a fixed coupler at the other end. It used the same mechanism that the 1615 switcher and the 1130 steamer used. The 520 had a cheap plastic pantograph that could be moved up and down but broke easily. The 520 ran in 1956 and 1957. It sold for $12.95.

The 520 was not a big seller for Lionel and they are not easy to find today, although many collectors ignore it because it was such a cheap item and lacks glamour. This combination of circumstances — an item that is scarce but available — makes the 520 sort of a sleeper for serious collectors. It is extremely difficult to find with the pantograph unbroken.

520 Electric.

STEAMERS

Steam locomotives had a unique style and charm and are still the favorite of many collectors today. Joshua Cowen loved them, too, and hated to see their era pass. In this section of the book all the steamers Lionel made in the postwar period will be discussed, with the exception of lowest priced models. They are covered in a chart on page 138.

One steam locomotive was offered in 1945. It was like the prewar 224, and came in a four-car freight set. All the cars in the set were sheet metal except for a new plastic Pennsylvania gondola.

The first year of any consequence in the postwar era was 1946, when the 726 Berkshire and the 671 and 2020 turbine were introduced. Externally different, the locomotives were quite similar mechanically and electrically. The turbine will be examined first.

TURBINES

Pennsylvania steam turbine.

1946

Although many items Lionel offered in 1946 were simply modified carry-overs of prewar items, the 671 and 2020 turbines were, with the exception of their E-units, entirely new.

The 671 and 2020 were exactly the same engine with different numbers, the 2020 being offered in 027. Anything said in this section about the 671 applies to the 2020.

The 671 was a model of the Pennsylvania's S-2, a direct-drive, pistonless, steam turbine that the railroad put in service in 1944 out of a misplaced confidence in the future of steam. They also wanted to keep their many on-line coal operators happy (about 50 per cent of the coal mined in the United States was transported by the Pennsylvania). Had they made more than one of the S-2s, which they didn't, the coal companies would have been happy indeed. The S-2 turned out to be an insatiable guzzler of fuel and water at speeds under 30 miles an hour. It performed fairly well at higher speeds but the trouble was there was a lot of work to be done under 30 miles an hour and the S-2 was uneconomical.

The biggest selling points that Lionel made with their "20 wheel" model S-2 was that it had knuckle couplers, smoke and eight-wheel double worm drive.

In a worm drive motor there was one reduction gear which reduced the speed of the axle in relation to the speed of the armature and eliminated the need for other reduction gears. The 671 and 2020, as well as the 726 Berkshire, had double worm drive, which meant that instead of having one of the four driving axles powered, they had two — the two outside ones. The four inside wheels were unflanged and rode above the track, only coming in contact with it occasionally, and the side rods drove the two inside sets of drivers.

1946 Turbine — double-worm drive.

Most prewar Lionel motors were spur driven. In spur drive, all the wheels ran directly off the motor and the side rods were for looks. Oiling side rods is not important on locos that have spur drive but it is extremely important on those that have worm drive.

Horizontal motor.

Besides being double-wormed the drive in the 671 also had two spur gears that transmitted the power from the motor to the worm-shaft. These were called idler gears and made the drive a combination spur and double worm.

The drive shafts on the double worm motor took up a good deal of space and demanded that the reversing unit be placed inside the loco horizontally rather than vertically. With the horizontal mounting, the solenoid plunger was spring loaded, as opposed to dropping by gravity in vertical mountings.

In 1946 a special smoke lamp and housing were made. The housing was a die-cast chamber that the smoke lamp fitted into. The bulb had a bayonet type base measuring ⅝-inch in diameter. The bulb was mounted horizontally. One side had a depressed area that served as a cup to hold the smoke pellet. The heat from the lamp changed the smoke tablet into a liquid.

There was a pellet made for the bulb-type smoke units. The regular SP pellets did not work well in the bulb-type smoke units.

At the base of the die-cast chamber there was a rectangular piece of metal that was moved up and down by a cam driven off the left front drive wheels. This created the puffing effect. Real turbines expelled smoke in a steady stream, but Lionel's puffing looked nice anyway.

The smoke housing took up a lot of space. Access to the bulb was through the front of the boilers. The bulbs burned out quickly.

The number 671 was rubber-stamped in silver on the cab below the window. The Pennsylvania keystone herald was on the boiler front with the Pennsy number in the middle. The herald came two ways, one with white lettering on a black background and the other with gold lettering on a red background. Most came with red and gold. Lionel didn't use the black and white herald until the late runs of 1946. Although more black and white versions were eventually made, in 1946 there were more turbines that had the red and gold herald.

The 671 came with a 671W tender and the 2020 came with both the 2020W and 2466WX tenders. They were plastic with metal trucks. "Lionel Lines" was rubber-stamped in silver on the sides. The tenders had four-wheel trucks.

671W tender.

The eight-wheel drive turbine — and the eight-wheel drive 726 Berkshire as well — were no better pullers than six-wheel drive engines. That was

because the eight-wheel drive locos had no more wheels on the track than the six wheel drivers. To improve the pulling power of the turbine, Lionel engineers wanted to put a weight above the drivers, but, with the big smoke unit, there was no room.

1947

This was the biggest single year of change for the 671. The casting was modified; the motor was switched to a single worm drive, with the spur gears eliminated; a new type of smoke generator was installed; and the reverse unit was mounted vertically and the motor was mounted at a 30-degree angle.

Single-worm drive turbine.

The frame casting was almost completely altered to accept the new motor and E-unit. There was more piping detail, which made the model look more like the real engine. This might have been one of the few times when Lionel actually added detail to a model rather than subtract it.

There was a new smoke unit that worked like a little hot plate. It used the SP smoke pellet and had a better type of action for pumping the smoke out. The new smoke generator, together with the new motor mounting, created enough room for a weight to be added. It was placed between the motor and E-unit.

With the installation of the new smoke generator, the headlight, which used to double as the smoke lamp, was changed. It was now an 18 volt screw-in bulb with a regular lens instead of the angular prism-type.

All the drive wheels came with nickel rims in 1947.

Prism-type lens.   Regular lens.

1948 and 1949

The tender for the 671 was changed in 1948, as Lionel brought out the Pennsylvania-style streamlined tender with a water scoop on the bottom. The tender had 12 wheels, was made of plastic and was numbered 2671W. The whistle was mounted horizontally to the frame. The scoop became a functioning part of the whistle, as it drew air into it. Without air, whistles don't whistle.

Also in 1948 there were a few early production tenders that had three backup lights. The real tenders had these lights and when Lionel designed their tender they planned for the lights.

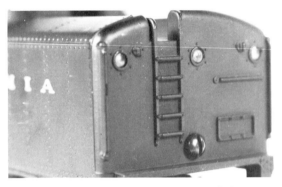

1948 2671W tender with back-up lights.

But since it was an added expense and since it was not that spectacular of a feature, the lights were dropped. The small run that was made had a one-piece clear lucite lens that fitted across all three openings. There was a hole in the frame of the tender that held the screw which held the light brackets.

2671W tender with bracket for light.

The tender on the 2020 changed its number from 2020W to 6020W in 1948 but otherwise it stayed the same. The 2020 did not get the Pennsy-style tender.

In 1948 the four flanged drive wheels were zinc with blackened steel rims. The four blind wheels were sintered iron and had no rims. In 1949 all the wheels were sintered iron without rims.

1950

Magne-Traction appeared and the frame was altered to accommodate it. The weight was removed from above the first and second drive wheels. Instead, a section of the frame was hollowed out between the first and second drive wheels to allow a round bar magnet to fit in. Running along the frame inside the drive wheels was a balanced metal plate. This transmitted magnetism to all eight of the drive wheels.

The locomotive number was changed to 681. The 2020 number was dropped completely and the turbine was only offered in O gauge. The number 681 was rubber-stamped in silver below the cab window. The side rods were changed so that the screw went into a turned steel insert. The screw used to go directly into the wheel. The counterweight on sintered wheels were recessed this year. Before they had stuck out a little.

1951

Sometime late in the year the lettering was changed. It was slightly smaller and it was heat-stamped in white. Heat stamping doesn't wear off as easily as rubber stamping.

1952

Because of the Korean War and the shortage of iron, Magne-Traction was dropped. The number reverted to 671. There was a large cavity between the first and second drive wheels where the magnet used to be. The lettering beneath the cab was rubber-stamped in silver again, perhaps because they had some left over. The number 671 appeared alone or with an "RR" printed below it, meaning it was a rerun of an earlier item.

This was the first year the turbine came with a streamlined, eight-wheel tender. It was still lettered "Pennsylvania" in white, heat-stamped lettering.

1953

Magne-Traction returned and so did the number 681, in white, heat-stamped letters. The tenders had white "Pennsylvania" markings and four-wheel trucks.

1954

A valve gear was added to the boiler, connected to the front driving wheel. This gear moved and gave a little more action to the engine. On the prototype S-2 the gear supplied oil to the bearing and was much smaller proportionally than it was on the model. A white line was painted along the edge of the running board on the side of the loco. The tender stayed the same.

1955

No changes to the loco or tender. It was discontinued the next year.

RATING

The turbines are common, but nevertheless are an interesting group to collect. There is a different, and collectable, model for each of the years it was made and to get them all is a challenge.

The 682 with the white stripe and oiler linkage is probably the collector's favorite. The linkage is often found disconnected or off completely.

BERKSHIRES

Lionel Berkshire.

1946

The 2-8-4 Berkshire, made by Lima, was the last steam locomotive to be made commercially in the United States. Lionel's model, the 726, was the biggest loco the company made in 1946. It used a modified boiler casting from the prewar 226E. A feed water heater was placed on the front of the boiler and some of the detailing was changed. The stack was moved about half an inch to the rear to accommodate the new smoke unit. The modifications, along with adding an extra driving axle, were supposed to make the 726 look like the New York Central's Berkshires, but it only bore a vague resemblance.

The trailing truck on the 726 was fitted with a drawbar. On the 226E there was simply a peg inside the cab and the drawbar on the tender hooked over the peg. To give the 726 more maneuverability on curves, the trailing truck was fitted with a drawbar which hooked to the short drawbar on the tender.

The steamchest and pilot were the same as that used on the 226E, but because the frame and smoke unit were new, the chest and pilot were mounted differently from the way they had been on the 226E. The 726 had a double worm and spur combination drive train similar to the turbine.

There were a couple of features that were unique to the 726. One was the manner in which the driving wheels and axles could be removed. It was a system, expensive in the assembly for Lionel, that was similar to that of the real locomotives. The drive wheels and bearings were completely removable. When the bottom of the

Berkshire pick-up assembly, 1946.

Berkshire pick-up assembly, 1947 through 1955.

pick-up assembly was taken off, the wheels and axles would fall out. On other types of assemblies made by Lionel, the axle rods were driven through the frame and were quite difficult to remove. Being easily removed, the wheels of the 726 were much more accessible for repairs. The roller pick-up assembly held the drive wheels in place.

The 726 had Baldwin disk wheels with nickel rims and nickel plated side rods. It used prewar, turned stanchions to hold the handrails on the body.

The smoke and headlight unit was the same as that used on the turbine, except that the units operated off 18 volts rather than 12. The motor in the Berkshire was larger than the motor in the turbine, but it made no difference in their relative pulling power.

The number 726 was rubber-stamped in silver on the cab below the window. The 726 came with a 2426W tender, which was a metal tender similar to a prewar 2226W except with postwar trucks. The early models had "Lionel Lines" rubber-stamped in silver on the side, but most of the tenders made in 1946 had white lettering. The tender had a die-cast whistle housing.

1947

As it was for the turbines, 1947 was a year of extensive changes for the 726. The same motor changes made by the 671 and 2020 were made on the 726. It was now a direct single worm motor mounted on a 30 degree angle. The E-unit was mounted vertically and the lever protruded from the top of the boiler. A ballast weight was placed between the first and second drivers and a new smoke generator was installed.

1946.

1947 and after.

The boiler casting on the 726 was changed, also. The sand dome was elongated about one-half inch. The eccentric rod bracket was enclosed behind part of the boiler casting. The handrail stanchions changed from the screw-type to the cotter pin-type.

The frame was completely changed so that the drive wheels were no longer easily removed. The pickup assembly was also changed, to the identical system used on the turbine.

Boiler castings.
1946.   1947 and after.

1948

The pilot was changed so that it had a simulated knuckle coupler and lift pin. The whistle housing was changed to plastic.

1949

The brush plates were changed, as Lionel decided to standardize them. The brush plates used on the GM Switchers, new in 1949, were installed in the 726. They did not have the protruding tubes the old plates had and took up less space. The old protruding tubes had contained the springs which supplied tension to the brushes.

1950

Magne-Traction was introduced and the number changed to 736. Spoked driver wheels replaced the Baldwin disk, reversing the process of the real Berkshires, which at the time were converting from the old spoked drivers to the Baldwin disks. The drive wheels were switched from zinc with steel rims to sintered iron without rims.

The Berkshire came with a plastic tender, number 2671WX, with six-wheel trucks. It was a streamlined Pennsylvania-style tender with Lionel Lines lettering. The plastic tender required that the draw bar of the locomotive be lengthened about a quarter of an inch so the cab would not hit the tender on curves.

1951

No changes in loco or tender.

1952

Magne-Traction was dropped and the number reverted to 726, which on some engines had the suffix RR. The headlight lens was changed from a flat, plastic disk to solid lucite. The tender went to four-wheel trucks and larger lettering with a different typeface.

1953

Magne-Traction came back from the war and so did the number 736. The lettering on the cab was changed from rubber-stamped silver to heat-stamped white, and it was slightly smaller. The color of the side rods was a brighter silver, as the plating changed from nickel to cadmium. There was a small wedge placed on the bracket below the headlight, which is a good way to tell the difference between the early and late Berkshires. The bracket protected the headlight from damage.

Boiler fronts.
1946 through 1952.   1953 and after.

1954-1966

The 736 remained the same through the years except that in 1955 the trailing truck went from die-cast to sheet metal, with plastic side frames. This was the same truck that was used on the Santa Fe-type Hudson in 1953. In 1957 the pickup assembly was made smaller and was mounted with only one screw. From 1961 onward the tender lettering read "Pennsylvania" instead of "Lionel Lines" and the tender had plastic, four-wheel trucks.

1966 was most likely the last year the 736 was made, although some leftover ones were reissued in 1968, which was the last year the Berkshire appeared.

746 NORFOLK AND WESTERN

Norfolk & Western

The 746 Norfolk & Western was brought out by Lionel in 1957. It was a model of the railroad's class J Northerns, the most powerful 4-8-4s ever made and the last of the streamlined steam locomotives to operate in the United States.

The 746 was the only Northern Lionel ever manufactured. It used the same running gear and frame as the 1957-model of the 736 Berkshire. The only change in the frame was that the eccentric crank was moved from the third driver to the second.

The boiler casting was new and a faithful reproduction of the real locomotive. It featured a plastic, bullet-shaped boiler front. The steamchest was also new, as was the trailing truck, which was more streamlined than the one on the 736. The pilot truck was the same one used on the 646 and 2046.

The 746 came with a 2046 tender with metal, four-wheel trucks. A red stripe outlined in yellow ran the length of the locomotive and tender. This 1957 version, with the stripe that ran the entire length of the tender, has become known as the long-striped version of the 746. Later tenders did not have as long a stripe.

The Berkshire wheel mechanism that Lionel used on the Norfolk & Western was too small proportionately compared to the actual locomotive.

1958 - 1960
The stripe on the tender was shortened. The stripe was now heat stamped, the earlier one having been silk-screened.

The 746 was offered in train sets from 1957 through 1959. In 1960 it was offered as a separate item only. All three years the tender came with metal trucks and it is not believed to have been made with plastic trucks. The 746 was discontinued after 1960.

The long-striped version of the 746 Norfolk & Western is preferred by collectors and is a harder to find than the short-striped version.

Next to the Hudson, the Norfolk & Western is the most prized of all the post war steamers.

K-4 PACIFIC-TYPE

1947 version of 675.

1947
The Pacific-type locos made by Lionel were not true Pacifics. Although their boilers were fairly good models of the K-4 Pacifics, they did not have the correct Pacific wheel arrangement. They were 2-6-2s. The real ones were 4-6-2s. The first two Pacific-types to appear after the war were the 675 and the 2025. They were the exact same loco, but the 675 was sold as an O gauge item and the 2025 as an 027.

The locos used the boiler casting from the prewar 225E, with extensive modifications to make it look more like a K-4. The Belpaire-type firebox was added to the boiler in front of the cab. The feedwater heater of the 225E was eliminated and a new Pennsylvania-type boiler front was added.

It had cotter pin-type stanchions, Baldwin disk drivers with nickel rims, and nickel-plated side rods. The engine came with a spur-drive motor.

Prewar 225E boiler casting.   Altered 225E casting with Belpaire firebox added.

The motor was spur driven in the 675 and 2025. They were one of three types of locomotives to have a smoke generator in 1947. The others were the Berkshire and turbine. But the generator used in the 675 and 2025 was slightly different in construction from the other two.

The early runs of the 675 and 2025 had their numbers heat stamped in white on the raised keystone that was part of the boiler front. Later runs used a red decal with the number 5690 in gold, 5690 being the number of the Pennsylvania prototype.

1948 and 1949
A new pilot with a simulated knuckle coupler and lift pin was placed on the locos in 1948. The size of the smoke stack was reduced and it had a thicker lip. The tender whistle housing changed from metal to plastic. The number of the tender with the 2025 changed from 2466WX to 6466WX, as the mechanical-type coupler replaced the coil-type. The number of the tender with the 675 remained 2466WX in 1948, but changed to 6466WX in 1949, when it also underwent the coupler change.

1950
The 675 was dropped. The number of the 2025 changed to 2035 as Magne-Traction was added. Spoked, sintered iron drivers replaced the disk drivers. The trailing truck was changed from a die-cast two-wheel to a sheet metal, stamped four-wheel. This made the locomotive a 2-6-4, still an incorrect configuration for the 4-6-2 Pacific.

The eccentric crank was different in 1950 from the crank used before and after that year. The end of the eccentric crank was crescent-shaped at the point where it fit against the wheel. Other years it was rectangular and used two pins.

The motor frame was changed to aluminum because of Magne-Traction. The aluminum showed behind the drivers and detracted from the appearance of the loco. The "X" designation was dropped from the tender because the extra handrail trim was dropped.

1951

There were two minor changes on the 2035. The armature gear bearing was switched from brass to sintered iron, and the magnets went from round to rectangular.

1952

Magne-Traction went off to war and the number 2025 came back. The O gauge 675 was offered again. Both locos had blackened steel frames, since the aluminum frame required for Magne-Traction was no longer needed. However, the sintered iron, spoked drivers remained, even though Magne-Traction was dropped. The 2025 came with the 6466W tender and the 675 came with the 2046W.

The 1952 catalog showed the 675 with a die-cast trailing truck and a 2-6-2 wheel configuration. It actually came with a stamped four-wheel trailing truck, just as the 2035 had the year before. It came with a 2046W tender, the only time a K-4 ever came with this tender.

RATING

The 1952 675 and 2025, with the sintered iron wheels, are the most difficult of the series to find. The next hardest to find is the 2035.

Lionel's model of the Pennsylvania's K-4 had one dubious distinction. It was, according to those who had to repair them, the most difficult locomotive to assemble that Lionel ever made. Because it was so difficult to assemble its place in the Lionel line was eventually taken over by the smaller Hudson-type locos first introduced in 1950.

PRAIRIE-TYPE

2026 Steam loco.

1954

The first 2-6-2 Prairie-type to appear after the war was the 224, which was identical to the prewar locomotive of the same number except that the postwar loco connected to the tender in a different way. The trucks also had knuckle couplers. It came with the 2466W tender and was included in the only set offered in 1945.

1946

The 224 ran again without change. The 1666 was introduced. This too was an exact duplicate of prewar model. In fact, the 1666 had been brought out the same year as the 224 before the war and the 224 was an O gauge version of it. The 1666 had nickel-rimmed drivers and a headlight and came with either a 2466T or 2466WX tender.

The 221 was also introduced in 1946. It had the same mechanism as the 1666 but had a streamlined, 20th Century Limited-style cowling. It was painted light gray and came with aluminum-finish drive wheels without rims. In some early models the wheels on both the pilot and trailing trucks were also aluminum-finish. The loco came with a 221T or 221W tender, which had New York Central markings decaled on.

221 Steam loco.

1947

The 224 was dropped. The 1666 ran again, although it was not cataloged. A number of changes were made. The number was rubber-stamped below the cab window. It had been lithographed onto a metal plate. The two-piece swinging bell was replaced by a fixed ornamental one. The steam chest and boiler were one unit and the pilot truck was made of sheet metal instead of being die cast. Taper pins were used in place of screws in many places and, as a consequence, the 1947 version could be assembled much quicker. It came with the 2466WX tender, the "X" designating extra handrail trim. This rubber-stamped version of the 1666 is difficult to find, although most collectors seem unaware of, or disinterested in, its scarcity.

The 221 ran again without mechanical change, but it was now painted black and the drive wheels had nickel rims, like the 1666.

1948

The 221 was dropped. The number of the 1666 changed to 2026 as smoke was added. Screws were used to secure the pilot to the boiler so that there was access to the smoke unit. A large compressor housing was placed on the pilot in front of the boiler and the sand domes were enlarged. The tender was the 6466WX.

2026 with compressor housing.   1666 without housing.

1949

The 2026 continued without much change. The smoke unit wire, which had hung down and sometimes shorted by coming in contact with the frame, was rerouted. This eliminated the shorting problem. A quick way to tell the difference between a 1948 model of the 2026 and a 1949 model is to look for the wire. If it is visible in front of the pickup assembly, it is a 1948 model.

1950

Magne-Traction was added and the number changed to 2036. The wheel arrangement was also changed, to 2-6-4. The drive wheels were rimless and sintered iron. Smoke was eliminated and so were the handrails and the eccentric rods. The trailing truck was stamped from sheet metal instead of being cast. The handrails were eliminated from the tender and the "X" was dropped from the 6466W number.

1951-53

Korean War shortages forced Magne-Traction to be dropped, smoke was added, and the number reverted to 2026. It came with either a 6466W or a 6466T tender and used the same boiler as the 1950 2036. There were no changes in 1952 or 1953.

1954

Magne-Traction returned and the number changed to 2037. It looked the same as the 2026 except for the method by which the number was placed under the cab. It was heat-stamped in white, rather than rubber-stamped in silver. A new, Santa Fe-style tender came with the loco. It was the same one brought out the year before for the 2055. It was numbered 6026T.

1955

The 2037 remained the same and a 2016 was introduced. The 2016 was the same as the 2037, only it did not have Magne-Traction or smoke, but it had a whistle. Both had headlights and the 6026-type tender.

1956

The 2037 was dropped, the 2016 was unchanged, and a new loco, the 2018, was added. The 2018 had smoke and, like the 2016, came with the 6026W tender.

1957

The 2016 was dropped, the 2018 continued unchanged, except that it came with the 1130T tender. The 2037 was reintroduced, with smoke and Magne-Traction, in both black and pink. The pink version headed the Girl's Train and came with the 1130T tender, a smaller model of the 2046 tender. The black version came with either the 6026W or 1130T tenders.

1958

The pink 2037 was unchanged, but the black came with the 6026W tender only. Some of these tenders came with plastic trucks. The 2018 was unchanged.

1959

The pink 2037 was dropped. The black continued without change, as did the 2018, except that both tenders came with plastic trucks.

1960

The black 2037 continued without change. The 2018 was dropped. Introduced was the 637, which was the exact same engine as the 2037 except for the number. It was given a three-digit number because it came in a Super O set. It had a 2046W tender with "Lionel Lines" markings.

1961, 1962, 1963

The 2037 and 637 ran again in 1961 with the only change being in tenders. The 2037 came with the 6026W tender with "Lionel Lines." The 637 had a 2046W tender with "Pennsylvania" replacing "Lionel Lines." Both tenders had plastic trucks. There were were no changes in anything in 1962 and 1963.

1964 through 1969

The 2029 was introduced and the 2037 and 637 were dropped in 1964. The 2029 was the same as the 2037 but without Magne-Traction. Instead, Lionel announced that the 2029 had "Track Gripper Wheels," which were rubber-rimmed and helped traction, but not as much as Magne-Traction did. The 2029 ran without significant change through 1969. There was no catalog in 1967 but some sets headed by the 2029 were sold through large retail chains. In 1968 the 2029 was made in Japan.

RATING

The Girl's Train engine, of course, is sought after by collectors, but none of the other Prairie-types are. They are all common and inexpensive. The rubber-stamped 1666, as mentioned, is hard to find but nobody cares.

SWITCHERS

1656 Steam switchers.

The first steam switcher Lionel offered after the war was the 1665 in 1946. It was similar to the prewar 1662, with the exception that the 1665 had postwar trucks and knuckle couplers. It had wire handrails and came with a 2403B tender (with bell), which had the same separate Bakelite coal pile as the prewar tenders did. The tender had a functioning backup light and a wire handrail along the steps leading to the coal bin.

There were two wires leading from the tender to the loco. These plugged into special receptacles in the cab. One carried the power to the front coupler and the other promoted a better ground. "Lionel Lines" was heat-stamped in white on the sides of the tender. The number 1665 was rubber stamped in silver under the cab window. The lettering on the tender was spaced almost its entire length, as it had been on the prewar version.

Lettering, 1946.

The 1665 was the only switcher produced in 1946, although the catalog also listed an 0-6-0 switcher, numbered 403. This was never made. No 0-6-0 switcher was made after the war. The 1665 was made in 1946 only. No switchers were made in 1947.

1948

The steam switcher was reintroduced with a new number, 1656. The boiler casting was changed somewhat, especially on the cab, where the roof was reinforced. The drive mechanism was redesigned and the engines could now operate on both O and 027 track. The gearing and wheels were improved on the 1656 and it no longer derailed going over O gauge switches. The gearing ratio was also changed to perform better at low speeds for switching.

The numbers beneath the cab came in two different styles. One style had serifed numerals and the numbers were fairly well spread out. The other style did not have serifs and the numbers were more condensed. Both were rubber-stamped in silver. The engine still had wire handrails.

The steam switchers, because of a high center of gravity and small wheels, were top heavy and would often roll over. The marker lights at the front of the boiler were located in a spot that made them vulnerable when the engine took a flop. As a consequence, it is extremely hard to find one of these switchers with unbroken marker lights. Another thing for collectors to look for on the switcher is the jewels in the marker lights, which were red, while in other Lionel engines they were green.

The tender with the 1656 was the 6403B. It had a bell and was die cast, with the coal pile being part of the casting. The steps had a wire handrail and the backup light functioned. The lettering on the tender said "Lionel Lines" and it came in two varieties: the scrunched up version and the elongated version. The bell clanger which had had a tendency to stick, was improved in 1948.

Condensed lettering, 1948.

1949

The 1656 switcher and the 6403B tender were unchanged. It should be noted that many experts believe the condensed lettering on the engine and tender was probably applied in 1948, while the more widely spaced letter appeared in 1949. However, that cannot be said with absolute certainty. All that is known for sure is that during the two years, 1948 and 1949, the lettering came two ways. The switcher was dropped in 1950.

1955

The steam switcher was reintroduced with the number 1615, reflecting several changes from the 1949 version. The boiler casting was changed to accommodate a new motor. The boiler now had, on the right side, a box-like protrusion which housed the brush plates of the new motor.

The locomotive looked quite similar to the 1656 but some detailing was eliminated. The simulated bell on top of the firebox was removed, as were the marker light jewels and the wire grab irons on the pilot.

The drive mechanism had a fabricated sheet metal frame, as opposed to the old zinc frame. The drivers were sintered iron, rather than cast zinc, and the side rods were cadmium plated rather than nickel. Overall the mechanism in the engine was very good. It was a good runner and a good puller and worked as well as the old switchers, perhaps better.

The front coupler was changed from the coil type to the magnetic armature type. The drawbar had a copper ground clip, which replaced the grounding wire.

The most disappointing feature of the 1615 was the tender. It was a plastic tender lacking bell, back up headlight or handrails. It was a cheap imitation of the old die-cast tender. It had metal trucks. "Lionel Lines" was heat-stamped in white, in an extended type face similar to prewar.

The switchers made in the early part of 1955 were rubber-stamped in silver. Those made later were heat-stamped in white.

The number on the cab was heat-stamped in white only.

1958

The number changed to 1625 as the front coupler became non-operating. The tender was the same, with the exception that the trucks, which had been metal, were now plastic. The switcher was discontinued after 1958.

THE HUDSON

1950 Hudson.

The New York Central's prototype Hudson was considered one of the best proportioned steam locomotives ever built. It was Joshua Lionel Cowen's favorite and he decided to have a scale model of one built.

When the 700EW was introduced in 1937 it represented the ultimate in model trains, combining the ruggedness and efficiency of mass production with the scale accuracy and attention to detail of handmade models. Volume I of this series — on prewar Lionel — goes into the 700EW in extensive detail, for those interested.

Considering the pride Joshua Cowen took in the original model, it was not surprising the company brought out the 773 Hudson for Lionel's golden anniversary in 1950.

The economic realities of the times made it impossible to duplicate the detail of the 700EW, but the 773 was nevertheless a fine piece of craftsmanship. It used the same basic boiler as the 700EW (and the later prewar 763EW), with some mounting variations. The handrail stanchions were changed to cotter pin-type and a different boiler front was used, the same one used on the postwar 736 Berkshire.

The 773 had an extensively modified frame, although the prewar crosshead guides were still present on the steam chest.

The 773's smoke unit was the same as the one on the turbines and Berkshires. It was driven by

a tab on the right hand crosshead. Smoke was one feature the postwar Hudson had that the prewar Hudson did not have, but there were some operators that could have done without it. The 773's smoke unit made a clanking sound that was annoying and occasionally today you will find the 1950 version of the loco with the smoke unit pumping assembly removed.

The 773 featured Magne-Traction and sintered iron wheels. But, unlike the prewar Hudson, the spokes on the wheels were simulated and the rims were not nickel. These wheels were not as attractive or realistic as the prewar wheels had been, but the Magne-Traction made a considerable improvement in the loco's pulling power.

The motor in the 773 was the same as that in the GM switcher, with a mounting modification. The gear ratio on the 773 was the same 18 to 1 as the prewar.

The pilot truck was changed so the big Hudson, originally designed for 072 track, could navigate O gauge curves. The wheels on the pilot truck were reduced in diameter. At the size they had been they would not have been able to swivel underneath the steam chest, something that was required of them on the sharper O gauge curves. On the less severe 072 curves the pilot wheels needed only to swivel up to the steam chest, but not under it. The steam chest was also modified.

The trailing truck was the same as the one used on the prewar except there was bolster cast into it and the drawbar mounted to the bolster.

The pilot itself, or cowcatcher, was also modified. It was raised a bit. On the prewar locomotive the pilot had a tendency to touch the center rails — especially if the track was uneven — and short out the engine.

The tender was numbered 2426 W. It was the same tender used on the late 763 and 226E before the war, but the postwar tender had postwar trucks and a slightly modified frame. The tender was die cast with a Bakelite coal pile. The whistle box was plastic, the die-cast whistle having been dropped from the line the year before. Sometimes collectors find they have a die-cast whistle with this tender and think it is the correct one, but it is not. The lettering on the tender read "Lionel Lines" and was heat-stamped in white. The tender was shown in the catalog with "New York Central" printed on the side, but this is not known to exist.

The locomotive had the number 773 rubber-stamped in silver beneath the cab window.

In spite of its quality, the 773 did not sell as well as expected and was discontinued after its 1950 run. The public in 1950 was enamored of the streamlined diesels and the Hudson apparently was too old-fashioned.

Surprisingly, the 773 was re-released in 1964 and was available through 1966. There were several changes on the 1964 version. It was minus the slide valve guides that had been on the rear of the steam chest, and the lettering on the cab was slightly larger, was rubber-stamped in white, and was a different style. The paint was more glossy than it had been.

1950 version with slide valve guides.   1964 version without the guides.

1950.   1964-1966.

The most disappointing feature on the 1964 version of the 773 was its tender. It was a plastic, Pennsylvania-type and was lettered "Pennsylvania." All this to go with the New York Central Hudson. In 1965, at least, they changed the lettering to read "New York Central," but they still used the Pennsylvania-type. In addition to everything else, the tender was too small proportionately for the loco.

The tenders in 1964, 1965 and 1966 were all equipped with four-wheel, plastic trucks.

There is a footnote to the postwar Hudson. The 1946 catalog showed two train sets which were led by a locomotive numbered 703. It was never made. It appears Lionel had plans to make one, but cancelled them. The locomotive would have been a cross between the 763 and 773. It would have had the Berkshire bulb-type smoke unit and the spoked drivers of the prewar Hudson.

SMALLER HUDSONS

NEW YORK CENTRAL-TYPE

2046 Hudson

During the postwar years Lionel made two types of Hudsons that were smaller than the 773. One type used the same boiler shell as the 726 Berk-

shire. The other type had a specially cast boiler so that it resembled the Hudsons used by the Santa Fe. The Berkshire boiler model, the 2046, appeared first and it will be discussed first.

1950

The 2046, with the 726 boiler shell modified slightly for mounting, used the same steam chest and pilot as the 726. A new four-wheel pilot truck was manufactured for the loco but the rear truck remained the same. The six-wheel drivers used on the 2046 were made of sintered iron, were spoked, and were approximately the same size as the driving wheels on the prewar 226E. Along with these wheels came a crescent-shaped eccentric crank that could not be put on backwards, a problem sometimes with eccentric cranks.

The reverse unit lever was moved from the center of the boiler, where it had been on the 726, to a spot just in front of the cab. The 2046 had a fixed, ornamental bell, rather than the swinging bell used on the Berkshire. Also missing was the ornamental whistle on top of the boiler, although it was shown with one in the catalog.

The 726's boiler front was modified for the 2046. It was a one-piece casting and the door did not swing open, nor did it look as authentic.

The motor mechanism was essentially the same as that used in the 2-6-2 2035 the same year, except that the reversing unit was moved behind the motor from in front of it. The 2046 had Magne-Traction.

The number 2046 was rubber-stamped in silver below the cab window.

The locomotive came with a Pennsylvania-type 2046W tender. This made the 2046 the first loco to come with the Pennsy tender other than the turbines. The turbine tenders had six-wheel trucks, while the 2046W had four. Also, it was the first time the Pennsy-style tender said "Lionel Lines" rather than "Pennsylvania." The lettering was approximately half the size as the Pennsylvania lettering and it was extended almost the full length of the tender.

Lettering, 1950.

The 2046 was dropped in 1951, as Lionel cut back production because of the Korean War.

1952

It reappeared without Magne-Traction and the number changed to 2056. The number was rubber-stamped in silver. The trucks on the tender were changed. The lettering was larger and of a different typeface.

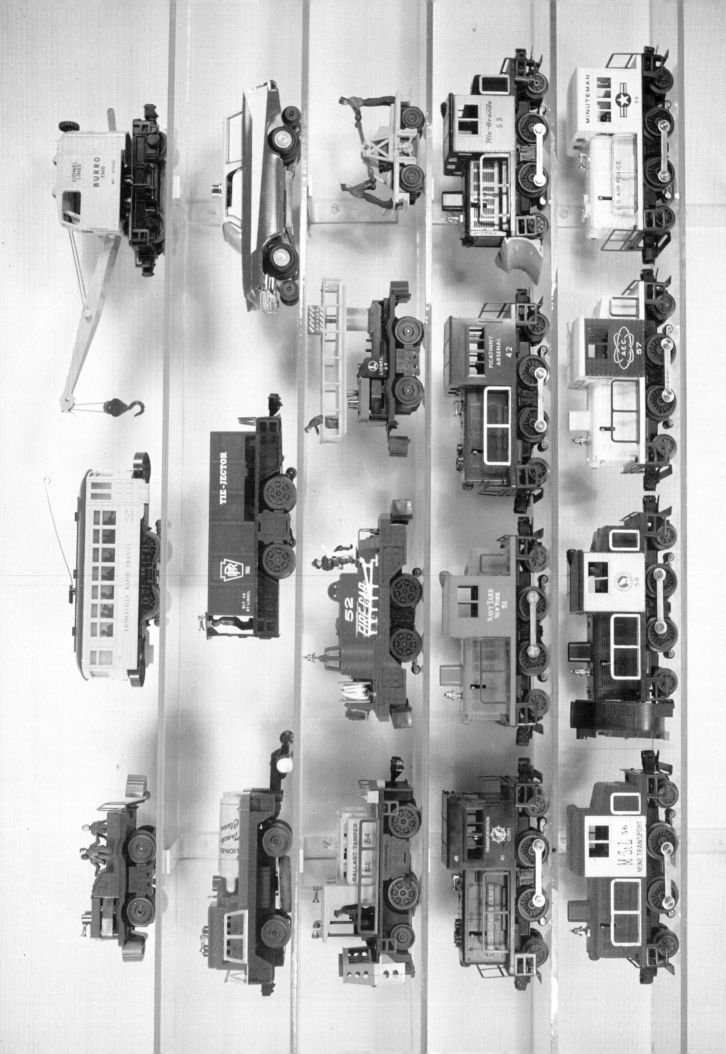

1953

Magne-Traction was put back on and the number reverted to 2046. The trailing trucks were changed to plastic on some of the later models and the side rods were cadmium plated instead of nickel. The number beneath the cab window was heat-stamped in white. There was no change to the tender.

1954

There was no change in the engine but it was offered in O gauge rather than 027 and the number was changed to 646. Some of the locos had rubber-stamped silver lettering, although most were heat-stamped in white. Same tender.

1955 through 1958

Everything remained essentially the same and then the loco was discontinued in 1959.

SANTA FE-TYPE

685 Hudson, 1953 version.

1953

The first of the Santa Fe-type Hudsons was the 685. The boiler was newly designed. On the Hudsons that the Santa Fe used the sand dome was shaped differently and the piping was different from that of the Hudsons used by the New York Central.

The boiler on the 685 was constructed as a one-piece unit, incorporating the cowcatcher, steam chest and boiler. The boiler front was the same as that used on the 2046, as were the drive mechanism, pilot and trailing trucks. It had a fixed, ornamental bell and an ornamental whistle. The advantage of the design, as far as Lionel was concerned, was that it allowed easy assembly and disassembly.

The 685 headed an O gauge set. There was also the exact same engine with a different number, 2055, which headed two 027 sets. The 685 came with a 6026W tender, which was of a new box-type design. It had simulated backup light. The 2055 came with either a Pennsylvania-style, 2046W tender, or a 6026W tender.

1954 through 1957

The number of the 685 changed to 665 in 1954. This reflected a change in the boiler front. It now had a feedwater heater and lower marker lights. Another 027 engine was introduced. It was the 2065, which was the same mechanically as the 2055 but had a feedwater heater and two illuminated marker lights. It came with either a 2046W or 6026W tender. The 2055, 2065 and 665 remained the same until 1957, when the 2055 was dropped.

685 without feedwater   685 with feedwater
heater   heater

1958

The 665 was unchanged, but the tender was a 6026W again. The 2065 was dropped.

1959

The 665 was unchanged. It was discontinued the next year.

1966

The 665 was reintroduced. It was identical to the 1959 model, except it came with a Pennsylvania-type tender again, this one with "Pennsylvania" lettered in heat-stamped white.

All the Santa Fe Hudsons came with heat-stamped lettering through their entire run, except for a few 2055s made in 1953 and some 665s.

RATING

The 773 Hudson, in either the 1950 or later version, is the most valuable of the postwar steamers. Of the two, the 1950 is more valuable. After the Hudson in value is the 746 Norfolk & Western. After the Hudsons and the Norfolk there is a precipitous drop in value, but next comes the 726 Berkshire, followed by the turbine and switchers.

POWERED UNITS

The powered units had their start with the 50 gang car, a popular item that was introduced in 1954 at the urging of many train enthusiasts. It sold for $7.95 and ran for 11 years, through 1964. The combination of low price and longevity, plus its play value, made the 50 gang car the biggest selling motorized unit Lionel ever made.

It used the same field coil and armature that was used in Lionel's whistle tender. It had rubber bumpers at each end. The bumpers would change polarity when they struck another object on the track and the gang car would change direction.

It came with an orange body and black frame. The first year it was made it came two ways, one extremely rare. The common way had blue bumpers and there were two blue men and one olive green man riding on top. When the car changed directions, the olive man swiveled around and faced the other way. The rare variation had gray bumpers and the man who swiveled was blue, while the other two were olive.

In 1955 the car was made the common way — with the blue bumpers, two blue men, and a swiveling olive man — but the simulated horn was moved to the right of the motor housing. It had been in the center of the housing. The horn was also switched from a two-piece mounting to a one-piece. In 1964 there were two minor changes. First, the bumper support bar now pointed down, and, second, the faces and hands of the men, which had been painted flesh color, were left unpainted. This 1964 version of the 50 hand car is the hardest to find besides the very rare gray bumper version.

Based on the success of the 50 gang car, Lionel soon followed with other small powered units. Here, in general chronological order, is a list of them:

60 TROLLEY

Ran from 1955 through 1958 using a similar power assembly to the 50 gang car. It operated the same way. It had bumpers and when it hit something it would reverse directions. The bumpers were commonly shaped out of spring steel, but a later, hard-to-find bumper was made of solid sheet metal. The trolley pole also changed directions. The car was illuminated and the body came in a medium and a light yellow. The roof was red. Through the years the "Lionelville Rapid Transit" lettering came in both blue and black.

41 ARMY SWITCHER

Modeled after gas turbine industrial switchers, this loco came in black with white lettering and ran without variation in 1955, '56 and '57. The frame was cast and the wheels were similar to the wheels used on the 681 turbine. It had a three-position reverse and operating couplers at both ends.

It used the same motor as the gang car and trolley and, like its little prototype, couldn't pull much. The attraction of the 41 Army Switcher — and the other small switchers that followed it — was that it was a self-propelling locomotive that was relatively cheap. They were of overall good quality, actually better than the 600 Katy and 610 Erie switchers brought out the same year.

51 NAVY SWITCHER

This was a model of a 30-ton, gear-drive diesel. It used the same chassis and mechanism as the 41 switcher, but the handrails on the front were shorter. It was unpainted blue plastic with white lettering, but there were two shades of blue, one a little darker than the other. Common, it ran in 1956 and 1957. The 30-tonners made by Lionel had weak window struts and are often found with them broken.

3360 BURRO CRANE

This also ran in 1956 and 1957. It had a die-cast frame with fixed couplers on both ends and could be used as a crane car in a set or could pull one or two cars of its own. The motor powered the hook up and down and swiveled the cab. No variations.

3927 TRACK CLEANING CAR

Made from 1956 through 1960, it was not self-propelling but did have a motor in it, which operated the mechanism which applied cleaning fluid to the track. It didn't do a very good job, but it kept busy. There was a manual on-off switch located behind the motor. The unit had to be pulled by a loco. No variations and fairly common.

42 PICATINNY ARSENAL

Identical to the 41 Army switcher except for its olive drab and white coloring. Sold poorly and ran in 1957 only. As a result, is among the scarcest of the small diesels.

53 RIO GRANDE SNOWPLOW

A 30-tonner with the addition of a snowplow, the Rio Grande came in black and yellow with black lettering. On the vast majority of them the "a" was backwards, but there is an uncommon variation with the "a" in "Grande" frontwards. These were probably the very last made. On the variation the yellow is lighter and the lettering a little smaller. Ran in 1957 and 1958.

55 TIE JECTOR

Introduced in 1957, the 55 tie jector had a new frame, but still used the same motor as the other small powered units. Ties were thrown out the left side of the car after it hit a trackside device which activated the mechanism. The wheels of the unit were almost identical to those on the GG-1, except the tie jector's were a little bigger. Ran through 1961.

56 MINNEAPOLIS & ST. LOUIS SWITCHER

A 30-tonner which ran in red and white in 1958 only. Had couplers at both ends.

52 FIREFIGHTER CAR

This car, which ran from 1958 through 1961, had the same basic chassis as the 55 tie ejector and functioned like the gang and trolley bumper cars.

54 BALLAST TAMPER

This used the same basic mechanism and the same trackside trip device to activate it as the 55 tie ejector. The tamper mechanism would then start pumping until tripped again. A popular item, which ran from 1958 through 1961 and again in 1966 without variation.

68 EXECUTIVE INSPECTION CAR

Ran from 1958 through 1961 without variation. It was unlike any of the other motorized units. Its motor was mounted sideways. It had both operating headlights and tail lights. There was a simulated mars light on the roof of the car, and, when turned from one position to another, this light operated as the directional control switch for the vehicle.

57 AEC SWITCHER

A 30-tonner with white plastic body and red cab with white lettering. The plastic was almost pure white when new but had a tendency to yellow and now almost looks yellow. Sometimes found with yellow blotches, because the plastic yellows unevenly. Ran in 1959 and 1960.

58 GREAT NORTHERN ROTARY SNOWPLOW

Same chassis and motor as other 30-tonners, but the worm gear ratio was changed somewhat so that it could both accelerate the loco and, through a series of pulleys, turn the snow blower on the front. The snowplow was belt driven from a pulley on top of the motor. Very much in demand by collectors, but extremely hard to find not busted.

69 MAINTENANCE CAR

Same motor and power chassis as 50 gang car except it had a platform on top with a blue man on it. The platform had a "Danger" sign, which would turn when the car switched directions. No variations in the three years it ran, 1960 through '62.

59 U.S. AIR FORCE SWITCHER

Identical to the 41 Army gas turbine switcher. Unpainted white plastic with blue and red lettering, couplers at both ends. Ran in 1962 and 1963.

65 HANDCAR

Made from 1962 through 1966 using an unpainted plastic body in either light or dark yellow. Had two rubber figures which contained a chemical to keep them pliable. This chemical reacted to the plastic and often melted it at the base of the men's feet. Used an HO motor to power it and sometimes it burnt out because it was too small to handle all the voltage available on O gauge. They are either broken, because they were fragile, or melted or burned out.

RATING

The 57 AEC switcher is probably the rarest of the series, followed by the 42 Picatinny and 59 Air Force. But the item most in demand by collectors is the 58 Great Northern snowplow, which holds the greatest appeal for them.

The 65 handcar in good condition is also very hard to find.

LARGE PASSENGER SETS

HUDSON

When, in the anniversary year of 1950, Lionel brought out the 773 Hudson, it was placed at the head of a set of three Irvington cars. The set sold for $85 and is now one of the most valuable of all the postwar passenger sets.

The 773 set included the 2426 die-cast tender and the 2625 Irvington, the 2627 Madison and the 2628 Manhattan. The set ran in 1950 only, and after that the Irvington cars were dropped. They were out of style, referred to by railroaders as "heavyweights," and the light, streamlined passenger cars had taken over.

There is some confusion among collectors as to what Irvington cars were produced when. Here is the postwar chronological order:

In 1946 a set of three cars was available. Each car had the Irvington name in block letters on the side. The number was 2625. These were sold in sets with the 726 Berkshire and the 671 steam turbine. The catalog had promised a set of Irvingtons headed by a 703 Hudson, but no such engine was ever made.

In 1947 the Irvington name was again available, along with the Madison and Manhattan. All were numbered 2625. The Madison was actually the only name new to Lionel, since a Manhattan car had been produced before the war. The Irvington and Manhattan had their names in plain block letters (from leftover prewar stamps), while the Madison had serif letters.

In 1948 all three cars were available again, but this time each had its own number. Irvington was 2625, Madison 2627 and Manhattan 2628. They came in two sets, one headed by the GG-1 and the other by the 726 Berkshire. The same was true in 1949.

A glance at the number sequence of the 1948 cars indicates that the number 2626 was skipped. That was because the 1946 advance catalog had listed a 2626 observation car that was never produced, or even shown in the regular catalog. This car had been given the name Sager Place, after the street on which the Lionel factory was located in Irvington, New Jersey.

Since Irvington and Sager Place refer to the location of the Lionel factory, and since Manhattan was where Lionel's home office was situated, the naming pattern of the Irvington cars seems clear. But what about Madison? Where did that name come from?

On August 25, 1880, in New York, New York, in a large wooden house on Madison Avenue between 103rd and 104th streets, a baby boy was born. His name was Joshua Lionel Cowen.

The prewar Irvington and Manhattan cars, incidentally, were both numbered 2623. The 1941 and 1942 catalogs also pictured a 2624 Manhattan observation car, but that was never produced. A 2624 Pullman was made, however. It is the rarest of the prewar Irvington cars.

All the postwar Irvingtons are highly prized, but the most coveted is the 1950 version which has people silhouetted in the windows.

Even rarer than these, but almost uncollectable, is a set of green Irvington cars made to match the green 2332 GG-1. It is not clear why these cars were made, but certainly no more than a handful were.

SUPER SPEEDLINER

The first postwar streamlined passenger set designed exclusively for O gauge appeared in 1952 and was called the Super Speedliner. The set, which was more than seven feet long, included a 2343 Santa Fe AA, a 2532 Silver Range Vista Dome, a 2531 Silver Dawn observation, and two Pullmans: a 2534 Silver Bluff and a 2533 Silver Cloud.

The 1952 catalog had the Super Speedliner Pullmans all mixed up. The catalog showed a picture of a car that was never made, the 2534 Silver Platter, and failed to show a picture of a car that was made, the 2533 Silver Cloud. Further, the Silver Bluff shown in the catalog had the wrong number. It was shown as 2533 — which was actually the number of the Silver Cloud — but it was produced at 2534, which had been the number originally assigned to the never-produced Silver Platter. The names were straightened out in 1953.

CONGRESSIONAL

The GG-1, discontinued after 1950, returned in 1955 at the front of the famous Congressional Set, considered by many to be the most handsome of the postwar passenger sets. It included the 2543 William Penn and 2544 Molly Pitcher Pullmans, the 2542 Betsy Ross Vista Dome and the 2541 Alexander Hamilton observation. The GG-1, numbered 2340, was in Tuscan red with gold

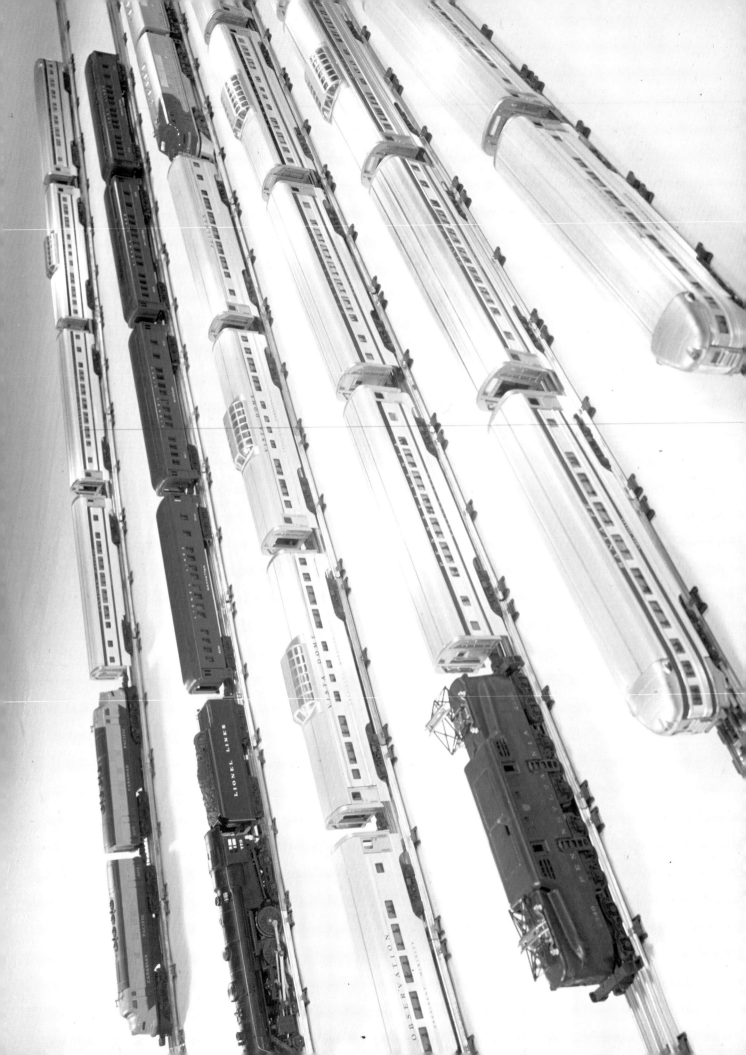

striping and the cars had matching-color side stripes. In 1956 the set remained the same but the number on the GG-1 changed to 2360. The Congressional Set was discontinued after 1956.

The Congressional set sold for approximately $100. It is not possible to give an exact figure because after 1954 Lionel dropped its Fair Trade price policy. Set prices thereafter were either not listed or, if listed, were merely suggested prices. Stores also made up their own sets after 1955.

Although Lionel included a Vista Dome car in its Congressional set, the Pennsylvania Railroad never used dome cars on its Washington-to-New York Congressional run. As a matter of fact, the high-sitting dome cars were not used on any of the Pennsy's electrified routes, because of clearance problems in tunnels and under the cantenary itself. Other railroads, with greater clearance, used dome cars on electrified runs.

CANADIAN PACIFIC

The Canadian Pacific Set was available in 1957 only and is extremely difficult to find. Included were a pair of 2373 Canadian Pacific AAs, three 2552 Skyline 500 Vista Domes, and a 2551 Banff Park observation. Two other cars with Canadian Pacific marking were offered but not included in the set. They were the 2553 Blair Manor and the 2554 Craig Manor Pullmans. The set cost over $100.

SUPER CHIEF

The Santa Fe Super Chief set was new in 1958. The aluminum passenger cars were the same ones that appeared in the Super Speedliner Set from 1952 through 1957, except they no longer had ribbing in the extrusion above the windows. The cars still had "Lionel Lines" on them. The ribbing had been taken out for the tape strips that appeared in the extrusion in 1955. In 1959 and 1960 the old Super Speedliner cars were offered separately with "Lionel Lines" in the extrusion but without the ribs.

The Super Chief that came out in 1959 had aluminum cars with red stripes on the sides to match the red and silver 2383 Santa Fe twin As. Included were a 2530 Railway Express baggage car, a 2563 Indian Falls Pullman, a 2562 Regal Pass Vista Dome and a 2561 Vista Valley observation. The set was available without change in 1960 and sold for around $100. In 1961 the set came with two vista domes and no baggage car. The set was discontinued the next year. Of all the Santa Fe Super Chief sets, the one with the two Vista Domes is the most valuable, since Vista Dome cars are more valued than baggage cars.

The 2562 Regal Pass Vista Dome car is named after an actual Santa Fe Vista Dome, one of the first built by the railroad. When that Vista Dome was new the Santa Fe wanted to show it off before putting it in service. An imaginative Santa Fe public relations man, Bill Burke, arranged, through the cooperation of the Chicago Tribune, to have public tours at a siding next to the Tribune loading dock on the lower level of Michigan Avenue. The only problem was how to get the new car the 25 blocks from the Santa Fe's Wentworth yards to the Tribune Tower. The North Western said the Santa Fe could use its tracks. It was to go on display on a Monday. On Saturday Burke called the yards.

"Get that coach over there, boys," he said.

"We're on the way," came the reply.

A few hours later Burke received a call.

"It won't get under the Clark Street bridge," the yard superintendent said. "It's too tall." At 15 feet 8 inches, the Vista Dome was taller than any other car in service.

"It's got to go under," said Burke. "Get it down. Lower the springs or whatever you have to do."

Another call came.

"We got it down to 15 feet 3 inches, but it still won't go under."

"Call the North Western," said Burke. Ask them to send a crew out there and cut the ground down. Take up the track and take out some dirt. We'll pay."

A few hours later there was another call.

"They cut the ground down and we got it under the bridge."

"Fine," said Burke.

"But now we've got another problem. We're at the first street crossing after the bridge and we lowered the car so much it won't clear the crossing."

"Jack it back up," said Burke. "We're going to get that coach to the Tribune by tomorrow."

They jacked it up and, finally, early the next morning, the Regal Pass arrived at the Tribune.

The 2530 Railway Express baggage cars which came with the Super Chief and other O gauge sets were brought out in 1954. The first cars had large doors that measured 1-13/16-inches wide and 1-5/8-inches high. These were made only a short time before Lionel started making the small-door version. These doors were 1-3/4 inches wide and 1-1/8-inches high. The large-door model looked better but constructing it involved cutting into the reinforcing extrusion which ran along the base of the car. This was a difficult process. By making the door smaller the hole for it could be punched out of the aluminum without hitting the extrusion.

LARGE SETS
Canadian Pacific
Hudson Passenger with extra pullman
Presidential
Congressional
Super Chief
Super Speedliner

The small-door 2530 is available but the large-door version is extremely rare.

Large door version.

Small door version.

The last O gauge passenger set to be offered in the postwar era was the Presidential. When it first appeared in 1962, it was pictured in the catalog with the 2383 Santa Fe AA and listed with the 2360 solid-striped GG-1. That first year the Presidential Set included two 2522 President Harrison Vista Domes, a 2523 President Garfield Pullman and a 2521 President McKinley observation. The following year the set was changed to include two Pullmans and one Vista Dome and the GG-1 was no longer included. The Presidential Set continued through 1966 and was listed at $125.

As a slight historical aside, it might be pointed out that the five years the set ran was about as long at the accumulated time served by the presidents the cars were named after. All died in office, two by assassination.

RATING

The Canadian Pacific, Congressional and Hudson are the most prized passenger sets of the postwar era. Next in desirability are the Super Chief with the red stripe and the Presidential sets. The most common set is the Super Speedliner made from 1952 through 1957. The Lionel Lines cars without the ribbing, made from 1958 through 1960, are actually harder to find than either the gold-striped Presidential cars or the red-striped Santa Fes, but they are not as much in demand because most collectors don't realize there is a difference between them and the more common ribbed versions of the Lionel Lines cars.

Lionel baggage car.

PASSENGER CARS
2552 *Canadian Pacific*
      Skyline 500
      Vista Dome
2562 *Santa Fe Regal*
      Pass Vista Dome
2543 *Pennsylvania*
      William Penn
      pullman
2521 *President*
      McKinley
      observation
2625 *Irvington pullman*

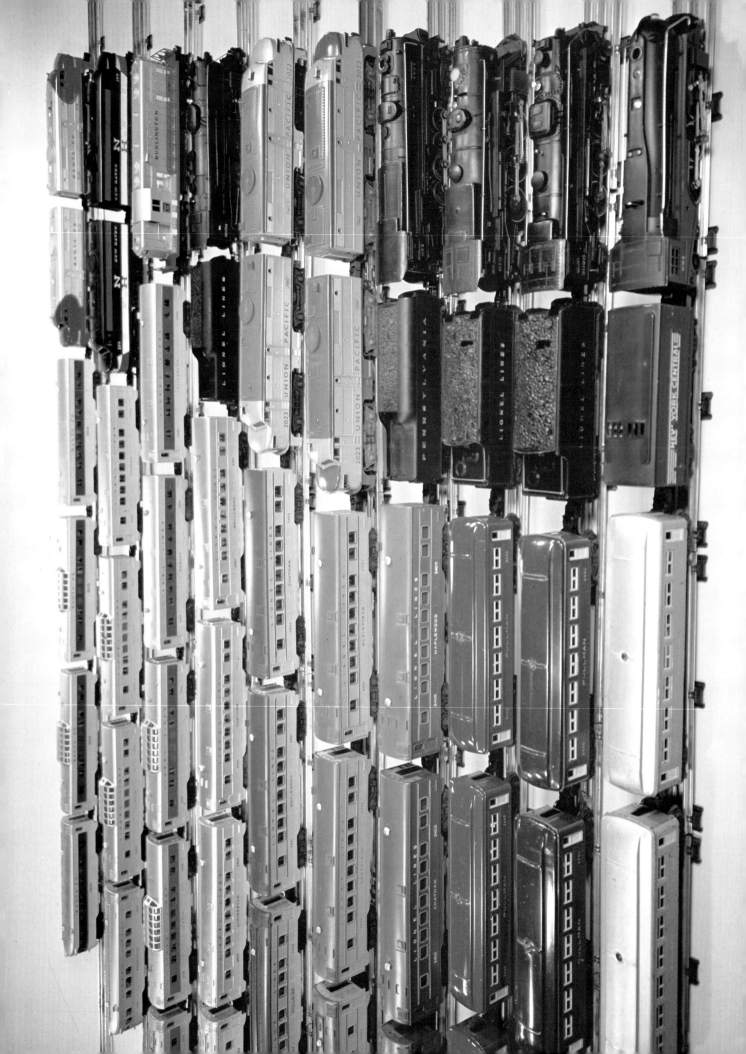

SMALL PASSENGER SETS

Anniversary set with gray nosed engines, 1950
671 set, 1948
675 set, 1947
2026 set, 1948
Empire State set, 1947

SMALL PASSENGER SETS (top to bottom)
Santa Fe set, 1962
New Haven set, 1958
Burlington GP-7 set with extra pullman, 1957
2056 set, 1952
Alco set, 1951

There is a rather general misconception about the small passenger cars shown on the opposite page. Many collectors, especially newer ones, think the cars were made only in 027 gauge. But that's wrong. The reddish brown sheet metal cars, shown in the third row from the bottom, ran in O gauge the four years they were made, 1946 through 1949, and the plastic streamline cars came both ways from 1948 through 1950.

SHEET METAL CARS

The sheet metal cars came in three different color schemes: powder blue with silver windows and roof; green with yellow window inserts and darker green roof; and reddish brown with gray windows. The lettering on all colors was rubber stamped in silver in 1946, and in white from 1947 on.

The blue cars ran in 1946 and 1947 only and were numbered 2430 Pullman and 2431 Observation. The green cars ran from 1946 through 1949. In 1946 and 1947 they were numbered 2440 Pullman and 2441 Observation. The numbers changed in 1948 to 6440 and 6441. This change in numbers reflected the change in couplers from coil to the armature-plate type. The reddish brown cars also ran through 1949 and were numbered 2442 Pullman and 2443 Observation the first three years. The last year the number changed to 6442 and 6443 because of the new couplers. The 64-numbered cars are a little harder to find than the others because they ran only one year.

PLASTIC STREAMLINE CARS

The plastic streamline cars were introduced in 1948, as Lionel moved to get a more contemporary looking car into their smaller sets. Through the years the cars came in many different colors and sets and the best way to consider these changes is on a year-by-year basis.

1948 and 1949

The first of the small plastic cars were green and are pictured in the fourth row from the bottom on the opposite page. They were the 2402 Chatham Pullman, the 2400 Maplewood Pullman and the 2401 Hillside Observation. This was an O gauge set headed by a 671 turbine. They also came in an 027 set headed by a 2025 steamer.

1950

The colors and numbers of the plastic cars changed, as the Anniversary Set was offered in 027. This set is pictured above the green cars. The set included a 2482 Westfield Pullman, 2481 Plainfield Pullman, and 2483 Livingston Observation. The set was shown in the catalog with a yellow Union Pacific Alco with a gray nose, but most were made without the gray nose. One of these rare gray nose Alcos is shown in the picture.

Lionel made their Alco specifically for these smaller streamline passenger cars, so that they would have a diesel to head them in sets. That is why the Alco is so much more under scale than the F-3.

There was also an O gauge set of cars offered in 1950. These were painted all-aluminum with black lettering. They were the 2421 Maplewood Pullman, 2422 Chatham Pullman and 2423 Hillside Observation. Both this set and the Anniversary Set had silhouettes in the windows. 1950 was the first year the silhouettes were offered.

1951

The only cars available were the painted aluminum ones. The numbers and names were the same but the roofs were now gray and there was a black stripe above and below the windows. The lettering was also black. These cars are pictured above the Anniversary Set. The set was headed by matching twin-A Alcos. This was an 027 set, as all the sets would be from then on.

1952 and 1953

The gray roofed cars were dropped and the all-aluminum cars returned with one car added, the 2429 Livingston. This was the first time Lionel offered a four-car passenger set in the postwar period. It was headed by a 2056 steamer and is shown in the picture above the gray-roofed cars. The same cars, minus the Livingston, were offered in a set headed by a Union Pacific Alco. The same two sets were offered in 1953, only the steamer was a 2055 and the Livingston was not included in the set.

1954

The same aluminum cars were offered but they now had red lettering and all the names and numbers were changed. The cars had new, mechanically operated couplers and only one pick-up roller. The cars were the 2434 Newark Pullman, 2435 Elizabeth Pullman and 2436 Summit Observation and a new car, the 2432 Clifton Vista Dome, the first Vista Dome offered in the plastic streamline series. The cars were offered in two sets in 1954 and three sets in 1955, although none are shown in the photograph on page 64.

1956

The all-aluminum cars were offered again, as separate items, and a new set was introduced. These were aluminum colored cars with a painted red stripe running along the window area. These cars were numbered 2444 Newark Pullman, 2442 Clifton Vista Dome and 2446 Summit Observation. The red-stripe set was headed by a silver Burlington GP-7, although the engine was hardly visible in the catalog and a lot of collectors don't realize the cars ever came with a geep. This set is shown on page 64 in the third row from the top. The set in the picture has five cars in it, including the 2445 Elizabeth, which was offered for separate sale only. The set normally came with only four cars.

The red-stripe cars were dropped in 1957, but the all-aluminum cars with red lettering continued. There was one change. The 2436 Summit Observation was dropped and a 2436 Mooseheart replaced it. The same cars were offered in many sets in 1958, including the one shown in the second row from the top on page 64. This set was headed by two New Haven Alcos and included two Clifton Vista Domes.

1959 through 1963

An aluminum colored set with a blue stripe in the window area was introduced in 1959 and the cars ran in sets or separately through 1963. These cars had blue Santa Fe lettering above the windows rather than "Lionel Lines." The numbers of the cars were 2412 Vista Dome, 2414 Pullman and 2416 Observation. The set shown on the top row of page 64 was cataloged in 1961 and was headed by two Santa Fe Alcos numbered 218. The set contained two Vista Domes.

1964 through 1966

The blue-stripe cars were dropped in 1964 and the cheapest version of the plastic streamline cars Lionel ever made was introduced. The cars were numbered 2404 Vista Dome, 2405 Pullman and 2406 Observation. The cars had no lights or window inserts. They were practically a skeleton version of the original cars. They came headed by a 212 Santa Fe twin Alco. The same cars ran in 1965. In 1966 lights and window stripe returned and the numbers changed to 2408 Vista Dome, 2409 Pullman and 2410 Observation. The cars were dropped the next year.

RATING

The most sought after cars in this series are the yellow Anniversary Set cars. These are followed by the green cars and the red-striped aluminum cars. The cars without lights or windows from 1964 and 1965 are hard to find, but nobody seems to want them.

Small streamline passenger car.

OTHER SETS

The Girl's Train, it turned out, was a dumb idea. It satisfied no one. Men and boys could be expected to dislike it, and any girl who was interested enough in trains to want one of her own would want a *real*-looking one, not some silly gimmick.

Potential buyers were therefore reduced to husbands who wanted something off-beat for their wives, and fathers who wanted something frivolous for a daughter who had no particular interest in trains. But most people don't spend $49.95 on something off-beat or frivolous at Christmas. At least they didn't the Christmas of 1957, when the Girl's Train came out. Dealers across the country were stuck with them. Lionel cataloged it again in 1958 in a fruitless effort to get rid of back inventory and then gave up.

The pastel consist of the Girl's Train was as follows: 2037 pink steam engine, 6462-500 gondola in pink frosting, 6464-510 light green New York Central boxcar (the catalog listed this color as robin's egg blue), 6464-515 buttercup yellow MKT boxcar, 6436-500 lilac hopper, and 6427-500 sky blue illuminated caboose.

Because so few were sold, the Girl's Train is a valuable collector's item today, even though many collectors don't like it. There are a few collectors who won't even have it, in spite of its value. It doesn't win votes from the women liberationists either, since to them it suggests an attitude that girls are too inferior to appreciate regular trains.

"It's insulting," says Polly Ann Connelly, an executive of the Woman's Center of Chicago. "Why did they think girls couldn't enjoy an ordinary train? They have women who are qualified engineers today and they certainly don't paint SD-45s pink for them."

In case anyone questions Ms. Connelly's credentials for talking about trains, it should be pointed out that she is an assembler at Electro-Motive's plant at LaGrange, Illinois, and is the first woman at EMD ever elected a union shop steward by her co-workers, all of whom are men.

ELECTRONIC

The electronic set, shown below the Girl's Train, was introduced in 1946 and was an outgrowth of Lionel's wartime technological development. It consisted of a 671 turbine, a 4671W tender, a 4454 boxcar, a 5459 dump car, a 4452 gon-

dola and a 4457 Pennsylvania N-5 caboose. The thing that made the electronic set different from conventional Lionel sets was its ability to uncouple or unload anywhere on the track, without the use of a remote control section.

Lionel built a special radio transmitter, which it used in conjunction with a regular transformer, that could plug into a standard household outlet. The transmitter sent out radio frequencies which were picked up by receivers on the cars. The engine and each car had its own receiver, either inside or under the frame. The tender, the nerve center of the loco, had two receivers, one inside and the other underneath. The receiver inside controlled the forward and reverse of the loco, the one below controlled the whistle. All the cars came with stainless steel axles.

The transmitter had colored buttons on it, a different color for each car, and things could be operated by pushing the desired buttons. Each car had a color decal on it that corresponded to the color on the transmitter.

In 1948 the set was offered with accessories and switches for the staggering price of $199.95. That same year the caboose changed to an SP-type with a plastic body. It was numbered 4357. In 1950 the set was cataloged with a turbine numbered 4681 and with a Pennsy-style 12-wheel tender. It is not known to exist that way. The gondola was always black with Pennsy markings and was 9 inches long. But it was shown as black with NYC markings, 10½-inches long and with a number 4462. It is not known to exist in the electronic version (with the receiver), but is common in the regular Lionel line.

The electronic set ran through 1950. Most freight cars Lionel made in 1946 and 1947 had provisions on their frames for mounting electronic receivers. The company planned to manufacture receivers in kit form so regular line cars could be converted to electronic cars. But after the electronic sets did not sell well Lionel cancelled plans to make the kits.

The 1950 advance catalog showed two cars designed for the electronic set that were never made. They were the 4456 hopper and 4460 crane car.

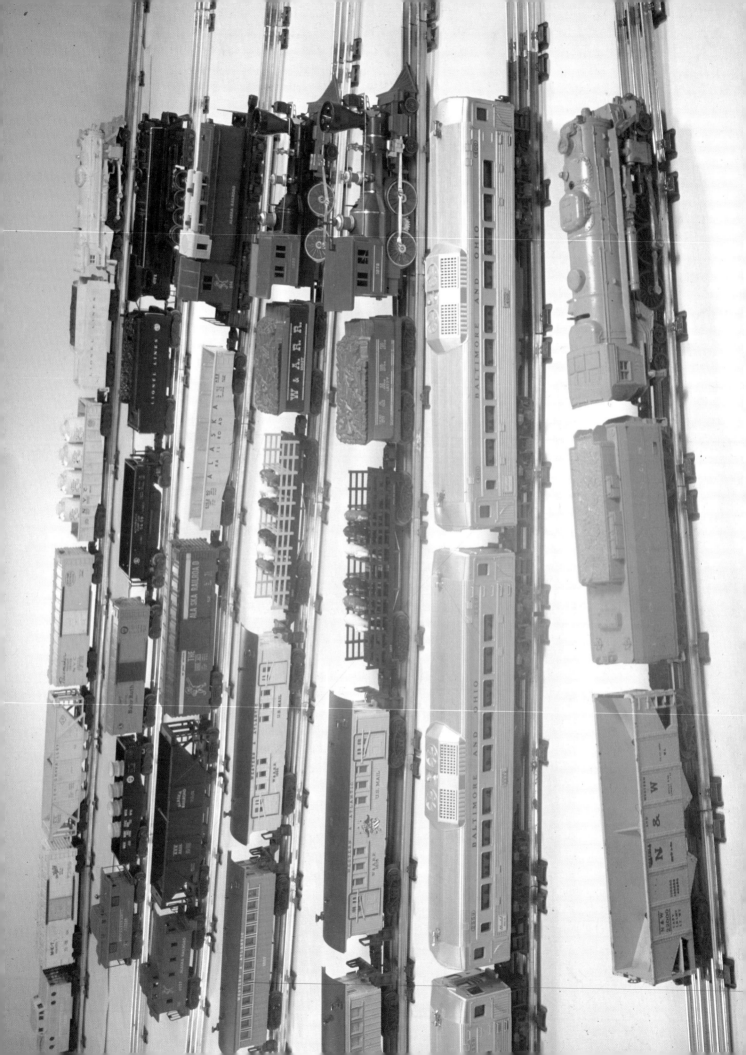

ALASKA

In 1959 Lionel came out with the Alaska outfit, in honor of the state which had been admitted to the Union the same year. The set came with the 614 Alaska diesel switcher, the 6162-50 yellow gondola with three red canisters, the 6825 trestle bridge flatcar, the 6465 tanker and the 6027 Alaska caboose.

Collectors have created their own Alaska Set, replacing the two less desirable cars, the 6825 and 6465, with the 6636 Alaska hopper and the 6464-825 Alaska boxcar. This creates a set with all the cars Lionel ever made with the Alaska name on them.

GENERAL

The General Set was new in 1959. Two versions were available, an 027 and a Super O. The Super O had an engine with headlight, smoke, Magne-Traction and a three-position reverse unit. The cars were illuminated and had operating couplers. The 027's loco had only a two-position reverse and a headlight. It did not have operating couplers or as much detail as the O gauge locomotive.

The 027 version came in two sets in 1959. One set came in a box called a Frontier Pack and contained a 1862 General loco and tender, the 1877 flatcar with six horses, the 1866 mail-baggage car and the 1865 passenger car. It had no track or transformer. The other 027 set had track and transformer but no flatcar or horses. In 1960 the 027 sets ran the same way except the engine had a black plastic headlight housing rather than one painted red. In 1961 the 027 Frontier gift set was dropped and the flatcar with horses was dropped from the other set, replaced by a 3370 sheriff and outlaw car. In 1962 the flatcar with horses returned, replacing the sheriff and outlaw car, and a 3376 giraffe car was added to the set, which was renamed the Prairie Rider, a circus train.

The Super O set was called the Five Star General and had a history similar to its 027 running mate, including the 1960 headlight change. In 1959 it was offered with the 1872 General locomotive, the 1877 flatcar with six horses, the 1876 mail-baggage car and the 1875W passenger car with whistle. There was also an 1875 car offered separately without the whistle. The set appeared this way in 1959, 1960 and 1961. In 1962 the set was changed to the Plainsman. The horse car was dropped and the new 3370 sheriff and outlaw car and the 6445 Fort Knox gold bullion transport car were added. Both the Super O and 027 General sets were dropped in 1963.

The 1962 catalog showed a red 6445 gold bullion transport car in the General Set. Elsewhere in the catalog it was shown by itself in silver, the

color it is always found in. It is not known to have come in red.

There was a special General Set made for Sears, probably in 1960. Uncataloged, it was the 027 version, except that the 1885 passenger car was blue instead of yellow and the 1887 horse car had yellow stakes instead of brown. The engine was numbered 1882. The Sears locomotive and tender were orange and black with gold trim. The set is often referred to as the Halloween Set.

The mail car in the Halloween Set was the same one that came with the regular General Set, a number 1866 in yellow with a brown frame. The yellow was painted on. There is an extremely rare yellow 1866 mail car that came with the Halloween Set, however. It is shown in the Halloween set pictured on page 68. This car had an unpainted lemon yellow body, no decal, and a black frame. It might be a one-of-a-kind item. It is in the collection of Frank Petruzzo of Oak Lawn, Illinois.

"I bought it at a TCA meet," says Petruzzo. "I think it might have been the prototype model of the car that Lionel was going to put in the Sears set, but for one reason or another they did not. I think maybe the prototype car was included in one regular production set."

BOY'S TRAIN

Frank Petruzzo is also the collector who owns the blue 2018 shown in the bottom row of page 68, along with the blue Santa Fe-type tender and a turquoise hopper with red Norfolk & Western lettering. This is part of an illogical "Boy's Train" set Lionel apparently planned to come out with in 1957 along with the Girl's train. A few eventually hit the street, but not many. Lionel cancelled their plans to make the train, and it was a good thing they did because it was just as dumb an idea as the Girl's Train was.

The entire Boy's Train consisted of the engine, tender, the hopper mentioned, plus a light tan boxcar with white doors and white MoPac lettering and the number 3494, a yellowish cream 6462 NYC gondola, and a 6417 round window caboose in light green with gold lettering. The MoPac markings on the boxcar with the number 3494 normally meant it was an operating boxcar, but on the Boy's Train the boxcar had no operating mechanism.

Edward Barbret of St. Clair Shores, Michigan, owns the whole set, except he has a black Norfolk & Western hopper instead of a turquoise one. Barbret came across his Boy's Train after seeing an advertisement in a local paper. Ed went to the advertiser's house. The ad had not specified what kind of train was for sale.

Girl's Train
Electronic
Alaska
Sear's General
Five Star General
Budd
Boy's Train

"I opened the box with the engine in it and I pulled a little of it out. My heart skipped a beat," says Barbret. "There was this blue 2018. At first I thought the engine had been repainted but then I saw the crisp Lionel numbers and the lettering on the tender. I knew I had something, but I didn't want to ask too many questions for fear if I did the guy might keep the train because it seemed so interesting. That happened to me once. So I just offered him a fair price for a 2018 freight set in good condition and he accepted. Then I got out of there. Since then I've been offered $2,500 for it."

BUDD CARS

Lionel brought out a motorized Budd passenger car in 1956 and numbered it 400. It sold well and in 1957 they came out with a Budd set, which consisted of a 404 motorized baggage car and two dummy passenger cars. The dummy passenger car was numbered 2559. A dummy 2550 baggage was offered separately. In 1958, the last year the Budds ran, Lionel switched things around and had the set consist of a 400 motorized passenger car, a 2559 dummy passenger and a 2550 dummy baggage.

The motorized version of these cars sold for $29.95 and the dummies for $12.95. More motorized cars were sold than the dummies and the dummies are now more rare. So, in spite of the fact that the dummies are of less intrinsic value than the motorized cars, they are now worth more to collectors, although all the Budd cars are prized. The most difficult to find is the 2550 dummy baggage, followed by the 2559 dummy passenger, the 404 motorized baggage and the 400 motorized passenger.

RATING

All the sets pictured on page 68 are prized by collectors. The rarest one, of course, is the blue Boy's Train, but that was a non-production model. Of the production models, the most sought after is the Girl's Train. That is followed by the Halloween set, which in turn is followed by the Budd set and the Five Star General, both equal in value.

The electronic set is hard to find in good condition, but it has never held great attraction for collectors because it is made up of common cars. It is one of the few sets that through the years did not increase much in value from its $200 selling price (with switches and accessories) of 1948.

SCOUT SETS

Scout Sets first appeared in 1948 and ran through 1952. They were decendents of the pre-war Winner and Lionel Jr. lines. They were inexpensive, designed as starter sets.

Scout sets were always freight sets and included a tanker, boxcar, gondola and caboose. Both three-car and four-car sets were offered, the three-car sets missing either a tanker or boxcar. The cars had stamped sheet metal trucks, plastic side frames and plastic couplers that were not compatible with standard Lionel couplers. The tanker and boxcar were designed specifically for the Scout set, while the gondola and caboose were cheaper versions of existing cars.

The Scout locomotive motor mechanism was unitized, meaning it was enclosed in a Bakelite housing and was not designed to be repaired. The reverse unit was different from the standard E-units and they did not work as well. It was hard to repair, too.

When the Scout engine was introduced in 1948 it was numbered 1001. In 1949 the number changed to 1110 as a new boiler was added, the same boiler used on the 1655 steamer. This boiler on the Scout engine has caused some confusion

among collectors, who sometimes mistake a Scout loco for a non-Scout, lower-priced engine. But even with the 1655-style boiler a Scout loco can be identified by the unitized motor mechanism and the words "Lionel Scout" on the tender.

Scout locomotives never had whistles, but they did have headlights every year except 1950.

The Scout name was last used in 1952, although sets that resembled them were made after that. The difference on these sets was a standard coupler. In fact, the absence of the standard coupler was the main reason the Scout sets were discontinued.

The Scout sets have limited appeal to collectors, mainly because they had little intrinsic value and lacked variety. There were some differences in colors and lettering on certain cars, but nothing that has really excited much interest.

The tank car came in gray and yellow with Sunoco markings. Both the tanker and boxcar continued to be included in low price sets after 1952 and eventually were upgraded to medium-priced sets in the late 50s. The Scout boxcars are discussed in more detail on page 90, the tank cars on page 97.

MILITARY AND SPACE

Neglected for many years by collectors — sometimes even scorned — the space and military items are now being vigorously pursued. Much of the old rejection of space and military pieces was based on the fact that they were cheaply made, had no actual prototype and, in fact, were not really railroad items. But interest in them picked up as newer collectors came into the hobby. These collectors had fond memories of the items from their chidhoods.

Space and military is a good category for collectors because prices have not leaped in this category like they have in others, but nevertheless there are rare items, little known variations and some elusive uncataloged pieces. All the items pictured on the next page will be discussed in this section, plus one or two others.

943 EXPLODING AMMO DUMP

1959 through 1961. When a missile hit this building a spring loaded mechanism would be tripped and the roof and sides would fly off, simulating an explosion. The mechanism was a mousetrap-type and it was cocked before the sides and roof were put on. It had hair-trigger tension and practically required the nerves of a demolition expert to assemble it without touching it off. But it was fun. Green roof and sides.

6470 EXPLODING TARGET CAR

1959 and 1960. Worked on the same mousetrap principle as the 943 ammo dump. This was provided with a pin that could be inserted through the roof and it would keep the car from exploding if so desired. It was made of unpainted red plastic with white lettering. The word "Explosives" was on the side. It had operating couplers.

448 MISSILE FIRING RANGE SET

1961 through 1963. Four missiles were mounted on launchers that comprised one launching base, the same one that was mounted on the 44 mobile missile launcher and the 6544 missile firing car. The rockets were fired manually at any of the exploding cars or buildings. The site was stationary. Base was unpainted gray plastic. Came with lichen moss, often used by Lionel for trees or bushes on their accessories.

6448 EXPLODING TARGET CAR

1961 through 1964. This car eventually replaced the 6470 and used the same mechanism and frame, but the sides of the car were made with white plastic and had red lettering. The words "Target Car" replaced "Explosives." This car also came with red sides and white roof.

6463 ROCKET FUEL CAR

1962 and 1963. A two-dome tanker in painted white plastic with red lettering. Had plastic trucks and the same construction as the 6465 Cities Service tanker.

3540 RADAR SCANNING SCOPE CAR

1959 and 1960. Used the standard 6511-type flatcar, which was the common flatcar used for the space and military items. On top of the flatcar were a radar screen and an antenna that rotated. The antenna was yellow and the base which contained the screen and panel was gray. A blue rubber man of the type used on the milk car and other accessories stood at the panel, which was illuminated in several colors by a celluloid strip.

6805 ATOMIC ENERGY DISPOSAL CAR

1958 and 1959. Unpainted red plastic flatcar with metal trucks, one of the few space cars that had metal trucks. The car carried two simulated concrete disposal cannisters in tan with "Danger — Radioactive Waste" printed on the side. Each cannister had a light that blinked independently of each other. The blinking lights were supposed to simulate an atomic reaction within the container. The power source for the lights was Super O rails secured to the top of the flatcar. The cannisters had grab-irons that are usually broken off nowadays. Also known to exist with gray cannisters.

3535 OPERATING SECURITY CAR

1960 and 1961. Black unpainted base with a rotating searchlight beacon mounted at one end. There was a red plastic housing, which was the same as the one used for the cab of the 520 electric switcher. Machine guns were mounted on the top of the cab rather than a pantograph.

44 U.S. ARMY MOBILE MISSILE LAUNCHER

1959 through 1962. A motorized unit using the same motor as the cheaper Alco locos and redesigned Alco trucks. The trucks had a special pickup shoe so that the missiles could be launched from a uncoupling track. The four missiles were mounted on one launching base, which was gray. The unit was blue with white lettering and had a man seated at a control panel. A red light above the man went on when the unit was operating.

6823 FLATCAR WITH MISSILES

1959 and 1960. Standard 6511-type flatcar in red. Two cradles were mounted on it to carry two IRBM-style missiles, the same type used on the 6650 missile launching car. An uncommon car, hard to find all together.

6844 MISSILE CARRYING CAR

1959 and 1960. Black car with white lettering. Contained a gray plastic base with six missiles of white plastic carried in an upright position. The missiles were removable and could be used on a missile firing car, such as the 44 Mobile missile launcher. Very hard car to find with all the missiles on it.

6175 ROCKET CAR

1958 through 1961. 1958 was the first year for the military cars. This car was commonly made of red plastic with white lettering, but also came in black with white lettering. Had a gray cradle, the same that was used with the 6801 boat car. Had a U.S. Navy rocket, the same one that came with the 175 rocket launcher. Red, white and blue lettering.

SEARS SET

Along the fourth row from the bottom of page 72 is an uncataloged set, headed by a 240 steamer, which was sold by Sears in 1961 or 1962. This is a rare set, including the steamer. The tender had no number and neither did the flatcar behind it. The flatcar was gray and similar to the horse car in the General Set. The green tank on top of the flatcar was different from the gray Marine Corps tank that went with the regular 6803 Military Transportation cars.

Flat car with tank.

The car behind the flatcar is a special version of the 3665 Minuteman car, which is discussed later in this section. Instead of carrying a missile which could be launched, as on the Minuteman car, the Sears car carried a cannon that could fire a shell. It was white plastic with a light blue roof that opened. It was numbered 3666.

The next car in the Sears set was the standard 6470 exploding target car. The caboose that came with the Sears set was a 6814 first aid medical car, which was a work caboose with a white cab and white bin which had stretchers and

oxygen tanks and a man. The regular 6814 first aid car had a gray frame, but the Sears medical car had a black frame.The Sears set did not come with a man, stretchers or oxygen units.

212 U.S. MARINE CORPS ALCO

1958 and 1959. This was a single-unit Alco with no front coupler or horn. It had Magne-Traction and a three-position reverse. There was also an uncataloged dummy A-unit made.

6413 MERCURY CAPSULE CARRYING CAR

1962. This car used the same chassis that the 6519 Allis-Chalmers car used (and which is covered in the section of this book on special load cars). But instead of carrying a nuclear heat exchanger, this car carried two silver-gray Mercury capsules. They were held down by two wires. It was made in 1962 only and very hard to find complete. Most of the time the capsules or their wires are missing.

3619 AERIAL OBSERVATION CAR

1962 through 1964. Used the same car body and roof as the 3665 Minuteman (and the 3666 Sears cannon). Instead of launching a missile (or a cannon shell) it launched a small helicopter, the same chopper that was used on Lionel's HO version of the helicopter launching car. The same mechanism was used on both gauges, too. The chopper was easily broken and even in good condition it did not perform well. The car body was unpainted yellow plastic and the roof was unpainted black plastic.

3349 TURBO MISSILE LAUNCHER

1962 through 1964. This car came commonly with a red plastic depressed center frame, but it also came with an olive drab frame.

6544 MISSILE FIRING CAR

1960 through 1964. Used the Allis-Chalmers 6519 chassis and the gray 44 mobile missile launching base. It had the exact same mechanism for firing the rockets manually as the 448 missile firing range set. The car was blue with white lettering.

6017-50 U.S. MARINE CABOOSE

1958 through 1960. An SP-style caboose painted blue with white lettering and no illumination. Plastic trucks.

470 MISSILE LAUNCHING PLATFORM

1959 through 1962. A stationary launching platform on a tan plastic base. It used the same launching unit that was mounted on the 6650 missile launching flatcar. The missiles were launched manually and the accessory came with a 6470 exploding boxcar.

3509-3519 SATELLITE LAUNCHING CAR

1961 through 1964. One of the best operating of the space and military cars. It used the same mechanism as the 3419 helicopter launching car, but the satellite functioned much better in the air than the helicopter. The car was sometimes cataloged in blue but that color never went into production. The car was always made in green. In 1961 there were a 3509, manually operated, and a 3519, remote controled, versions made. The same was true in 1962. In 1963 and 1964 only the remote control 3519 was made. There was also an uncataloged 3510 in red made in 1961 or 1962. This was a manual version.

There was a preproduction model of the 3509 made in blue and a picture of it is shown. The difference between the blue preproduction model and the green production model was that the preproduction number was decaled, the radar dish was a darker yellow, and the satellite top was chrome-plated plastic.

6530 FIRE PREVENTION TRAINING CAR

1960 and 1961. This was the same body as the 3530 GM generator car, only without anything inside. It came in red with white lettering and apparently was an attempt to use the 3530 dies again. The car did not do anything.

3512 OPERATING FIREMAN AND LADDER

1959 through 1961. Had a red superstructure with a fireman sitting behind a fire nozzle. At the other end of the car was a metal extension ladder. There was a light at the base of the ladder. The light, the ladder and the fireman rotated. Two stamped sheet metal ladders hung on the side. They were the same ladders that were used on the 494 beacon tower.

1805 MARINE CORPS SET

In 1960 Lionel offered a special 1805 Land, Sea and Air gift pack. This set consisted of all the cars shown on the second row of page 72, except for the Big Bertha cannon car. The cars in the set were all standard cars, except they were in olive drab with white U.S.M.C. markings and they had their own numbers. The set was offered in 1960 only and all the cars in it are rare.

The Marine Corps set was headed by a 45 U.S. Marine Mobile Missile Launcher, which was the same as the 44 Mobile Missile launcher except for the olive drab color. The caboose in the set was a 6824, which was the same as the 6814 First Aid medical car, only in olive. The stretchers and oxygen tanks were white.

The other cars in the second row of the photograph will be described in their standard versions.

3419 OPERATING HELICOPTER CAR

1959 through 1965. 6511-type flatcar in blue plastic with a double-prop helicopter. Had a windup, spring-loaded mechanism that launched the helicopter and which could be operated manually or by a remote control section of track. The helicopter was quite fragile. The Marine Corps version was numbered 3429.

6650 IRBM MISSILE LAUNCHING CAR

1959 through 1963. Red flatcar, blue launching base and black launching pad. The rocket was launched by a spring catapult. The whole assemblage could pivot on the car. The Marine Corps version was numbered 6604.

3830-3330-6830 OPERATING SUBMARINE CAR

1960 through 1963. The flatcar was light blue. It came both painted and unpainted and held a gray plastic submarine. In 1960 the 3830 had a submarine with a windup propeller that operated in the water. The same year there was a 3330, which was the same car but the sub was assembled from a kit. The 6830, also offered in 1960, had a sub that did not have an operating propeller. The 3330 and 6830 were dropped in 1961 and only the 3830 ran through 1963. The Marine Corps version was numbered 3820.

6651 FLATCAR WITH CANNON

1961. An uncataloged car with the standard 6511-type frame and olive drab coloring and white USMC markings. It did not come with the Marine Corps set. It was offered in some department store specials. The cannon fired shells and was supplied with four of them. The barrel of the cannon was the same as the one used in the 3666 cannon car in the Scars set, but the mounting was different.

3665 MINUTEMAN CAR

1961 through 1964. The body used on this car was in essence the same one used on the 3530 generator car, and it used the same basic mechanism that the 6650 missile launch car used. The mechanism was a diaphragm elevation power unit, which permitted the launching device to rise slowly as the roof of the car opened. The car sides were unpainted white plastic and the roof was unpainted dark blue plastic. There was blue and red lettering on the sides. There was also a 3665 made without any lettering at all. Some are also known to exist in the colors of the 3619 copter car.

175 ROCKET LAUNCHER

1958 through 1960. Used a sheet metal base painted tan, and a vibrator-type motor to move the gantry away from the rocket launching area. There was a gray plastic launch pad area with a spring-loaded, solenoid-tripped launching mechanism. Atop the gantry was a manually operated boom of yellow plastic. The gantry moved back and forth on Super O rails on the same wheels as the pilots of many locos. The rocket was made of white and red plastic with U.S. Navy markings. The accessory worked well and the gantry, which was electrically operated from a control panel, moved smoothly. It was somewhat fragile and is hard to find without something being broken.

419 HELIPORT

1962. This was the same structure as the 465 dispatching station, only now it had a helicopter launching pad on the roof. The building didn't have a control board inside or men at panels, but the colors were the same as the dispatching station. The roof contained the same helicopter launching unit used on the 3419 flatcar. There was a wire ring which was pulled to launch the helicopter. Made only one year.

3545 OPERATING TELEVISION MONITOR CAR

1961 and 1962. Used the same superstructure on top of the flatcar as the 3540 radar scanning car, except that instead of an antenna there was a yellow television camera with a blue rubber man sitting behind it. The camera rotated. There was another rubber man at a monitor panel. The car was unpainted black plastic, the superstructure was blue.

6512 CHERRY PICKER CAR

1962 and 1963. A flatcar with a boom on top, the same boom that was used for the 3512 fire and ladder car. It had a metal extension ladder but at the end there was an orange plastic compartment that contained a gray plastic man who was supposed to be an astronaut. The man was on a turntable and could swivel from view, making it appear he had boarded a rocket. The ladder was operated manually with a crank. The car usually came in black but there is a rare variation in blue.

3470 AERIAL TARGET LAUNCHING CAR

1962 through 1964. An unusual and interesting item. It used the ordinary 6511-type flatcar in unpainted blue plastic, although there were two shades of blue, a darker one being more common than a lighter one. There was a white superstructure with red lettering on it. One end of the superstructure was rounded and housed two batteries. The other end of the superstructure had a high, circular section which housed a blower. On top of the blower was a large saucer-shaped platform. Into this fitted a round, white balloon, with a target painted on it in red.

When the blower was activated by a switch, a jet of compressed air shot out of the saucer platform, sending the balloon a few inches aloft. The air swirled around the balloon and created a vacuum under it and kept it hovering above the saucer, even when the train was moving. The car was designed to be used with the 3349 turbo missile firing car, which fired a whirling disk that could knock the balloon out of the vacuum and onto the floor. The blower nozzle on the car was normally clear plastic but some were made with red plastic.

6820 AERIAL MISSILE TRANSPORT CAR

1960 and 1961. A flatcar with a non-operating helicopter. Identical to the 6819, except that the helicopter carried one missile instead of two. The missile was the same as that used on the 44 mobile missile launcher and other items. The car was blue both years, although shown in red in 1961.

6407 FLATCAR WITH REMOVABLE MERCURY CAPSULE

1963. Unpainted red plastic flatcar. Carried a large white plastic missile with red markings. The missile rode on the same cradle used on the boat carrying car. The cradle was gray. The rocket was held to the car with an elastic band. The capsule end of the rocket was blue and removable and was actually a pencil sharpener. This is the rarest of the space and military cars and ran for only one year.

RATING

As mentioned, the rarest car in the space and military category is the 6407 flatcar with the rocket and removable capsule. The one pictured above is in the collection of Hunter J. von Unshuld of Chicago. Von Unshuld also owns the rare uncataloged Sears set shown in the fourth row on page 72.

Generally, cars with loads are extremely difficult to find intact, the loads usually having been lost along the way. The items were also fragile, so that if the loads have not been lost, they almost always have been broken. The service sets — Army, Navy and Marine — are more valued than the other, mixed car sets, with the Navy being hardest to find.

ROLLING STOCK
BOX CARS

2454 Pennsylvania
2454 Baby Ruth
6454 Pennsylvania

6454 New York Central
6454 New York Central
6454 New York Central

EARLY STYLE

These 9¼-inch boxcars are almost two inches shorter than the more popular 6464 series and are considered less colorful. As a consequence, they have been largely overlooked by collectors. That is ironic, because the cars are of top quality and many of them are more difficult to find than 6464 cars which are more valued.

There is considerable confusion about what cars in this group were made when, and this confusion has contributed to the neglect collectors have shown the series. Even the catalog seems little help in identifying the cars. The 1948 catalog, for instance, included a disclaimer that Lionel reserved the right to alter lettering and emblems on its boxcars. When the cars *were* shown, they were poorly illustrated and what was illustrated was not necessarily what was being made.

The cars were cataloged between 1946 and 1953 but the best way to determine when a car was made is by inspecting the frames, doors, couplers and trucks. Each of them made changes

through the years. The frames and doors will be discussed here. The couplers and trucks are discussed in the coupler section.

The frames used on the 9¼-inch boxcars made in 1946, 1947 and the early part of 1948 had four large holes, which had been intended for the receiving unit of the electronic set. These early frames had footsteps on all four corners.

In 1948 a new frame appeared. This still had footsteps but had only two small holes. In 1949 the frame had three additional small holes and one large hole in the center. This was the same frame that was used on the operating cars that were introduced the same year. The additional holes were for securing the operating mechanism. The same frame was used through 1953, except that the footsteps were eliminated after 1950.

The doors used in 1946 and 1947 were die-cast and the same ones that were used on the Pennsylvania double-door automobile car. Both the right-hand and left-hand doors of that double-

6454 Santa Fe
6454 Erie
6454 Southern Pacific

3464 Santa Fe (operating)
3464 New York Central (operating)
3474 Western Pacific (operating)

door unit were used on the 9¼-inch boxcars. The right-hand door had a simulated destination board and a latch with a handle. The left-hand door had a receiving latch on the right side. When the right-hand door appears on the small boxcar it looks fine, but the left-hand door does not. The receiving latch is on the wrong side.

In 1948 the right-hand (latch-and-designation board) door was a bit different. There was a hollow, die-cast pin attached to the inside of the door. That was because it was the door that had been used on the merchandising car from the year before. That pin had been attached to the operating mechanism. In 1948 Lionel used the door on standard boxcars, too.

In 1949 both the right-hand and left-hand doors had the pin but it was no longer hollow. The small boxcars were now operating as well as non-operating and the pin was part of the operating mechanism. Lionel used the same doors on both type of 9¼-inch cars. The door remained the same in 1950 and 1951. In 1952 the door was changed to plastic but had the same general appearance as the die-cast door with the latch and destination board. Lionel used only this type door in 1952 and 1953.

There is one other general statement that can be made about the early boxcars. All cars produced in 1948 and after came with the same 6454 number regardless of road name.

2454-6454 Pennsylvania

Running in 1946 only, the 2454 had a plastic body, metal doors and coil-type couplers of either the 1945 or 1946 style. It was cataloged in Tuscan with white lettering but was not made in Tuscan. It was made in orange with a brown door and in orange with an orange door. Both versions are hard to find, but the orange door version is harder.

The Pennsylvania, now numbered 6454, ran again in 1949 and continued through 1953. The years the 6454 ran have been deduced from the appearance of the cars rather than from the catalog, because the 6454 Pennsylvania was never cataloged. Some cars have a number of features discontinued in 1950, thus establishing the belief that it was made in 1949, and other cars contain features that appeared in the later years. All the cars had the magnetic couplers, and others made the same frame and door changes that have been discussed. Sometime in late 1952 or 1953 some cars were made with black plastic doors.

2454-6454 BABY RUTH

This was new in 1946 and was the exact same car as the orange 2454 Pennsylvania. It was cataloged in orange with an orange door and Southern Pacific or Lionel markings, but it was made with a brown door and Pennsylvania markings. It ran the same way in 1947, then was dropped.

In 1948 it reappeared with the 6454 number and the new type coupler. It had the same color scheme but the color of the orange was noticeably darker. This dark orange 6454 Baby Ruth car is rare. It was made in late 1948 only.

The Pennsylvania and Baby Ruth cars were the only ones that had the 2454 numbers. All the other small boxcars had 6454 numbers. However, some 6454 cars came with the coil-type couplers in 1948. The orange New York Central car shown in the color photograph has a 6454 number and coil couplers.

6454 NEW YORK CENTRAL

Ran in 1948 in all-brown with white lettering, the way it was shown in the catalog. But it also ran in bright orange with black lettering and a brown door; and in burnt orange with white lettering and a brown door. The burnt orange was probably made for a short time in 1949, too.

6454 SANTA FE

This car was made in 1948 but was never cataloged with a 6454 number. It was all-orange with black lettering and brown doors. Possibly this car was available the early part of 1949. The 3464 operating car made in 1949 was identical except that it had black doors.

6454 ERIE

This car was not cataloged until 1950, but it was probably made in 1949, since, like the Pennsylvania, it exists with a number of features that were discontinued in 1950. The car continued through 1953 and experienced the standard frame and door changes. Although it was dropped from the catalog in 1953, collectors — as in the case of the Pennsylvania — believe the Erie was made that year, because there are 6454 Eries that have unpainted black plastic doors. These were likely made in 1953 as replacement bodies only.

6454 SOUTHERN PACIFIC

Like the Erie, the Southern Pacific was not cataloged until 1950, but for the same reasons collectors think it was made in 1949. In 1950 it was shown in orange with a brown door, but it was made in reddish brown with a reddish brown door and white lettering. The 1951 catalog showed the Southern Pacific in orange, but it was made in brown again. No one interviewed had ever seen an orange S.P. The car was not cataloged after 1951 but it was made in 1952 and 1953.

The Southern Pacific came in three different shades. The first cars were brown. Those made in late 1950 and 1951 had a reddish tone to the brown. The ones made in 1952 and after were maroon, almost the color of the Lehigh Valley hopper.

RATING

The two most difficult cars to find in the early non-operating series are the 2454 all-orange Pennsy and the dark orange 6454 Baby Ruth. Next would be the 6454 New York Central in burnt orange.

OPERATING CARS

These boxcars had the same bodies as the 6454 cars and the same mechanism as the later 6464-type operating boxcars. There were three early operating boxcars: the 3464 Santa Fe, the 3464 New York Central, and the 3474 Western Pacific.

3464 SANTA FE

This was the first of the small operating boxcars. Introduced in 1949, it came in orange with black lettering. It had either a brown painted door or a blackened metal door. In 1950 and 1951 it came with the black door only; the steps were removed from the frame in '51. In 1952 the car was made of unpainted orange plastic that was a slightly lighter shade than the painted orange. It had black plastic doors.

The plunger assembly housing changed in 1952. Before, the plunger housing was made of sheet metal and furrowed into the frame. In 1952 the housing was made of Bakelite and press-fit onto the frame. The car is often found with this housing either missing or broken. All the later 6464-type operating cars came with this Bakelite housing.

3464 NEW YORK CENTRAL

This car was cataloged in 1952 only. It was tan, with a blackened metal door and white lettering. Even though the car was not cataloged until 1952, it was made in 1950 and 1951. The car came with footsteps in 1950, without them in 1951. Most of the cars sold in 1952 were left over from the production run of 1951. If they were actually made in 1952 they should have had the Bakelite housing and plastic door.

3474 WESTERN PACIFIC

This car first appeared in 1952 and always came with a plastic door and the Bakelite plunger housing. It ran through 1953. It was shown in the catalog both years in white with black lettering and a red feather across the side. It is not known to exist that way. It was made with a silver body, yellow feather and black lettering. The large feather was a two-piece decal.

RATING

The Western Pacific is the hardest operating boxcar to find in good shape because the silver paint and large decal were marked up easily.

The 9¼-inch boxcars are an excellent group to collect. They are interesting and, as noted, there is wide-spread misunderstanding about them.

MERCHANDISE CARS

3454 Merchandise car.

3854 Merchandise car.

3454 PENNSYLVANIA

Lionel made two operating merchandise cars. Both were activated by a section of remote control track. When the track was energized, the door would open and the mechanism inside the car would throw boxes out one at a time. The car came with five Bakelite cartons with "Baby Ruth" stamped on them. After the mechanism operated five times the door would close. It was quite similar to the operation of the milk cars. Both the large and small operating merchandising cars used the same mechanism.

The 3454 was cataloged in 1946 in Tuscan with white Pennsylvania markings, but it is not known to exist that way. It was made in silver with blue Pennsylvania lettering. The car was 9¼-inches long and used the same body as the 2454 boxcar. It had a hatch at one end of the roof for loading the boxes. The 3454 ran in 1946 and 1947.

3854 PENNSYLVANIA

Also available in 1946 and 1947, this car was 2¼-inches longer than the 3454. It came in dark brown with white Pennsylvania markings. It used the same Bakelite body as the prewar Pennsylvania scale and semi-scale boxcars. A hatch was placed on the roof for loading the boxes. The car was so long that an extra pair of pickup shoes was placed on the trucks. Normally each truck would have one pickup shoe, but the 3854 trucks had two. The extras were located closer to the middle of the car, to insure they stayed within the special section of track needed to operate the car. Because the car was so long, one of the regular pair of shoes sometimes extended beyond the section of track and the unloading mechanism would not work.

RATING

The handsome scale look of the 3854 has made it one of the most sought after of all the Lionel postwar boxcars. The smaller 3454 is also hard to find in good condition, but not nearly as desirable.

3854 pickup assembly.

6464 SERIES

Lionel introduced a newly designed boxcar in 1953. It was, at 11 inches, 1¾-inches longer than the earlier type boxcars had been. It was also higher. It would become known to collectors as the 6464 car, since all numbers in the series started with 6464. It was probably the most popular car Lionel ever made.

There were several reasons for its popularity. First, everybody seems to like boxcars, and then these particular boxcars were large and came in a great variety of colors and road names. But as much as everyone seems to like them, the 6464 cars can still drive collectors crazy. There are 29 different number designations and so many variations, major and minor, that no one seems to know them all. This section will examine each of the 29 cars and touch on as many variations as space or information permits. There undoubtedly will be omissions but it is hoped they will not be important ones.

There are a couple of generalizations that can be made about the 6464 cars. All of them made before 1955 had doors which had a single block in the middle. This block represents the order

Boxcar doors.
1953-1955.   1955 and after.

board on real cars. But in 1955 Lionel made a special door for the State of Maine car. This door had three additional blocks, one above the original and two below it. The smooth surfaces of these blocks were used for lettering that was unique to the State of Maine car (see the unit on the 6464-275), but eventually it became the only type of door Lionel made, although after 1955 they continued to put single-block doors on some 6464 cars until the supply was exhausted.

Another general change occurred on the cars in 1959, when Lionel began using a different style body casting. The casting was thinner than the earlier one. It had a thinner roof. The cars with the early casting and those with the late look almost exactly alike. The inside of the roof of the early 6464 cars had a smooth surface. The later ones had a rough surface. By opening the boxcar door and running a finger along the roof, a person can determine the texture, and this is the quickest way to tell the difference between the two castings. The later casting broke easier than

the early ones, which used perhaps 15 per cent more plastic. All 6464 cars made in 1959 or after had the thinner casting. A good deal of the riveting detail was eliminated on the sides of the cars in the later castings. For the most part the rivets that were eliminated were the second rows from each end.

Plastic trucks began appearing on the cars in 1958, although the metal trucks lingered on some cars for a time.

6464-1 WESTERN PACIFIC

The first in numerical sequence of the 6464 series and one of four cars brought out in 1953, the Western Pacific was shown in the catalog with a white body and black lettering. It was actually produced in silver with blue lettering. It is also known to exist with both black and red lettering. Elliot Smith, a 6464 expert from New York City, has an orange 6464-1 with a brown door and black lettering but it is a preproduction model. There is also a preproduction powder blue Western Pacific with black lettering. The 6464-1 ran again in 1954 and then was dropped.

6464-25 GREAT NORTHERN

The Great Northern was cataloged in orange with black lettering and a red and white Great Northern herald. The car is not known to exist with this lettering. It was produced with an orange body and white lettering and herald. Ran without change in 1954 and then dropped.

6464-50 MINNEAPOLIS & ST. LOUIS

This car was made from 1953 through 1956 in Tuscan with white lettering. In 1953 it was shown in the catalog in green with yellow lettering, but it is not known to have been sold that way. The Kusan Manufacturing Company made a proportionately similar boxcar and painted it green with yellow lettering and sometimes collectors mistake this car for a Lionel 6464-50. It is quite similar to the version shown in the Lionel catalog. If Lionel had ever made the green M. & St. L., it probably would have been the same color as the 6464-75 Rock Island.

6464-75 ROCK ISLAND

This car came in dark green with gold lettering in 1953, the same as it was shown in the catalog. It ran the same way in 1954 with no significant changes, then was discontinued. In 1969 it was reissued as part of a group Lionel called their "Famous Name Rolling Stock" grouping. It was made of unpainted green plastic and gold lettering that was so shiny it looked as if it were gold plated. It had the later style body casting and the four-block door.

6464-100 and -250 WESTERN PACIFIC

In 1954 Lionel made two Western Pacifics. One was a regular production model and the other was a very limited run, perhaps a promotion for the Western Pacific Railroad. The production model was silver, had a yellow feather, and was numbered 6464-100. The one that never went into regular production is shown in the photo below. Only three are known to exist. The one shown belongs to Matt Volpe of Chicago.

Rare Western Pacific.

In 1955 the orange Western Pacific with a blue feather was made. The number on the car was 6464-100, but the number on the box was 6464-250. The parts list also referred to the car as 6464-250 and -250 would have been the next number in the 6464 sequence.

In 1966 Lionel finally made the blue-feather car in large numbers. It was numbered 6464-250. Lionel seemed to realize the car was wanted by collectors; the 1966 catalog said the car was "back by popular demand." But the catalog kept up its tradition of never getting things quite straight with the Western Pacific blue feather car. The photograph in the catalog was of a 1955 version Western Pacific, complete with the number 6464-100 on it and metal trucks. The car produced had the number -250 on it, was of a darker shade of orange than the 1955 version, and the words "cushion underframe" were higher on the right side than they had been.

The 6464-250 had plastic trucks and the 1955-style door and 1959-style body. Even though it was not an exact duplicate of the earlier blue feather car, it resembled it closely. It is in demand by collectors, although, of course, not as much as the extremely scarce original run 6464-100 made in 1955.

6464-125
NEW YORK CENTRAL PACEMAKER

In 1954 Lionel started making boxcars with two and three-tone color schemes. Before, they had basically been solid colors with contrasting lettering or heralds. The 6464-125 Pacemaker was the first of the multi-tones, with the top half of the car being red, the bottom half gray and the door red. The lettering and herald were white. The 1954 catalog showed the red on top running around the ends, but it was never made with red ends. They were always solid gray, as was the roof.

With the introduction of the multi-tones, Lionel for the first time began casting the bodies of the boxcars in the predominant color of railroad's color scheme. Boxcars had previously been cast out of clear plastic, or any kind of scrap plastic available, and all the colors were painted on. By using colored plastic, one paint color could be eliminated. Most collectors don't differentiate between the two techniques of achieving road name colors, but discriminating collectors do. They feel the unpainted plastic cars give a little bit cheaper look than the painted cars. Also, the stamping of letters did not adhere as well to unpainted plastic as to painted. 6464-125 Pacemakers, when found nowadays, are often found with the lettering off.

The 6464-125 was made in 1954, 1955 and 1956 with no changes. It was a popular car and in 1955 Lionel made it in both the non-animated and animated versions. All the multi-tone cars sold well and Lionel kept making more of them. In 1956, for instance, five of the six new 6464 cars were multi-colored. The one that was not, the Katy, was not a good seller.

6464-150 MISSOURI PACIFIC

This car probably had more variations than any other boxcar. There might be as many as 15, some of them quite minor, but nevertheless detectable. The three main changes will be discussed here.

The car was introduced in 1954 and ran again in 1955 and in 1957. The 1954 version was cast in blue plastic with a gray stripe painted in the middle of the sides. The ends and roof were gray and the door was yellow plastic with a gray stripe which matched the stripe on the body. The lettering was black and the word "Eagle" appeared to the right of the door; this is the reason the 6464-150 is referred to as the Eagle car.

The masking job on the Eagle car in 1954 was not good and the line where the gray met with the blue was not sharply defined. Some of these early castings were of a darker blue than the later ones were, a blue so dark as to be almost purple. Many collectors are not aware of this early casting.

In 1955 the appearance of the car remained essentially the same, except the door was all-yellow and the gray stripe on the side of the car was about an eighth of an inch narrower. The "Eagle" lettering was therefore smaller, too. There were grooves in the side of the body at the point where the gray and blue met and this made the masking job easier, although the grooves were really put in the casting to help the masking of the State of Maine car, which, with its three colors, created an even more difficult masking assignment. In any case, the grooves helped in the masking of the Eagle car. Some of the lettering on the side of the Eagle car was rearranged in 1955.

In 1956 only the animated Eagle car ran, and then in 1957 the 6464-150 returned. The 1956 animated car, numbered 3495-150, was painted differently from the previous non-animated cars. Instead of being made of blue plastic, the animated car was made of gray plastic and the blue was painted on. This was also true of the 6464-150 Eagle car that ran in 1957. Among other changes on the 1957-version of the Eagle were the 1955-style door and the placement of the word "Eagle," which now appeared at the far left. It was smaller than it had been in 1955.

There were a number of other minor changes on the 6464-150 Missouri Pacific, among them some riveting detail.

It is hard to say which 6464-150 Missouri Pacific is hardest to find. Probably the one most desired by collectors is the first one, the one made in 1954, simply because it was the first.

6464-175 ROCK ISLAND

This all-silver version ran in 1954 and 1955 and is most common with blue lettering. However, there was a small production run with black lettering and there is a possibility some were made with red lettering. The car used the same letter-stamping as the green 6464-75. The black lettering may have been made in 1954, but most collectors believe it was made in 1955, because of so many other odd things happened that year.

6464-200 PENNSYLVANIA

This car, made in 1954 and 1955, is relatively hard to find. It was maroon with white lettering. Although it did not sell well in 1954 and 1955, it was reissued in 1969 and sold better and is easier to find today. The 1969 version had a silghtly more brownish tint to it than the previous versions. It also had the 1955 doors and 1959 body casting. There are also rivets missing under the letters "V-A-N-I-A."

6464-225 SOUTHERN PACIFIC

Painted all-black with white lettering and a yellow and red herald. This is the only boxcar Lionel made that was all-black (the New Haven had an orange door). It ran in 1954, 1955 and 1956 with no known variations. There is a possibility that the 1956 car was made with the 1955-style doors, but it is believed that the 1956 cars were merely carry-overs from those made in 1955.

6464-275 STATE OF MAINE

Introduced in 1955, there were many variations of this car over the years. The earliest model had a white plastic body with the blue and red painted on the sides. The roof and the ends were also painted blue. The door came two ways: a solid red plastic and a white plastic with painted red and blue stripes.

The four blocks on the State of Maine's special door had the following letters on them. The block above the original order board had the word "of" on it, the original middle block had "and" on it (part of the road name — Bangor and Aroostock), and the bottom two blocks had the larger letters "D" and "U," the middle letters of the word "Products."

The early red door version of the State of Maine car always came with the white plastic body. A later body casting in 1955 was made of blue plastic. This simplified the painting because only the red and white on the sides had to be painted on. The blue of the roof, ends and side could remain unpainted. This unpainted blue plastic was the same as that used for the Missouri Pacific car in 1955, and the body sides, as mentioned, had the same grooves as the Missouri Pacific. The door with this blue plastic version in 1955 was always red, white and blue.

The white plastic on the State of Maine cars from 1955 has a tendency to yellow and therefore these cars look different now from the others.

The 6464-275 was discontinued in 1956 and when it was reissued in 1957 it no longer had the grooves in the sides. Lionel had come up with a silk screen process that eliminated the need for the grooves. The process had first been used on the State of Maine operating car in 1956. The new 6464-275 was made of blue plastic and so was the red, white and blue door. The car ran in 1958 and 1959. Some were made in late 1959 with no number.

6464-300 RUTLAND

The Rutland was made in 1955 and 1956 and there were five main versions. The most common was made of yellow plastic with green roof and ends. The bottom half of the sides were also green. The word "Rutland" was written on the left side of the door in green and the letters were spaced evenly apart. The herald on the right had the word "Rutland" going through it. Inside the perimeter of the herald was written "Green Mt. Gateway." The door was unpainted yellow plastic, It was the early type door.

A second version had the yellow plastic door painted green on the bottom half, the way the real railroad did it. A third version had the door made of white plastic and the entire door was painted yellow. This made the color of the door somewhat darker than the yellow plastic door. It is quite uncommon. A fourth version had the lettering in a brighter green than the other cars and the spacing of the word "Rutland" was irregular.

The fifth version used a yellow plastic body, but the green painted on it was a high glossy kind, as opposed to the dull green of the other models. The herald was different, too. It was more solidly green inside, rather than yellow outlined in green. The car was cataloged this way in 1955 and some were made, but not too many. It is one of the hardest to find of the variations. The green door version and the green herald version are also hard to find.

It is hard to say when the different versions were made and why, but they all were.

6464-325 B&O SENTINEL

Made in 1956 only. All boxcars made in 1956 and after with metal trucks had the push-clip type method of holding the trucks to the frame. Before that, the horseshoe system was used. The 6464-325 had an aluminum finish with a light blue stripe across the lower part of the sides. The lettering was dark blue and "Sentinel" was written on the left side. Above that it said "Baltimore & Ohio Fast Freight Service." It had the yellow, black and green B&O herald on the right side. There are no known variations. It is one of the most sought after of all the 6464 cars because not many were sold. It was, except for the Katy, the least colorful of the 6464 cars introduced in 1956.

6464-350 KATY

Maroon body with white lettering and unpainted maroon plastic door of the 1955 style. It had metal trucks. It is as hard to find as the Sentinel but is generally not as hotly pursued because of its subdued color scheme. Made in 1956 only with no known variations.

6464-375 CENTRAL OF GEORGIA

This had an unpainted maroon plastic body with a silver roof and a silver oval on the side of the car. It had a Central of Georgia herald in yellow on the right side. It ran without change in 1956 and 1957, then was dropped. It was reintroduced in 1966 with the 1959 body frame and metal trucks. Otherwise the same. Discontinued after 1966.

The B&O Sentinel, the Katy and the original run Central of Georgia were never offered in sets.

6464-400 B&O TIME-SAVER

In 1956 the B&O Time-Saver had a dark blue unpainted plastic body, silver roof and an orange triangular stripe along its side. The stripe tapered down to a B&O herald on the right side. The lettering inside the stripe was blue, the lettering outside was white. Made again in 1957 without change and then discontinued. Reintroduced in 1969 with a blue plastic that was slightly lighter. The orange and herald were a bit brighter, too. A row of rivets under the "H" in Ohio was omitted in 1969. It always came with metal trucks.

6464-425 NEW HAVEN

Introduced in 1956, the early runs came with metal trucks. The body of the 6464-425 was made of black plastic, but it was also painted black over that, for some unknown reason. It had an orange door and white lettering. The catalog showed the big "N" on the left side with a full serif. It was made with a half serif. It ran the same way in 1957. In 1958 the trucks were changed to plastic and the orange on the door was slightly darker. The big change this year was the serif on the "N." It was finally full, as shown in the catalog.

The 6464-425 was discontinued after 1958 but was reissued in 1969. It had the light body casting. It had the same black body and orange door color scheme as the earlier model, with the white lettering. The serif was full. Most of these black New Havens made in 1969 have the 6464-425 number stamped on them, but a few were inadvertently stamped with the number 6464-725, which was the number used on the orange New Haven first made in 1962 (see 6464-725 section).

6464-450 GREAT NORTHERN

Made in 1956 and 1957 with olive green plastic body and an orange stripe through the middle. The stripe was outlined in yellow. The lettering was mostly yellow, although there was some green lettering inside the stripe. It had a three-color Great Northern decal on the right side. Dropped in 1958. Reintroduced in 1966 with later style trucks and body. The green was a little lighter, but otherwise everything was the same. Dropped the next year.

6464-475 BOSTON & MAINE

One of four new cars introduced in 1957. Unpainted light blue plastic body, black unpainted plastic door and black and white road herald to the right of the door. Some of the other lettering was in black and some was in white. It ran again in 1958 with plastic trucks and then again in 1959 with the lighter body casting. Discontinued the next year but reintroduced in 1965, without change. It ran again in 1966 and the blue plastic was considerably darker. Ran this way through 1968.

It should be noted here, perhaps, that each run of the body casting produced a slight color change. It is extremely hard to get color to be exactly the same each time. These little changes in the color of the plastic are ignored by many collectors, who do not consider them legitimate variations. Other collectors do consider them variations. For instance, the only significant changes in color of the 6464-475 Boston & Maine came in 1966, when the blue was painted on a gray plastic body. This can be considered a color variation. For the other years, the B & M cars made in 1958 and 1959 were slightly darker in color than and 1959 were slightly darker in color than those made in 1957, but most collectors don't consider them real variations. These collectors generally feel they would go crazy if they tried to collect each slight change in color from run to run — not just for the B & M, but for the rest of the 6464 cars and other rolling stock.

6464-500 TIMKEN

Ran in 1957 and 58 in unpainted yellow plastic body with a white stripe running down the middle. The lettering was blue-gray and it had an orange and white decal on the right side. Inside the decal were the words "Roller Freight." In 1957 the trucks were metal, in 1958 they were made in both metal and plastic. It was discontinued until 1969, when it had all the later changes and the yellow plastic was slightly lighter and the lettering was black rather than blue-gray.

6464-510 PACEMAKER

Brought out in 1957 to go in the Girl's Train. Its body was painted a pastel, bluish-green and its door was a light yellow. It had black lettering. It used the heavy plastic body of the earlier 6464 cars, but the late style door and metal trucks. It was available in the Girl's Set only, never separately.

6464-515 KATY

This was the other boxcar made for the Girl's Train in 1957 and 1958. Its color scheme was just the opposite of the Pacemaker: the body was a light yellow and the door a bluish-green. It, too, had the early, heavy, body casting, metal trucks and late doors. Like the 6464-510 Pacemaker it was available in the set only, making them the only two 6464 cars never available separately.

6464-525 MINNEAPOLIS & ST. LOUIS

This had a red plastic body with the red painted on. It was rather a dull red, with white lettering. It had the heavy plastic body casting and metal trucks. It was made the same way in 1957, when it was introduced, and in 1958. In 1964, when it was reissued, it was painted a bright, glossy red. It now had the lighter plastic body casting and plastic trucks. On some of these later castings, there was some riveting detail missing through the "M & St. L" herald. It ran without change in 1965 and 1966, then was dropped from the line.

6464-650 DENVER & RIO GRANDE

This car was made with an unpainted yellow plastic body, silver roof and silver bottom stripe. A black stripe separated the yellow and silver on the sides. It had black lettering. Some 6464-650 Rio Grandes are known to exist with an unpainted yellow plastic roof, probably from an early 1957 run. It was shown that way in the 1957 catalog. In 1958 some cars came with plastic trucks. It was dropped the next year. In 1966 it was reintroduced with the yellow slightly lighter than it had been. The row of rivets following the technical data on the left side was omitted.

6464-700 SANTA FE

The Santa Fe Shock Control was made in 1961. It was painted bright red with a glossy finish — like the 6464-525 Minneapolis & St. Louis from 1965 and 1966. It had white lettering. No known variations. A silver door version has been reported, but for the most part door variations on 6464 cars have been ignored in this book. There has been some counterfeiting of doors. They can be so easily switched around that it is impossible to tell if they are genuine or not. It is quite possible that Lionel put odd-colored doors on different cars occasionally. These are legitimate variations, but because so much cheating has taken place, door variations on the 6464 cars, unless otherwise noted, are disregarded by most serious collectors.

6464-725 NEW HAVEN

This was introduced in 1962 with a body painted orange over gray plastic, unpainted black plastic door, and black lettering. This car used the later, thinner, body shell and plastic trucks. It ran through 1966. The catalog always showed the car with the number 6464-735 on it. Also, the box the car came in always had the number 6464-735 on it. But the number stamped on the car was always 6464-725. It is not known to exist with the -735. After being dropped in 1967, the car came back unchanged for one year in 1968.

The black 6464-425 New Haven was reintroduced in 1969, but some of them were accidentally stamped with the 6464-725 number, the number always before stamped on the orange New Haven. No orange New Havens were made in 1969.

6464-825 ALASKA

This car is much sought after. It was produced in 1959 and 1960, then dropped. It was painted dark blue over a gray plastic body, yellow striping and lettering. It is considered hard to find, but it is not as hard to find as some collectors believe. What is hard to find is one in good condition, since the slightest chip makes the gray show through the dark blue.

6464-900 NEW YORK CENTRAL

Introduced in 1960, the car ran through 1963, was dropped, ran again in 1965 and 1966 and then was dropped for good. Its gray plastic body was painted jade green and it was an authentic reproduction of the New York Central boxcars of those years. The usually demure New York Central became a bit flashier just before its merger with the Pennsylvania.

RATING

Only regular production run cars are being considered in the 6464 rating in this book. Of these, the 6464-100 Western Pacific with the blue feather is the hardest to find. Next is the 6464-325 Sentinel, 6464-350 Katy and the solid herald 6464-300 Rutland.

OPERATING BOXCARS

3484 Santa Fe
3494-150 Missouri Pacific
3494-550 Monon

3494-1 NYC Pacemaker
3494-275 State of Maine
3494-625 Soo Line

Lionel's operating boxcars used the same bodies as their 11-inch and 9¼-inch non-operating counterparts. The first ones made were the smaller ones, and these were followed by the 6464-type in 1953.

It was the development of a new uncoupling system in 1948 that allowed the operating boxcars to come into being. Until 1949, the electromagnetic couplers had worked through the use of an electromagnet on each truck. Then Lionel placed an electromagnet on a remote control section of track and put a plunger under the coupler. When the car went over the electromagnet the operator could energize it. The electromagnet would pull down the plunger, which in turn would open the coupler.

Lionel engineers realized this same technique could be used on other things. They got the idea to place a man in a boxcar and connect him to a metal plunger which protruded from the bottom of the car. The spring-loaded door mechanism was also connected to the plunger. When the

car was stopped over the electromagnet and it was activated it would draw down the plunger, which would trip the mechanism, opening the door and pushing out the man. The door had to be closed manually. It was an efficient system and inexpensive. An operating boxcar cost only 50 cents more than the $4.50 non-operating boxcar.

The large operating boxcars used the same bodies and frames as the 6464 cars. They always used the heavy body casting and metal trucks. The Pennsy and Santa Fe used the one-block door, the others used the later, four-block door.

3484 PENNSYLVANIA
Cataloged in 1953 only, but it is so common many collectors feel it was also made in 1954.

3484-25 SANTA FE

This car was cataloged in 1954 only, but it came three diffrent ways. Most commonly found in orange with white, heat-stamped lettering, it is also known to exist with white, rubber-stamped lettering and black, heat-stamped lettering. It was shown with black lettering in the catalog, but this is a rare variation.

3494 PACEMAKER and
3494-150 MISSOURI PACIFIC

Both these cars were cataloged for one year only, the 3494 in 1955 and the 3494-150 in 1956.

3494-275 STATE OF MAINE

It was introduced in 1956 and ran through 1958. It was the same as the 6464-275 State of Maine car but was never made with grooved sides. It always came with the red, white and blue door. Some were made without numbers.

3494-550 MONON and
3494-625 SOO LINE

Both cars were available in 1957 and 1958. Monon was unpainted maroon plastic. The Soo used the same plastic and painted it brown.

3428 U.S. MAIL

New in 1959, this car used the same mechanism as the other cars, but the man in the car was designed differently. He had a magnet stuck in his belly button and a mail bag with a metal backing was stuck to the magnet. When the man was activated he would go forward and then stop abruptly and the mailbag would continue out the door and onto the ground.

This car had the late style body and door and it had plastic trucks. It ran again in 1960, was dropped, and was reintroduced in 1965 with no change. It ran again in 1966 and then was dropped for good.

RATING

Because the Monon and Soo were brought out late, and because they were rather colorless, they did not sell well. They are the most difficult to find of the operating cars and among the most coveted of all the rolling stock items.

Another car that is extremely rare is the Santa Fe with the black lettering. Many collectors are not aware of it.

3428 Operating U.S. Mail car.

AUTOMOBILE BOXCARS

6468 Baltimore & Ohio
6468X Baltimore & Ohio
2458 Pennsylvania

6468 New Haven (half serif)
6468 New Haven (reversed)
6468 New Haven (full serif)

2458 PENNSYLVANIA

Lionel's first scale-type automobile car — or double-door boxcar — was the prewar 2758, originally introduced in 1941. This same car was reissued in a set in 1945 with the number 2458 and knuckle couplers. It used the same prewar body in 1945 and 1946, with the prewar number on the side, even though it was listed in the catalog with its proper postwar 2458 number. By 1947 all the cars had the correct number on the side.

The car was dark brown with Pennsylvania markings in white. This was the only postwar boxcar to be made entirely of metal. It ran through 1948 without change. Common, but handsome.

6468 BALTIMORE & OHIO

Introduced in 1953, the 6468 used the same body as the 6464 series cars, except for the double doors. It was blue with white lettering. It ran through 1955. In 1955 another B&O automobile car was available. It was exactly the same as the

6468 except it was painted Tuscan red and had white lettering. It was numbered 6468X. It was included in a Santa Fe 027 freight set in 1955.

6468-25 NEW HAVEN

This car ran in 1956, 1957 and 1958 and is known to have come three different ways. One way had a black "N" with a full serif, and the "H" was white. Another way had a black "N" with a half serif. A third variation had a white "N," with full serif, and a black "H." This third variation is the rarest of the New Havens.

RATING

The rarest of all the automobile cars is the Tuscan red 6468X Baltimore & Ohio. Actually, the New Haven variation with the white, full-serifed "N" and the black "H" is probably as rare as the 6468X but because the variation is so subtle collectors don't get as excited about it as they do the 6468X.

SCOUT-TYPE BOXCARS

6054 Baby Ruth	6014 Airex	6014 Wix
6014 Bosco	6044 Airex	6036 Chung King
6050 Libby's	638-2361 Van Camps	6024 Whirlpool
	6050 Savings Bank	6050 Swift

The picture on this page shows a number of cars that evolved from the Scout boxcars. They all have standard trucks and couplers, in metal or plastic. The cars were used as promotional cars for private companies.

The cars came in white, red, orange or unpainted blue plastic. Many times the same car came in different colors and it is impossible to say exactly how many brand names were made in what colors.

Sometimes a brand name car appeared with more than one number, and sometimes a number overlapped brand names, being used on two or three different ones. It all got to be quite confusing. For instance, the Airex cars in the photo have different numbers, while the Bosco car has a number that is the same as one of the Airex cars.

RATING
The 6014 Wix and the 6036 Chung King Express are two hardest to find of the Scout-type boxcars.

GONDOLAS

6462 New York Central
6462 New York Central
6562 New York Central

1002 Lionel
1002 Lionel
1002 Lionel

Almost every freight set Lionel made had a gondola and consequently there are not many that are hard to find. There were two types of gondolas: the small ones, which were 9-inches long from coupler end to coupler end, and the larger ones, which were 10½-inches long.

SMALL

The first new gondola made after the war — in fact, the first new freight car — was the

2452 Gondola.

2452 Pennsylvania in black with white lettering. It came out in 1945. It was the only car that was not a prewar carryover. The plastic body was painted black and the underframe was sheet

metal. The car had a brakewheel at each end, footsteps in all four corners, and came with four wooden barrels.

In 1946 an 027 version was introduced and was numbered 2452X. It was identical to the other except it had no brakewheel or barrels. In 1948 the number was changed to 6452 in the catalog but the number 6462 appeared on the side of the car. The 6452 number was rubber-stamped on the bottom of the frame. In 1949 the number 6452 came on the sides.

Also in 1948, the ubiquitous 1002 gondola was introduced. The floor was altered to accept Scout-type trucks. The car came commonly in blue with white lettering. It also was made in silver with black lettering, yellow with black lettering, and red with white lettering. The silver, yellow and red are the favorites among collectors.

In 1949 the gondola was available in black only. This small gondola was made through 1969 and was available at different times in black, white, green and light blue. It had different numbers, loads and trucks, but it was always the same car.

LARGE

The first of the large gondolas came out in 1949. It had a plastic body and sheet metal frame. It was painted black and bore New York Central markings in white. There was a brakewheel at each end and footsteps in each corner. The trucks were metal. Six wooden barrels came with it. It was numbered 6462. Several other numbers followed the 6462, but they were essentially the same car, sometimes with different loads.

6462

The car ran as described above in 1949. In 1950 the black car came both with and without brakewheels. Also there was a 6462 available which was painted a dull red and came with brakewheels and footsteps.

In 1951, 1952 and 1953 only the black car was available and it no longer had footsteps or brakewheels. Most were unpainted black plastic, although a few were painted black, the way they had all been in 1949 and 1950.

In 1954 a green 6462 was introduced, a light green painted over the plastic. It had no brakewheels or footsteps. In 1955 the black car was dropped, but the green still ran and an unpainted red plastic car was introduced.

In 1956 the red and green cars were made again, but now the serifs on the New York Central lettering were longer than they had been. Both cars — and all the 6462 cars that had come before them — came with six wooden barrels, but the barrels in 1956 and after were the same as the ones that came with the barrel car.

In 1957 the green 6462 was dropped and the red car now came with four white cannisters instead of the six barrels. This car was dropped the next year. The pink gondola that ran with the Girl's Train was numbered 6462-500 and ran in 1957 and 1958.

6002

This car ran in 1950 only. It was black with white lettering. It is hard to find

6562

This was the same car as the 6462, only it came with four red cannisters instead of barrels. It ran in 1956, 1957 and 1958. It came in red with white lettering in 1956 and 1958 and in black and white lettering in 1957. There was a rare variation that ran in 1956. It was a gray car with red lettering and is pictured at the top of the page. In 1957 plastic trucks were introduced, and in 1958 the floor was changed so the trucks could mount directly to the body.

6062

This gondola was the same as the others except it carried three orange cable reels. It ran from 1959 through 1964. The body was red in 1959 and black after that.

6162 and 6342

This car ran from 1961 through 1969 in either blue or black, but always with white cannisters. In 1959 there was, for one year only, a 6162-50 in yellow plastic with dark blue Alaska markings and three white or red cannisters.

The 6342 was the gondola made for the culvert loader in 1956, '57, '58 and '59.

RATING

The two hardest to find of the large gondolas are the 6562 New York Central in gray with red lettering and the 6462-500 pink Girl's Train gondola. Next is the 6162-50 Alaska.

Of the smaller gondolas the three shown in the picture are the most sought after.

CRANE CARS

2560 Sheet metal
2460 Gray Cab
2460 Black cab

6460 Red cab
6560 Gray cab
6560-25 Red cab

Essentially, Lionel made only two crane cars during the postwar period. One was the 027 gauge 2560; the other was the larger 2460 and its descendants, which ran in both O gauge and 027.

2560 LIONEL LINES

This car ran in 1946 and 1947 in 027 sets. It was the same small, sheet metal crane that ran before the war with the number 2660. It was shown in the catalog with an all red cab. It is not known to exist that way. The number 2560 and "Lionel Lines" was rubber-stamped on the back of the cab. The cranes made in 1946 had the same Bakelite boom that the prewar version did. The boom came in three colors, brown, green and black. Black is the hardest to find. In 1947 all the 2560 cars had plastic booms.

2460-6460-6560 BUCYRUS ERIE

New in 1946, the 2460 was a completely new design. It had a die-cast frame and a plastic cab and boom. It used the same type six-wheel trucks that were used on the Irvington cars. The lettering had serifs and was heat-stamped in white. There were two cab colors, one a glossy gray with black lettering and the other a dull black with white lettering.

1947 through 1950

All the cabs were black after 1946. Everything else was the same as the 1946 version. Some collectors think there was a variation on the 2460, a variation that had a cab with a gray, plastic exhaust stack. There was no such variation, although sometimes a cab with a stack turns up on a 2460 car. What has happened in those cases is that someone has put the cab from the 182 Crane accessory onto the 2460 car. The two cabs are interchangeable and the 182 cab does have a stack. But Lionel never put the 182 cab on the 2460. An easy way to check this is by the box Lionel made for the 2460 crane. A crane with a stack will not fit into the box. No crane cars were made in 1951.

1952 and 1953

The Bucyrus Erie crane was reintroduced with four-wheel trucks and a new number, 6460. It was all-black with white lettering. The lettering was now sans serif and instead of the words "Lionel Lines" on the cab forming one continuous arch, only the word "Lionel" was arched. "Lines" was written in a straight line below "Lionel."

1954

Everything remains the same except the cab was available in red with white lettering as well as black. The red was a dull red and was painted over gray plastic. The number was still 6460. This was the last year for die-cast frames.

1955

Like many other items in the Lionel line, the crane car underwent extensive changes in 1955. The frame was now unpainted black plastic. The number was changed to 6560 and it was available mainly in unpainted red plastic, although some were made in unpainted gray plastic. The cab casting was changed and a smoke stack was added, the first time a Lionel crane legitimately had one. The handle on the crank wheel was shortened and the hook was smaller and instead of being turned to the side it pointed in line with the boom.

The method of securing the cab to the car frame changed. Before, the cab was attached to the underside of the frame by means of a steel tube which was clamped in place by a horseshoe washer. In 1955 a speed nut replaced the washer. It was quicker to assemble and cheaper to make but it was not as strong.

The changes made in 1955 cut costs and generally cheapened the product, but one of the cost cutting steps resulted in an improvement. Until 1955, Lionel used screws to attach the cab body to the cab base (as opposed to the car frame, which was below the base of the cab). In 1955 Lionel clipped the cab to its base. This was cheaper but it was better because the screws stripped and did not hold.

1956

Only the red cab was available. For some reason some of the frames were numbered 6560-25, although most retained the 6560 designation.

1957 and 1958

Available in red only, numbered 6560.

1959 through 1969

Plastic trucks replaced the cast trucks and the crank wheel was made into a solid casting in 1959. Available in red only. Remained the same every year through 1969, except for 1965, when it wasn't cataloged.

RATING

The gray, 12-wheel 2460 made in 1946 is the most difficult to find of all the crane cars. Next is the painted red 6460 made in 1954. This car was cataloged in only one set, which was headed by the Seaboard GM switcher.

The cars listed in this section were the only crane cars Lionel made after the war, although there seems to be a great deal of confusion over the matter, even among experienced collectors. Most people think there were more crane cars made than there were. The various cab bodies on the cranes were interchangeable and this has led to quite a bit of swapping. For instance, some collectors think that there is a 12-wheel 2460 crane with a red cab. These exist, but they were never made by Lionel. People have simply taken the red cab off a 6460 and placed it on a 2460 frame.

OIL TANK CARS

2855 Sunoco
2855 Sunoco
6555 Sunoco

6415 Sunoco
6425 Gulf
6315 Gulf

Lionel threw together a train set in 1945 that consisted of mostly prewar cars with postwar trucks and knuckle couplers. Two of the cars in the set, the 2758 Pennsylvania double-door boxcar and the 2755 Sunoco tank car, still had their prewar numbers, even though they had the new coupler. Lionel hadn't even bothered to change the numbers on the cars.

2755

The 2755 Sunoco had a sheet metal tank body, Bakelite dome, stamped sheet metal ladders, wire handrails, and die-cast frame. It also had footsteps at all four corners. The Sunoco decal was a yellow diamond with "Sunoco" printed in black inside the diamond and a red arrow going through it. Above the word "Sunoco" was the word "Gas" and below was the word "Oil," both printed in black.

The postwar numbering of the tankers started in 1946. They follow.

2555-6555

This was the exact same car that was produced in 1945 under the number 2755. Apparently Lionel decided to use up all its old 2755 decals in 1945, before coming out with the 2555 decal in 1946. It ran again in 1947, but most frames didn't have footsteps in the corners and the decal was changed. It only had the word "Sunoco" inside the diamond, printed in dark blue against a yellow background. It was the same in 1948. Some came with the number rubber-stamped on the

frame and no number on the decal.

In 1949 non-coil couplers were added and the number changed to 6555. Otherwise it was the same. Large, single-domed tankers discontinued after 1950. It came with both types of Sunoco decals.

2855

First produced in 1946, this car was supposed to have had the same die-cast frame and body as the prewar full-scale tank car had, but it didn't. But the catalog said it did and Lionel charged more for it than they did the 2555, $7.50 as opposed to $5.50.

All that was done on the 2855 that was different from the 2555 was that the sheet metal tank car was painted black. It used the same yellow, three-word herald but the other lettering was white, to show up against the black car. People were paying two dollars for a paint job.

The 2855 came in both black and gray in 1947. It made the same changes in the frame as the 2555 did and the same change in the decal, eliminating the words "Gas" and "Oil" from above and below "Sunoco." So it was exactly like the 2555 again, but again it sold for two bucks more. A small quantity of the 2855s were produced in black in 1947, but most were in gray, although there were not too many of either sold. It is rubber-stamped on the bottom of the frame. The cars were discontinued after 1947.

2465-6465-6463

The 2465, introduced in 1946, was the first of the two-dome tank cars after the war and the first tank car Lionel made with a plastic body. The sheet metal frame was the same as the one used on the boxcar in 1946, but there were four large rectangular holes punched out of the frame to simulate the kind of open frames that real tank cars have.

2465 Sunoco, 1946 version.

The 2465 was painted silver and had a Sunoco decal, which had black lettering and yellow background and red arrow. Another decal to the right of the herald had the technical information printed on it in black, but the 2465 number appeared nowhere on the body. It was rubber-stamped on the bottom of the frame. The car had wire handrails, and footsteps on all four corners.

The handrails ran only along the catwalks on the sides of the car, although the catalog showed them running around the ends, too. Another error in the catalog was in showing the double domer with ladders running down from each dome. It was never produced that way. The catalog also showed, in one picture, the tanker with the Sunoco decal in the middle, rather than off to one side. It was never made with the decal in the middle.

The color of the lettering changed from black to blue in 1947 and then in 1948 the decals were dropped and replaced by silk-screening. When the new coupler was added in 1948 the number of the double-domer changed to 6465 but it was otherwise unchanged. It looked like the decal version, but was a little duller and had less tendency to chip off. In 1951 the footsteps were eliminated from the frame.

The car remained essentially the same through 1956. It was dropped in 1957, but reappeared in 1958 with a new herald, that of Gulf Oil, and with some design changes. The number was still 6465. The wire handrails were eliminated and replaced by plastic ones cast into the body. The frame used a different stamping and the body was not screwed onto the frame but secured to it by metal tabs which bent over. The tab system of holding the tank to the frame was first used on the scout tank cars of 1948. And the mountings

between the frame and the body were round now instead of rectangular. The Gulf Oil 6465 came in either all-black or all-gray. The same car came in gray, orange or black with Lionel Lines markings.

In 1959 the only double domer available was gray plastic with no oil company herald. It just said "Lionel Lines." The next year the Cities Service herald appeared in white against a bright unpainted green plastic body. This same year,

6465 Cities Service — later type casting.

1960, there was an uncataloged version which was the same as the cataloged car except that it had non-operating couplers and was numbered 6045.

Things stayed the same until 1962, when another two domer was added to the line, the 6463 Rocket Fuel car in white with red lettering. It was identical to the 6465. It ran again in 1963, while the 6465 herald was changed from Cities Service to Lionel Lines. This was all-orange and the Lionel logo was on the left side. The 6463 Rocket fuel car was dropped in 1964, but the Lionel Lines two-dome tank ran unchanged in 1964, '65 and '66 before being dropped.

6415-6425

The 6415, brought out in 1953, was the first three-dome tank car Lionel ever made. It was bigger than any previous tanker. It used a new frame and came in a plastic tank body painted in bright aluminum and it bore the Sunoco herald, silk-screened on.

The frame of the 6415 did not really hold the trucks to it, as other frames did. The trucks were attached through the frame and onto the body. There was a metal handbrake wheel at one end of the frame, metal ladders and, for the first time on a tank car, handrails running around the ends of the car, just as on a real tanker. It was a nicely proportioned car and ran off and on without much variation for the next 16 years. It is only too bad that it was not offered with a larger variety of company names.

There was no change in the car in 1954 and 1955. In 1956 the Sunoco herald was dropped and replaced by Gulf. The number was changed to 6425, but other than the herald it was identical in every respect to the 6415, except that the aluminum paint was a bit duller.

The 6425 was dropped from the line in 1959 and no triple-domers were on the market until 1964, when the Sunoco came back with its old number, 6415. It had the dull aluminum paint and plastic trucks and ran through 1969 without change, except it was given metal trucks again the last year.

6315

Brought out in 1956, the 6315 was a chemical tank car with a black plastic body painted orange outside the center area, black lettering, and Gulf herald. It used the same frame and chassis as the 6415 and 6425, but it was a single-dome car with a metal catwalk at the top. The catwalk had metal ladders running down both sides of the tank body. There were also metal handrails around the entire car.

There were a couple of minor variations. Some cars had shiny orange paint and some had dull. The shiny ones are harder to find. The 6315 tanker is probably the most popular tank car with collectors; they like the extra detailing the platform on top offers. Lionel only made it in the Gulf herald. It would have been nice if they had offered it in more variety. American Flyer offered it in six or seven different company names.

The car was discontinued after three years and then was reissued in 1963 with the same number. This time, however, the car was all-orange, made of orange plastic instead of black. It had Lionel Lines markings rather than Gulf, and had plastic trucks. It ran this way until 1966, when the Gulf label was put back on. It was discontinued after 1969.

1005 Sunoco.

SMALL TANK CARS
1005-6035-6015-6025
The 1005 Sunoco single-dome tank car was made for the Scout train in 1948. It was shown in the catalog in dark blue with a three-color

Sunoco decal and white lettering, but it was not made that way. It was made in unpainted gray plastic and the lettering was black, although some may have been made with blue lettering. It had handrails and ladders that were cast into the plastic. It had Scout trucks. The frame was sheet metal and was connected to the tank by tabs. It was slightly smaller than the two-dome 6465 tank car.

6035 Sunoco.

It ran unchanged until 1952, when it was upgraded by putting on a better coupler and taking it out of the Scout set and putting it into an 027 set. The number was changed to 6035. In 1954 the number was changed to 6015 and the Scout-type trucks and couplers were replaced by standard trucks and couplers. It was unpainted yellow-plastic with Sunoco marking.

In 1955 the small tanker was available separately for the first time. Previously they had come only in sets. The number was changed to 6025 in 1956, when it was given the Gulf herald and came in either black or gray plastic. It used metal trucks and couplers. The gray was available in 1957 again, but also, with the same 6025 number, in all-orange Gulf. It came with either plastic or metal couplers.

In 1958, the last year the tank cars ran, the 6025 came in black plastic with Gulf herald and white Lionel lettering. There is a possibility the orange 6025 was made that year but not cataloged.

RATING
Of all the tank cars, the black 2855 from 1947 is the hardest to find. Next in scarcity is the black 2855 from 1946. Next is the gray 2855 from 1946. All three of these cars are uncommon.

Most of the rest of the tankers are common, whether they be single, double, or triple-domed, or chemical cars. The favorite among collectors of these are the 6465 Cities Service, the 6425 Gulf, and the 6315 shiny-coated Gulf.

LOG CARS

2411 "Big Inch" flat car
3451 Log car (operating)
3461 Log car (operating)

3361 Log car (operating)
6361 Log car
3362 Helium tanks (operating)

2411-6411 FLATCAR

1946 through 1950. Used the same frame as the work caboose. It is shown in the photograph above carrying blackened steel pipes, the way it came in 1946, when it was called the "Big Inch" flatcar. Every year after that it came with logs and was simply referred to as a flatcar. It was numbered 2411 in 1946 and 1947, and 6411 after that, reflecting a change in the couplers.

3451-3461 LOG DUMP CAR

New in 1946. It used a die-cast frame and sheet metal log bed and stakes. It was a great all-around improvement over the prewar log dumper. The 3451 came with a painted black frame and a blackened log bed and, in 1946 and 1947, either silver lettering or white. There were five wooden logs supplied with the dumper and they were in their natural color. It always came with the 1946-style coupler assemblies. The frame was made so the electronic receiving unit could be fitted to it.

In 1948 the lettering was enlarged and came in white only.

The number was changed to 3461 in 1949 when the couplers were switched from coil to non-coil. There were no other changes until 1954, when the frame was painted green and the logs were stained dark brown for the first time. Lionel used up their old inventory of 3461s in 1955, then dropped it.

3361-3362-3664
OPERATING LUMBER CAR

Introduced in 1955. It was merely the 6362 rail truck car with a log dumping mechanism added. The rails for holding the trucks on the 6362 were left on the frame of the 3361. It came in unpainted gray plastic with black, serifed lettering.

The car used a newly designed solenoid dumping mechanism that lifted the bed in even stages. The old mechanism would raise the bed too fast

if too much voltage was applied and the logs would overshoot their bin; if not enough voltage was applied the bed would not raise at all. The new system raised the bed a little each time the control button was pressed.

1956 through 1960

The lettering was changed to sans serif in 1956, then back to serif in 1958. No log dumpers ran in 1960.

1961

The 3362 was introduced. It was unpainted dark green plastic with white lettering. It had a new cargo — helium tanks, which were made of wood, painted aluminum, and slightly fatter than the old logs, and had tapered ends. It had a spring-loaded mechanism that was tripped by an electromagnet in the uncoupling track section.

1962 and 1963

The 3362 ran unchanged and then was dropped.

1965 through 1969

The log dump car was reintroduced with the number 3364. It was the same as the helium dump car but came with three dark stained logs, which were the same size as the helium "tanks" but did not have the tapered ends.

6361 TIMBER TRANSPORT CAR

1960 and 1961. 1964 through 1969. The same basic car as the 6362, with sheet metal frame, plastic trucks and a dark green plastic body with white lettering. Had three realistic wood logs secured by blackened brass chains. It was dropped in 1962 and 1963, then ran without change through 1969.

RATING

All the log cars are common. The 3461 with the green frame is a little harder to find than the others, but the 6361 with the real logs is the most sought after because it looks so authentic.

COAL DUMP

3459 *Silver bin*
3469 *Black bin*
3359 *Twin dump*

3459 *Green bin*
3559 *Sheet metal*

Lionel offered two automatic coal dumping cars in 1946. One of them, the 3559, was the same car that had been made before the war except it had postwar trucks. The other, the 3459, was a new design.

The 3559, since it was a rerun, was one of the few cars in the 1946 catalog that actually came the way it was shown, with a red dumping bin and black frame. Two tabs which had been on the ends of the frame on the prewar version were removed in 1946 to accommodate the new couplers. It ran unchanged through 1948.

The new 3459 was shown in the catalog with a silver dumping bin and frame and blue Baltimore & Ohio markings. It was not made that way. It was made with a black frame, unpainted aluminum bin and blue lettering. In late 1946 they started painting the aluminum bin black.

The 3459 used a die-cast frame and an electromagnetic solenoid to activate the dump bin, similar to the operation of the log dump car. The action was fragile and the cars are often found broken today.

In 1947 the 3459 continued with the black frame and bin, but the bin was now sheet metal. In 1948 they started painting the bins on the 3459 green, then late the same year started painting them black again. There is no known reason for this except that Lionel might have wanted to get rid of some green paint. Lionel also experimented with painting the bins yellow in 1948, although

they made only a few. Lionel often experimented with colors, painting 10 or 15 items one color and then deciding it was not quite right. They then disposed of them through regular sales.

The number of the 3459 was changed to 3469 in 1949 because new non-coil couplers were added. It was painted all-black with white lettering. It had one other mechanical change besides couplers. The hinge pin on the bin door was larger and stronger than it had been. The dumping door on the 3469 is not interchangeable with the 3459 unless the hinges are changed.

The 3469 continued without change through 1955, after which it is discontinued.

The 3359 twin-bin dump car was introduced in 1955. It was longer — 11½ inches as opposed to 9½ inches — than the single bin, but it was cheaper for Lionel to manufacture since it had a sheet metal frame and its two bins were plastic. The underbelly was red plastic and it tabbed onto the frame. The bins were unpainted gray plastic with black lettering. The mechanism worked similar to the 3361 long dump car of 1955. Both bins would not dump at the same time. They dumped in sequence.

The 3359 coal dumper ran through 1958 without change.

RATING

The silver 3459 is the hardest to find of production run dumpers.

HOPPERS

6456 *Lehigh Valley*
6456 *Lehigh Valley*
3456 *Norfolk & Western*

6456 *Lehigh Valley*
6456 *Lehigh Valley*
2856-2956 *Baltimore & Ohio*

The first hopper offered after the war was the prewar, semi-scale 2956 B&O, which was available in 1946 and 1947 with postwar trucks and couplers. The catalog both years said the B&O had a postwar number of 2856, but it didn't. The car still had the number 2956 on it. The catalog also showed the B&O in gray, but it wasn't. It came in black only. There is a theory among some collectors that Lionel never even offered the car after the war and that those that exist with postwar trucks have them because operators put them on the prewar cars.

Other than the questionable semi-scale carryover, postwar hoppers can be classified into an early, twin-bin type and a later, larger, covered hopper. The small hoppers are pictured on this page.

2456-6456

The prewar hopper was dropped in 1948 and in its place came the twin-bin 2456. It had a plastic body painted black with Lehigh Valley markings in white. This car is hard to find but most collectors don't know it, so it has not been aggressively sought after. The car was made in 1948 only; in 1949 the number changed to 6456 because the new couplers were added.

The 6456 ran through 1955, changing colors several times, but always with the Lehigh Valley markings. In 1951 it was available in maroon with white lettering as well as black. The interior was changed slightly in 1951; the reinforcing

1948-1950 with corner gussets and molding plug.

1951 and later without corner gussets
and molding plug.

gussets were removed and the molding plug was removed. In 1954 the black and maroon versions were dropped and the gray model appeared with maroon lettering. There was also a glossy red version with yellow lettering, and a less common glossy red with white lettering. The black and the red hoppers were cataloged again in 1955, but the red was probably not made.

6476

In 1956 this cheaper version appeared. It still had metal trucks, but tabs replaced screws for holding the truck frames to the body. In 1957 the car had plastic trucks, which attached to a metal plate on the body, and was available in three colors, all unpainted plastic: red with white lettering, black with white lettering, and gray with black lettering. The road name on all remained Lehigh Valley.

6446-25 Norfolk & Western
6436 Lehigh Valley
6346 Alcoa Aluminum

6536 Minneapolis & St. Louis
6636 Alaska
6736 Detroit & Mackinac

From 1958 through 1969 the 6476 was made in many different colors, some with road names and some without. The plastic trucks attached directly to the body without a metal plate. Some of the cars made through the years were a yellow Lehigh Valley, a gray Santa Fe, a black Lehigh Valley, and a khaki with no road name.

3456 OPERATING HOPPER

When Lionel introduced the 456 coal ramp accessory in 1950, it came supplied with a 3456 operating hopper. The car was identical to the 6456, except it had operating hatches. The 1950 catalog showed the car with Lehigh Valley markings, but it is not known to have been made that way. It was made with Norfolk & Western markings. It ran through 1955, always in black with white lettering.

The first of the big hoppers appeared in 1954 with the introduction of the 6446-25 Norfolk & Western. These cars were modeled after the covered hoppers that were used by real railroads to transport grain, cement or other materials that required protection from the elements.

6446-25 NORFOLK & WESTERN

The first hopper was gray with black lettering and metal trucks. The roof was removable and had 12 hatches that opened and closed. The next year, 1955, the car was cataloged in black with white lettering. The gray was not cataloged but may have been available. In 1956 no N&W was cataloged but the black version was available without the roof.

Glossy red 6456 with white lettering.

RATING

The glossy red 6456 with white lettering is the most difficult small hopper to find. The next most difficult is the glossy red 6456 with yellow lettering. Also hard to find is the 2456 Lehigh Valley in black and the 2956 die-cast hopper with postwar trucks and couplers.

Norfolk & Western covered hopper.

Lionel had begun cutting expenses across the line in 1955 and the most expensive part of producing the cement hopper was the roof. Without the roof, however, the long, high hoppers had a tendency to warp, so Lionel added a brace that was inserted into holes on each side of the car.

In 1957 the original gray 6446-25 with the roof returned. It was dropped in 1958 and did not come back until 1963. It had the roof again, but it did not have the -25 suffix on the side. It had plastic trucks. Although it did have the roof, it also had the holes in the side for a brace. It was numbered 576446.

6436 LEHIGH VALLEY

New in 1955, this was actually the first cataloged hopper without a roof. It came in maroon with white lettering. It also came in an uncataloged version — in black. The maroon version was offered in 1956 and 1957. The lilac Girl's Train 6436-500 Lehigh Valley was also available in 1957 and was the only Lehigh Valley available in 1958. It was dropped in '59.

In 1963 the Lehigh Valley returned in both an open and a covered version. Both were red with white lettering. The open version was numbered 6436-110, the covered was cataloged as 6446-60. But those were numbers used in the catalog only. The sides of the cars merely had the number 6436 on them.

The red Lehigh Valley was made again in 1964 and was available through 1968. This is the most common of the covered hoppers. The red hoppers made in 1963 have "New 3-55" written on the center panel. The red hoppers made after that do not.

6346 ALCOA ALUMINUM

A covered hopper available in 1956 only but probably available in 1957, too. It was aluminum colored with a three-color Alcoa herald on each side.

6536 MINNEAPOLIS & ST. LOUIS

New in 1958, it was an open hopper, red with white lettering. Ran again in 1959, then was dropped, and then revived in 1963, when it had a shinier red finish than before.

6636 ALASKA AND
6736 DETROIT & MACKINAC

Both open hoppers. The Alaska, in black with yellow lettering, was offered in 1959 and 1960. The Detroit & Mackinac, in red with white lettering, was made in 1960, 1961 and 1962.

RATING

The most valued of the regular production hoppers are the 6436-500 lilac Lehigh Valley, the 6636 Alaska and — even though it was made for three years — the 6536 Minneapolis & St. Louis. The M. & St. L. is an unusual case. It ran for three years but still did not sell as well as the popular 6346 Alcoa, which was cataloged for only one year. The red 6436 Lehigh Valley with the "New-55" is rare but it looks so much like the other red Lehigh Valleys that collectors have tended to ignore it.

The Norfolk & Western Railroad, about 1956, had Lionel make up 30 hoppers for a special display. They were made in pink, silver, lilac and bronze and are probably the rarest of all the hoppers.

Lehigh Valley open hopper.

SEARCHLIGHT CARS

6520 with green generator
6520 with orange generator
6520 with maroon generator

3650 Searchlight extension car
  (dark gray frame)
3530 Generator car
6822 Nightcrew searchlight car

6520-3520-3620

1949 through 1956. The 6520 was the first searchlight car, other than the 2420 work caboose, that Lionel made after the war. The car used the same die-cast, depressed center frame as the 2461 transformer car. It was painted light gray with black lettering. The simulated generator was shown in the catalog as green, but only a few of these unpainted green plastic generators were made in 1949. Most were unpainted orange plastic. There was an extremely small number made with unpainted gray plastic generators, but those were not even considered a production run. In 1950 the car was available with orange generator only, and in 1951 the generator was unpainted maroon plastic.

The searchlight housing was die-cast and painted crackle gray. The light could be turned on and off by remote control.

In 1952 the number was changed to 3520 and the orange generator returned. The searchlight rotated continuously because of a new vibrating system. The remote control was eliminated in 1954, the searchlight was made of gray plastic and metal, and the number changed to 3620.

3650 SEARCHLIGHT EXTENSION CAR

1956 through 1959. Used the same frame as the 3520. It came in light gray and dark gray with black lettering. The dark gray, shown in the color picture, is harder to find. Instead of a generator in the center, there was an operating reel of wire. The searchlight was removable and was secured to the car by a magnet. A small die-cast handcrank fit into a hole next to the reel and is usually missing when the car is found today. There was a small dark gray plastic generator at the end of the car opposite the light.

3530 OPERATING GM GENERATOR CAR

1956 through 1958. Equipped with the same portable searchlight as the 3650, but without the magnet. Included was a power pole to which the light attached. The car itself was unpainted blue plastic with a metal frame and either blue or black belly tanks. It was an accurate reproduction of a car made by General Motors to provide power at emergencies.

Inside the car were a simulated generator and a fan. When the door was opened the circuit was completed, a light inside would turn on, and the fan would start rotating and make the sound of a humming generator. It never sold well and it is difficult to find with all its components intact.

6822 NIGHT CREW CAR

1961 through 1969. This was a 6511-type flatcar in unpainted red plastic, white lettering and plastic trucks. There was a blue rubber man mounted in the middle of the car. The base was gray plastic and the same one used on the 6812 track maintenance car. The base might also have been made in black.

RATING

The hardest searchlight car to find is the non-production run 6520 with the unpainted gray plastic generator. Of the production run cars, the 6520 with the green generator is the hardest to find. That is followed by the dark gray 3650 searchlight extension car. The most common is the 6520 with the orange generator.

STOCK CARS

3656 Lionel (operating)
3356 Horse car (operating)
3366 Circus car (operating)

6356 New York Central
6376 Circus car
6556 MKT

The operating cattle car came out in 1949 and was the most popular of all the stock cars Lionel made. It ran for seven years, but it was not a particularly realistic looking car. It was pretty stubby and out of scale, but kids didn't mind; they loved the action. Which just goes to show that beauty is only skin deep. The later stock cars, especially the bi-level cars, were longer and better looking.

3656 OPERATING STOCK CAR

1949 through 1955. A 9¼-inch stock car with plastic body painted orange, a sheet metal frame and metal trucks. It had the Lionel logo on the side in white lettering, although a small number were made in 1949 with black lettering. Some of the cars made in late 1949 and all of the cars in 1950 had an Armour sticker on the center door. There were also doors on the ends of the car for the cattle to pass through once the action started.

Both the car and the corral it came with had their own vibrating mechanisms. These moved the cows from the car through the corral and back through the car again. Nine cows came with the outfit, but only five could fit into the car at one time.

In 1949 and 1950 the corral deck was made of aluminum and the corral gates were orange plastic. In 1951 and later the corral deck was made of tin and the gates were yellow plastic. The base was green. On these later corrals the ramps that led to the car had a tendency to stick.

Both Lionel O and 027 gauge track hooked onto the corral base to make sure it lined up properly.

One of the problems with the cattle car was that the cows fell over a lot when the car was moving around the track. This problem was corrected on the horse car by making the sides of the walkway higher.

6656-6646 NON-OPERATING CATTLE CAR

1950 through 1954 and 1957. When it was introduced in 1950, the 6656 had the same body as the operating cattle car, only without the operating doors and mechanism. The car was painted yellow, although the catalog showed it in brown, a color that is not believed to have been made. The car had the Armour sticker and the footsteps at all four corners. After 1950 the Armour sticker wasn't used. In 1953 the footsteps were removed and the shade of yellow was slightly darker. 1954 was the last year for the 6656.

In 1957 the cattle car was reissued with the number 6646. It was orange plastic with black lettering and plastic trucks. It was discontinued the next year.

3356 OPERATING HORSE CAR

1956 through 1960 and 1964 through 1966. The horse car replaced the operating cattle car and it had an improved operation. It was quieter and not as erratic, and had higher sides on the walkway to prevent the animals from falling over. The car was 11¼-inches, two inches longer than the cattle car. It was unpainted green plastic with yellow Santa Fe markings. It had nine black horses.

The end doors of the car folded out and became the ramp, rather than having the ramp on the corral. The corral itself was simplified and was almost all plastic. It was green with white fencing and brown walkways.

3366 CIRCUS CAR

1959 through 1962. Same car and corral as the horse car. The car was unpainted white plastic with a red catwalk and red lettering. The horses were white instead of black. The troughs were gray and the other area red. The white plastic had a tendency to yellow. The doors were broken easily on both the horse and circus cars.

6356 NYC BI-LEVEL STOCK CAR

1954 and 1955. Newly designed in 1954. 11¼-inches long. Metal frame and plastic body painted yellow with black lettering. Bore New York Central markings and metal trucks and couplers. On the real railroads this type of car was used to carry small animals such as pigs and sheep. It had four sliding doors.

6376 CIRCUS CAR

1956 and 1957. Same as the 6356 New York Central, which it replaced. Unpainted white plastic with red lettering and red catwalk on the roof. Hard to find now with the lettering unspeckled because it did not adhere well to the unpainted plastic.

6556 KATY

1958. Same as the 6376 and 6356, only painted dull red with white lettering and white doors and the Katy markings. Metal trucks. It was only shown in one set, headed by a Virginian rectifier, although it was listed for separate sale. This is the rarest of the postwar bi-level stock cars.

6434 POULTRY CAR

1958 and 1959. This was the original version of the animated chicken sweeper car. The frame and body were altered versions of the bi-level stock car. The car was painted red with white lettering and a plain gray plastic door. The car was illuminated with two lights. It had white plastic sheets lithographed with chickens on both sides.

RATING

The 6556 Katy is the hardest to find and most valued of all the stock cars. Next is the 3366 operating circus car and the 6376 circus car. The small 6646 made in 1957 is also hard to find but seems to cause no great excitement among collectors.

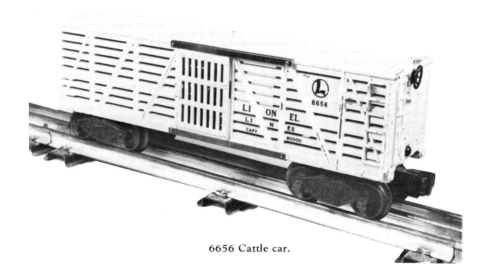

6656 Cattle car.

REFRIGERATOR CARS

3462 Lionel (operating)
3662 Lionel (operating)
3672 Bosco (operating)

6472 Lionel
6672 Santa Fe
6572 Railway Express

Lionel made two types of refrigerator cars after the war . . . operating and non-operating. The operating cars will be discussed first.

OPERATING
3462 — 3472 — 3482

Introduced in 1947, the 3462 was the first car Lionel made with a human figure involved in action. It used essentially the same body as the 2454 small boxcars. It came with a trackside platform and it worked well. At $8.95, it was cheaper than most operating cars or accessories. It was 8¾-inches long.

It came with a plastic body painted all-white — or eggshell, as Lionel called it — and black lettering. The frame was sheet metal and the doors and door frame were made of aluminum and were a separate unit from the plastic body. This made the unpainted aluminum doors a different color from the white body.

The mechanism inside the car was ingeniously simple and efficient. Five milk cans could be loaded into a hatch on the end of the roof. The cans would roll down a chute towards a spot inside the doors where a rubber man was mounted on a steel base. The cans would roll toward the man one at a time. Since the bottom of each light aluminum can was magnetized, the magnet would afix itself when it struck the steel base on which the man stood. The can would then stand upright. When the mechanism was activated, the doors would fly open and an arm behind the man would push him and the can onto the metal platform, where the magnet on the can would afix itself again and the man would pop back into the car. The doors would close.

The car was made in both dull white and glossy white. Most were dull. The one in the photograph above is glossy.

The car operated on a standard remote control section of track that came with all train sets in 1947.

1948
The outside of the car remained the same but some internal changes were made.

1949
The number was changed to 3472 when mechanical couplers were introduced.

1950 - 1953
More detailed plastic doors replaced the aluminum in 1950 and the hatch on top of the car opened wider than before, making loading easier. The body was now made of unpainted white plastic. No changes the next three years.

1954
There were extensive internal changes and the number was changed to 3482. The frame was a new stamping, and used a simpler tab and screw system of attaching to the body. The operating

mechanism had a stronger coil spring and the entire action worked with less vibration. But the car, as it had been before, was still too heavy. The number 3482 appeared only on the right side of the door. The number 3472 still appeared on the left side.

1955

In spite of the overhauling made the year before, this was the last year the car ran, because the new, larger operating milk car was introduced this year. The number 3482 appeared on both sides of the door.

3662-3672
1955

This car was 2½-inches longer than the small milk car. Its construction was similar to the 6672 non-operating refrigerator car in that the roof and ends were one piece. It came with unpainted white plastic sides. The roof, ends and doors were unpainted brown blastic. The lettering was black. The 6672 non-operating refrigerator car had a plastic frame, but the 3662 had a metal frame to promote a ground.

The mechanism was similar to the smaller operating car but was now mostly plastic. Its door system was much improved over the old system, using one spring for both doors. The new car had metal strips above and below the doors. These strips protruded and protected the doors if the car fell on its side. There were now seven plastic cans instead of five metal ones and they were not magnetized. The car ran unchanged through 1958.

1959

The 3662 was still unchanged. The 3672 Bosco car was introduced. It used the same brown roof and doors as the 3662 but the sides were made of dark yellow plastic. It had brown lettering which said "Corn Products Refining Company." It also had a Bosco decal. The Bosco cans were made of yellow plastic with the word "Bosco" in red. The Bosco platform had a brown base and a yellow superstructure.

1960 through 1966

Both the 3662 and 3672 ran unchanged in 1960 and then were dropped. The 3662 reappeared with plastic trucks and couplers in 1964 and ran the same way in 1965 and 1966 before it was dropped for good.

RATING

The Bosco car is the most valuable of the operating refrigerator cars, but it is not necessarily the hardest to find. At least as hard to find, and probably harder, is the 3462 with the glossy white paint job shown in the picture. But it is not as glamorous as the Bosco car and therefore not as sought after by collectors.

NON-OPERATING
6472-6482 LIONEL LINES

Introduced in 1950, the 6472 was the same car as the operating milk car but had no mechanism. It ran through 1953 and was dropped. The car reappeared in 1957 numbered 6482. It had plastic trucks and was offered in one set only. It is a hard car to find, but nobody seems much interested in it.

6672 SANTA FE

Introduced in 1954. Fine detailing and realistic looking. It came in two shades of brown, one reddish and the other chocolate. The lettering was black in 1954 and blue in 1955 and 1956. It was dropped after 1956.

6572 RAILWAY EXPRESS

Made in 1958 and 1959. It was the last reefer Lionel made. Painted dark green with gold lettering and a Railway Express decal. It came with metal trucks. Sometime in the middle 1960s Madison Hardware of New York City, a large Lionel retailer, had the company make up a special run. The Madison Hardware version is a lighter shade of green than the previous production runs and has plastic trucks. It is fairly common.

RATING

By far the most difficult to find of the non-operating refrigerator cars are the original production runs of the 6572 Railway Express cars with the metal trucks. Next in scarcity is the black-lettered 6672 Santa Fe.

FLAT CARS

6511 Pipe car
6430 Piggy back transport
6816 Bulldozer

6416 Boat loader
6500 Airplane car
6469 Liquified gas car

The 6511 flatcar, which was brought out in 1953, eventually became the mainstay of the Lionel rolling stock. It was used many different ways with many different numbers. There were at least 60 cars into which the 6511 evolved. Here are some of them:

6511 PIPE CAR

1953 through 1956. At 10½-inches, this car was longer than any previous Lionel flatcar. It was made of black plastic painted dull red. It had 11 metal side stakes and carried a cargo of five silver-gray plastic pipes. It had die-cast ballast weights mounted to the body, and trucks mounted to the weights. These made the car heavy enough to be used near the front of a long train. In 1954 the die-cast weights were replaced by sheet metal ones, not as heavy, but sufficient to keep the car on the tracks. In 1955 the car came in both unpainted brown plastic and unpainted red plastic. In 1956 it was made in red plastic only.

In 1955 there was a number variation, the 6311. It was the same car as the 6511 and came in both brown and red, but it had only six stakes instead of 11.

6414 AUTO LOADER and 6416 BOAT LOADER

This was the exact same car as the 6511 except that a sheet metal superstructure was added. The superstructure fit into the old stake holes. The 6414 auto car ran from 1955 through 1966 and is extremely common. No picture is shown. The frame was red plastic and the superstructure black. It had metal trucks until 1957 and plastic after that. It had "Auto-Loader" rubber-stamped in white on the side of the superstructure until 1964. Then it became a sticker. Some were printed in white, others in yellow. In 1964 the autos were cheapened a great deal.

The 6416 boat loader ran in 1961 and 1962, same car, same colors as the car loader. It had four boats which were originally used on HO gauge cars. The colors of the boats were blue and white.

6430 PIGGY BACK TRANSPORT

1955 through 1958. This was the 6511 with a sheet metal stamping which secured the trailers. The car was unpainted red plastic with white lettering. The car had metal trucks and the 6511 stake holes were plugged up. It came with two green "Lionel Lines" trailers in 1955. In 1956 the load was changed to two Cooper-Jarrett trailers, which were white. The Cooper-Jarrett trailers were gray in 1957 and 1958.

The piggy back cars were not made in 1959 or 1960, but in 1961 one was reintroduced with the number 6440. It was shown in the catalog in red with white Lionel markings and in blue with white Lionel markings, but it is doubtful any blue cars were ever made. The red car had plastic trucks. It carried two gray plastic trailers which had two wheels rather than four wheels. The 6440 ran in 1961 only.

The 6431 was new in 1966 and was very similar to the 6430 from 1956, except it had plastic trucks. It was so similar to the 6430, in fact, that the number 6430 still appeared on the side of the car. The number 6431 was used in the catalog and was stamped on the box, but not on the car. The trailers on the car were the same as the ones on the 6430, but now a tractor was provided for them. The tractor did not fit on the flatcar. It was meant to be played with separately. The tractor was not made by Lionel. It was made by the Midge Toy Company of Rockford, Illinois.

6800 and 6500 AIRPLANE CAR

1957 through 1963, except 1961. This car was introduced as 6800 in red plastic with white lettering. Metal trucks. It carried a Lionel-made model of a Beechcraft Bonanza, which was yellow and black. Some had the yellow on the top half of the plane, others had the yellow on the bottom half. In 1958 the car had plastic trucks. In 1962, after not being made a year, the car came back as 6500 in unpainted black plastic with white lettering. The plane changed colors to red and white, but still came in two top-and-bottom combinations. There was white heat-stamped lettering on the red wing. This is harder to find than the yellow and black airplane.

6816 BULLDOZER and 6817 SCRAPER

1959 and 1960. A 6511-type car with red frame and white lettering. The 6816 carried an unpainted orange plastic bulldozer with black Allis-Chalmers markings. It was an excellent model of a bulldozer, made by Lionel. Held to the flatcar by an elastic band.

The 6817 carried an unpainted orange plastic model of a scraper with Allis-Chalmers markings. This, too, was an excellent Lionel-made model. Both the 6816 and 6817 are much sought after by collectors because both the pieces of equipment they carried were fragile and it is hard to find them unbroken. Also, they were the kinds of loads more likely to be seen on railroad cars than many Lionel was making at the time.

6826 CHRISTMAS TREE CAR

1959 and 1960. Used the same unpainted red plastic 6511-type flatcar as the Allis-Chalmers cars, only it came with a bundle of simulated Christmas trees which were made out of some kind of fuzzy and fragile material. They were held onto the car by an elastic strap.

6469 LIQUIFIED GAS TANK

1963. This was a 6511-type flatcar which had appeared earlier as a miscellaneous car, numbered 6467 and 6477, first with no load, then with pipes. The 6469 had high black bulkheads at each end and carried a tank made out of heavy cardboard and covered with glossy white paper. It had black lettering and an Erie herald. The car is hard to find in good condition but not particularly sought after, since a lot of people don't know it was made.

RATING

All the flatcars with removable loads are hard to find complete or intact. Two of the hardest are the 6816 bulldozer and 6817 scraper. Others that present the collectors with difficulty are the 6500 airplane, the 6826 Christmas tree and the 6416 boat loader. Most of the 6511-type flatcars were used to carry military and space loads.

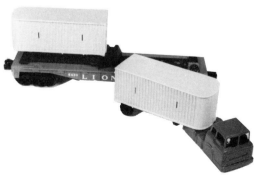

6431 with tractor.

BARREL CARS

3562-1 Black
3562-25 Gray
3562-50 Yellow

3562-25 Gray
3562-75 Orange

The operating barrel car, numbered 3562, was introduced in 1954 and was designed to go with the 362 operating barrel loader. The car was actually a high-sided gondola with panel sides. There was a conveyor running down the middle.

1954

The car had a plastic body and sheet metal frame and it always came with Santa Fe markings. It came in three color combinations painted over the clear plastic body: gray with blue lettering, gray with red lettering and black with white lettering. Each color combination had its own number suffix. The car came with six wood barrels, a plastic unloading bin, CTC track clip, platform extension clip and two rubber track spacers and a control button.

The conveyor on the 3562 was operated by vibration, similar to the operation of the cattle car. The barrels would be jiggled along to the end of the car, where a cam pushed them over the side. There was a blue rubber man attached to the cam arm and he moved along with it, making it appear he was kicking the barrels out. The system worked efficiently except for one problem. When the car was moving around the track, the rhythm of the train could cause the ramp to start vibrating and the barrels would start dropping. This problem was eliminated the next year.

1955

The black car with white lettering was discontinued and so was the gray version with red lettering. The gray with blue lettering continued and was joined by a yellow car with black lettering. This car had a clip that held the cam in a closed position, preventing the barrels from falling out when the car was moving.

Most of the yellow cars were unpainted yellow plastic, but some early ones were painted yellow, and this yellow was darker than the unpainted.

1956

The gray barrel car was dropped and only the unpainted yellow 3562 was available.

1957

The yellow continued and was joined by an unpainted orange plastic car with black lettering. Still numbered 3562.

1958

The yellow was discontinued and only the orange was available. This was the last year.

RATING

The barrel car was a popular item. The most common versions are the gray version with blue lettering and the yellow. The most difficult to find is the gray car with red lettering. This is an extremely rare car. The black car is also had to find.

DEPRESSED CENTER CARS

2461 Transformer car
6561 Wire cable car

6461 Transformer car
6561 Wire cable car
6418 Bridge girder car

Depressed center cars were used by the railroads, generally, to carry loads that were unusually high or heavy. The height part applied, generally, to Lionel models, too, although weight was not really a factor.

2461 and 6461 TRANSFORMER CARS

1947 through 1949. Introduced as 2461 with die-cast body painted light gray. This was Lionel's first depressed center car. It had coil couplers and black "Lionel Lines" on the side, although some were made with no lettering on the side. Those, however had the number rubber-stamped on the bottom. The transformer was made of clear plastic painted red. It had four plastic electrodes on top which are usually missing today. There was a decal on top of the transformer that said "Transformer Car" in white. Sometimes the decal was placed on both sides, sometimes on only one side. In 1948 the transformer was changed to black. In 1949 the number was changed to 6461, the transformer remained black, but the couplers were changed to the mechanical type.

6561 CABLE CAR

1953 through 1956. Same as the 6461, with slots added that an elastic band could fasten to in order to hold down the cables. The car was still gray with black lettering. The cables were dark gray plastic and had one turn of aluminum wire to simulate a loaded cable. In 1954 the color of the reels was unpainted orange plastic.

6418 MACHINERY CAR

1955 through 1957. Model of a 150-ton-capacity depressed center car made by the Pennsy. Die-cast frame painted light gray, with four sets of standard metal trucks. Each pair swiveled independently of the others. Came with two orange plastic girders and two elastic guy lines. In 1955 the girders said "Lionel" in raised letters, which were the same color as the girder. In 1956 and 1957 the girders were a lighter orange, almost pink, and the lettering said "U.S. Steel" in black. Some girders in 1957 were black and were used on the 214 girder bridge. The car girders had 6418 in raised, white numerals. The bridge girders did not.

6518 TRANSFORMER CAR

1957 and 1958. A picture is not shown of this car, but it was the same as the 6418 with a different load. It carried a black transformer like those on the 2461 and 6461. The number 6518 appeared on the transformer. The load looked too small on the huge depressed center car.

RATING

The hardest depressed center car to find is the 1947 model of the 2461 with no lettering on the side. Next would be the 6418 machinery car with the orange girders and black lettering. All the transformers themselves are hard to find with the electrodes intact.

SPECIAL LOAD CARS

6445 Gold reserve car
6362 Rail truck car
6475 Pickle car

6519 Allis Chalmers
6475 Libby pineapple car

As Lionel made an ever-increasing variety of rolling stock, some of the cars defied precise classification. The cars on this page might have been put in two or three different categories, but they seem to fit most appropriately into a category of their own. Perhaps that's the authors' way of saying they didn't know where else to put them.

6445 FORT KNOX CAR

1961 through 1963. No variations. This car had almost the same body as the aquarium car, except it had a simulated safe door with a combination lock on it. It had a slot for coins on the top and the coins could be retrieved by unscrewing the body. There were plastic gold bars inside. The body was painted aluminum with black lettering. In 1962 the catalog also showed the car in red and yellow lettering but it is not known to exist that way.

6362 RAILWAY TRUCK CAR

1955 through 1957. Had rails molded onto the flat bed for the cargo of three trucks. It came in bright unpainted orange plastic with black lettering. "Lionel Lines" was serifed in 1955, unserifed in 1956 and serifed again in 1957. The serifed version is more common. In 1955 it was shown in reddish brown with white lettering but it is not known to exist that way. Had the same body as the 3361 log car.

6519 ALLIS-CHALMERS

1958 through 1960. A reproduction of a real car Allis-Chalmers had built to haul heat exchangers to nuclear plants. Orange plastic body

with dark blue lettering. Came in two shades of dull orange. A darker shade is not as common as a medium shade. Plastic trucks and metal hand brakewheels and two wire tie-down lines. Usually found with the hand brakewheels broken. The heat exchanger was unpainted gray plastic. Later a missile firing car and a mercury capsule car used the same chassis.

6475 PICKLE CAR

1960 through 1962. Came in unpainted tan body and sides and painted brown roof and green lettering. Plastic trucks. On the yellow plastic pickle barrels there were simulated slats and bands painted in brown. The word "Pickles," was printed in red, but only on one side. A small number were made without the bands and slats, but with the word "Pickles." There was also a small number made, perhaps for the Heinz Company, that had the word "Heinz" written in red rather than "Pickles."

6475 LIBBY PINEAPPLE

1960 or 1961. Came in an uncataloged set and it is hard to determine exact year. Same as the pickle car except it was unpainted blue plastic with white lettering. There were two shades of blue. The vats were unpainted gray plastic covered by a silver label that had "Libby" in red and "Crushed Pineapple" in blue.

RATING

The most difficult cars to find in the special load group are the Heinz pickle car and the Libby pineapple car.

ACTION CARS

3424 Wabash
3444 Cop and Hobo
3435 Aquarium

3434 Chicken sweeper
3370 Sheriff and Outlaw
3376 Giraffe

Joshua Lionel Cowen once said that kids wanted action connected with their model railroads, or else, he said, they would get bored and "set fire to the curtains." These cars gave them action and, it is assumed, preserved draperies throughout the world.

3424 OPERATING BRAKEMAN

1956 and 1957. Unpainted blue plastic body with white lettering and white unpainted plastic door. Heavy-style casting, late door, metal trucks. Brakeman made of blue rubber in 1956 and white rubber in 1957. The blue plastic car was lighter in 1957 than it was in 1956. It was cataloged with an orange door but never made that way. It came with two tell-tail poles, which on real railroads warned a man on a roof of a car that an obstruction, such as a tunnel, was approaching. The tell-tales were simply a series of ropes strung from a pole above the track. On the Lionel version the poles were clipped to a spot on the track and when the pickup shoe passed over the spot the brakeman was electrically flattened. He popped up again when the car passed the second tell-tale.

3444 COP AND HOBO

1957 through 1959. No variations. Unpainted red plastic gondola car with Erie markings in white. Tan plastic simulated crates on the inside. Metal trucks. Two men were made of soft rubber and when they were activated looked as if they were a cop chasing a hobo. They were

attached to a belt that was actually a piece of 16mm film. That was cheap material for Lionel to employ and it was effective. There was a vibrating motor to propel the belt, the motor later used in the 345 culvert unloader and the 464 lumber mill. There was an on-off switch in the middle of the crates.

3435 AQUARIUM

1959 through 1962. Illuminated. Had four windows, two on each side, with clear, undulated plastic to give the distorted look of water. Used the same motor and film belt as the 3444, but the film was 35mm and had fish painted on it. Switch was on bottom of the car. When activated, the fish swam by the windows.

The car had a new body casting made of clear plastic painted green. The most common version had yellow lettering with a simple Lionel "L" between the two windows. An uncommon version with yellow lettering had the "L" and also had "Tank 1" written under one window and "Tank 2" written under the other. Some cars came with gold leaf lettering instead of yellow and the gold leaf came three ways, all uncommon: (1) with a gold circle around the "L" and "Tank 1" and "Tank 2" written under the windows; (2) with the writing under the windows but no circle around "L"; (3) with the gold circle but without the writing under the windows.

3434 CHICKEN SWEEPER

1959, 1960, 1964 through 1966. Same car as the 6434 non-operating poultry car introduced the year before and which was similar to the double-decker stock cars, except there was a panel on the side with pictures of chickens and it had a single, not double, door. The operating version was tan with a gray door. The mechanism was a modified version of the animated boxcar's. The man was suspended on a hair spring. He swung back and forth with a broom. He had to be pushed back in manually. Plastic trucks appeared in 1964.

3376 GIRAFFE

1960 through 1964. Used almost the same plastic body as the 6656 stock car. Blue plastic with white lettering. The giraffe was yellow plastic. It was mechanically operated and worked in conjunction with the tell-tale. A plastic arm protruded from the side of the car above the truck. When this hit an arm on the tell-tale base, the giraffe would drop into the car through his hatch on the roof. When the arm passed the tell-tale, the giraffe would pop back up. For a time in 1962 the giraffe car was made in green. There was also an uncataloged 3386 giraffe car made after 1966 which had non-operating couplers and arch-bar trucks.

3370 SHERIFF AND OUTLAW

1961 through 1964. No variations. Used a similar car body as the giraffe car. Green plastic with yellow lettering. Two portions of the roof were cut out, one for a sheriff and one for an outlaw. When one figure was up the other was down and visa versa, simulating a gun fight. Mechanically operated off a cam on the wheels of the car. Continuous action, simulating a gunfight, as the car went around the track. Made originally for the General Set.

RATING

All the action cars are popular with collectors. The aquarium car is the most sought-after.

Another view of the Lionel showroom layout. Photo courtesy of Carstens Publications.

CABOOSES

SOUTHERN PACIFIC-TYPE CABOOSES

6457 Lionel
6017 Boston & Maine
6017 Boston & Maine

6657 Rio Grande
6059 Minneapolis & St. Louis
6058 Chesapeake & Ohio

6557 Lionel
6017 Santa Fe
6017 Santa Fe

Lionel, from 1947 through 1969, made a model of the caboose used by the Southern Pacific Railroad, although Lionel made it in many more road names than just the SP. They made it, as a matter of fact, in more road names than any other caboose they ever manufactured.

During the course of its 23-year history, the SP-style caboose underwent a number of changes, and therefore its evolution, collectors have found to their frequent perplexity, was often murky and difficult to follow. The caboose was used in every form from a highly detailed top-of-the-line item to an unadorned Scout-type car. The SP caboose will first be traced in this section on a year-by-year basis from 1947 through 1954. Starting in 1955 Lionel made so many versions of the caboose that an accurate report of all of them would take up more space than is available in this book.

1947

The first Southern Pacific-type cabooses, the 2257 and 2357, appeared in 1947, although they were not illustrated in the catalog until 1948.

The plastic 2257 was painted either bright red or brown, with SP markings in white. It was not illuminated and brake wheels comprised the only trim. It had a coil-type coupler at only one end.

The 2357 was the top-of-the-line SP caboose, with illumination, clear plastic window inserts, stamped sheet metal ladders, tool boxes, coil-type couplers at both ends and a plastic smokestack painted brown. The plastic body was brown with white SP markings.

1948

The 2357 continued without change. The 2257 had its number changed to 6257 as mechanical couplers replaced the coil. The old 2257 was still used in the catalog, however. There was a 6257X caboose which came in a switcher set and had couplers at both ends. It came in either bright red or dull red and with SP markings.

A 6357 caboose was introduced and it was priced between the top-of-the-line 2357 and a low-priced 6257. It was included in 027 sets and had one mechanical coupler, illumination, window inserts and a brake wheel at both ends. It was dull red with SP markings.

1949

The 6257 and 6357 continued without significant change. The 2357 changed its number to 6457 because it received mechanical couplers. The SP marking was replaced by a Lionel "L" inside a circle. Same color.

1950

The 6257 and 6357 continued without change. The paint on the 6457 was now semi-gloss and the chimney was blackened and die-cast.

1951

No change in any of the three cabooses.

1952

The 6257 was unchanged, the 6457's color was changed to reddish brown, and the 6357 was painted maroon and had the Lionel logo. It also had a die-cast chimney.

1953

The 6457 was dropped and the 6357 became the top SP caboose. It was unchanged from the year before, as was the 6257.

1954

Some of the 6257s have the Lionel logo, others still have the SP.

1955 through 1969

The 6257 was available almost every year with either SP or Lionel markings. The number 6257 was always on the side. In most cases the body was unpainted red plastic. In 1963 a 6257 was made with a die-cast chimney.

The 6357 was made through 1961 and then dropped. It was made in bright red with Santa Fe markings in 1960, similar to the one shown on the middle shelf of page 115.

6657 DENVER & RIO GRANDE

Lionel introduced their first SP-style caboose in a road name other than SP or Lionel in 1957. It was the 6657 Denver & Rio Grande and had the same features as the 6357 made the same year. It ran again in 1958 and then was dropped.

6557 SMOKING CABOOSE

The 6557 smoking caboose was made in 1958 and 1959. It was a standard 6357 with a liquid-type smoke generator. The generator must be used with a number 55 lamp; other lamps cause serious damage to the unit. An interesting thing about the smoke cabooses was the placement of the brake wheels, which was on the right as you look at the rear of the caboose. On all other SP-style cabooses it was on the left.

6007-6017-TYPE

Lionel made another SP-style caboose not yet mentioned. The main difference between it and the 6257 was that it did not have brake wheels. Its only interest to collectors is that it was made in a number of different road names. It was the cheapest caboose Lionel made, other than Scout cabooses. It was usually unpainted plastic and had no trim at all. The first caboose of the kind was made in 1950 and was numbered 6007. In 1951 the number was changed to 6017. Most of the cheaper road name cabooses ran for only one year and are relatively hard to find.

Since the frames of all SP cabooses were interchangeable with the body castings, collectors could improvise rather freely. The middle row of the photo on page 115 shows the results of some of these improvisations. Detail has been added to the cabs and they have been placed on a 6457 chassis. Many collectors make these changes in order to dress up the attractive but unadorned Lionel road name cabooses.

On the bottom row of page 115 are examples of the way the cabooses were made by Lionel. The caboose on the far left is a rare 6017 Boston & Maine with the dark, Alaskan-blue body, as opposed to the usual Boston & Maine blue shown above it. The dark blue version was made in 1959 only.

Not shown in the picture on page 115 are a 6167-85 Union Pacific, a painted gray 6017 with black lettering, a 6057-50 orange Lionel Lines, a 6017-50 USMC and a 6017-200 U.S. Navy. These, together with the ones shown, comprise all the cheap road name cabooses without brake wheels that Lionel made.

BODY CASTINGS

There is a final point of interest about the SP-style cabooses. Through the years, they were made with three basic different body castings. The first was used between 1947 and 1955 and can be identified by a bead of plastic which reinforces the roof beneath the smokestack.

The second appeared first in 1955 and has different detailing on the cupola and no ladder slots. The smoking caboose used this style, which was in general used until 1959, although sometimes appearing a bit later. It was also used on the Scout cabooses in 1948.

The third style had thicker, stronger steps, ladder slots and curved grabirons on the cupola. This style was used between 1959 and 1969.

RATING

The most sought after SP-style cabooses are the 6657 Denver & Rio Grande and the 6557 smoking caboose. The red 6357 Santa Fe is probably the hardest to find, but few collectors are aware of it.

PENNSYLVANIA-TYPE CABOOSES

6417 Pennsylvania
6417-51 Lehigh Valley
6427 Virginian

6427 Lionel Lines
6417-51 Lehigh Valley
2457 Pennsylvania

SHEET METAL TYPE

Lionel had come out with a good model of the Pennsylvania Railroad's N5 caboose in 1941 as part of the prewar scale-detailed series. The caboose was brown, with red window trim, and was numbered 2757. In 1945 Lionel included the caboose, now numbered 2457, in the only set they offered.

The caboose had postwar trucks and couplers but everything else about it except the color was the same as the prewar caboose, including the side stampings, which said the caboose was made 4/41. The car was made entirely of sheet metal and was painted bright red with black trim and white lettering. There was a hand brakewheel at each end, frosted window panes and a die-cast stack mounted on the roof. It was illuminated and had underframe detailing which included a brake cylinder and tool box.

Some of the cabooses have "Eastern Division" written on the side. These were made in late 1945 or early 1946 and usually have footsteps that extended beneath the end platform. Cabooses without the "Eastern Division," as they all were in 1947, usually do not have the footsteps. Discontinued after 1947.

There was an 027 version of the 2457. It was numbered 2472 and came out in 1946. It was the same color as the 2457 but had no window inserts, end windows in the cupola, brakewheels, smokestack or lights. It came with "Eastern Division" on it. It ran unchanged in 1947 and was dropped.

PORTHOLE TYPE

These round-windowed cabooses were built by the Pennsylvania Railroad and they were the only railroad to ever use them, although Lionel used several different road names on their models. Lionel's model was an excellent one.

1953

Introduced as number 6417 in Tuscan red with Pennsylvania markings in white. Came with metal trucks and operating couplers at both ends. The body was plastic with the ends — the deck, handrails, steps and railings — a separate casting in black plastics. The illuminating light was mounted on a spring clip that attached to the bottom of the frame and could be removed without taking the caboose apart.

1954

The 6417 continued unchanged. The 6417-53 and the 6417-51 were introduced. The 6417-53 was the same caboose, only with Lionel Lines markings. The 6417-51 had Lehigh Valley markings and was painted light gray with maroon lettering. Only year it was cataloged, but collectors think it was made in 1955 also. An extremely low number were made in Tuscan red, probably a test run checking the Lehigh stamping.

1955

The 6417-51 Lehigh dropped, 6417 Pennsy continued, Lionel Lines changed its number from 6417-53 to 6427, as it now only came with one coupler.

1956-57

The Pennsy and Lionel lines continued in Tuscan in 1956. The Pennsy also only had one coupler but its number didn't change. In 1957 they continued without change, but the 6427-500 sky blue caboose was brought out for the Girls Train. It had Pennsylvania markings. A very small number of these were made in light yellow — no more than the few Lehigh Valleys made in Tuscan.

1958

The 6417 Pennsylvania was dropped, the 6427 Lionel Lines and the 6427-500 Girls train continued without change. The 6427-60 Virginian was introduced in dark blue with heat-stamped yellow lettering, one coupler, and metal trucks. Came in one set headed by the Virginian rectifier and also offered separately. Ran this year only.

1959 through 1961

In 1959 all the porthole cabooses were dropped except the 6427 Lionel Lines, which acquired plastic trucks and a little more brownish shade of Tuscan. The 1960 catalog showed a caboose with Santa Fe markings but it is not known to exist.

1962 through 1968

In 1962 the number changed to 6437 and the markings were switched to Pennsylvania. No changes the rest of the run. A very rare caboose was made in 1963. It was numbered 6447. It was the same as the 6437 but it had no light. It came in an O gauge set headed by a 637. Collectors overlook this rare item because it looks exactly like the common 6437, except for the number.

RATING

The three most sought after Pennsylvania cabooses are the Tuscan Lehigh Valley, followed by the Virginian and the gray Lehigh Valley.

Showroom layout control panel.   Photo courtesy of Carstens Publications.

BAY WINDOW AND WORK CABOOSES

6517 Lionel Lines
6419 Norfolk & Western
6219 Chesapeake & Ohio

6517-75 Erie
6119 Delaware, Lackawanna & Western
6130 Santa Fe

BAY WINDOW

The bay window caboose was introduced in 1955 in red with white lettering and Lionel markings. The light bracket was the same as the one used on the N5-C Pennsylvania caboose and the trucks and couplers were the same as those used on the 027 passenger cars after 1953. This was the only time Lionel ever used passenger trucks on a freight car. The caboose came two ways: some had two lines under "Built by Lionel" and others did not have the lines. The version without the lines is harder to find. The Lionel Lines caboose ran through 1959.

In 1966 the bay window caboose was reintroduced, this time with the Erie name and the number 6517-75. This was appropriate because the Erie was the first railroad in the country to have the bay window caboose and for a while was the only one. The Erie, made in 1966 only, is, along with the Tuscan Lehigh Valley, the most prized of all postwar cabooses.

WORK

Lionel made two versions of a work caboose, one of much higher quality than the other. The better one, shown by itself in the photograph below, was introduced in 1946 and ran through 1957. The cheaper model, shown in several versions in the photograph at the top of the page, was introduced in 1955. The better caboose will be discussed first.

2419-6419 and 2420-6420

Both the 2419 and 2420 were introduced in 1946. They were the same car except the 2420 had a searchlight and the 2419 did not. The caboose was made with the same die-cast frame that was used on the 2411 "Big Inch" flatcar. It required quite some handwork to assemble. It had handrails and ladders, metal brakewheels at both ends of the cab and a die-cast metal smokestack on the roof. The cab was made of heavy plastic. There were operating couplers at both ends and two tool boxes in front of the cab.

2420 with searchlight.

Both the 2419 and 2420 came with Delaware-Lackawanna markings on the side of the cab. The side of the frame had "Lionel Lines" in black. The 2419 was painted light gray and the 2420 was painted dark gray. On each model both the metal frame and the plastic cab were painted, so the shade of gray on the frame in most cases matched the shade of gray on the cab.

The numbers of the cabooses changed to 6419 in 1948 and 6420 in 1949 because of coupler changes. In 1951 both were dropped, but the 6419 appeared again in 1952 — only now some of the cabs were unpainted gray plastic, rather than painted, and they did not quite match the gray of the frames. By 1953 all the cabs were unpainted and mismatched.

In 1957 a 6419 was made with N&W markings. It combined the die-cast frame of the better caboose with the snap-on cab of the cheaper caboose. It had a smaller smokestack and no ladder. The same caboose came with Delaware & Lackawanna markings in 1957. The N&W was dropped the next year, the D L&W the year after.

In both 1956 and 1957 there was a 6419 catalogued in orange but it is not known to exist. The D L&W with the die cast frame and snap-on

cab was reissued in 1963 with plastic trucks and a new number of 6429. It was dropped the next year.

CHEAPER MODELS

The cheaper line of cabooses introduced in 1955 had stamped sheet metal frames and only one handrail, which was a part of the frame stamping. One bin replaced the two tool boxes. The bin end had the only operating coupler and the cab was secured to the frame by tabs rather than screws. The cab and bin were made of unpainted gray plastic. None had a rear coupler. These cabooses were made in many colors and road names through the years. One of the colors was orange, but it should not be confused with the 6419 orange that was shown in the catalog in 1956 and 1957 and was never produced.

RATING

The Erie is the rarest of the bay window cabooses.

The 6429 D L&W made in 1963 only is the hardest of the better work cabooses to find. Next hardest is the 6419 N&W, followed by the 2419 made in 1946 and 1947. The three cheaper cabooses shown in the photograph are the hardest to find of their type.

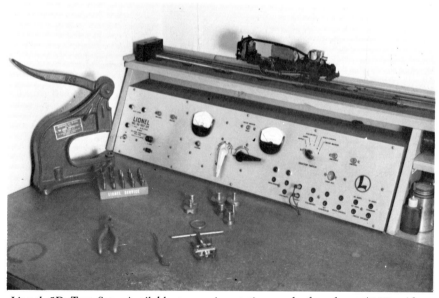

Lionel 5D Test Set. Available to service stations only for about $100. Also shown: ST(Service Tool) 350 riveting tool, quartering dies, track pliers and ST 301 wheel puller.

ACCESSORIES

Like the operating cars, accessories, in Joshua Cowen words, "gave the little nippers" plenty of action. This was good not only for the little nippers, but for Lionel, because accessories became an ever-increasing source of revenue for the company in the postwar years. Cowen himself seemed fascinated with them.

"J. L. Cowen is undoubtedly one of the biggest fans of his own products," a magazine once said of him. "He is likely to stand in his showroom and, with absolute absorption, stare at an accessory for minutes at a time, occasionally giving off a whistle of surprise."

All the accessories shown on the opposite page will be examined in this section, as well as all the other major accessories.

OPERATING

97 COAL ELEVATOR
1946 through 1950. Identical to the coal elevator made before the war. Silver superstructure, yellow housing, red roof, black Bakelite base. Had an electric drive motor and a series of worm gears that drove the conveyor bucket chain. It carried the coal from the unloading bin to the hopper housing, where it was held. Stayed there until a button was pushed and a hatch opened on the other side and the coal poured out. It was noisy and inefficient, spilling almost as much coal as it moved, but it was impressive looking and popular. Two separate tracks were needed to make it operate.

164 LOG LOADER
1946 through 1950. This used the same type of motor as the 97 coal elevator. Had a Bakelite base painted light green, a red Bakelite roof and a yellow and silver superstructure. A log car dumped the logs into one side of the log loader. The logs were picked up by a chain lift which had tabs that slid under the logs. A log was picked up and flipped over the top onto an inclined plane, where they were stored awaiting the arrival of a log car. When a button was pushed, a gate lowered and the logs rolled onto the log car. Two lights under the roof illuminated the accessory. It was large and noisy and required two tracks to operate, but it was handsome, interesting to watch, and popular.

182 MAGNETIC CRANE
1946 through 1949. Black base, aluminum superstructure, black cab with white markings. Used the same sized motor as the 38 water tower and the OO gauge Hudson. It was the same

cab as the 2460 crane car except that the 182 had a gray smokestack on the roof. The base of cab was die-cast and had a catwalk with wire handrails. The boom was the same as the one on the 2460 crane car and the magnet was the same as the 165 prewar crane. In fact, in 1946 there were some leftover 165 cranes sold and

the picture in the catalog was actually that of the prewar crane with the number 182 on it. A red light went on inside the cab when the magnet was turned on. Hard to find in good condition because they were fragile and got plenty of use. Came with a bag filled with steel blanks.

Steel blanks.

282-282R PORTAL CRANE
1954 through 1957. Lionel actually made two separate versions of the portal crane. The 282 ran in 1954 and 1955 and the 282R ran in 1956 and 1957. Both had a superstructure made of unpainted gray plastic. The crane was designed to span track. At the bottom of each of the legs was a flanged wheel. Lionel apparently intended the crane to travel on some kind of track but they never produced any track for it.

The 1954 and 1955 version had a swivel base made of maroon plastic and had handrails. The cab was painted black and had white lettering. No number appeared on the cab. "Lionel Lines" was arched in two lines towards the rear. The cab had a gray plastic chimney that was glued to the roof. The body was screwed to the base and there was wire detail on the boom. The boom was the same as the one on the 182 crane. The magnet either came blackened or with a silver colored plating and was not as detailed as the 182.

Electromagnet from 182 crane.   Electromagnet from 282 crane.

The 1956 and 1957 version had a body that clipped to the base rather than screwed on. The smokestack was molded onto the body and the cab had the number 282R on it. The wire detailing on the boom was eliminated and the mechanical gearing was improved.

The control unit was the same for all four years the crane ran. It had levers instead of the buttons that the 182 crane had. But the 282-282R did not work as well as the 182. There was a slippage problem. The crane used a five-conductor compound cable that was covered by bleached, gray rubber. The bleach caused the rubber to dry out and it cracked. It is almost impossible to find a 282 crane with original wiring that does not have a cracked cover. Collectors prefer the 182 to either the 282 or 282R.

364 LOG LOADER

1948 through 1957. Made entirely of stamped sheet metal. It was painted crackle gray and was 27 inches long. In 1951 the paint was changed to hammer tone gray enamel. The logs were dumped at one end and rolled onto the conveyor belt, which carried them to the other end, where they rolled to the edge and fell onto a log car.

The conveyor belt was red cloth. It had a light with two green lenses and one red. Although not as interesting to watch as the 164 log loader, the 364 worked well and sold well. It used the same mechanism as the 397 diesel coal loader. An advantage of this accessory was that it required only one track.

397 OPERATING DIESEL-TYPE COAL LOADER

1948 through 1957. The 1948 catalog showed the diesel coal loader with a red bin, yellow diesel housing and a 70 yard light. Only a small number of them were made with the yellow diesel housing. Most of the housings were blue. An even smaller number were made with the light. The base was painted gray. The bin was painted a dull red over black plastic, although some bins were left unpainted black. In 1949 the diesel housing was painted light blue on all the models; the base was hammer tone gray; the bin was unpainted red plastic. In 1950 the brush plate and the conveyor superstructure were changed somewhat, reducing a tendency of coal to get stuck in the belt and jam it.

The bin was connected to a cam and the floor of the bin was stepped and would snap back with each quarter turn of the cam. At each snap, the coal was jiggled up a step toward the rear of the bin. When it got to the highest step at the rear it dropped into a hole, where enough was gathered to be picked up by ridges on the conveyor belt and carried up. There was a clear plastic deflector at the end of the conveyor which prevented lumps of coal from flying off the end. The deflector was easily broken and so the coal

often would go flying anyway. In spite of this, the 397 coal loader was an improvement over the 97 coal elevator and could be loaded and unloaded from the same track.

456 OPERATING COAL RAMP AND HOPPER CAR

1950 through 1955. Designed as companion pieces to the 397 operating coal loader. The hopper car would be pushed up the ramp and coupled to the end pier. Electromagnets between the rails opened the hopper hatches at the press of a button and the coal would fall into the storage bin. If an operator had the 397 coal loader, he could position the storage bin on the 456 above the 397 and dump the coal into it. The conveyor on the 397 could then go into action, dumping the coal into another car and completing the complicated operation. The coupler on the end pier operated by remote control and when a button was pushed the hopper on the 456 would roll down the ramp. There was a light atop the end pier and it went on when the hopper was released. The car was a standard hopper with operating hatches. It is known to exist only with Norfolk and Western markings.

The ramp had a stamped sheet metal base and plastic support piers, except for the end one, which was sheet metal. The entranceway, around the steps, was die-cast and the surface on which the track was afixed was aluminum. The stanchions were stamped metal and the railings were made of steel wire. The whole thing was painted a dark blue-gray. In 1952 the color changed to a light gray and the handrails were made out of fishing line. The accessory was quite large, 35 inches long, and was almost impossible to use on a small layout. But it was still a popular item, and it required skill on the part of the operator.

455 OPERATING OIL DERRICK

1950 through 1954. When introduced, had a sheet metal base painted red, a stamped, sheet metal superstructure painted olive green, and an unpainted orange plastic diesel unit which was the same as that used on the searchlight car. The drive housing for the pump was made of unpainted maroon plastic. The parts on the base of the derrick were black.

It came equipped with a hand-operated winch that nowadays is often found broken. The pump beam actually went up and down and drove the rest of the action and was activated by a solenoid controled by a bi-metal device. There was a light bulb situated beneath an oil bubble device which simulated oil being pumped out of the well and into a pipe.

The derrick came with four aluminum oil drums and a Sunoco sign that hung on the side. The 1950 catalog shows the sign saying "Sunoco

Dynafuel," but it did not say that. It said "Sunoco Oil Derrick No. 455." The accessory came with an on-off switch. In 1953 Lionel began making the derrick with a red top, above the elevated platform. The 1952 catalog showed a red top but it wasn't made until the following year. The red top versions are harder to find than the others. When they started painting the tops red they changed the green at the bottom from dull to glossy.

There was a working model made by Lionel in 1950, before the first production run. This model had a corrugated roof over the pump.

This was a well-designed accessory and one of the few oil-related ones Lionel ever made.

Derrick usually found with this sign missing.

362 BARREL LOADER
1952 through 1957. Made with an unpainted gray plastic base and unpainted brown plastic superstructure. There was a sheet metal conveyor area that was a light yellow. There was a rubber figure mounted on the platform. The figure was blue on the early models and white on the later ones. It came with six wooden barrels that were placed at the lower end of the ramp. When the accessory was activated the barrels moved up the ramp by means of vibrations, similar to the method used on the cattle loader. The barrels started their journey up the ramp in an upright position, but when they hit a depression in front of the man, they fell over, giving the impression he had knocked them on their sides. The barrels would continue up the ramp and roll off into a gondola car. The accessory was good looking and trouble free. In 1954 a special barrel car was designed that would unload the barrels onto the bottom of the ramp, making the cycle complete.

The photograph in the 1952 catalog made the barrel loader look as if it were made of sheet metal. But it is not known to exist in sheet metal.

497 COALING STATION
1953 through 1958. Combined the coal elevator and the coal ramp in one operation and required only one track. Like the coal elevator it raised the coal to an overhead position. It wasn't as interesting as the other coal accessories but it operated better than any of them. It clipped to the track in the same manner as the operating cattle loader.

The mechanism was supported by four metal columns that spanned the track. The accessory had a dark green plastic roof, red sheet metal sides and a unpainted maroon plastic hopper and bin. The color of the roof changed to a lighter green in 1954. It was almost chartreuse.

Any Lionel dump car could be used with the accessory but none was provided with it. The coal was dumped into the bin, which was hoisted by pulleys to the hopper, where the coal was dumped into another car. This accessory spilled very little coal, while other Lionel coal accessories spilled a lot.

415 DIESEL FUELING STATION
1955 through 1957. This accessory had a sheet metal base painted gray, a white plastic building and a red plastic roof. It was illuminated and there was a plastic sanding tower on the base. When the train approached the station a man came out of the house and simulated the action of attaching a metal fuel hose to the engine and giving it fuel. The man returned when the train left. A button activated the man.

Rather dull action and the item was not a big seller. The building was later used on the 114 and 118 newsstand.

352 ICE DEPOT
1955 through 1957. The superstructure was unpainted red plastic, and it also came in unpainted brown plastic. Both colors are about equal in availability. Used white plastic building with red, unpainted plastic roof. The roof was shown all three years in blue but it was always made with a red roof. The man was made of blue plastic and had orange arms and an orange paddle. The arms and paddle were one unit and that unit came off easily. Five plastic ice cubes were provided with the accessory and they were loaded into a car by the man.

There was a modified 6464 box car provided with the accessory. It was made of unpainted orange plastic and had black lettering which said "Pacific Fruit Express" on the side. The car had a roof hatch that opened to accept the cubes. The 1955 catalog showed the car in white. It is not known to exist in white.

6352 PFE boxcar.

464 OPERATING LUMBER MILL

1956 through 1960. Had a stamped sheet metal frame, white plastic building, light gray plastic roof, dark gray plastic shed area and red door.

The saw mill was a fascinating accessory to watch. Logs would disappear into the mill only to reappear from the opposite side mysteriously changed into boards.

The logs were pushed one-by-one into the mill by a series of tabs that stuck up from a conveyor belt. The boards were stacked one on top of the other inside the mill. The bottom board straddled two shelfs and rested directly over the belt. The tab that pushed a log stuck up high enough so that when it went into the mill it went right between the two shelves and made contact with the bottom board, pushing it out the other side. That meant for a while the tab was pushing two pieces of wood, the log on the bottom and the board on the top.

When the log reached the middle of the mill it rolled down an incline away from the conveyor. By this time the board was out the other side, creating the illusion that the log had been run into the mill and cut and shaped instantly into a piece of lumber. To begin the cycle again, the logs had to be taken out a rear door of the mill and the boards had to be stacked back up inside. The mill was noisy but interesting. The grating noise the accessory made sounded like a real saw mill.

342 CULVERT LOADER

1956 through 1958. No variations. It used a heavy gauge, stamped sheet metal base painted black; orange and black crane; simulated concrete foundation made of tan plastic; a red plastic building with a dark gray roof; and a gray culvert track.

The driving mechanism was the same as that used on the 464 lumber mill. A claw-like apparatus on the crane picked up the culverts from a loading area and delivered them to a gondola. A special 6342 gondola car was provided with the accessory. It had a ramp built into it so the sections of pipe would roll to the end and make room for each succeeding section. The car was unpainted red plastic with white New York Central markings. A disadvantage to the culvert loader was that the gondola had to be unloaded by hand and culvert sections placed back on the loading ramp. That's why they introduced the 345 culvert unloader the following year.

345 CULVERT UNLOADER

1957 and 1958. Designed as a companion to the culvert loader, it had the same color scheme. This accessory unloaded the culverts from the gondola and placed them on a ramp behind a tower. Instead of the crane having a clamping device, however, the unloader was equipped with a magnet which attached itself to the culverts. Both the unloader and loader could be operated separately, but there was also an extension ramp supplied that connected the two and the culverts would roll from the 345 unloader platform to the 342 loader to make a continuous operation.

The unloader came with the same 6342 gondola car with ramp as the loader. Like the loader, the unloader was rather temperamental and would malfunction easily. The unloader is a little harder to find than the loader because it was made for only two years instead of three.

In 1969 there was a 348 culvert unloader made that was the same as the 345 except that it was manually operated. It was the first made for Sears around 1962 or 1963. The manually operated one sold for $22 in 1969, while the electrically operated unloader cost $18.95 in 1958.

350 ENGINE TRANSFER TABLE

1957 through 1960. No variations. Both the base and the moving transfer table were blackened-stamped sheet metal. There was a yellow plastic shed on top of the moving table. The shed housed the motor, which was the same as that used on the 397 coal loader. It was a modified gear box motor. It drove, through a series of gears, two wheels at each end of the transfer table. The wheels were the same type that were used on the 55 tie jector.

The table worked well, moving an engine from one track to a parallel track, but it could only handle one diesel unit at a time. Therefore AA or AB combinations wouldn't fit.

334 DISPATCHING BILLBOARD

1957 through 1960. Unpainted tan base, green and white departure boards. Clock and loud speaker on top were simulated. No variations. The board gave the name of a train, the arrival and departure times, and the track number. When a button was pushed, the man mounted on the front would move across the board from left to right and then back again, and, as he did so, the train name, time and number changed. There were six different combinations.

Operated by a vibrator-type motor similar to the one used in the saw mill.

128 ANIMATED NEWSSTAND

1957 through 1960. No variations. The base was unpainted gray plastic. The newsstand was green plastic with a red plastic roof. The fireplug was red. The stand was illuminated by a lantern that stood on the right side of the stand. The men were made of gray plastic and the dog of white plastic. When the piece was activated the man inside the stand moved from the front to the rear and back again, while the man outside moved in a semi-circle away from the newsstand and then back facing it again. The dog ran around the fire plug in one direction and back in the other. It worked with a vibrating type of motor with a complicated set of gears. It was a well engineered piece, but was not particularly popular. It sold for $6.95 and is hard to find with the newspaper in the hand of man standing outside.

264 OPERATING FORK LIFT

1957 through 1960. No variations. Used a vibrator-type motor. Black sheet metal base; unpainted brown, raised deck area; and a specially designed fork lift truck. The truck was connected to the metal base through a slot. The truck, at the press of a button, would move over to a loaded timber flat car, grip and lift a board, turn around and take the board over to the platform and then return for another board. After all the boards were unloaded from the flatcar and piled onto the platform the car had to be reloaded by hand to start the process over again.

192 RAILROAD CONTROL TOWER

1959 and 1960. No variation. Used the same superstructure as the 197 radar tower and the same base, only now the superstructure was green instead of black. The base was gray plastic and the ladder orange. The building was green with clear plastic windows and a green roof. Inside were simulated control panels with dials and switches. The interior was illuminated. Two blue rubber men were mounted on swivel discs and revolved inside the house.

There was a three-balled anemometer for indicating wind velocity on top of the roof. It was made of white plastic and quite often one or more of the balls are found missing. The accessory, which was nice looking, was nevertheless fragile and is hard to find in good condition. The light bulb inside the tower was placed too close to the plastic roof and as a result frequently melted a hole in the roof. It is handsome and hard to find, two qualities which make it desired by collectors.

375 MOTORIZED TURNTABLE

1962 through 1964. Used the same yellow plastic shed that was used on the 350 transfer table. The turntable itself was made of sheet metal stamping painted black. Had a complicated system of gears, which were made of sheet metal and housed in the shed. The motor was small and battery operated, using two D-cell batteries. The accessory was inexpensively made and did not look good, but it operated well. A disadvantage was that the trains had to climb a $3/4$-inch incline to get on the table. Also, it could not handle F-3 double units.

STATIONS AND TOWERS

115 STOP STATION

1946 through 1948. Same as prewar version. Stamped sheet metal building with red enamel base and roof, cream colored building, red trim on windows and doors. Had lights and the same stopping unit as prewar version. The skylight was removable and the doors swung open. This was a good model of a small city station.

137 STOP STATION

1945 and 1946. This was a carryover item from before the war. It was embossed and made of sheet metal. It was cream colored with a red roof.

156 ILLUMINATED STATION PLATFORM

1946 through 1949. Another prewar carryover. It had a green bakelite base and red bakelite roof, which was supported by three metal uprights painted aluminum. Four sheet metal lithographed signs clipped onto the railing. Extra fence lengths were available to connect a series of stations, making them look like one long station.

157 ILLUMINATED STATION PLATFORM

1952 through 1955 and 1958 and 1959. Same as the 156 except it was made of plastic and came in different colors.

132 STOP STATION

1949 through 1955. Had unpainted maroon plastic base, simulated brick deck, simulated wood walk around the back, white plastic building, green door and window inserts and a removable green plastic roof. The station boards said "Lionelville." The station was illuminated. It had the same train stop-control device mounted inside as the 115. The color of the plastic varied slightly through the years but not significantly. This was a good model of a rural or suburban station.

There was also a 133 station introduced in 1957.

133 STATION

1957, 1961, 1962 and 1966. This was the same as the 132 stop station except this one did not have the train-stopping mechanism.

256 FREIGHT STATION

1950 through 1953. A nicely detailed station similar in construction to the 132 stop station. Many parts were interchangeable with the 132, including window inserts and doors. Came with three lithographed signs mounted on a picket fence. Many different signs.

356 OPERATING FREIGHT STATION

1952 through 1957. Same as the 256, except it had a vibrating metal deck. Two men on baggage trucks moved around on the deck, in and out of the station.

257 OPERATING FREIGHT STATION

1956 and 1957. Same as 256 but with battery activated diesel horn mounted inside the station.

445 OPERATING SWITCH TOWER

1952 through 1957. Unpainted white plastic building with clapboard siding and a green plastic roof and window trim. The base was maroon. The station was illuminated and ran without significant change every year.

There were two figures that were operated by a solenoid inside the tower. As the train approached it came in contact with a track trip and the action started. Although there were two figures, only one was visible at a time, to give the impression there was only one man involved in the action.

When the train approached, a man visible on the upstairs deck disappeared inside the building. Then the second man came out of the building and went down the stairs with a lantern. It all gave the appearance of one man seeing the train coming and running down the stairs to flag it down. The first year the accessory was shown in the catalog with brown sides and white trim but it is not known to have been made that way. It would have been more realistic looking if it had.

465 DISPATCHING STATION

1956 through 1959. The building was unpainted red plastic with clear plastic windows and a printed paper background simulating a control panel. It was illuminated from behind. It had a dark gray unpainted plastic roof with a yellow plastic microwave antenna on the top. The roof was held on by two screws disguised to look like ventilators. The base and columns were made of unpainted tan plastic.

There was a speaker inside and it faced downward, so that the sound came out underneath the building. The speaker unit was inside and operated with four D-cell batteries. A crude, toy microphone was provided with the accessory. The mike had a couple of buttons, one to start and stop the mike, and one to start and stop the train.

The building itself was later used on the 419 heliport, covered under the space and military section of this book.

WATER TOWERS
38 WATER TOWER

1946 and 1947. A good reproduction of a large city water tower, detailed well enough for scale layouts. The tank was amber-colored plastic, which was transparent. It had a dull red roof. At the top of the tank was a reservoir for water, which was poured through a hole in the roof. This reservoir was hidden from view by the roof itself, which slanted down over it.

This is one of the most unusual accessories Lionel ever made and the man who designed the works was Joshua Cowen. When Cowen was first shown a model of the tank it contained no water. "Where's the water?" Cowen asked. The engineers had thought that a tank containing real

Lionel water tower prototype.

water was unfeasible, since they did not want water spilling out of the spout and splashing on the tracks. Cowen then designed a tank which contained water and could be made to look as if it were emptying when it really was not. It had a recirculating water pump, not unlike some Cowen had invented at the turn of the century, before he started Lionel.

The outside wall of the tank was in reality two walls, one 3/16ths of an inch away from the other. The area between the walls was a storage area for water. It held about the same amount of water as the reservoir under the roof. After the reservoir under the roof was filled, the water drained through the pump, filling the storage area on the sides. Lionel supplied tablets to color the water, making it dark enough to be visible between the transparent walls.

38 Water Tower with tank removed to show pump.

When a button was pushed, the spout lowered and at the same time a small motor operating the pump was started. The water was then pumped from the outer chamber to the reservoir above. As the chamber emptied it gave the impression of water draining out of the tank and into a tender, but actually it was just being transferred to the reservoir. After the control button was released, the pump would stop and the spout would raise. Slowly the water from the upper reservoir would drain back down into the side chamber.

This is a rare item. Many collectors have never seen it. When it is found, it is usually rusted.

30 WATER TOWER

1947 through 1950. Same as the 38 except it did not fill with water. Had a gray base in 1947, a black superstructure, a gray tank base and a brown roof. The tank was amber colored and the spout black. Some color variations in 1947 had a red roof. In 1948 the superstructure was an unpainted brown plastic and so was the base of the tank. It no longer had a filling plug in the roof. Ran unchanged through 1950.

138 WATER TOWER

1953 through 1957. The base was plastic instead of die-cast, as the other towers had been. The tank was unpainted brown plastic in 1953 but it was no longer translucent. The roof was unpainted gray plastic and the spout was black plastic. In 1954 the tank changed color to a reddish brown and the roof to orange. No changes thereafter.

193 WATER TOWER

1953 through 1955. Model of a tank similar to the one at the Lionel factory. Plastic tank painted silver on top of a red sheet metal superstructure, silver roof, gray plastic base. A few of the superstructures were painted black, but these are rare. The superstructure was the same as the one used on the 455 oil derrick.

Collector Bill Vagell at the Lionel water tower, 1974.

BRIDGES

313 BASCULE BRIDGE

1946 through 1949. In 1946 the bascule bridge was reintroduced. It was the same as the prewar bridge. It had a silver superstructure and green base. The bridgetender's shack contained the motor and was painted yellow with a red roof. Used the same motor as the log and coal elevators.

There was a counterbalancing spring mounted in the foundation piers of the bridge. The spring could be adjusted so that it pulled against the die-cast base of the bridge, barely allowing it to sit flat. This meant that a small motor, which without the springs would be too weak to lift the heavy spans, could be used in operating the structure. On real bridges the lifting action is aided by the use of a counterweight. The Lionel bridge had what looked like a counter weight, but it was really just an empty sheet metal cube.

The tension of the spring had a tendency to warp the base opposite the shack. The bridge came with track permanently mounted. The rails were made to accept both O and 027 gauge track. The part of the span that supported the track was made of Bakelite. The rest of the superstructure was made of stamped sheet metal.

There was a light with a red lens at the top of the superstructure. When the bridge was moving up or down the light went on. When found now, the lens is usually missing.

A black framework was provided to secure the track when the bridge was used on a temporary layout. The frame is often missing when the bridge is found today because it wasn't necessary for permanent layouts and the owners would discard it.

One button controlled the entire operation. When it was pushed the bridge would raise and the train would be stopped in either direction. When the bridge reached its maximum height, the bridge would begin to go down. The whole raising and lowering operation took about 45 seconds. When the bridge arrived in the lowered position the train would start again.

In 1947 the gear box and motor mechanism were changed. All the gearing was placed in the bridge tower rather than the bridge tender's shack. The new mechanism had more reduction gears and raised the bridge slower, putting less strain on the motor. In 1948 the light lens screwed in rather than snapped in, as it had done.

213 RAILROAD LIFT BRIDGE

This was a bridge that was pictured in the 1950 catalog but the bridge was never produced. There was one working model made, but it was an extremely complicated design and to produce it would have been an engineering problem of immense proportions.

OTHERS

There are several other accessories that appear in the color photograph, including some that are rather unusual.

145 GATEMAN HOUSE

1950 through 1966. Green sheet metal base, unpainted white plastic house, dark red plastic roof and red plastic door. Man painted blue came out of his house with lantern as the train passed. The 145 gateman is probably the most popular trackside accessory Lionel ever made.

154 FLASHING SIGNAL

1945 through 1966, and 1969. Sometimes shown in the catalog with red base but almost always was made with black base. Only a few made in red. In 1950 a very few made with an orange base. Also in 1950 the crossbuck section changed from die-cast to plastic and bulbs from the screw-type to the bayonet type. "Stop" was rubber stamped until 1950, in raised letters thereafter.

252 CROSSING GATE

1950 through 1963. Black base, white gate, two red lights on gate, copper light bracket inside. In 1952 light bracket changed to tin. Worked just like a real crossing gate. Solenoid engaged cam that pulled gates down. When trains passed and solenoid released, weights at ends pulled gates back up.

151 SEMAPHORE

1947 through 1969. Made with black base, some early ones made with green base.

153 BLOCK SIGNAL

1945 through 1959. Prewar carryover, die-cast green enamel base, sheet metal pole die-cast light fixture assembly. One light bulb green and the other red. Through 1949 the bulbs were opaque. From 1950 through 1953 they were clear. From 1954 they were opaque again. The accessory made possible running two trains on the same track. Effective at crossovers and switches. One train would stop the other.

148 DWARF SIGNAL

1957 through 1960. Model of type of signal used in real freight yards. It was manually operated. Toggle switch changed the color of the light from red to green. Many people don't realize it was manually operated. Sold poorly because it was overpriced at $5.95 the first two years. It is hard to find, although there is no big demand for it.

450 SIGNAL BRIDGE

1952 through 1959. The red and green light bulbs were opaque in 1952 and 1953, and clear after that.

452 GANTRY SIGNAL

1961 through 1963. Kind of a freak. It's the same as the 450, except there's only half of it. It was top-heavy but was held upright by a clip device which attached to the track.

26-260 BUMPER

1948 through 1969, except 1968. Spring-cushioned aluminum shock absorber. The first ones were painted gray in 1948; later that year and from then on they were painted red. In 1952 the number changed to 260 and the shock absorber changed to black plastic. In 1958 the casting was changed to accommodate Super O track.

394 BEACON TOWER

1949 through 1966, except 1965. Sheet metal superstructure painted bright red in 1949. Aluminium beacon which was fragile and revolved around a stem pin. In 1950 the superstructure was still red, although some were painted green and these are now hard to find. In 1952 the superstructure changed to aluminum and was unpainted. In 1954 the superstructure changed back to sheet metal and was painted silver. The beacon changed to die-cast and was rotated by a vibration motor. In 1958 the superstructure was changed to red and things remained the same for the rest of the run.

35-56-58-64 STREET LAMPS

These are the four most desirable of the postwar street lamps. Three of them are shown in the photograph on page 122, the 56 being the exception. They were all prewar carryovers and they all ran from 1946 through 1949 except the 58, which ran in 1950 also.

RATING

With the possible exception of the 38 water tower, no accessory can be considered rare, although there are some rare variations. All the prewar carryover accessories are sought after, however. They were made of sheet metal and Bakelite and had a heavy feel to them that the later postwar accessories lacked. Of these, the 97 coal elevator, the 313 bascule bridge and the 164 log loader are the most sought after.

Of the exclusively postwar group of accessories, the 38 water tower is truly rare. The 397 diesel coal loader with the yellow bin and 70 yard light is a rare variation. The regular 397 is common. The 352 icing station, the 342 culvert loader and the 345 culvert unloader are in demand. So are the 464 lumber mill and the 497 coaling station. The 192 control tower is hard to find in good condition.

TRUCKS, COUPLERS & TRACK

1945

Lionel introduced the scale-type truck. It had a sheet metal bolster — the part of the frame that spanned the space between the wheels — and die-cast side frames, which were staked onto the sheet metal bolster. The coupler itself had an electromagnetic coil behind it that, when energized, opened the coupler jaw. The whole assembly was rigidly mounted to the bolster. A fiberboard plate holding the pickup shoe broke rather easily, so it is hard to find an unbroken one today.

The coupler assembly was complicated, with many parts, and was expensive to assemble. Lionel actually reverted to an assembly they dropped after 1939 and which was almost impossible to repair.

Most of the 1945-type trucks found today have sintered iron wheels, which was the most common way they were made. But some of the early 1945 trucks had die-cast zinc wheels and thick, turned steel axles. Some of these early zinc wheels had swirled backs.

1945 and 1946 unitized assembly.

1946 - 1949 with clip on coupler.

1946 and 1947

The coupler head and the bottom plate became one unit, the same unitized assembly they had developed in 1940, but for some unknown reason had abandoned in 1945. In 1946 the coupler head extended about 1/16th of an inch further out from the car than it had in 1945. The bolster was changed slightly in 1946. A stop tab stuck out from the rear and this prevented couplers with pickup shoes from pivoting too far.

The 1945-type truck was made in a limited quantity in 1946 until they exhausted the parts. By 1947 the supply was exhausted.

1948 and 1949

The mechanical-type coupler was introduced on most 027 gauge equipment in 1948. The coil coupler continued unchanged on O gauge equipment. The cars with mechanical couplers began with 6400 numbers and the cars with coil couplers had 2400 numbers. The mechanical coupler required a special 6019 magnetic uncoupling section of track. The mechanical coupler was cheaper to make and did not uncouple over switches, which the coil-type coupler had a tendency to do. The mechanical coupler had a large hole near the back of the base plate and a small hole in the center of the armature for the return-spring rivet.

Things were the same in 1949 but the mechanical couplers were used on all freight cars O or 027 gauge, except the O gauge crane car. The coil coupler was still used on most passenger cars.

1948 mechanical type.

1950 version with rivet mounting.

1950 and 1951

The big hole in the back of the base plate was off to one side and there was an added hole directly behind the first small hole in the armature. The new hole made it easier to assemble trucks which had roller pickup assemblies. All roller pickup trucks, incidentally, used a brass roller through 1950. After that they used a steel roller with riveted axles.

1952

The coupler assembly remained the same, but the truck construction changed. The center of the bolster area was embossed, where it had been flat. The side frames were held to the bolster more securely. The top of the frame was depressed into the bolster and the depression is visible on the side of the frame. It is a good way to tell a truck made in 1952 or after. The trucks and couplers remained the same in 1953 and 1954.

Side frame and bolster, 1946-1951.

Side frame and bolster, 1952 and after.

1955

A small tab was added to the armature plate, making it easier to open the coupler by hand.

1955 and after type with manual uncoupling tab.

1957 plastic truck with flared axle.

The coupler pin was a little looser and more cheaply made and would disengage sometimes when it wasn't supposed to. This was the year Lionel also began using a more inexpensive method of holding the truck to the car. A turned brass rivet had been used previously, secured by a horseshoe clip. Now they started using a sheet metal spring clip, which was not as durable. There was no change in the trucks or

1955 truck with spring clip.

couplers in 1956. The cheaper trucks were used throughout the line in 1956. They had been used on only the less expensive cars in 1955.

1957

The plastic truck was introduced on some models, primarily on the 027 cars and less expensive trains. The metal trucks were still used on the boxcars and the larger freight cars.

The plastic truck was a different design, modeled after Timken roller trucks. The side frame, bolster and couplers were all one piece. It no longer had the bottom plate. The coupler had a sintered iron disk that operated the jaw. All in all, the plastic trucks were simplified and worked very well. On most of the plastic trucks the bolster was held to the frame by means of a rivet.

Plastic truck introduced in 1957.

The wheels on plastic trucks were slightly different. The flanges were higher and the wheel, from the flange out, was wider. This change compensated for the loss of weight suffered by adding the plastic trucks.

Some of the metal trucks made in 1957 had that small tab eliminated.

1958

The metal trucks were just about phased out. They were still used on certain freight cars with lights or on the whistle tenders. The 1957-type plastic truck continued without change

A new plastic truck was added to the line. It was a model of an arch-bar truck and was used on the General Set. Later this truck was used incorrectly on more modern equipment.

Arch-bar type truck.

1959 through 1962

The plastic trucks were used on just about everything. The metal trucks were used only on the operating horse and circus cars, and the operating Bosco and milk cars. These cars required pickup shoes, for which the plastic trucks had no provisions.

1963 through 1965

The axles mountings were changed slightly on the trucks and the knuckle was now plastic, where it used to be metal. The plastic knuckle no longer required a metal rivet and spring. There was now a one-piece plastic unit incorporating the spring, knuckle and hinge. But the plastic hinge was not strong enough and broke upon impact with other cars.

Starting in 1963 many of the better freight cars came with only one operating coupler. Before, all the more expensive cars came with two operating couplers.

1966 through 1969

The plastic knuckle and plastic spring were still used, but Lionel went back to using a metal hinge pin.

SIX-WHEEL
PASSENGER CAR TRUCK
1946

Truck used on Irvington cars and tenders.

Introduced in 1946 on the Irvington car. The trucks were models of the Pennsylvania-style passenger trucks used on the heavyweight older style passenger cars. Lionel also used the trucks on the Bucyrus Erie crane car and two tenders.

Truck used on crane car.

The bolster on the trucks was stamped sheet metal. The side frames were made of acetate plastic and were tabbed onto the sheet metal behind them. The trucks had roller and pickup shoes mounted to the front and center axles. The coupler itself was articulated, swiveling independently of the trucks.

The truck used on the crane car differed somewhat. The coupler arm was not articulated and the bolster had a brass mounting boss on top of it. This boss was threaded and screwed onto the car frame. The six-wheel trucks always came with coil-type couplers and had pickup shoes.

1947 through 1951

There was no change in 1947. In 1948 the six-wheel trucks were used on the Pennsylvania-style tender, which came with the 671 turbine. The coupler arm was articulated and slightly shorter than the one on the passenger cars.

The truck ran through 1951. It is often found with the plastic side frames broken.

SCOUT-TYPE

Scout truck.

1948 through 1952. This truck had a sheet metal stamping similar to the six-wheel trucks with plastic side frame. It had a black plastic coupler mounted to the bolster. The coupler was not compatible with a standard Lionel coupler, but there was a conversion coupler available.

After 1949 Lionel put the standard coupler on the Scout trucks at the factory and used this converted truck on some cheaper train sets. The Scout-type coupler was still used on Scout sets.

SMALL PASSENGER CAR TRUCKS

Coil type.

1948 through 1953

These trucks were the same general size and construction as the freight trucks, but they were very well detailed on the side frames. The bolster was the same as the one on freight trucks. The major difference was that the coupler arm extended further on the passenger model and was articulated. These passenger car trucks were first used on the 2400-series streamline passenger cars. They were first made with coil-type couplers and pickup shoes. The roller pickup changed from brass to steel in 1951.

Mechanical type.

1954

The side frames were the same but they were mounted differently and the construction of the bolster changed. The couplers were mounted directly to the bolster, rather than to the base plate. It was more rigid, although still articulated, swiveling from a different point. This was really a modified version of the mechanical coupler made for O gauge passenger cars in 1952.

There was no change in this coupler after 1954. There was one freight car that used this truck. It was the bay window caboose introduced in 1955. Caboose trucks were different from other freight trucks because people rode in cabooses and a softer ride was required.

O GAUGE PASSENGER TRUCKS
1952 through 1966

Introduced on the aluminum passenger car, which were the only cars to ever use these trucks. The truck had a heavy sheet metal bolster and the side frames were die-cast. These trucks, even though they had only four wheels, were larger than the six-wheel trucks used on the Irvington cars. They were an excellent reproduction of the type truck, used on real aluminum cars. The lighter weight aluminum cars required only four-wheel trucks.

Lionel's model had an extremely long, articulated coupler arm. The trucks had a unique, wireless pickup roller. The top of the roller spring

Truck for large streamline passenger cars.

rubbed against a metal plate, passing the current from the roller to the inside of the car without the use of a wire. Trucks used on the baggage car had no roller pickup.

In 1952, the first cars produced had a wire without the sliding pick-up.

TRACK

Lionel's three-rail track was efficient, relatively trouble-free and versatile. Layouts could be designed that included reverse loops and crossovers with no need of special wiring. But it was admittedly unrealistic. The company's main competitor, American Flyer, changed to two-rail track after the war. This change was in itself an inducement to some toy train operators to buy American Flyer. The Flyer track was more realistic looking than Lionel's but it was still far from perfect. The ties were too big and too widely spaced.

Lionel, in 1957, decided to add to the line a new track, one that would be more realistic looking than Flyer's. It was called Super O and had narrow plastic ties placed close together. There was still a middle rail but it was reduced to a thin piece of copper that blended in with the brown ties. The two outside rails were flatter on top, like the prewar T-rail track. The curve on Super O was more gradual than regular O gauge. It took three sections to make a 90 degree turn, as opposed to the normal two sections. The diameter of a circle of Super O track was 38-inches; regular O was 31-inches.

O gauge, 027, T rail and 072 track are covered in detail in Volume I of this series.

SWITCHES

The best switches Lionel made were in O gauge, and they came in both remote control and manual versions. They had a heavy Bakelite base and a motor mechanism which could be placed on either side of the track, making it more versatile in tight quarters. There were indicating lights on both the switch itself and on the controller and they showed whether the switch was straight or curved.

The switches had a fixed voltage feature which enabled the switch to receive power independently of the track. That meant if a train was running at a slow speed, and consequently little power was being fed to the third rail, there was a separate power source feeding the switch motor to keep its action strong. The switches also had a non-derailing feature.

The O gauge remote control switches ran from 1946 through 1969. The only change in the switch came in 1950, when the lamp socket was changed from a screw-in type to a bayonet type. They were numbered 022.

The O gauge manual switches were made like the automatic and ran from 1946 through 1959. They were numbered 042.

027 switches had a painted black sheet metal base. From 1946 through 1951 the motor housing was made of plastic. After 1951 a newly designed base made of plastic was used. The O gauge non-derailing feature was added to the 027 switches in 1952, but switches made from then on did not seem to work well with steam locomotives made in the early postwar years. 027 switches were made through 1969, in both remote control and manual versions. They were numbered 1122.

Sometime in the late 1940s, Lionel made a switch that was a cross between an O gauge switch and an 027. The number was 022A. It had an 027 controller, no sliding contacts and no fixed voltage plug. Everything else was just like the 022 switch. Very few of these 022A switches were made. They are hard to find.

Both manual and remote control switches were available in Super O. They had the fixed voltage and non-derailing features of O gauge but resembled the 027 switches in weight and quality. They were available from 1957 through 1966.

(continued from page 5)

attention to the product itself. This led to great raging arguments at times between Joshua Cowen on one hand and Larry and Raphael on the other. The younger Cowen and Raphael would insist that certain economizing steps be taken on the product; Cowen was reluctant to see such things as wire handrails removed.

Lifespan tests of some of Lionel's locomotives indicated that, with proper maintenance and normal use, they could last indefinitely. This delighted Joshua, but not Lawrence.

"I have a tendency to worry about turnover," said Lawrence, a balding, serious-looking man of 38 when he assumed the presidency of Lionel in 1945. His background had been in finance before joining his father in the business in 1938.

After a decision was made on which road name was to be used on a new item, a prototype model was made and then displayed at the annual Toy Fair. The amount of interest shown at the Toy Fair was the final factor in determining whether the model would actually be produced, or what its final form would be. Occasionally a prototype model would be made and then never produced because of lack of orders at the Toy Fair. These prototypes have become the envy of all collectors.

Lionel celebrated its 50th anniversary in 1950 and Joshua Cowen brought back the Hudson. It could not be the scale work of excellence that the 700E had been, but the 773 was a good model nonetheless. Cowen estimated that Lionel would have had to sell the old 700E for $150 in 1950 to show a profit. 1950 was also the year the company introduced Magne-Traction, another development that set off the ebullient Cowen.

"It's positively wonderful," he said to some visitors in the showroom one day. "A train can take a curve at the equivalent of 180 miles an hour without jumping track. Amazing!"

The Union Pacific Alcos were introduced in 1950, too. There is a story Joshua Cowen liked to tell about the first U.P. diesel the company built. It was Cowen's habit to get the first sample of every new item. He just liked to look them over. But sometimes there would be something wrong with that early model, Cowen would discover it, and subordinates would get rather nervous.

"The first Union Pacific diesel we built, I picked it up and the cab came off. It seems if there's a defective piece, I will get it. Not long ago I turned a knob on a new transformer and it didn't work. It's the darndest thing I ever saw. I can stick my hand in a box containing 10,000 wheels and if there is a bad one I will get it."

Some of Lionel's innovations took longer to develop than many people thought. Whistles and horns seemed to have presented the biggest problems. Charles Giamo developed the first whistle in 1934, following experiments with cuckoo whistles, Japanese flutes and various air chambers, but it took years to achieve the proper tone. Magne-Traction took four years to develop and it took at least that long to develop a nontoxic smoke pellet.

The anniversary year was a good one for Lionel. They had net sales of $21.5 million and a net profit of $2.2 million. The diesels were selling well. Even comedian Jack Benny had one, but he came by his in an unusual fashion. A Benny radio script of December 17, 1950, had the following dialog in it, starting with announcer Don Wilson:

DON: *And now, ladies and gentlemen, let's go out to Jack Benny's home in Beverly Hills. At the moment, Jack is out doing his Christmas shopping and Rochester is just leaving to do his.*

(SOUND: WINDOW CLOSING)

ROCH: *Oh, oh. What's this on the desk? Hm... a letter in Mr. Benny's handwriting. "Dear Santa . . . Christmas is almost here and it would make me very happy if you gave me a train." . . . Hee, hee, hee. When Mr. Benny wants a train, he wants a TRAIN. This letter isn't addressed to Santa CLAUS. It's addressed to Santa FE . . . Well, they may send him one; he's mentioned them enough.*

Well, the Santa Fe did not send Jack Benny a real train, but an alert member of their public relations department did send him Lionel's model of the F-3, which Benny proudly displayed thereafter.

In 1952 Joshua Cowen's good friend, Arthur Raphael, retired. Sometimes, when Raphael's wife and daughter were out of town, Joshua Cowen, whose own wife had died in 1946, would stay with his friend. But Cowen's visits could be disconcerting. While Raphael was out, Cowen, the incurable tinkerer, would reroute the wiring in the apartment. During one stay, Cowen had the bathroom light hooked up with the phonograph, the doorbell operating the toaster and had installed a jump-out boxing glove to surprise Raphael's wife on her return.

Around that time Cowen and Raphael were attending a company function when an elderly salesman from San Francisco approached Cowen and told him he had one of those original crude, wooden gondolas Cowen had hand-built in 1900. He showed it to Cowen.

"I'll give you a thousand dollars for it," said Cowen.

"I wouldn't sell it, Mr. Cowen," said the salesman. "But I'm leaving it to you in my will."

Cowen thanked the man and after he walked away, turned to Raphael.

"I'll outlive that fellow if it's the last thing I do," he said.

He very well might have. Up until his retirement in 1958, when he was made chairman emeritus of the board of directors, Joshua Cowen remained amazingly active and youthful in attitude. He would be riding in a car, for instance, and see Lionel trains in a store window. He would have the driver stop, and then Cowen would walk to the window and study the trains in that curiously intense way he had, as if seeing them for the first time.

The half-decade from 1955 through 1959 was particularly outstanding from a collector's point of view. Those years saw the introduction of the rarest of the F-3's, including the Canadian Pacific, Baltimore & Ohio, Milwaukee Road, Rio Grande and New Haven; the Budd cars; the Norfolk & Western Js; the Northern Pacific and Minneapolis & St. Louis geeps; the Great Northern and Virginian electrics; the General and Congressional sets; and the Jersey Central FM.

But the times, inevitably, were changing and the change was bringing trouble for Lionel, although the signs were not always easy to discern.

America had become an increasingly mobile society since the end of World War II. People relocated more readily than they had in the past and they often moved into small quarters. Large train sets were too much trouble to move and store, so people sold them or gave them away. The popularity of HO gauge increased as the sales of O decreased, and although Lionel went into HO in 1957, they were too late with too little.

Americans were becoming air conscious. Air travel was soaring and the railroads were beating down the doors of the Interstate Commerce Commission to cut back passenger service. A whole generation of little boys was growing up and going to airports with their dads to watch planes take off, rather than going downtown to the depot to watch trains arrive. There were no longer the highly publicized announcements of new passenger trains. Instead, there were highly publicized announcements of a series of ever larger and faster airplanes: the DC-6s and 7s, the Boeing Stratocruisers, and, eventually, the turbo-props and jets, the DC-8s and Boeing 707s.

In addition, an economic recession started in 1957 and continued through 1958 and into 1959. Lionel sales had risen steadily in the immediate postwar years and by 1953, aided by some government contracts during the Korean War, sales hit an all-time peak for Lionel of $32.9 million. Then, as government contracts decreased, sales averaged around $22 million the next three years. In 1957 net sales were down to $18.7 million with a net profit of $842,000, down from the $1.5 million profit the year before. In 1958, the year Joshua Lionel Cowen retired at age 78, net sales fell to $14.4 million. The company, for the first time in years, declared a loss of $469,000. Seventy per cent of the loss was attributed to Airex, a Lionel fishing equipment subsidiary.

For several years before 1958, Lawrence Cowen had been reporting to the Lionel stockholders that the company was looking to diversify, while at the same time bidding for more government contracts. The company was especially interested in the electronics field. It was apparent that management felt Lionel could not survive as a toy train company only.

Then Joshua Cowen was out and Lawrence Cowen wanted out. He would be more comfortable in the investment business on Wall Street, where he had spent his early years, than in the corporate acquisition game. The Cowens put their stock up for sale in 1959.

Someone who *was* comfortable at the acquisition game, was almost made for it by temperament, was Roy M. Cohn, who in October of 1959 headed a group that bought controlling interest in Lionel. He announced that the company would embark on an immediate and aggressive diversification program.

Only 33 years old when he became chairman of the board of Lionel, Roy Cohn was already nationally known. In August of 1954 he had resigned as the chief investigator of the U.S. Senate's anti-subversive committee headed by Sen. Joseph R. McCarthy of Wisconsin. In that position Cohn, like his boss, had been almost constantly embroiled in controversy and had attracted both great support and feverish opposition. Since the McCarthy days, Cohn had been involved in fight promotion, the restaurant business, publishing, investments and his law practice. Cohn was 5-feet, 8-inches tall, had deceptively sleepy eyelids and a photographic memory. He had graduated from Columbia Law School before his 21st birthday, still too young to be admitted to the bar. A man of unquestioned talents, Cohn was once described by *Time* magazine as "precocious, brilliant and arrogant . . . he moves at a dog trot and speaks like a machinegun."

Cohn, of course, brought in new members of the board of directors, including George Sokolsky, a newspaper columnist and long-time supporter of Cohn and Senator McCarthy, and Isabel Brandaleone, Joshua Cowen's daughter. Directors Joseph Bonanno, Charles Giaimo and Phillip Marfuggi were off the board. They were still officers, though, along with Ronald Saypol, Mrs. Brandaleone's son-in-law and an experienced toy merchandiser. Saypol's father, Irving, was an appellate court judge in New York and had been, in 1950, the U.S. Attorney for the southern district of New York. While U.S. attorney he had prosecuted the Rosenberg spy trial and had appointed as his first assistant a 23-year-old lawyer named Roy Cohn, whose father, Albert, was an appellate division judge and an influential member of the New York Democratic organization.

The new law firm for the Lionel Corporation was Saxe, Bacon & O'Shea of New York City. A partner in the firm was Roy Cohn.

Cohn began immediately to implement the acquisition program he had announced. In June of 1960 the company acquired Anton Electronics of Brooklyn and Intercontinental Manufacturing of Dallas, both space-related firms. At the end of the year, Lionel acquired Telerad Manufacturing Corporation. These companies were all acquired in exchange for Lionel stock. The Lionel stockholders statement of 1960 declared the company to be operating in the black, based on the sales of its subsidiary companies. Net sales were listed as $31.3 million, with a net profit of $681,236. In 1959, the last year of the old management, the company had shown a loss of $1.2 million on sales of $15.7 million.

The man issuing the 1960 stockholders report was John B. Maderis, who had been elected president of Lionel in August of 1960. Maderis, 58, had just retired as a major general and commander of the Army's missile program at the Redstone Arsenal, Huntsville, Alabama. He had no experience in toy trains, but Cohn wanted him for his connections within the government missile program. Lionel wanted contracts.

Maderis, who everyone called "the general," was given a five-year contract at a salary of $50,000 a year, plus an option to buy 20,000 shares of Lionel common stock at 95 cents a share. In addition, the company was obligated to retain Maderis as a consultant for an additional five years at $10,000 a year, and, on January 9, 1961, the board of directors approved the purchase of his airplane. It paid $65,800 in cash and took over Maderis's remaining payments amounting to $66,663.

In theory it seemed a good idea to hire someone like Maderis, with his contacts within Army and the government space industry. But the trouble was Maderis had quit the Army in a dispute over what he considered the inadequate missile program. He was, while president of Lionel, in the process of writing a book which was highly critical of the very people to whom he was supposed to endear himself.

Lionel continued, during 1961, to swallow companies faster, apparently, than it could digest them. It was becoming clear that Lionel trains were merely peas in a huge corporate shell game. In 1960 the company had abruptly dropped a lot of its best items and replaced them with cheaper units. Supervisory personnel, as well as skilled workers, were being laid off in slashing economic cutbacks. The cutbacks, in the view of many old Lionel employees, seemed to apply to the bottom but not to the top. Irving Schull, the curator of the popular Lionel museum, was being forced to sell off the collection. Morale was low.

In 1961 the Lionel catalog was led by scientific kits instead of trains. About the only items left from the 1950s were the GG-1, the Santa Fe F-3 and the Berkshire. More cuts in personnel were made. After Lionel bought Dale Electronics, many of Dale's supervisory personnel were transferred to Hillside, further lowering morale. It was a long way from the days when Joshua Lionel Cowen used to walk through the factory, bubbling enthusiasm and calling employees by their first names.

Cohn's frenetic activities continued. He did not restrict himself to Lionel business, either. He still had his law practice and was involved in, at one time or another, five travel agencies, two airline insurance companies, a savings and loan institution, a swimming pool company and the 5th Avenue Coach Lines, a New York City bus company. He also promoted the Floyd Patterson-Ingemar Johansson heavyweight championship fight in 1960 and was involved in the promotion of an upcoming Patterson-Sonny Liston fight.

Lionel acquired Dale Electronics along with Pacific-Western and Sterling Power. They were all part of Hathaway Instruments, Incorporated, which was merged with Lionel in October of 1961, after a stormy meeting of the stockholders. In many ways, the meeting was typical of the Cohn years. About 100 shareholders were at the Essex House in New York City. Many were in an angry mood. At one point, a stockholder demanded to know why Medaris's salary had been raised to $60,000 a year in 1961 while no dividends were paid for 1960.

"We have only been out of the woods for two years," said Cohn, adding that Maderis was of great value to the company.

A stockholder named John Gilbert wanted to know about the voting procedure. Director George Sokolsky engaged in a loud exchange with Gilbert and ended up telling him, "Just behave yourself."

"You should behave," Gilbert replied. "Maybe all directors over 65 should resign."

"I'll take care of this situation," said Cohn, and cracked down his gavel.

"A ham actor!" Sokolsky shouted at Gilbert.

"He's a reactionary newspaperman!" yelled Gilbert.

"Don't yell," said Cohn.

"You have a microphone. I haven't!" yelled Gilbert.

Another acquisition that took place in 1961 was one with M. Steinthal & Company, the manufacturer of parachutes. The owners of the company, Martin and Augustus Steinthal, were to receive $800,000 in Lionel stock, but, they said, they never did. Instead they received only $247,800 and later sued Cohn. They eventually won a judgment of $552,200. The judgment was against Cohn himself and not the Lionel Corporation because, the judge ruled, Cohn had personally guaranteed payment in writing after the board of directors of Lionel would not.

General Maderis's stockholders report for 1961, the first full year he was president, reported sales of $55.3 million but a net loss of $1.8 million, an all-time Lionel high. Things were not going well for the general. Nor for Lionel. In April of 1962, with losses still growing and the train business declining, Maderis was kicked aside. He was made vice-chairman of the board of directors, a post of no power. Melvin Raney took over as president and chief operating officer in July of 1962.

The 1962 catalog was a potpourri of trains, model cars, science labs, chemistry sets, phonographs and tape recorders. Morale in the Hillside plant sunk lower. At year's end the net losses for the new, space-age Lionel Corporation were $4.8 million — and counting. Sales were down to $41.5 million

By March of 1963, the Lionel corporation was a shambles. It was top-heavy with executives from the many mergers and acquisitions and these high-salaried officials had ill-defined areas of responsibility. Business was stumbling, employees were grumbling and stocks were tumbling. Roy Cohn announced he was quitting. He said he was granting options on his 55,000 shares of stock to Victor Muscat, who represented a three-man group which included Robert Huffines and Edward Krock. The three of them were involved in Defiance Industries and had become big corporate conquerors of the '60s.

Cohn sold at a loss, giving up his shares and voting rights in return for an interest-free loan of $281,275, which he apparently wanted to finance the April, 1963, heavyweight rematch between Sonny Liston and Floyd Patterson.

Roy M. Cohn presided over his last annual meeting of the Lionel stockholders on Monday, May 6, 1963, at the Essex House hotel on Central Park South in New York City. The stockholders approved the transfer of control from Cohn to the Muscat-Krock-Huffines group. Victor Muscat became board chairman. Several months later the Muscat group, seeing better opportunity elsewhere, sold out to a group headed by A.M. Sonnabend of the Hotel Corporation of America. That meant there were three different operating officers of the Lionel Corporation during 1963 — Raney, Muscat and Sonnabend. No one was paying much attention to trains. The 1963 catalog was printed in black and white. Lionel had a net loss of $6.5 million. In the four years since Roy Cohn had become chairman of the board, Lionel had lost more than $14 million. It had not paid a single dividend. The stock had dropped from 15 when he bought it, to 6½ when he sold.

The Roy Cohn era was over, although legal after-affects would linger for years. There was one final incident, however, that seemed to sum up the whole turbulent period.

While Cohn was conducting his final meeting as chairman of the board, a New York City deputy sheriff named Edward A. Pichler was standing in the lobby of the hotel. He had tried unsuccessfully to approach Cohn as he was going into the Lionel meeting. Pichler held in his hand a judgement for $9,303.46 against Cohn. A Civil Court judge had ordered Cohn to pay that amount to a William P. Rosensohn, a partner of Cohn in the promotion of the 1960 fight between Patterson and Ingemar Johansson. Rosensohn said the money was the balance of the percentage due him in the promotion.

Pichler looked around and saw Cohn's $10,000 gray Cadillac limousine parked in front of the Essex House. The car had air-conditioning, a telephone and an extension phone. Pichler ordered it driven to a garage on East 46th Street, where it was to be held for public auction.

Three days later Cohn appeared in court and asked that a new hearing on the matter be held. He said the contested $9,303.46 was to be paid to Rosensohn only after he accounted for ticket sales in that amount. The judge granted Cohn a new hearing. Asked why it had taken three days for him to do something about getting his car back, Cohn said he had not discovered it was missing until then. He said he had another one just like it.

Roy Cohn, like him or not, had style.

A. M. Sonnabend, the man who took over Lionel in late 1963 after Muscat and his partners sold out, died a short time later. In March of 1964, Robert A. Wolfe, a former Lionel officer and toy company executive, was elected president and chief operating officer. He announced a program of consolidation, rather than diversi-fication, and said there would be more emphasis placed on toy production. He said that in recent years Lionel had been in "corporate chaos."

On September 8, 1965, Joshua Lionel Cowen died at the age of 85.

Gradually, Robert A. Wolfe led Joshua Cowen's old company to firmer financial footing, but not through the sale of trains. The 1966 catalog contained an opening statement by Wolfe. It said, "Here at Lionel we've been making toys that are good, clean fun for almost 60 years."

What he meant was that the company had been making toys for almost 70 years. The mistake perhaps indicated the relative interest the Lionel executives had in the train aspect of the corporation. In 1968, the only train set the company offered was manufactured at the Hagerstown, Maryland, plant of the Porter-Spear Company, a Lionel subsidiary. So were all the accessories. That same year, the 2029 locomotive was made in Japan. In 1969 the motors and reversing units for all the locomotives were made in Japan.

Ronald D. Saypol, the former Lionel officer who had arrived and departed during the Cohn era, returned as president of the corporation in 1968, while Wolfe moved up to chairman of the board. Lionel got out of the train business completely after 1969, having entered into a licensing agreement with General Mills, who leased the Lionel name and made the trains themselves.

Fundimensions, a toy division of General Mills, purchased the molds, tools and dies from Lionel and moved them from the Hillside plant to a 97,000-square-foot building in Mount Clemens, Michigan, where, by April of 1970, production of Lionel trains began again. General Mills also leased 40,000 square feet in the basement of the Hillside plant. There they made track, accessories, and some rolling stock.

The Lionel line increased in quality and quantity each year after General Mills took over and the leasing arrangement has been profitable for both sides. In 1974 Lionel entered into a new five-year agreement with General Mills. The arrangement called for Lionel to receive 3.5 per cent of the net sales of the items covered by the agreement. Lionel received $1 million in advance, which represented a minimum royalty of $200,000 for each of the five years. Royalties in 1974 amounted to $480,600, so General Mills paid Lionel an additional $280,000. In 1975 the royalties came to more than a half-million dollars.

Back in 1950, when Lionel was approaching the apex of its postwar sales, a company executive, differentiating between Joshua Cowen's preoccupation with the quality of the product as opposed to Lawrence Cowen's concern with profits, said:

"J.L. is the father of the baby. Larry is simply the pediatrician."

Well, the father died, and then so did the doctor, and it appeared for a time that the child would, too. But it survived, barely, and, as the decade of the '80s approached, it appeared the child might live a long, full life.

SCOUT LOCOS

	Years	Cat.	Boiler	Motor	Reverse	Smoke	Light	Magne-Traction	Rubber Tires	Whistle
1001	1948	Yes	Plastic	Scout	Scout	No	Yes	No	No	No
*1001	1948	No	Metal	1655	3-Pos	No	Yes	No	No	No
1101	1948	No	Metal	1655	3-Pos	No	Yes	No	No	No
1110	1949, 51-52	Yes	Metal	Scout	Scout	No	Yes	No	No	No
1120	1950	Yes	Metal	Scout	Scout	No	No	Yes	No	No

SCOUT-TYPE LOCOS

	Years	Cat.	Boiler	Motor	Reverse	Smoke	Light	Magne-Traction	Rubber Tires	Whistle
233	1961-62	Yes	Plastic	Scout	Scout	Yes	Yes	Yes	No	Yes
234	Not known to exist.									
235	1961	No	Plastic	Scout	Scout	No	Yes	Yes	No	No
236	1961-62	Yes	Plastic	Scout	Scout	Yes	Yes	Yes	No	No
237	1963-66	Yes	Plastic	Scout	Scout	Yes	Yes	No	Yes	No
238	1963-64	Yes	Plastic	Scout	Scout	Yes	Yes	No	Yes	Yes
239	1965-66	Yes	Metal	Scout	Scout	Yes	Yes	No	Yes	Optional
240	1961 ?	No	Plastic	Scout	Scout	Yes	Yes	No	Yes	No
241	1965	No	Metal	Scout	Scout	Yes	Yes	No	Yes	Yes
242	1962-66	Yes	Plastic	Scout	Scout	No	Yes	No	Yes	No
243	1960	Yes	Plastic	249	2-Pos	Yes	Yes	No	No	Yes
244	1960-61	Yes	Plastic	249	2-Pos	Yes	Yes	No	No	No
245	1959	No	Plastic	Scout	Scout	No	Yes	Yes	No	No
246	1959-61	Yes	Plastic	Scout	Scout	No	Yes	Yes	No	No
247	1959-61	Yes	Plastic	249	2-Pos	Yes	Yes	No	No	No
248	1958	No	Plastic	249	2-Pos	No	No	No	No	No
249	1958	Yes	Plastic	249	2-Pos	No	No	No	No	No
250	1957	Yes	Plastic	2034	3-Pos	No	Yes	No	No	No
251	1959 ?	No	Metal	2034	3-Pos	No	Yes	No	No	No
1050	1959	No	Plastic	Scout	No	No	Yes	No	No	No
1060	1960-61	No	Plastic	Scout	No	No	Yes	No	No	No
1061	1964, 1969	Yes	Plastic	Scout	No	No	No	No	Yes	No
1062	1963-64	Yes	Plastic	Scout	Scout	No	Yes	No	With or Without	No
1130	1953-54	Yes	Plastic	2034	3-Pos	No	Yes	No	No	No
1654	1946-47	Yes	Metal	1654	3-Pos	No	Yes	No	No	Optional
1655	1948-49	Yes	Metal	1655	3-Pos	No	Yes	No	No	Yes
2034	1952	Yes	Metal	2034	3-Pos	No	Yes	No	No	No
6110	1950	Yes	Metal	Scout	Scout	Yes	No	Yes	No	No

*This loco is a mis-numbered 1101.

LIONEL
Postwar
Price & Rarity Guide No. 3
1945-1969

Since our postwar book appeared in 1976, much has happened to our hobby. The number of collectors has increased dramatically and prices, not surprisingly, have increased also — some would say frighteningly.

This is particularly true in the most collectable categories, such as the F-3s, FMs, and some of the steamers. By far the biggest increase in prices were for those items in legitimate *Mint* condition in their original boxes. For instance, the authors saw a *Mint* B&O F-3 with original box sell at an auction for $7,000. Five years ago that price would barely have reached $2,000.

There are several factors involved in the spectacular increase in prices, some specifically linked to the train collecting hobby, others related to larger sociological trends. The heated economy of the country in general and Wall Street in particular during the 80s was certainly reflected in train prices. More people with more money were getting involved in toy trains — literally speculating in train futures. These new venturers into the hobby drove the prices up at a quicker pace than ever before.

In addition, the sheer number of collectors and the lengthening years they have been in the hobby have led to ever-increasing numbers of large and sophisticated collections. The demand for the rarest items increases, and the prices go up. Then, as these top items are acquired, pressures increase to obtain mint items in their original boxes. After a collection of *Like New* items with original boxes is acquired, the next level is boxed sets.

As we head toward the mid-point of the 90s, boxes and boxed-sets are the buzzwords driving the hobby. Because of this new and feverish interest in individual boxes and boxed sets, we have included sections on both these relatively uncharted categories in our guide. This added significantly to the cost of production, but since the authors and publisher wanted this book to be as complete and useful as possible, economic considerations were set aside.

The economy has slowed and prices are dropping but they are still at their highest point in history. Demand for toy trains in top condition is still very strong, especially in postwar Lionel.

A quick look at demographics will explain why. The average age in our hobby is 46. In 1953, when Lionel sales peaked, this 46-year old was 6. Chances are he had some trains but not all the ones he wanted. Today, some 40 years later, he is financially able to obtain all those trains he missed. This is in keeping with the theory that people tend to collect the toys they had as kids. If that is true, it would explain the drop in demand for prewar trains and cause concern for the future of the hobby. Who's going to want all these trains in 20-30 years, ask the cynics. Hot Wheels and Barbie Dolls will be the hot items.

We don't agree. Today, Roman coins and Civil War items are still fervently sought-after and cherished. Toy trains will be desirable as long as people appreciate quality and tradition.

One downside to the rapid growth has been the emergence of unscrupulous practices. Fakes, mail-order fraud, and reproduction parts passed off as original all have had a damaging effect. In 1986, we exposed the practice of changing the colors of cars by the use of chemicals and other techniques. Recently, we introduced a new magazine, the *Toy Train Revue Journal*, to keep collectors informed of all that is going on in the hobby – both the good news and the bad news. We know of instances where unsuspecting collectors have paid hundreds of dollars for a Lionel load car, only to get a reproduction load instead of an original.

"The key is to educate," says Frank Hare, a former president of the TCA. "Tell how these guys fake cars. There are hundreds of thousands of dollars in profits involved. If collectors aren't educated and told what to look for, these guys will keep getting away with it."

The primary purpose of train collecting should be to have fun and experience the camaraderie. Some collectors have suggested open discussions about the unsavory issues should be discouraged because of the bad name it gives the hobby. We don't agree. Discouraging public discourse does not solve the problem. Quite the opposite, it encourages the fraud merchants to operate with greedy impunity. We believe it would be irresponsible for us to ignore practices which are damaging the hobby and costing innocent collectors thousands of dollars. The best defense is to expose and educate. That is what we have done and that is what we will continue to do.

If location is the key in real estate, then condition is the key in toy train collecting. The high prices are paid for only items which are genuinely *LN* or *Mint*. There is a huge drop-off after that.

The prices in this guide are based on *LN* without the box. As with our other guides, we have a chart showing how much to add or subtract from *LN* depending on condition. While this chart may have been fairly accurate in the mid-80s, it is nothing more than a loose guide today. Because of today's wide range of prices, there is a huge and impossible-to-gauge gap between *Mint* and the other categories. That's why we call this a guide.

With the exception of *Mint,* prices are falling from their artificially inflated levels of the late 80s. Lionel Postwar and MPC prices appear to be leveling off, while prices in Prewar O gauge are staying even and those in Standard gauge are flat and falling.

A certain amount of cooling among train prices is probably not a bad thing, especially if prices have been inflated by cold-eyed speculators. As one art dealer said recently, "A person buying to speculate tends not to have an emotional interest in art."

The same could be said about train collecting. And even though this is a price guide, it seems to the authors that less emphasis on prices is always a healthy thing. In the world of toy trains, we need fewer calculator operators and more train operators.

About This Guide

One Price

TM Price and Rarity Guides list only one price. That price is the asking price for items in *Like New* condition without their original box. We feel this is a reasonable standard of condition for collectors to aspire to in acquiring items of the postwar period, and enough items are for sale in this condition that an adequate sampling of asking prices can be made to arrive at an accurate average. Below is a chart to be used to calculate how much to add or subtract from the item if it is in better or worse condition than *Like New*.

Like New comes from the grading standards established by the Train Collectors Association and the Toy Train Operating Society, two nationwide clubs for toy train collectors. Those standards are as follows:

TCA and TTOS Grading Standards	
Mint	Brand new, unmarred, all original and unused.
Like New	Free of any blemishes, nicks, or scratches; original condition throughout, little sign of use.
Excellent	Minute nicks or scratches. No dents or rust.
Very Good	Few scratches, exceptionally clean; no dents.
Good	Scratches, small dents, dirty.
Fair	Well-scratched, chipped, dented, rusted or warped.
Poor	Beat-up, junk condition, some useable parts.

TM Price Chart	
Condition	Add or subtract to listed price
Mint boxed	+30% or more
Like New	Price Listed
Excellent	-10%
Very Good	-25%
Good	-40%
Fair	-50% or more

Determining Prices

We send an inventory list of items to postwar experts across the country. They pick the areas where they are strongest and assign a price and rarity rating for each item within their expertise. We also observe prices at train meets and watch the prices advertised in magazines and the newsletters of collecting organizations. After all the prices have been noted, we take a consensus and print the resulting price.

Still, determining prices is a fallible undertaking. The actual sale price of an item is almost always lower than the asking price, because the seller anticipates a low initial offer as prelude to the negotiation dance. We do not use the sale price because it is not feasible to be present on a consistent basis each time an item is sold. We would then be left with the task of having to ask the buyer (if he could be found) and seller what the sale price was.

This is a faulty method because sellers tend to exaggerate on the high side and buyers tend to exaggerate on the low side. On the other hand, asking prices, both printed and at meets, can be noted with accuracy.

The final sale price will always be subject to several variables, including how eager the buyer is to buy and the seller to sell, the region of the country where the sale is made, the interpretation of condition by the parties involved, and the law of supply and demand. Under certain conditions, then, a price in this book may appear high or low to one side or the other in a deal. That is the reason we call this the TM Price *Guide*, not the TM Price *Mandate.*

Determining Rarity

We also ask our experts to give an indication of how rare an item is. Although it is often true that the rarer an item, the higher the price, it is by no means an inflexible truth. There are items which turn up with regularity but are in such great demand that they cost dearly. Conversely, some items are hard to find but have a low price tag because collectors just are not that interested in them. But we believe knowing how rare items are is important in assembling a collection.

The system goes from 1, the most common with little or no collector interest, through 5, the rarest. To have a great collection, one should have some of the items that carry a rarity rating of 5 and most of those that carry a rating of 4. Plus or minus signs are used to fine tune the ratings.

No price is listed for **5X** or **5P** items because when so few items exist, sometimes only one, it is impossible to get a consensus. When a price is listed that was arrived at by less than the usual number of reported sales, an * appears after the price. If an * appears without a price, it indicates no sales were reported. Plus and minus signs are used fine-tune the ratings. The following is our code to rarity:

5P	Prototypes of which there were one or two made. *Examples: 6346-56 Alcoa hopper with decal, 6416 Boat Loader w/ decals and painted over 6414 Auto Loader*
5X	Pre-production mock-ups, factory mistakes, toy show paint samples, or special items of which less than 50 were made. *Examples: 3459 coal dump car painted yellow, 6464-515 Katy blue with black lettering*
X	Item of dubious origin. Most likely a fake but absolute proof of fraud is lacking. More information is requested from our readers. *Examples: 6464-825 with white lettering and stripe, 2365 blue with white lettering*
5	Extremely desirable and essential glamour item which is either one or two or all three of the following: high–priced, in great demand, and extremely difficult to find. Usually a rare variation made early or late in the production run and then only for a short time. *Examples: 2338 with orange stripe through the cab, 2023 with gray nose, 2332 in black.*
4	A regular production run item, but part of a far lower then normal production run. Orders did not justify larger production. Usually cataloged for less than two years. Very collectable and hard to find but likely to turn up at a large meet. High-priced and in great demand but easier to find than a 5. *Examples: 2242 New Haven F-3, 2330 GG-1, 6427 Virginian caboose, 58 GN snowplow*
3	A quality item and part of a normal production run, usually cataloged for more than two years, and available at medium or large meets. Moderate collector interest. *Examples: 52 fire car, 2056 steamer*
2	Big sellers that were cataloged for a long time. Easy to find and usually among the first items a collector acquires. *Examples: 2018 steamer, 6446-25 N&W Hopper, 2024 C&O Alco*
1	No collector interest. Made in huge numbers. Very common. Low priced. *Examples: 152 crossing gate, 6076 gray/black*

Note: In an effort to better pin-point the rarity of certain items, we have initiated the use of plus signs after the rarity rating designation.
Example: (4+) indicates the item is harder to find than a 4 but not quite as rare as a 5. The + designation is not to be confused with the 5+ designation which was used in the first edition of this guide to designate paint samples, mock-ups, and factory mistakes. "5X" is the new designation for this category.

Variations

In most cases, we list only major variations. Major variations are worth more than normal versions. Minor variations – which are worth no more than normal versions – are not listed.

Major variations are usually made for a short time early in a production run before some change was made in the decorating process that changed the rest of the cars in the run. A major variation could also be part of a limited run made for a special set.

All major variations have the following characteristics: the unusual version is easily recognizable from the normal version, they exist in sufficient numbers to be obtainable, and they are accepted as collectable variations by the majority of experienced collectors. Examples would be a solid-shield Rutland boxcar, long-stripe Norfolk & Western tender, 6464-1 Western Pacific in silver with red lettering, and the 2465 Sunoco tank car with the decal in the center. These are major collectable variations and are important to collectors. They are included in this book.

Examples of minor variations would be slight differences in the external color of the item and the color of the plastic mold. Couplers, doors, and trucks are not considered because all can be easily switched.

In most cases we ignore these minor variations. Listing them would only serve to confuse the reader, clutter the guide, and make essential information harder to find.

Minor variations not listed are worth no more than the common or normal version.

Trend Arrows ▲ ▼

Trend Arrows indicate growth or decline in value or demand. If an item is "hot" and on the upswing, an up arrow will appear. Conversely, if an item is losing value and interest is dropping, a down arrow will appear. If there is no discernible trend up or down, no arrow will appear.

How To Use This Guide

Items are listed by category in numerical order. Information is listed as follows: catalog number, roadname or type of item, years in the consumer catalog, color, rarity rating and price. The number in parentheses is the rarity rating. The number on the extreme right in bold face is the average asking price.

Colors

The purpose of listing colors is to identify the item, not describe it in detail. The dominant color – usually the body of a locomotive or boxcar and the walls of buildings – is listed first, followed by the color of the roof, if different, and the color of lettering or graphics.

Beware and Be Aware

Our first Postwar Guide, published in 1986, exposed the practice of chemically altering the color of a car or engine and selling these fraudulent items as rare color samples for large amounts of money. Since the TM expose in 1986, traffic in these fakes has been greatly curtailed. However, collectors should still have a healthy skepticism about unusual colors. Beware, too, of unusual combinations of couplers, frames, doors, and trucks because each can be switched.

It is highly unlikely a major, legitimate variation is going to suddenly turn up after going undetected by thousands of collectors for more than 30 years.

Many fine reproductions and repaints have been made of the more desirable locos and cars. Some are not identified as reproductions and are difficult to tell from the original. Reproduction parts are also being made and Lionel has re-issued a number of postwar items with interchangeable parts. Unmarked reproduction parts being passed off as originals pose a serious threat to our hobby.

Approach every deal with a healthy skepticism and If you have doubt, seek the advice of an experienced collector before you buy.

Notice to Non-Collectors

The prices listed are those a collector would ask another collector to pay if the items were in almost new condition and the items were being sold one-at-a-time.

A non-collector most often is selling a group of items at once, and that lowers the price.

Rare indeed is the non-collector who has trains in almost new condition and who, in order to get the prices listed in this book, would lug the items to and from train meets, over a span of months, to sell them one-at-a-time. The collector is doing the non-collector a service by purchasing the whole group.

The non-collector's main concern should be with getting a fair price. The way to arrive at a fair price is to consider condition, establish a price using the chart on the preceeding page, then deduct 30 to 40 percent.

Abbreviations

A	An "A" preceding the designation for years produced indicates the item appeared in the advance catalog.
HS	Heat-stamped
FM	Factory mistake
MB	1955 Door
RS	Rubber-stamped
SB	1953 Door
SM	Service manual
U	Uncataloged
NDV	No difference in value
*	No sales reported
*	An * after the price indicates the price listed was arrived at using less than the usual number of reported sales.

Appraisal Service

If you have trains you wish appraised. send a list. Include the number of each item and a brief descrption as to color and condition. Send to TM Books and Video, Box 279, New Buffalo, Michigan 49117. Phone: 1-219-879-2822.

Update

McComas and Tuohy's Lionel Postwar book blazed the trail for the many Postwar Lionel books which have been published since 1975. Research has yielded much new information but very little is in conflict with the original text – strong testimony for the thoroughness of the research. However, there are some minor additions and corrections we would like to make:

Page 16
Second column, first paragraph:
Text indicates the version with a gray roof was not made in 1954. It was.

Page 32
Second-to-last sentence, third paragraph under *Rating:*
The number for the UP should be 635, not 634.

Page 37
Tenth paragraph:
Vagell took the eight GG-1s in 1962, not 1963.

Page 57
Fourth paragraph, seventh line:
The ends of the bumper support bar began to point down in 1956.

Page 73
Fourth paragraph, under Sears Set, third line should read:
"...was sold by Sears in 1964."

Page 90
Last sentence, last paragraph, should read:
The 6014 Wix and 6014 Chun King Orient Express are the two hardest to find of the Scout-type boxcars.

Page 109
Last sentence, first paragraph, should read:
The 6440 ran in 61,62, and 63.

Additional Information

The *Toy Train Revue Journal* is the *Wall Street Journal* of train collecting. It is a price guide, market report, and tip sheet all rolled into one magazine. The *TTRJ* provides quarterly price updates and also contains useful articles on market conditions, trends in collecting, "what's hot and what's not", and layout building. It is the essential companion for the toy train collector and operator. For subscription information, call: 1-800-892-2822.

Acknowledgements

Joe Algozzini contributed mightily to all three guides in this book. Joe is one of the most knowledgeable collectors in the hobby and provided essential information. He is a dedicated researcher and tireless worker. Joe also established lines of communication with other knowledgeable collectors. They include Gregory Hake, who researched the box guide, along with Bill Logsdon, Dan Mega, Bob Bretch, and Drew Bauer.

Other contributors include Don Corrigan, Bernie Puralewski, Bob Caplan, Ken Banaszek, Harry Lovelock, Charlie Weber, Terrel Klaassen, Dick Meerly, Steve Patterson, Bob Jacobson, Ed Holderle, Richie Shanfeld, Ed Dougherty, Lou Palumbo, Rogers Piercy, and Joe Sadorf.

Contents

Diesels

F-3 Units

Note: Most reproductions have silk-screen lettering; however, some 2345 reproductions exist with heat-stamped lettering.

2240	**Wabash AB** 56 Gray/blue/white	(3)	1200▲
2242	**New Haven AB** 58,59 Silver/black/orange	(4)	1700▲
2243	**Santa Fe AB** 55-57 Silver/red	(3)	500
2243C	**Santa Fe B Unit** 55-57 Silver/red	(3)	225

2245 **Texas Special AB** 54,55
1. Silver trucks/red pilot/portholes (3) 850▲
2. Black trucks/silver pilot/A unit with (5) 1750▲
   portholes/B unit solid portholes
   late 55 only
Note: Extremely rare solid porthole A units known to exist. Possible dealer replacement shells.

2333 **Santa Fe AA** 48,49 Silver/red
1. RS larger lettering (3+) 1000
2. HS smaller lettering (3) 900

2333	**Santa Fe** Clear bodies (Vol. 5, pg 65)		5X

2333 **New York Central AA** 48,49
Dark gray/gray/white
1. RS larger lettering (4) 1300▲
2. HS smaller lettering (3) 1250▲
Note: Original NYC's had black decals and original Santa Fe's had red decals. Replacement decals are available and can be applied to either.

2343	**Santa Fe AA** 50-52 Silver/red	(2)	775

2343C **Santa Fe B Unit** 50-55 Silver/red
1. Screen roof vents 50-52 (4) 350
   matches 2343
2. Louver vents 53-55 (3) 300
   matches 2353

2344	**New York Central AA** 50-52	(3)	825

2344C **New York Central B Unit** 50-55
1. Screen roof vents 50-52 (4) 400
   matches 2344
2. Louver vents/matches 2354/53-55 (3) 350

2345 **Western Pacific AA** 52 (4) 2750▲
Silver/orange/black

2353	**Santa Fe AA** 53-55 Silver/red	(3)	750

2354 **New York Central AA** 53-55 (3+) 800
Dark gray/gray/white

2355 **Western Pacific AA** 53 (4) 2650▲
Silver/orange/black

2356 **Southern AA** 54-56 (4) 1600
Green/gray/yellow

2356C **Southern B Unit** 54-56 (4) 400
Green/gray/yellow

2363 **Illinois Central AB** 55,56 Brown/orange/yellow
1. Black lettering (4) 1450
2. Brown lettering (4+) 1500

2367	**Wabash AB** 55,56 Gray/blue/white	(4)	1400

2368 **Baltimore & Ohio AB** 56 (4) 2850▲
Blue/white/black

2373 **Canadian Pacific AA** 57 (4) 3000▲
Gray/maroon/yellow

2378 **Milwaukee Road AB** 56
1. No yellow stripe along roof (4) 2800▲
2. Yellow stripe along roof (4+) 3250▲
3. A unit no stripe, B unit with stripe (4+) 3150▲

2379 **Rio Grande AB** 57,58 (4) 1800▲
Yellow/silver/black

2383	**Santa Fe AA** 58-66 Silver/red	(3)	725

FM Units

Note: Watch for Jersey Central reproductions being sold as originals. The best way to tell an original is by checking the spacing between Jersey and Central. On the original, there is more space between the words on one side than there is on the other. On reproductions, the space between the words is the same on both sides.

2321 **Lackawanna** 54-56
1. Gray body maroon roof 54 (3+) 900
2. Gray body gray roof 55,56 (3) 700

2322	**Virginian** 65,66 Blue/yellow	(3+)	975

2331 **Virginian** 55-58
1. Yellow/black both colors (4) 1600
   painted on gray plastic body
2. Blue/light yellow/both colors (4+) 1400
   painted on/gray mold
   Note: Gray mold version is rarer but does not command as much money as the black/yellow version.
3. Blue/yellow - yellow only painted (3+) 1100
   on blue plastic mold
   Note: The yellow on the second version is much lighter than the yellow on the third version, which is almost gold.

2341 **Jersey Central** 56 Orange/blue/blue stripe
Note: Originals are heat-stamped; reproductions are silk-screened
1. Glossy finish (4+) 3500
2. Dull finish (4) 3200

GP-7s and GP-9s

Note: Originals have HS lettering. Reproductions have RS lettering or are silk-screened. Known reproductions include 2337, 2339, 2349, 2347, 2365.

2028 **Pennsylvania GP-7** 55 Tuscan
1. Yellow RS lettering/gold frame (4) 500
2. Gold RS lettering/gold frame (4+) 500
3. Gold RS lettering/tan frame (5) 800▲

2328	**Burlington GP-7** 55,56 Silver/black/red	(4)	500▲
2337	**Wabash GP-7** 58 Blue/gray/white	(3+)	450▲

2338 **Milwaukee Road GP-7** 55,56
1. Orange stripe through cab (5) 2500▲
2. All-black cab (3) 375

2339	**Wabash GP-7** 57 Blue/gray/white	(3+)	450

2346 **Boston & Maine GP-9** 65,66 (3) 400

2347 **Chesapeake & Ohio GP-7** U65 *Sears* (5) 3000
Blue/yellow

2348 **Minneapolis & St. Louis GP-9** 58,59
1. Red/white (4) 500
2. Red/yellow X

2349 **Northern Pacific GP-9** 59,60 (4) 500
Black/gold/red

2359 **Boston & Maine GP-9** 61,62 (3) 350
Blue/black/white

2365 **Chesapeake & Ohio GP-7** 62,63
Dummy couplers
1. Blue/yellow (3) 425
2. Blue/white X

Alcos

Note: The later Alcos, those made in 1957 and beyond, often turn up with cracked pilots. Be sure to check pilots before buying.

202	**Union Pacific A** 57 Orange/black	(3)	125
204	**Santa Fe AA** 57 Blue/yellow	(4)	225

205 **Missouri Pacific AA** 57,58 Blue/white
1. Blue/white (2) 175
2. Dark blue/white (4) 250

208	**Santa Fe AA** 58,59 Blue/yellow	(3)	200
209	**New Haven AA** 58 Black/orange/white	(4)	650▲
210	**Texas Special AA** 58 Red/white	(3)	175
211	**Texas Special AA** 62,63,65,66 Red/white	(3)	150

212 **US Marine Corps A** 58,59 Blue/white
Fixed rear coupler only. No coupler
opening in front
1. E unit/Magnetraction (3) 225
2. No E unit/no Magnetraction (4) 275

212T **US Marine Corps** 58,59 Blue/white (4) 550▲
Dummy unit made to match 212. Fixed
couplers front and rear

212	**Santa Fe AA** 64-66 Silver/red	(3)	175
213	**Minneapolis & St. Louis AA** 64 Red/white	(3)	250▲

215 **Santa Fe AB** U64,65 Silver/red/black-yell stripes
1. With 218C dummy unit (3) 200
2. With 212T dummy unit (2) 150

216	**Burlington A** 58 Silver/red	(4)	350▲
216	**Minneapolis & St. Louis A** U Red/white	(3)	150

| 217 | **Boston & Maine AB** 59
 Black/blue/white | (3) | **200** |

217	**Boston & Maine AB** 59 Black/blue/white	(3)	**200**
218	**Santa Fe AA** 59-63 Silver/red	(3)	**200**
218	**Santa Fe AB** 61 Silver/red	(3)	**175**
218C	See 223 entry		
219	**Missouri Pacific AA** U59 Blue/white	(3)	**225▲**
220	**Santa Fe A** 61 Silver/red	(2)	**125**
221	**Rio Grande A** 63,64 Yellow/black	(2)	**90**
221	**USMC A** U64 Olive drab/white	(4)	**350▲**
221	**Santa Fe A** U64 Olive drab/white	(4)	**400▲**
222	**Rio Grande A** 62 Yellow/black stripes	(2)	**90**
223,212	**Santa Fe AA** U64 Silver/red		*****
223,218C	**Santa Fe AB** 63 Silver/red	(3)	**225**
224	**US Navy AB** 60 Blue/white	(3+)	**300▲**
225	**Chesapeake & Ohio A** 60 Dark blue/yellow	(3)	**185**
226	**Boston & Maine AB** U59 Black/blue/white	(3)	**225▲**
227	**Canadian National A** U59,60 Green/yellow	(3)	**250**
228	**Canadian National A** U60,61 Green/yellow	(4)	**225**
229	**Minneapolis & St. Louis A** 61 Red/white	(3)	**150**
229	**Minneapolis & St. Louis AB** 62,63A		
	1. Red/white	(3)	**225**
	2. Olive drab uncataloged	(5)	**500***
230	**Chesapeake & Ohio A** 61 Blue/yellow	(2)	**125**
231	**Rock Island A** 61-63		
	1. Black/red stripe and white stripe	(3)	**150**
	2. Black/red stripe/no white stripe	(3)	**175**
	3. Black/white stripe/no red stripe	(4+)	**400▲**
232	**New Haven A** 62 Orange/black	(3)	**125▲**
1055	**Texas Special A** U59,60 Red/white	(2)	**85**
1065	**Union Pacific A** U61 Yellow/red	(2)	**85**
1066	**Union Pacific A** U64 Yellow/red	(2)	**85**
2023	**Union Pacific AA** 50,51		
	1. Yellow/gray nose, roof & trucks 50	(5)	**3000▲**
	2. Yellow/gray roof & black trucks 50	(3)	**300**
	3. Silver/gray roof & black trucks 51	(3)	**300**
2024	**Chesapeake & Ohio A** only 69 Blue/yellow	(2)	**125**
2031	**Rock Island AA** 52-54 Black/white	(4)	**450**
2032	**Erie AA** 52-54 Black/yellow	(4)	**400**
2033	**Union Pacific AA** 52-54 Silver/black	(3)	**350**
2041	**Rock Island AA** 69		
	1. Black/white lettering/red stripe	(3)	**200**
	2. Black/no lettering, no red stripe	(3+)	**225**

GM Switchers

600	**MKT** 55 Red/white		
	1. Black frame/black rails	(3)	**175**
	2. Gray frame/yellow rails	(3+)	**225▲**
	3. Gray frame/black rails	(4)	**250▲**
601	**Seaboard** 56 Black/red/white		
	1. Red stripes/rounded ends	(3)	**200**
	2. Red stripes/squared ends	(3+)	**225**
602	**Seaboard** 57,58 Black/red/red	(3)	**225**
610	**Erie** 55 Black/yellow		
	1. Black frame	(3)	**225**
	2. Yellow frame	(4+)	**400▲**
	3. Lionel dealer replacement shell with raised nameplate	(4)	**250▲**
611	**Jersey Central** 57,58 Orange/blue	(3)	**225**
613	**Union Pacific** 58 Yellow/gray/red	(4)	**300**
614	**Alaska** 59,60 Blue/yellow Came with dynamic brake unit		
	1. *Built by Lionel* in blue raised letters	(3)	**350**
	2. *Built by Lionel* in yellow raised letters	(4+)	**500▲**
616	**Santa Fe** 61,62 Black/white/safety stripes		
	1. No dummy horn, bell, or E unit slot	(3+)	**250▲**
	2. Has dummy horn, bell, & E unit slot	(4)	**350▲**
617	**Santa Fe** 63 Black/white/safety stripes	(4)	**350**
621	**Jersey Central** 56,57 Blue/orange	(3)	**250**
622	**Santa Fe** 49,50 Black/white (operating bell)		
	1. Large *GM* decal	(3+)	**375**
	2. Small *GM* decal	(3)	**350**
	3. Large *GM* decal *Built by Lionel* in white	(4)	**425**
	4. Same as 3 plus small decal	(4+)	**450**
623	**Santa Fe** 52-54 Black/white		
	1. 10 Handrail stanchions	(3+)	**300**
	2. 3 Handrail stanchions	(3)	**250**
624	**Chesapeake & Ohio** 52-54 Blue/yellow		
	1. 10 Handrail stanchions	(3+)	**350▼**
	2. 3 Handrail stanchions	(3)	**275▼**
633	**Santa Fe** 62 Blue/yellow		
	1. No safety stripes	(3)	**150**
	2. Safety stripes	(3+)	**185**
634	**Santa Fe** 63,65,66 Blue/yellow		
	1. Safety Stripes	(2)	**125**
	2. No Safety Stripes	(3)	**150**
635	**Union Pacific** U65 Yellow/red	(4)	**200**
645	**Union Pacific** 69 Yellow/red	(3)	**175**

6220	**Santa Fe** 49,50 Black/white (operating bell)		
	1. Large *GM* decal, 1949	(4+)	**375**
	2. Small *GM* decal, 1950	(4)	**350**
6250	**Seaboard** 54,55 Blue/orange/white-blue		
	1. Decal	(4)	**400**
	2. Rubber-stamped	(4)	**400**

	*Note: Fewer rubber-stamped versions
	   produced but decal version with decal
	   in excellent condition is more desirable.*		

GE 44-Ton Switchers

Note: All are difficult to find in Like New condition because they have a tendency to flake and are usually found with broken screw holes.

625	**Lehigh Valley** 57,58 Red/black/white	(3)	**250**
626	**Baltimore & Ohio** 57 Blue/yellow	(4)	**450▲**
627	**Lehigh Valley** 56,57 Red/white	(2)	**225**
628	**Northern Pacific** 56,57 Black/yellow	(3)	**250▼**
629	**Burlington** 56 Silver/red	(4)	**500▲**

Budd Cars

400	**Baltimore & Ohio** 56-58 Silver/blue	(3)	**375**
404	**Baltimore & Ohio** 57,58 Silver/blue	(3+)	**425**
2550	**Baltimore & Ohio** 57,58 (dummy)	(4+)	**550▲**
2559	**Baltimore & Ohio** 57,58 (dummy)	(4)	**500▲**

Electrics

GG1s

2330	**GG-1** Dark green/5 gold stripes 50	(4)	**1600**
2330	**GG-1** Nickel-plate		**5P**
2332	**GG-1** 47-49 single motor		
	1. Black/5 silver stripes	(5)	**2000**
	2. Black/5 gold stripes	(5)	**2000**
	3.Dark green/5 gold stripes/ decaled keystones	(3)	**1000**
	4. Dk green/5 gold stripes RS keystones	(4+)	**1600**
	5. Dk green/5 silver stripes RS keystones	(4+)	**1700**
2340-1	**GG-1** Tuscan 55, 5 gold stripes *Congressional Set*	(4+)	**2000**
2340-25	**GG-1** Brunswick Green 55 5 gold stripes	(4)	**1800**

(Continued on next page)

2360-1 **GG-1** Tuscan 56-58, 61-63
1. 1956/5 gold stripes/RS/small (4) **2000**
   PRR keystone
2. Same as 1 but large *PRR* keystone (5) **2200**
   usually found on solid-stripe versions
3. 1957,58 Solid stripe/RS/OB (3) **1500**
   marked 2360-10/large *PRR* keystone
4. 1961-63 Solid stripe/painted/ (3) **1500**
   HS markings
5. Late 1963 Solid stripe/painted/ (3) **1500**
   decaled markings
6. Very glossy finish/5 gold stripes **5P**
   Note: Variations exist having to do with louvres,
   shape of headlights, and steps. NDV.

2360-25 GG-1 Brunswick green 56-58 (4) **1600**
5 RS gold stripes

Other Electrics

520 **Box Cab** 56,57 Red/white
1. Black plastic pantograph (3) **150**
2. Copper plastic pantograph (4) **175**

2329 **Virginian** 58,59 Blue/yellow (4) **750**

2350 **New Haven EP-5** 56-58 Black/white/orange
Note:The major variation of the New Haven has to
do with the color of the N and H. The common
version has a white N and orange H. The rare
version has an orange N and black H. Both
versions come with either the nose trim painted
or a decal. The versions with the painted nose trim
are far more sought after than the decal versions.
1. White *N* orange *H*/nose trim decal (3) **475**
2. White *N* orange *H*/painted nose trim (4) **900**
3. Orange *N* black *H*/nose trim decal (4) **1500**
4. Orange *N* black *H*/painted nose trim (5) **1750**

2351 **Milwaukee Road EP-5** 57,58 (3) **650**
Yellow/black/red

2352 **Pennsylvania EP-5** 58,59 (3) **600**
Tuscan/gold

2358 **GN EP-5** 59,60 Orange/green/yellow (4+) **1000**

Note: Difficult to find EP-5s in Like New condition due to
flaking and fading. Beware of repaints, particularly Milwaukee
Road because of no decal. 2352 does not bring price
commensurate with its rarity because of its drab color
scheme.

Powered Units

Note: High prices, restorations and reruns have lessened the
demand. Beware of repaired window struts. Like New, 54, 55,
and 3360 must be complete with track actuator.

41 **US Army** 55-57
1. Unpainted black plastic with white (3) **150**
   lettering
2. Yellow lettering **X**

42 **Picatinny Arsenal** 57 Olive drab/white (4) **400**

44 **US Army** 59-62 Blue/white/gray (3) **225**

45 **US Marines** 60-62 (3+) **275**
Olive drab/white/gray

50 **Gang Car** 54-64 Orange/blue
1. Gray bumpers (54 only). Men in (5) **800**
   reversed colors
2. Same, blue bumpers (3) **75**
3. Horn changed to solid type used (1) **75**
   on later F-3's, attached off-center.
   Blue bumpers

51 **Navy Yard** 56,57 Blue/white (2) **200**

52 **Fire Car** 58-61 Red/white (3) **250**

53 **Rio Grande** 57-60 Black/yellow
1. *a* printed backwards (4) **350**
2. *a* printed correctly (5) **800**

54 **Ballast Tamper** 58-62,66,68,69 (3) **250**
Black/yellow

55 **Tie-Jector** 57-61 Red/white (4) **250**
Some came with a horizontal opening
behind man, some didn't. NDV

56 **Minneapolis & St. Louis** 58 (4+) **550**
Red/white

57 **AEC Switcher** 59,60 White/red/white (4+) **750**

58 **GN Rotary Snowplow** 59-61 (4) **600**
Green/white

59 **Minuteman** 62,63 White/blue (4+) **600**

60 **Lionelville Trolley** 55-58 Yellow/red/blue
1. Yellow/black lettering 55 (3+) **200**
2. Yellow/blue lettering (3) **175**
3. Roof vents (4) **275**
4. Yellow/red lettering *
Note: Some of these cars may actually be faded
black cars since black pigment has red in it.
5. The first versions off the production (5) **350**
   line had black silhouettes of motormen at
   each end of the trolley. They would appear
   and disappear according to which direction
   the car was traveling. However, the motormen
   silhouettes were rather indistinct and Lionel
   soon discontinued putting them on. The
   motormen remained available for separate
   sale and today trolleys exist with motormen,
   but they almost always were put on by
   collectors.

65 **Handcar** 62-66 (4) **450**
1. First versions were made of light yellow
   plastic which had a tendency to melt
   and are almost impossible to find in Like
   New condition. This version came with
   two sizes of rectifiers: thick (extends
   through slot in chassis wall) and thin
   (clipped to chassis wall). The thick version
   (two rubber-tire wheels) is harder to find
   than the thin version (one rubber-tire
   wheel). NDV
2. Dark yellow (4) **450**

68 **Executive Inspection Car** 58-61
1. Red/cream (3+) **325**
2. Red throughout **5P**
3. Blue/cream stripe **5P**

69 **Maintenance Car** 60-62 Dk gray/black(3) **300**

3360 **Burro Car** 56,57
1. Yellow (4) **300**
2. Brown **5P**

3927 **Track Cleaning Car** 56-60 (4) **175**
Orange/blue, complete with 2 bottles,
brush, and wiper

Steamers
The Hudson

773 4-6-4 50, 64-66 S, MT
1. 1950/2426W tender/has slide valve (5) **2200**
   guide/silver RS *773* on cab/white,
   HS *Lionel Lines* lettering on tender
2. 1964/736W tender/no slide valve (4) **1500**
   guide/larger, thicker *773* RS in white
   on cab/HS *Pennsylvania* on tender
3. 1965,66/same as 65 version but with(4+) **1600**
   New York Central on 736W tender

Berkshires

726 2-8-4 2426W 46 (4) **850**
Turned stanchions, *Atomic Motor* double
worm drive, horizontal motor, Baldwin drivers

726 2-8-4 2426W 47,49 (3) **650**
Cotter pin stanchions, single worm drive
and slanted motor, Baldwin drivers

726 2-8-4 2046W 52 Korean War issue
Spoked drivers, no Magnetraction
1. 726RR stamped on cab (3) **400**
2. No RR (4) **500**

736 2-8-4 2671WX 12-wheels 50,51 (3) **450**
Diecast trailing trucks/Magnetraction/
smoke/rubber-stamped cab number

736 2-8-4 2046W 8-wheels 53-55 (2) **400**
Diecast trailing trucks/Magnetraction/
smoke/heat-stamped cab number

736 2-8-4 2046W,736 55-66 (2) **400**
Sheet-metal trucks with plastic side frames/
Magnetraction/smoke/HS cab number

746 4-8-4 *Norfolk & Western* 746W 57-60
1. Short stripe tender (4) **1400**
2. Long stripe tender (4+) **1700**

Turbines

671 6-8-6 671W 46-49
1. Dbl worm drive/horz motor/, 46 (3) **350**
   671W
2. Sgl worm drive/slanted motor/,47 (3) **350**
   671W
3. 2671W with back-up lights, early 48 (5) **500**
4. 2671W , later 48 and 49 (2) **300**
   no back-up lights

671 6-8-6 2046W-50 52 S (2) **300**
No Magnetraction

671RR This version came with or without RR (re-run)
printed below 671. NDV

| 671R | 6-8-6 4671W 46-49 | (4) | 400 |

Electronic Control Set
Engine and tender only. White on black
electronic control decals. See Sets

681 6-8-6 50,51,53
1. 2671W, 12-wheel tender/50 (3) 300
2. 2046-50, 8-wheel tender/51,53 (2) 250

682 6-8-6 2046W-50 54,55 (4) 550
White stripe and oiler linkage

2020 6-8-6 2020W,2466WX 46 (2) 250
027 gauge version of 671
Double worm drive/horizontal motor

2020 6-8-6 2020W,6020W 47-49 (2+) 225
Single worm drive & slanted motor

4681 6-8-6 4681W 50 **Not known to exist**

Smaller Hudsons

646 4-6-4 2046W 54-58 S, MT
1. Diecast trailing trucks/*646* RS silver (4) 300
2. Plastic side frames on stamped (3) 275
   trailing trucks/larger *646* RS in silver
3. Same as 2 but *646* HS in white (3) 275

665 4-6-4 54-59,66 S, MT
Same as 685 but with feedwater heater
and lower marker lights. Both HS and RS
cab number. NDV. Plastic side frames on TT.
1. 6026W *Lionel Lines* (3+) 225
2. 2046W *Lionel Lines* (3+) 225
3. 736W *Pennsylvania* 66 (3) 200

685 4-6-4 6026W 53 Smoke, Magnetraction
1. *685* RS in silver below cab window (4) 300
2. *685* HS in white below cab window (3) 275

2046 4-6-4 2046W 50,53
1. Early 1950/*2046* RS in (3+) 250
   silver/metal TT
2. Later 1950/*2046* HS in (3+) 250
   white/metal TT
3. 1953/*2046* HS in (3) 250
   white/plastic TT

2055 4-6-4 2046W,6026W 53-56 S, MT
1. 1953/*2055* RS in silver/6026W (3) 250
2. 1954-56/*2055* HS in white/2046W (2) 225

2055 4-6-4 6026W Blue Boy's Train *
Locomotive only

2056 4-6-4 2046W 52 S, no MT (3) 325
Lionel Lines in larger lettering than on 2046W

2065 4-6-4 2046W,6026W 54-56 S, MT
1. 1954/*2065* RS in silver/2046W (3+) 275▲
2. 1955,56/*2065* HS in white/6026W (2) 250

The General

1862 4-4-0 1862T 59-62 Gray/red (3+) 275
No smoke, no MT, no whistle, headlight
*Note: Red or black headlight housings are
interchangeable. NDV*

1872 4-4-0 1872T 59-62 Gray/red (4) 400
Smoke, MT, whistle, headlight, oper. couplers

1882 4-4-0 1882T U60 Black/orange (4) 750
MT but no smoke or whistle/sold by *Sears*
Note: See Set Chapter as Generals
usually are sold in sets.

K-4 Pacific Type

675 2-6-2 *Lionel Lines* 47-49
1. Early 47/*675* HS on boiler front/ (4) 250
   Baldwin disc drivers/2466WX/2466T
2. Late 47/red decal *5690* on boiler (3) 225
   front/*675* RS on cab/2466WX/2466T
3. 48/2466WX/2466T (3) 225
4. 49/6466WX (3) 225

675 2-6-4 2046W 52 (3+) 225
Sintered iron spoked drivers/5690 decal

2025 2-6-2 2466WX,6466WX 47-49
Die-cast trailing truck/Baldwin disc drivers
1. Early 47/2025 HS on boiler front/ (3) 175
   2466WX
2. Later 47/red *5690* decal/2466WX (2) 150
   2025 RS on cab
3. 48,49 6466WX (2) 150

2025 2-6-4 6466WX 52 No Magnetraction (2) 125
Spoked drivers/5690 or 6200 on red decal

2026X 2-6-2 6466T U49 (5) 400
Same as 2025 but no smoke

2035 2-6-4 6466W 50,51 (3) 175
Magnetraction/spoked drivers/
stamped four-wheel trailing truck

Prairie Type

221 2-6-4 221W,221T *New York Central* 46,47
1. Gray/aluminum-colored wheels/46 (4) 225
2. Gray/black wheels/46 (3) 200
3. Black/black drivers with nickel rims (3) 200

224 2-6-2 2466W,2466T 45,46
1. Black handrails, 1945 (4) 200
2. Stainless handrails, 1946 (3) 175

637 2-6-4 2046W 59-63 (3+) 175
Magnetraction/2037 boiler casting

1666 2-6-2 2466WX,2466T 46 (2+) 125
Number plates, Nickel-rimmed drivers

1666 2-6-2 2466WX U47 RS number (3+) 150

2016 2-6-4 6026W 55,56 (2) 85
Same as 2037/no Magnetraction or smoke

2018 2-6-4 6026W,6026T,1130T 56-59 (2) 85
Smoke/no Magnetraction

2018 2-6-4 6026W Blue Boy's Train *

2026 2-6-2 6466WX 48,49 Wire handrails/smoke
1. Visible smoke-unit wire/1948 (3) 175
2. Hidden smoke-unit wire/1949 (3) 175

2026 2-6-4 6466W,6466T,6066T 51-53 (2) 125
Cast handrails/no smoke/no Magnetraction

2029 2-6-4 1060T,243W 64-66 (2) 100

2029 2-6-4 243W *PRR* markings 68,69 (4) 175

2036 2-6-4 6466W 50 (2) 100
Magnetraction/smoke

2037 2-6-4 6066T,6026T 53-64, (2) 100
6026W,243W 57-63

2037-500 2-6-4 1130T-500 57,58 (4+) 1000
Pink Girl's Loco
Either RS (left) or HS (right) numbers. NDV

Switchers

1615 0-4-0 1615T 55-57
No bell, back-up light, or handrails
1. Silver RS numbers, early 1955 (3+) 275
2. White HS numbers, later 1955-57 (3) 225

1625 0-4-0 1625T 58 (4) 325▲
No bell, back-up light, or handrails/
dummy front coupler

1656 0-4-0 6403B 48,49
Tender has handrails, back-up light, and
bell. Some come mis-numbered 6043B.
1. Sans-serif numerals on cab & *Lionel* (4) 400
   Lines lettering on tender condensed
2. Serif numerals on cab and lettering (4) 400
   on tender elongated

1665 0-4-0 2403B 46 (4+) 475▲
Similar to prewar 1662. Usually found with
red and green marker lights broken. Tender
has handrails, back-up light, and bell. Number
rubber-stamped in silver on cab/elongated
heat-stamped lettering on tender

Scout and Scout Type

233 243W, 233W 61,62 S, HL, MT (2) 75

234 Not known to exist but 234T does exist

235 1130T U61 S, HL, MT (4) 70

236 1130T, 1050T 61,62 S, HL, MT (3) 60

237 1130T 63-66 S, HL
1. Narrow white stripe (2) 50
2. Thick white stripe (4) 60

238 243W 63,64 (3) 75

239 243W, 242T 65,66 (2) 75▲
HS and RS numbers. RS rarer but NDV

240 242T U64 2P, S,HL, RT *Sears* 9820 (4) 400▲
See Sets

241	1130T U65 Diecast, S, 1 RT *JC Penney*		
	1. Thick white stripe	(4)	125▲
	2. Narrow white stripe	(2)	80
242	1130T, 1062T, 1060T 62-66		
	1. Thin-sided walkway	(2)	65
	2. Thick-sided walkway	(2)	50
243	243W 60 HL, RT	(3)	80
244	244T, 1130T 60,61 S, HL	(2)	60
245	1130T Timken trucks U59 2P	(4)	125▲
246	1130T, 244T 59-61,A62, HL, MT	(1)	60
247	247T A60,A61, S, No MT	(3)	75
	Blue stripe *B&O*		
248	1130T U58	(4)	75
249	250T 58	(4)	100
	Red stripe/*Pennsylvania*		
249	250T U58	(4)	100
	Liquid smoke unit, large smokestack		
250	250T 57	(3)	100
	Red stripe/*Pennsylvania*		
251	1130T U66	(4+)	250▲
1001	1001T 48		
	Only plastic Scout locomotive. Some diecast 1101s show up rubber-stamped *1001*		
	1. Plastic/White HS *1001* on cab	(3)	60
	2. Plastic/Silver RS *1001* on cab	(4)	125
	3. Diecast 1101 RS *1001*	(4)	150▲
1050	0-4-0 1050T U59	(4+)	225▲
1060	1060T A60,A61	(3)	60▼
1061	1061T, 1062T A63,A64,69		
	1. 0-4-0/no tire on drive wheel/1061T	(2)	50▼
	2. 0-4-0/1062-50/1061T	(2)	50▼
	tire on drive wheel		
	3. 2-4-2/tire on drive wheel/1062T	(4)	60▼
	4. 2-4-2/tire on drive wheel/ number	(4)	90▲
	printed on paper and glued to cab,		
	one geared drive wheel instead of two		
1062	1061T, 1062T 63,64		
	1. No tire on drive wheel/1061T	(2)	50
	2. Tire on drive wheel (1062-50)/1062T	(3)	60
1101	1001T U48 Scout, diecast, 3P		
	1. Heat-stamped 1101	(2)	75
	2. RS 1001	(4+)	150▲
1110	1001T Scout 49,51,52 diecast		
	1. Wire handrails	(3)	60
	2. No wire handrails	(2)	50
	3. Same with hole in boiler front	(3)	75
	over light, silver reverse lever		
1120	1001T 50 Scout	(2)	50
1130	1130T, 6066T 53,54		
	1. Plastic boiler/3P/1130T or 6066T	(2)	60
	2. Die-cast boiler/3P/6066T	(4)	75

1654	1654T, 1654W 46,47 Diecast, 3P	(3)	60
1655	6654W 48,49 Diecast, 3P	(3)	60
2034	6066T 52,3P	(3)	60
6110	6001T 50 Diecast, 2P, MT, no light	(3)	60

Passenger Cars

Sheet-Metal Cars

Note: Sets consist of 2 Pullmans and 1 Observation. Cars came with both silver and white lettering. Silver is rarer. Prices are for white lettering. Add 20% if silver lettering.

2430	Pullman 46,47 Blue/silver	(3)	100
2431	Observation 46,47 Blue/silver	(3)	100
2440	Pullman 46,47		
2441	Observation 46,47		
	1.Blue/silver	(3)	80
	2.Green/cream	(3)	80
2442	Pullman 46-48 Brown/gray	(3)	90
2443	Observation 46-48 Brown/gray	(3)	90
6440	Pullman 48,49 Green/cream	(3+)	85
6441	Observation 48,49 Green/cream	(3+)	85
6442	Pullman 49 Brown/gray	(3+)	85
6443	Observation 49 Brown/gray	(3+)	85

General Cars

1865	**Western & Atlantic** 59-62	(2)	75
	Yellow/brown		
1866	**Western & Atlantic** 59-62	(2)	75
	Yellow/brown		
1875	**Western & Atlantic** 59,60	(4+)	400▲
	Yellow/Tuscan		
1875W	**Western & Atlantic** 59-62 (whistle)	(4)	250
	Yellow/Tuscan		
1876	**Western & Atlantic** 59-62	(2)	150
	Yellow/brown		
1885	**Western & Atlantic** U60	(4)	300
	Sears Black/brown/white		

Small Streamline Passenger Cars

GREEN/YELLOW 48,49			
2400	Maplewood Pullman	(4)	150
2401	Hillside Observation	(4)	150
2402	Chatham Pullman	(4)	150
ALUMINUM/BLUE 64,65 (no lights)			
2404	Santa Fe Vista Dome	(3)	60
2405	Santa Fe Pullman	(3)	60
2406	Santa Fe Observation	(3)	60
ALUMINUM/BLUE 66			
2408	Santa Fe Vista Dome	(3)	60
2409	Santa Fe Pullman	(3)	60
2410	Santa Fe Observation	(3)	60
ALUMINUM/BLUE/BLUE STRIPE 59-63			
2412	Santa Fe Vista Dome	(3)	75
2414	Santa Fe Pullman	(3)	75
2416	Santa Fe Observation	(3)	75

ALUMINUM/BLACK 50,52,53			
2421	Maplewood Pullman	(3)	100
2422	Chatham Pullman	(3)	100
2423	Hillside Observation	(3)	100
2429	Livingston Pullman 52,53 only	(4)	125
ALUMINUM/BLACK/BLACK STRIPE/GRAY ROOF 51			
2421	Maplewood Pullman	(4)	100
2422	Chatham Pullman	(4)	100
2423	Hillside Observation	(4)	100
ALUMINUM/RED 54-58			
2432	Clifton Vista Dome	(3)	60
2434	Newark Pullman	(3)	60
2435	Elizabeth Pullman	(3)	60
2436	Summit Observation	(3)	60
2436	Mooseheart Observation 57,58 only	(4)	100
ALUMINUM/RED/RED STRIPE 56			
2442	Clifton Vista Dome	(4)	80
2444	Newark Pullman	(4)	80
2445	Elizabeth Pullman (sold separately) 56	(5)	325
2446	Summit Observation	(4)	80
YELLOW/RED 50			
2481	Plainfield Pullman	(5)	400▲
2482	Westfield Pullman	(5)	400▲
2483	Livingston Observation	(5)	400▲

Large Streamline Passenger Cars

PRESIDENTIAL 62-66			
2521	McKinley Observation	(4)	250
2522	Harrison Vista Dome	(4)	250
2523	Garfield Pullman	(4)	250
2530	**Railway Express Agency Baggage Car** 54-60		
	1. Small doors	(3)	250
	2. Large doors	(5)	800▲
SUPER SPEEDLINER 52-60			

Note: Some plates are glued on, some are secured by rivets; others by hex nuts. Some plates have dots, others do not. Different methods of wiring are used to connect the lights to the pick-up assemblies. None of these minor variations affect the price. The only important variation has to do with the channel along the side of the car. Most are ribbed. A few are smooth. If smooth, add 20% to the prices listed.

2531	Silver Dawn Observation	(3)	100
2532	Silver Range Vista Dome	(3)	100
2533	Silver Cloud Pullman	(3)	100
2534	Silver Bluff Pullman	(3)	100
CONGRESSIONAL 55,56			
2541	Alexander Hamilton Observation	(4)	400▲
2542	Betsy Ross Vista Dome	(4)	400▲
2543	William Penn Pullman	(4)	400▲
2544	Molly Pitcher Pullman	(4)	400▲
CANADIAN PACIFIC 57			
2551	Banff Park Observation	(4)	450
2552	Skyline 500 Vista Dome	(4)	450
2553	Blair Manor (separate sale only)	(5)	600▲
2554	Craig Manor (separate sale only)	(5)	600▲
SUPER CHIEF 59-61			
2561	Vista Valley Observation	(4)	300
2562	Regal Pass Vista Dome	(4)	300
2563	Indian Falls Pullman	(4)	300

Note: Prices for cars with plain window inserts. Add $75 -$125 for Like New with all boxes and components, including inserts with people in silhouette but beware of reproductions. The original Irvington cars had heat-stamped lettering, and it has dulled with age. Reproductions have silk-screened lettering, which is bright, and the rivets around the area of the lettering have been removed to accommodate the silk screen.

2625	Irvington	(4)	350
2625	Manhattan 47 only	(4+)	350
2625	Madison 47 only	(4+)	350
2627	Madison	(4)	325
2628	Manhattan	(4)	325

Military and Space

3309 **Turbo Missile Launching Car** 63,64 (2) **75**
Red/white one missile, arch-bar trucks, two fixed couplers, no missile holder

3330 **Flat Car with Operating Submarine Kit** 60,61
1. Submarine assembled (3) **90**
2. Submarine unassembled (4+) **175**

3330-100 Operating Submarine Kit (4+) **500**

3349 **Turbo Missile Launching Car** 62-65
Missile holder/Timken trucks/no number or lettering on car
1. Red/white/2 operating couplers (2) **85**
2. Olive drab/one operating coupler (4) **500▲**
   and one fixed coupler

3409 **Helicopter Launching Car** 61,62 (3) **100**
Blue/white
Note: Manually cocked and released. Gray Navy helicopter with one propeller, yellow tail assembly. Flatcars are available and so are reproduction helicopters.

3410 **Helicopter Launching Car** 61,62 (3) **125**
Blue/white, Yellow unmarked helicopter/one propeller

3413 **Mercury Capsule Car** 62-64 (4) **275**
Red/white, Gray base/red launcher/parachute inside of white/red rocket with gray nose

3419 **Helicopter Launching Car** 59-65
Note: Helicopters with 2 props are more desirable than helicopters with one propeller.
1. Light blue/gray *US Navy* copter (3) **200**
   with 2 props/large winding mechanism
2. Same as 1 but dark blue (2) **200**
3. Same as 2 but small winding (2) **175**
   mechanism
4. Light blue/small winding (3) **175**
   mechanism
5. Light blue/small winding (3) **200**
   mechanism/yellow copter/one propeller
6. Same as 4 but dark blue (3) **175**

3429 **USMC Helicopter Launching Car** 60 (4) **500▲**
Olive drab/same mechanism as 3419/gray, one prop gray helicopter with *USMC* markings. Included in *1805 Land, Sea, and Air Gift Pack.*

3470 **Target Launcher** 62-64
Note: Blower nozzle turns up in many different colors. NDV
1. Dark blue flat (2) **75**
2. Light blue flat (4) **100**

3509 **Satellite Car** 61,62 Green/white (3) **75**
Manual operation/black/silver satellite/ gray superstructure/yellow microwave disc

3510 **Satellite Car** A62 Red/white manual (3) **100**
Lionel only on side/no number/plastic Timken trucks/fixed couplers/black & silver satellite/ gray superstructure/yellow microwave dish

3519 **Satellite Car** 61-64 Green/white (2) **75**
Gray superstructure/yellow dish/operated by remote control

3535 **AEC Security** 60,61 Red/white (3) **125**
Gray plastic roof gun usually missing/gray rotating searchlight/same cab as 520 electric

3540 **Operating Radar Car** 59,60 (3) **150**
Red/wht, Gray base/yell dish/blk & silver radar

3619 **Helicopter Recon Car** 62-64
1. Operating Yellow/black roof/red and (3) **150**
   black lettering/same body & roof as
   3665 and 3666/red copter
2. Same w/darker yellow body (4) **200**

3665 **Minuteman** 61-64 White/blue with rocket
1. Dark blue roof (3) **175▼**
2. Light blue roof, 1964 (4) **200**

3666 **Cannon Box Car** U64 (5) **500▲**
Sears Set 3-9820, Wht/lt blue roof/blue lettering/ oper. cannon fires silver painted wooden shells.
Beware: Reproduction roofs available

3820 **Operating Submarine** 60 Olive/white (4) **250**
USMC markings on car/*US Navy* markings on gray sub/part of 1805 *Land, Sea, and Air Gift Pack*

3830 **Operating Submarine** 60-63 (3+) **175**
Blue/white, Gray sub/*US Navy* markings

6175 **Flat Car with Rocket** 58-61
Same gray cradle used with 6801 Boat Car/ *US Navy* rocket/red/white/blue lettering
Same rocket that came with 175 launcher
1. Red/white 58 (3) **110**
2. Black/white 59-61 (2) **100**

6402-Type (mold 1877-3) Flat Car/green tank (4) **275**
U64 *Sears*

6407 **Flat Car with Large Missile** 63 (4+) **500▲**
Red/white, Gray cradle is same used on 6501/ holds large white-red rocket/removable blue nose with and without pencil sharpener/ reproduction sharpeners available

6413 **Mercury Capsule Carrying Car** 62,63
Blue/white, 2 gray unlettered Mercury capsules secured by bands/reproduction capsules available/same chassis as 6519
Note: Brakewheels may be added
1. Blue/white (4) **150**
2. Aqua/white (4+) **200**

6448 **Target Car** 61-64
1. Red sides/white lettering (2) **50**
2. White sides/red lettering (3) **60**
Note: Solid white can be made by combining 1 and 2

6463 **Rocket Fuel** 62,63 White/red (3) **50**

6470 **Exploding Boxcar** 59-63 Red/white (2) **50**
Spring-loaded

6480 **Exploding Boxcar** 61 Red/white (4) **65**

6512 **Cherry Picker** 62,63 Black/white (3) **125**
Gray base holds black metal ladder/original vestibule orange/repros exist in both orange and black

6544 **Missile Launching Car** 60-64 Blue/white
Gray launching mechanism/usually found with brakewheels broken/used 6519 chassis and 44 launching base/same firing mechanism as 448 range set
1. White lettered console (2) **150▲**
2. Black lettered console (4) **375**

6630 **Missile Launcher** U60-64 *Sears* (3) **90**
Blk/wht/blue base w/black missile firing ramp

6640 **USMC Missile Launcher** 60 Olive/wht (3) **200**
Flat comes both with and without lettering. NDV

6650 **Lionel Missile Launcher** 59-63 (3) **80**
Red/white, Blue launcher/same as 6630/black launching pad, white/red missile with blue nose

6651 **USMC Cannon** U65 Olive/white (4) **185▲**
Came in *JC Penney* set headed by 221 *USMC* Alco

6803 **USMC Tank & Microwave Truck** 58,59(4) **250**
Gray microwave dish truck and tank

6804 **USMC Trucks** 58,59 Red/white (4) **250**
Gray microwave dish truck and truck with 2 guns

6805 **Radioactive Waste** 58,59 Red/white (2) **135**
Metal trucks
Note: Reissued 9234 in 1980. Reissued containers are gray plastic/originals are black plastic painted gray. Sometimes found with tan containers which were made for the 462 derrick platform.

6806 **USMC Radar Truck and Navy Hospital Truck** 58,59 (4) **250**
Red/white/1 gray USMC radar dish truck and 1 *US Navy* hospital truck

6807 **Flat with USMC Boat** 58,59 Red/wht (4) **175**
Large gray amphibious boat

6808 **Flat with USMC Truck and Tank** 58,59 (4) **300**
Red/white, Gray searchlight truck & two-gun tank

| 6809 | **Flat with 2 USMC Trucks** 58,59 | (4) | 250 |
| | Red/wht, Gray cannon truck & *Navy* hosp. truck | | |

6814	**First Aid Medical Car** 59-61, U64 White/red		
	Man, 2 stretchers, oxygen tank unit		
	1. Black RS serif *Lionel,*/gray frame	(3)	175
	2. White HS serif *Lionel*/black frame/	(4)	200
	no tray insert/no man or stretchers		
	oxygen unit/*Sears* U64		

6819	**Helicopter** 59,60 Red/white	(3)	65
	Gray *Navy* one-prop helicopter/carries 2		
	missiles, reproduction helicopters available		

6820	**Navy Helicopter** 60,61		
	Gray *Navy* one-prop copter with 2 missiles/		
	repro copters available		
	1. Light blue/white	(4)	175
	2. Dark blue/white	(3)	150

6823	**ICBM Missiles** 59,60 Red/white	(3)	75
	2 red/white IRBM-type missiles/same		
	missiles as on 6650		
	Note: Missile and rocket parts interchangeable;		
	therefore all color combinations are possible.		

| 6830 | **US Navy Submarine** 60,61 Blue/white | (3+) | 125 |
| | Gray non-operating sub with black lettering | | |

6844	**Missile Carrying Car** 59,60		
	6 white missiles/gray missile holder		
	base/reproductions of gray base available in		
	gray and black		
	1. Black/white	(2)	65
	2. Red/white	(4+)	600▲

Rolling Stock

Action Cars

3357	**Cop and Hobo Car** 62-64		
	Known as Hydraulic Platform Maintenance		
	Car. Comes with cop, hobo, and platform.		
	Reissued in 1982 as 7901		
	1. Blue/white	(3)	75
	2. Prototype (Vol. 5, p. 91)		5P

3370	**Sheriff and Outlaw** 61-64		
	1. Green/yellow	(3)	75
	2. Decal version (Vol. 5, p. 71)		5P
	3. Arch-bar trucks/blue car/no lettering		5P
	4. Same but green car/no lettering		5P

3376	**Operating Giraffe Car** 60-64, 69		
	1. Blue car/white lettering	(2)	60
	2. Green car/yellow lettering	(2+)	75
	3. Blue car/yellow lettering	(4)	500▲
	4. Mock-up (Vol. 5, p. 90)	(5+)	
	5. Decal version mock-up	(5+)	
	Note: Giraffe comes two ways: yellow with brown		
	spots and solid yellow. NDV		

3386	**Operating Giraffe Car** U66		
	1. Blue, white lettering	(2+)	75
	2. Bongo and Bobo (Vol. 4, p. 39)		5P

3424	**Wabash** 56-58 Two tell-tale poles		
	1. Blue/white/blue man	(3)	100
	2. Same but white man	(3+)	125

3434	**Operating Chicken Car** 59,60 64-68		
	Brown/white		
	1. Blue sweeper man	(3+)	150
	2. Gray sweeper man	(3)	140

3435	**Aquarium Car** 59-62 Green		
	Reissued in 1981 as 9308		
	1. Yellow lettering/no circle around	(3)	200
	L/no tank designation		
	2. Same as 1 but gold lettering	(3+)	250
	3. Gold lettering/circle around L/	(5)	1200
	Tank No. 1 and *Tank No. 2*		
	4. Same as 3 but no circle around L	(5)	800▲
	5. White lettering		X

| 3444 | **Erie Animated Gondola** 57-59 | (2) | 100 |
| | Red/white, reissued in 1980 as 9307 | | |

6473	**Horse Transport Rodeo Car** 62-66, 69		
	1. Yellow/red lettering	(2+)	25
	2. Yellow/brown lettering	(3)	40

Operating Barrel Cars

3562	**AT&SF** 54-58		
	1. Black/white/black trough, 54 3562-1	(3)	185
	2. Black/white/yellow trough, 54 3562-1	(3)	185
	3. Gray/red, 54 3562-25	(4)	325▲
	4. Gray/red, 54 3562-1	(5)	1000▲
	5. Gray/blue, 55 3562-25	(2)	75
	6. Painted yellow/black 3562-50	(4)	150
	7. Unpainted yellow plastic/blk, 55,56	(2)	75
	3562-50		
	8. Unpainted orange plastic/blk 57,58	(3)	110
	3562-75		
	9. White/black		Not Known To Exist

Boxcars

Early-Style Boxcars

X2454	**Pennsylvania** 46 Orange/black 9 1/4"		
	1. Orange door	(4+)	250
	2. Brown door	(3+)	225

| X2454 | **Baby Ruth** 46,47 | (2+) | 35 |
| | Orange/black lettering/brown door | | |

4454	**Baby Ruth** Electronic Set 46,47	(4)	250
	Orange/black lettering/brown-painted doors		
	Note: Black doors questionable		

| 6454 | **Baby Ruth** 48 | (4+) | 300 |
| | Dark orange/black lettering/brown doors | | |

6454	**New York Central** 48,49		
	1. Brown/white/brown door	(2)	75
	2. Bright orange/black/brown door	(4)	200
	3. Burnt orange/white/brown door	(2)	75

| 6454 | **Santa Fe** U48,49 | (2) | 50 |
| | Orange/black lettering, brown doors | | |

6454	**Southern Pacific** 50,51		
	Made in 49,52 and 53 but not cataloged		
	1. Brown/white/large circular herald	(3)	75
	with 1/16" break in outside circle		
	between *R* and *N* 1949		
	2. Same with small herald	(3)	75
	no break in outside circle 1950		
	3. Reddish brown/white/small herald/	(2)	75
	no break/51-52		

| X6454 | **Erie** 50-53 Brown/white/brown doors | (3) | 65 |
| | Made in 49 also but not cataloged | | |

X6454	**Pennsylvania** U49-53		
	1. Tuscan/white/Tuscan doors	(4)	100
	2. Tuscan/white/black plastic doors	(4+)	125

Scout-Type Boxcars

638-2361	**Van Camps Pork & Beans** U62,63 Bank slot		
	1. Light red/white-yellow	(4)	60
	2. Dark red/white-yellow	(3+)	50

1004	**Baby Ruth** 48,49,51,52 Orange/blue		
	1. Blue outlined *Baby Ruth*	(1)	12
	2. Solid blue *Baby Ruth*	(1)	12

| 6004 | **Baby Ruth** Orange/blue 50 | (3) | 15 |
| | Blue outlined only | | |

6014	**Airex** SM59, A60 Red/yellow-white		
	1. Regular style lettering	(3)	85
	2. Bold style lettering	(4)	125

X6014	**Baby Ruth** 51,52,54-56 *PRR*		
	1. White/black 51,52	(2)	14
	2. Red/white 54-56	(2)	14

6014	**Bosco** 58		
	1. White/black	(4)	75▲
	2. Red/white	(1)	15
	3. Orange/black	(2+)	15

| 6014 | **Campbell Soup** U69 Red/white | | X |

| 6014 | **Chun King** U Red/white | (4) | 200 |

6014	**Frisco** 57,58 White/black		
	1. White/black	(1)	15
	2. Red/white	(2)	15
	3. Orange/black	(4)	50▲

| 6014 | **Wix** U59 White/red | (4) | 225▲ |

6014-85	**Frisco** 69		
	1. Orange/bright blue	(2)	20
	2. Orange/dark blue	(2)	20

6014-335	**Frisco** 63-66,68 White/black		
	1.With coin slot	(4)	100
	2.Without coin slot	(1)	10

6024	**Nabisco Shredded Wheat** 57 Orange/black		
	1. No bank slot	(2)	25
	2. Bank slot		5P

6024-60 RCA Whirlpool U57,58 Red/white   (3+)   85

6034   Baby Ruth 53,54 *PRR*
1. Orange/dark blue   (2)   12
2. Orange/blue   (1)   12

6044   Airex U A59,A60
1. Blue/yellow-white   (1)   25
2. Dark blue/yellow-white   (5)   350
3. Teal blue   (4)   150

6044-1X Blue Plastic/No lettering   (5)   1500*
Blue plastic shell, *McCall/Nestle's* decal
Note: Reproduction decals available

6050   Libby's Tomato Juice 63,63
1. With green stems   (2)   75
2. Without green stems   (4)   125
3. Without white lines between   (3)   100
   tomatoes

6050   Lionel Savings Bank 61 White/green
1. *Built by Lionel* spelled out   (4)   150▲
2. *Blt by Lionel*   (3)   35

6050   Swift 62,63 Red/white
1. Bank slot   (2)   25
2. No bank slot   5X
3. Minus two rows of rivets left of door   (3)   35

6464 Boxcars

The 6464 boxcars are the most popular category of Lionel's postwar rolling stock. Their splashy graphics make them some of the best-looking cars Lionel ever made in the postwar era. There are so many variations – both major and minor – that they present an endless challenge to collectors. The category also contains some of the rarest and most valuable items of the postwar era.

To understand the variations, the collector must be familiar with the different body and door types that were used. The identification and labeling of the different body types, which has become the accepted standard of the hobby, was first published by Charles Weber of Norristown, Pennsylvania.

Doors used in 1953, 1954, and early 1955 had a single, large block in the middle. Those used in 1955 through 1969 had three additional blocks. The first door is called the 1953 single block (SB) door and the second is called the 1955 multiple block (MB) door.

Body Type 1, SB Door
In 1953, the first body type had four rows of rivets to the left of the door (rows 1 through 4) and four rows of rivets to the right of the door (rows 5 through 8). The rows to the right of the door were not interrupted but three of the rows to the left of the door were interrupted by smooth areas. The rivets were removed because they interfered with the heat-stamping process used in applying graphics. Row 4 was the only row on the left side that was not interrupted.

The Type 1 body type comes with the SB door only.

Body Type 2A, SB Door
In 1954, the increase in the size of graphics necessitated more changes in the rivet detail. The middle portion of row 2 and all of row 7 were removed.

Most Type 2As come with the SB door but some 2As were still being used in 1955 after the MB door was introduced so Type 2A exists with both SB and MB doors. The most common examples of Type 2A with MB doors are the 6464-125 NYC, 6464-150 Missouri Pacific and the 6464-275 State of Maine.

Body Type 2B, MB Door
In 1955, the only change on the body had to do with the roof. The Pacific Fruit Express car was introduced and it used the same mold as the 6464 boxcars. To make the PFE, Lionel altered the die to make an opening for the ice hatch. When the die was used again to make 6464 boxcars, a plug was inserted in the die to cover the opening but a thin plastic ridge was discernible on the roof. This third body type is called 2B.

It was a transition year for doors. Lionel started using the multiple-block doors about mid-way through the year. So Type 2B exists with both MB and SB doors.

Body Type 3, MB Door
A new mold was introduced in 1958. The result was a boxcar made of lighter weight plastic with ribs on the underside of the roof. The thin line from the ice hatch was gone and the rivet detail changed slightly, for no apparent reason. The change had to do with row 7. Two rivets were added to the top and two rivets were added to the bottom.

In 1960, the number of rivets changed in row 3. They were almost all removed.

As with other categories, we recommend the collector concern himself with only major variations, i.e. those that can be readily seen on the exterior of the car and those generally accepted by the majority of experienced collectors.

6464-1 Western Pacific 53,54 Type 1
1. Silver/blue   (3)   150
2. Silver/blue inside roof ribbing   (4+)   600▼
3. Silver/red   (5)   1500*
4. Silver/black   5P
5. Orange/white   5P
6. Orange/silver   5P
7. Powder blue/black   5P
8. Dark blue/white   5P
9. Orange/black   5P
10. Silver/light blue feather RS both sides   X

6464-25 Great Northern 53,54 Type 1
1. Orange/white   (2)   125
2. Same, red/green decals   (5)   600*
   To be legitimate, decal must be applied over smooth surface. If traces of heat-stamping can be detected under decal, it was applied outside the *Lionel* factory.
3. Tuscan/white   5P

6464-50 Minneapolis & St. Louis 53-56 Type 1
1. Tuscan/white   (2)   100
2. Dark green/gold   5P
3. Tuscan/yellow   5P
4. Light bluish green/black   5P
5. Copper primer/Tuscan and white   (5)   500

6464-75 Rock Island 53,54,69
1. Dark green/gold Type 1 53,54   (3)   125
2. Dark green/gold Type 4 69   (2)   110

6464-100 Western Pacific 54,55
1. Orange/white/blue feather   (5)   5000*
   1954 Type 1
2. Same but no *1954* Type 1   (5)   2000*
3. Silver/blk/yellow feather Type 1 54   (4)   200
4. Silver/blk/yell feather Type 2A 54,55 (3)   150
   Long feather or short feather. NDV
5. Orange/white or gray/blue feather   (4)   1000*
   Type 2A 54,55

6464-125 New York Central 54-56
1. Gray-red/HS white, 54, gray top   (4)   135
   row of rivets, SB no cedilia Type 2A
2. Gray-red/RS white red top row   (3)   125
   of rivets, SB, cedilia, Type 2A 55,56
3. Same as 2 but no cedilia   (4)   200
4. Same as 2 but MB   (3)   125
5. Lilac/red Type 2B   5X
6. Pink/red Type 2B   5X

6464-150 Missouri Pacific 54,55,57   (3)   150
1. Blue-gray/RS black, gray stripe on SB door/no *XME*/3/4-inch *Eagle* and *New 3-54* to right/6464-150 to left/ no grooves/no *Built by Lionel*/blue plastic/painted gray stripe/Type 2A/ early 54 first run
2. *New 3/54* moves to the left/*BLT by*   (3)   150
   Lionel and *XME* are added to the right/ late 54 second run
3. White shell painted blue-gray/   (3+)   150
   grooves/5/8-inch *Eagle*/BLT by Lionel and *XME* to right/*BLT 3/54* and *6464-150* to left/ gray stripe on SB door/early 55
4. Same as 3 but blue plastic   (2+)   125
   shell/early 55
5. Blue-gray/RS black solid yellow SB   (5)1500▼
   door, *XME*, 5/8 inch *Eagle* to right, *New 3-54* and *6464-150* to left, grooves/Built by Lionel, MP seal in first panel to left of door, blue plastic, painted gray stripe/ Type 2A, 55
6. Same as 4 but white plastic SB door (4)   250
   painted yellow/last run 1955
7. Blue-gray/RS black/solid yellow   (2)   125
   MB door/*XME*, 1/2 inch *Eagle* and *New 3-54* to left/*6464-150* to right, no grooves/*Built by Lionel*/gray plastic painted blue/Type 2B/57
   Note: The 6464-150 has more variations than any other boxcar. The seven listed above represent a reasonable number to collect. The number is limited to keep the collector (and the authors) from going crazy. The variations listed are in chronological order. Many more variations – all worth about $150 – were made by Lionel by interchanging the various kinds of doors, using grooves, not using grooves, changing the sizes of the Eagle and using different shades of blue paint and plastic.

6464-175 Rock Island 54,55
1. Silver/blue   (3)   125
2. Silver/black   (5)1200▲

6464-200 Pennsylvania 54,55,69
1. Tuscan/white Type 1   (3+)   175
2. Tuscan/white Type 2A   (4)   185
3. Tuscan/white Type 4   (3+)   165

6464-225 Southern Pacific 54-56
1. Black/white, red/yell herald Type 2A (3+) **185**
2. Same but Type 1 (5) **1500***
3. Black/white, white herald Type 2A (5) **2000***

6464-250 Western Pacific 66
1. Orange/white Type 4 (3+) **200**
2. Same but Type 3 (5) **1000▲**

6464-275 State of Maine 55,57-59
1. Red-white-blue/white-black (3) **125**
   Type 2A, 2B
2. White body, painted red and blue (4) **150**
   stripes, solid red door Type 2A
3. Red-white-blue, no 6464-275, same
   shell used on 3494-275 Type 2B (4+) **250**
4. Red-white-blue Type 3 (3) **110**
   Note: 2A is HS, 2B both HS and RS. NDV

6464-300 Rutland 55,56
1. Green-yellow/RS green-yell, yellow (2) **125**
   plastic door Type 2A
2. Same, wht plastic door painted yell (3) **150**
3. Irregular spacing HS MB Type 2B 56 (3+) **175**
4. Yellow body and door models, RS (5) **1200▼**
   yellow-green, yellow and green SB door
   Type 2A
5. Yellow body painted glossy green, (5) **3500▲**
   solid yellow plastic SB door, solid shield
   herald, Type 2A

6464-325 Sentinel
1. Type 2B 56 (4+) **750▲**
2. Decaled one side only **5P**

6464-350 Katy 56 Type 2B
1. Maroon/white (4) **375**
2. Pink/black **5X**

6464-375 Central of Georgia 56,57,66
1. Maroon plastic, painted silver (3) **150**
   oval & roof red-white lettering 3-56 built date
   Type 2B 56,57
2. No built date Type 4 66 (2) **100**
3. Gray plastic painted red, painted (5) **2500***
   silver oval and roof, red/white lettering,
   3-56 built date Type 4 66
4. Red decal lettering, silver oval Type 2B **5P**
   Note: Types 2B and 4 come with both maroon and
   red lettering. NDV

6464-400 B&O Time-Saver 56,57,69
1. Blue-silver-orange/blue-white, Built (3+) **165**
   5-54 Type 2B
2. Same, built 2-56 Type 2B (4) **200**
3. Two different built dates: 5-54 on (5) **1500***
   one side and 2-56 on the other Type 2B
4. Blue-silver-orange/blue-white Type 4 (3) **125**
5. B&O markings Timken colors Type 4 (5) **1200***
6. Solid green/white Type 4 (5) **1200***

6464-425 New Haven 56-58
1. Blk/wht, half-serif N Type 2B 56,57 (3) **100**
2. Blk/white, full-serif N Type 2B 57,58 (2) **100**
3. Black/white, Type 3, 58 (2) **75**

6464-450 Great Northern 56,57,66
1. Olive-orange/yellow stripe Type 2B (3+) **165**
2. Same but Type 3 (5) **1500***
3. Same but Type 4 (3) **150**
4. White lettering, white stripe Type 4 **X**
5. White lettering, yellow stripe Type 4 **X**

6464-475 Boston & Maine 57-60,65,66,68
1. Blue/black-white Type 2B (2) **90**
2. Same but Type 3,4 (2) **85**
3. Purplish/black-white, 66 (4) **150▲**
   Note: This car comes in many different shades of
   blue w/ and w/o built dates (harder to find). NDV

6464-500 Timken 57,58,69
1. Yellow/blue-gray Type 2B (3+) **135**
2. Decal markings (Vol. 5, p. 25) **5P**
   Type 2B
3. Yellow/black Type 4 (3+) **135**
4. Same as 3 but Type 3 (4) **200**
5. Yellow/red Type 4 **5X**
6. Green/white Type 4 **5X**
7. Green/red Type 4 **5X**
8. Green/gold Type 4 **5X**
9. Beige/black Type 3 (4+) **400▼**

6464-510 NYC Pacemaker 57,58 Girl's Train Type 2B
1. Bluish green/black (4) **700▲**
2. Sky blue/black (5) **900***
3. Yellow/black **5X**

6464-515 Katy 57,58 Girl's Train Type 2B
1. Yellow/black (4) **700▲**
2. White/black **5+**
3. Beige/black **5P**
4. Blue/black **5X**

6464-525 Minneapolis & St. Louis 57,58,54-66
1. Red/white Type 2B (2) **90**
2. Red/yellow Type 2B **5X**
3. Red/white Type 3 (3) **125**
4. Red/white Type 4 (2) **90**
5. Red/yellow Type 4 **5X**
6. Bright-pink purple/white **5X**
   (Vol. 5, p. 2) Type 4
7. Raspberry-gray/white Type 4 **5X**

6464-650 Rio Grande 57,58,66
1. Yellow-silver/black/roof painted
   silver/built date/Type 2B (3) **135**
2. Same but no built date Type 4 (2) **100**
3. Same as 2 but yellow-painted roof, (5) **1500▲**
   built date
   Note: The rare painted yellow-roof version is on a
   gray Type 4 body mold. Type 2s with a yellow
   roof (unpainted) are created by removing the
   silver paint.

6464-700 Santa Fe 61,66
1. Red/white Type 4 (3) **150**
2. Same but Type 3 (5) **1500***

6464-725 New Haven 62-66,68,69
1. Orange/black Type 4 62-66, 68 (2) **85▼**
2. Black/white Type 4 69 (4) **200**

6464-825 Alaska 59,60
1. Blue/yellow, yellow stripe Type 3,4 (4) **250▲**
2. Blue/white, white stripe (Vol. 5, **X**
   p. 26) Type 3,4
3. Blue/white, yellow stripe (Vol. 5, **X**
   p. 26) Type 3,4
4. Blue/white, white stripe, white door **X**
5. Blue/yellow, yellow stripe, yellow (5) **350***
   door Type 4
   Note: Types 3 and 4 came in both blue and gray
   · body molds. NDV

6464-900 New York Central 60-63,65,66
1. Jade green/black-red-white Type 4 (3) **125**
2. Same but Type 3 (5) **1200***
3. No red lettering or black trim around **5X**
   NYC Type 4
4. No red lettering or white date Type 4 **5X**
5. Yellow/black-red-white (Vol. 5, **5X**
   p. 24) Type 4

Automobile Boxcars

X2458 **Pennsylvania** 45-48 Dk brown/white (3+) **125**

2758 **Pennsylvania** U45,46 (3) **100**
Note: Cataloged as 2458. Lionel had left-over
2758 bodies so they were fitted with a postwar
frame and trucks and sold as a 2458.

6468-1 **Baltimore & Ohio** 53-55 Blue/white (3) **85**

6468X **Baltimore & Ohio** 55 Tuscan/white (4+) **500**
027 Santa Fe freight set

6468-25 **New Haven** 56-58
1. Black N with full serif, H in white (2) **125**
2. Same, darker orange and (3) **150**
   Tuscan doors
3. Black N with half serif, H in white (2) **100**
4. White N with half serif, H in black (4) **350***

Operating Boxcars

3428 **United States Mail** 59,60,65,66 Type 3 (3) **100**
Red/white/blue/gray man or blue man. NDV

3484 **Pennsylvania** 53,U54 Type 1 Tuscan/white
1. Non-painted man 53 (2) **75**
2. Man with flesh tones painted on (3) **75**

3484-25 AT&SF 54,56
1. Orange/HS black/Type 1 2A 2B (5) **1500***
2. Orange/RS white/Type 1 (3) **115**
3. Orange/HS white/Type 1 2A 2B (3+) **125**

3494-1 NYC Pacemaker 55 Type 2A (3+) **150**
Gray/red/white

3494-150 Missouri Pacific 56 Type 2B (3+) **150**
Blue/gray/yellow door

3494-275 State of Maine 56-58 Type 2B
1. Line above and below B.A.R. (3) **125**
   and 3494275
2. No line above or below B.A.R. and (4) **250**
   3494275 omitted, 56 only

3494-550 Monon 57,58 Type 2B Maroon/white
1. Built Date (4) **400**
2. No built date (4+) **425**

3494-625 Soo 57,58 Type 2B (4) **400**
Tuscan/white

6352-1 Pacific Fruit Express 55-57 Type 2B
1. Lettering includes CU. FT. (3) **100**
2. No CU. FT. (4) **150**
Came with 352 Ice Depot and 5 cubes of ice.
Original cubes have bubble, reproductions don't

Early-Style Operating Boxcars

3464   **AT&SF** 49-52
     1. Orange/black, 1949
       a. Brown painted door   (2)   35
       b. Blackened metal door   (3)   35
     2. Unpainted orange plastic/black   (4)   65
       plastic doors
     3. *NYC* Tan/White   (5) 1000▲

X3464   **New York Central** 50-52   (3)   50

3474   **Western Pacific** 52,53 Silver/black   (4)   100

Cabooses

Early Cupola Type

2457   **Pennsylvania** 45-47 Red/white
     1. Tool box, generator, steps and 2   (3)   50
       couplers, *Eastern Div.* lettering
     2. Same, no steps   (2)   45
     3. Brown/white left-over inventory   (4)   85
       from the prewar 2757 caboose.

2472   **Pennsylvania** 45-47 Red/white
     1. Late 1945 trucks, sintered iron   (2)   40
       wheels, one coupler, *Eastern Div.* lettering
     2. Same, 1947 trucks   (1)   40
     3. Same as 1 without *Eastern Div.*   (3)   40
       lettering

4457   **Pennsylvania** 46,47 Red/white   (4)   175
     Electronic Set

Southern-Pacific Type

1007   **Lionel Lines** 48-52 Red/white   (1)   8

2257   **SP** 48 No light, 1 coupler, brake wheels
     1. Bright red/white   (2)   8
     2. Brown/white   (4)   8

2357   **SP** 48 Brown/white
     2 operating couplers, 2 ladders, 2 tool boxes,
     2 brakewheels, light
     1. Red stack   (4)   100
     2. Brown stack   (2)   30
     3. Black stack   (2)   30
     Note: Though not in the 47 catalog, both the 2257
     and 2357 were available in 1947.

4357   **SP** 48 Brown/white Electronic Set   (4)   125

6007   **Lionel Lines** 50 Red/white   (2)   10

6017   **Lionel Lines** 51-61
     Common, inexpensive caboose made in
     many colors and shades. Major colors:
     1. Red/white metal trucks   (1)   5
     2. Tuscan/white metal trucks   (2)   5
     3. Tuscan/white Timken trucks   (1)   5
     4. Light Tuscan/white Timken trucks   (1)   5
     5. Brown/white Timken trucks   (1)   5
     6. Olive drab/U   (5)   500*
     Note: 6007 and 6017 were the cheapest
     cabooses Lionel made other than Scout cabooses.
     Similar to the 6257 but without brakewheels.
     Usually unpainted plastic and no trim.

6017-50   **US Marine Corps** 58 Blue/white   (3)   75
     Box marked 6017-60

6017-85   **Lionel Lines** Gray/black   (3)   40

6017-100   **Boston & Maine** 59,62,65,66
     1. Dark blue/white 59   (5) 600▲
     2. Blue/white   (2)   75

6017-185   **AT&SF** 59,60 Gray/red   (3)   60

6017-200   **US Navy** 60 Blue/white   (4)   100

6017-225   **AT&SF** U60 Red/white   (3)   65

6017-235   **AT&SF** 62 Red/white   (4)   70
     6017-235 stamped on box only

6027   **Alaska** 59 Dark blue/yellow   (3)   100

6037   **Lionel Lines** 52-54
     Scout caboose with magnetic couplers
     1. Brown/white   (1)   5
     2. Light brown/white   (1)   5
     3. Tuscan/white   (1)   5
     4. Red/white   (1)   5

6047   **Lionel Lines** 62
     1. Various shades of red/white   (1)   5
     2. Unpainted Tuscan plastic   (4)   10

6057   **Lionel Lines** 59-62
     1. Red/white   (1)   5
     2. Brown/white   (2)   6
     3. Orange-red/white   (1)   5

6057-50   **Lionel Lines** 62 Orange/black   (3)   35

6058   **Chesapeake & Ohio** 61 Yellow/black
     1. Painted black frame, rails   (2)   60
     2. Unpainted frame, no rails   (3)   60

6059   **Minneapolis & St. Louis** 61,62,65-67,69
     1. Unpainted dark red plastic/white   (1)   30
     2. Unpainted red plastic/white   (1)   30

6059-50   **Minneapolis & St. Louis** 63,64
     1. Painted dark red/white   (3)   45
     2. Unpainted red plastic/white   (2)   30

6067   Not known to exist. Lionel parts list shows
     this car but part number for body is 6257

6157-125   No Lettering
     1. Red   (1)   5
     2. Light red   (1)   5
     3. Brown   (1)   5

6167   **Lionel Lines** Red/white 63   (1)   5

6167-25   No Lettering Red 64   (1)   5

6167-50   No Lettering Yellow 63   (2)   6

6167-85   **Union Pacific** 64-69 Yellow/black   (3)   50

6167-100   No Lettering 64 Red   (1)   7

6167-125   No Lettering 64
     1. Brown   (1)   7
     2. Red   (1)   7

6167-150   No Lettering Yellow   (1)   10

6257   **SP and Lionel markings** 48-56   (1)   8
     Note: Previously 2257. Very common. Made in
     many colors & variations, none worth more than $8.

6257X   48,49
     1. Bright red/white   (4)   35
     2. Dull red/white   (4)   35
       Same as 6257 but with 2 couplers. Came in
       1425B set with 1656 switcher

6257-100   **Lionel Lines** 56-63   (1)   5

6357   **SP and Lionel markings** 48-61
     1 coupler, light, inserts, 2 brakewheels
     1. SP Dull red/wht, 2357 on side, 6357 (5)   35
       RS on base
     2. Same, 6357 on side   (2)   25
     3. SP Bright red/white   (2)   25
     4. *Lionel* Maroon/white   (2)   25

6357-50   **AT&SF** Red/white 60   (5) 1200*
     Came in rare 2555W set, called both the
     Over and Under and the *Father and Son* set.

6457   **Lionel** 49-52 (previously 2357)
     2 couplers, light, inserts, ladders, tool boxes,
     smokestack
     1. Brown/white 49   (3)   40
     2. Semi-gloss brown/white 50   (3)   40
     3. Reddish brown/white 52   (4)   50

6557   **Lionel** 58,59 Tuscan/white   (4)   275
     Smoking caboose

6657   **Rio Grande** 57,58 Yellow/silver/black (4)   250
     Not made with smoke unit by Lionel

N5C Pennsy Type

6417   **Pennsylvania** 53-57
     1. Tuscan/white *New York Zone*   (2)   75
     2. Same as 1 but no *New York Zone*   (4)   300

6417-25   **Lionel Lines** 54 Tuscan/white   (2)   40

6417-50   **Lehigh Valley** 54
     1. Gray/red   (2)   75
     2. Tuscan/white   (5) 1500

6427   **Lionel Lines** 54-60 Tuscan/white   (2)   50

6427-60   **Virginian** 58
     1. Blue/yellow   (4) 300▲
     2. Dark blue/white   X
     Note: Reproduction Virginian cabooses exist.
     Originals are heat-stamped with rivet detail.
     Reproductions are silk-screened with rivet detail
     removed.

6427-500   **Pennsylvania** 57,58 Sky blue/white   (4)   500
     Girl's Train

6437   **Pennsylvania** 61-68 Tuscan/white   (3)   45

6447   **Pennsylvania** 63 Tuscan/white   (4)   400

Bay Window

6517   **Lionel Lines** 55-59 Red/white
     1. *Blt 12-55* and *Lionel* underscored   (4)   **125**
     2. *Blt 12-56* and *Lionel* not underscored (2)   **85**

6517-75 Erie 66 Red/white   (5)   **600▼**

6517-1966 Train Collectors Association   U66   (4)   **500▼**
     Orange/white

Work Cabooses

Note: Cabs, tool boxes easily switched

2419   **DL&W** 46,47 Lt. gray/black   (2)   **75**

2420   **DL&W** 46-48
     1. Dark gray/blk HS serif *Lionel Lines*   (4)   **125**
        Note: Variations exist having to do with style of
        lettering, couplers, color of frame, and shade of
        gray. NDV
     2. Black/RS sans-serif *Lionel Lines*   *****
        factory repaint

6119   **DL&W** 55,56
     1. Red cab and tray, white HS serif   (2)   **40**
        Lionel, black painted frame
     2. Same as 1 but gray tray   (1)   **40**
     3. Same as 1 but sans-serif *Lionel*   (1)   **40**

6119-25 DL&W 57
     Orange cab and tray, black HS *Lionel*
     1. Glossy orange painted frame   (4)   **50**
     2. Flat orange painted frame   (2)   **45**

6119-50 DL&W 56   (2)   **50**
     Brown cab and tray, white HS *Lionel*
     brown painted frame

6119-75 DL&W 57   (3)   **50**
     Gray cab and tray, black HS sans-serif *Lionel*
     on glossy or flat gray painted frame

6119-100 DL&W 63-66
     White or gray lettering, serif and sans-serif. NDV
     1. Red cab, gray tray, white RS serif   (1)   **30**
        Lionel black painted frame
     2. Same but no *Lionel* on blue metal   (4)   **40**
        frame, *Built by Lionel* HS on cab

6119-125 No Lettering 60   **X**

6120   No Lettering U61,62
     1. Yellow cab and tray, black painted   (1)   **20**
        frame, no stack but hole for one
     2. Same but without hole for stack   (2)   **25**

6130   **AT&SF** 65-68
     1. Painted red cab and tray, white   (1)   **30**
        RS serif, *Lionel* black painted frame
     2. Same but unpainted gray tray,   (5)   **60**
        blue frame
     3. Unpainted red cab and tray   (3)   **40**

6219   **Chesapeake & Ohio** 60 Blue/yellow   (4)   **100**

6419   **DL&W** 48-50 52-57
     1. Painted gray cab, tool boxes and   (2)   **50**
        frame, black HS serif *Lionel*
     2. Same but black RS sans-serif   (5)   **60***
        Lionel Lines (factory repaint)
     3. Same as 1 but unpainted gray cab,   (2)   **50**
        tool boxes and frame
        Note: Numerous minor variations. NDV

6419-25 DL&W 55 Gray/black   (3)   **50**

6419-50 DL&W 56,57 Gray/black   (3)   **60**

6419-75 DL&W 56,57 Gray/black   (3)   **50**

6419-100 Norfolk & Western 57,58   (4)   **225**
     576419 on cab
     Unpainted gray plastic cab, molded tool
     boxes and frame, black HS serif *Lionel Lines*

6420   **DL&W** 49,50   (4)   **150**
     Dark gray/black, searchlight

6429   **DL&W** 63 Gray/black   (4)   **300**

6814   **First Aid Medical Car** 59-61 White/red
     Man, 2 stretchers, oxygen tank unit
     1. Black RS serif *Lionel,*/gray frame   (3)   **175**
6824-50 2. White HS serif *Lionel,*/black frame/   (4)   **200**
        no tray insert/no man, stretchers or
        oxygen unit/*Sears* U64

6824   **USMC First Aid Medical Car** 60
     1. Painted olive drab and gray tray,   (4)   **225**
        white RS *USMC*, olive drab
        painted frame, tray insert, white
        HS 6824 on car. Came in
        Land, Sea, and Air Gift Pack 1805
6119-125 2. Same except white RS serif *Lionel*   (4)   **225▲**
        on black painted frame, no tray insert,
        no "6824"on tray. Came in *JC Penney*
        set 19334

Coal Dump Cars

3359-55 Lionel Lines Twin Dump 55-58   (3+)   **75**
     Black/red frame/two gray bins

3459   **Lionel Lines** 46-48
     1. Black/white   (2)   **75**
     2. Unpainted aluminum bin,   (3)   **500***
        blue lettering
     3. Same but blank on one side/FM   (4)   **450***
     4. Painted green bin, white lettering   (3)   **100**
     5. Painted yellow, black lettering   **5X**

3469   **Lionel Lines** 49-55 Black/white   (2)   **75**

3559   **Coal Dump** 46-48 Black/red   (2)   **50**

5459   **Electronic Set** 46-48 Black/wht/decal   (4)   **150**

Crane Cars

2460   **Bucyrus Erie** 46-50 6-wheel trucks
     1. Glossy gray cab/black lettering 46   (4)   **350▲**
     2. Black cab/white lettering 46-50   (2)   **100**

2560   **Lionel Lines** 46,47
     1. Green, brown or black   (2)   **75**
        Bakelite boom 46
     2. Black plastic boom 47   (2)   **75**

4460   **Bucyrus Erie** 50 6-wheel trucks   Never Made

6460   **Bucyrus Erie** 52-54
     1. Black cab/white lettering 52-54   (2)   **75**
     2. Red cab/white lettering 54   (3)   **90**
        (6460-25 on box)

6560   **Bucyrus Erie** 55-64,66,68,69
     1. Gray cab/black lettering   (2)   **100**
        Lionel used a screw to attach the trucks
        (not a horseshoe clip) on the first run.
        A number of different frames and cabs were
        used on these early versions. They were
        molded plastic in either an orange/red
        (4) **125** or black (5) **225**. A few had no
        printing at all on the frames or printing
        without the 6560 number
     2. Red cab/white lettering   (1)   **90**

6560-25 Bucyrus Erie Red/white 56   (3)   **110**

Depressed Center Cars

2461   **Transformer Car** 47-48
     1. Light gray/blk/red transformer/2462 (3+)   **90**
        RS on frame
     2. Same but no lettering *2461* RS   (4)   **250▲**
        on bottom
     3. Same as 1 but black transformer   (3)   **80**

6418   **Bridge Girder Car** 55-57 Gray
     Four 4-wheel trucks. O gauge only.
     Will not negotiate 027 switchers
     1. Orange girders/*Lionel* in   (3)   **100**
        raised letters
     2. Pinkish-orange girders/black   (2)   **100**
        US Steel
     3. Black girders/raised lettering   (3)   **100**
        US Steel

6461   **Transformer Car** 49 Gray/black   (3)   **85**
     Insulators usually broken. Repros are flexible.
     Originals are brittle and yellowed with age.
     Applies to 2461 also

6518   **Transformer Car** 56-58 Gray   (3+)   **110**
     Black transformer with white lettering.
     Four 4-wheel trucks. O gauge only.
     Will not negotiate 027 switches

6561   **Cable Car** 53-56 Gray/black lettering
     Two plastic reels wound with aluminum wire
     1. Orange reels   (2)   **75**
     2. Gray reels   (2)   **75**
     3. Dark gray reels   (3)   **85**

Flat Cars

1877 **Fence and Horses** 59-62
1. Brown/yellow, 2 each white, black (2) **65**
   and brown horses, plastic arch-
   bar trucks, 2 operating couplers
2. Same, Timken trucks (2) **75**

1887 **Fence and Horses** U60 *Sears* (4) **175**
Brown/yellow. Same as 1877, plastic
arch-bar trucks, 2 operating couplers

2411 **Big Inch Flat Car** 46-48 Light gray/black
Same frame as 2419 Work Caboose.
1. 46 and 47 came with metal pipes. (4) **125**
   Original pipes have ridge inside. Reproductions are smooth inside
2. In 47 and 48 came with 3 wood (2) **50**
   logs, stained or unstained

3460 **Flat with Trailers** 55-57 (2) **60**
Unpainted red/white, 2 dark green *Lionel
Trains* vans. Original vans have *Fruehauf*
labels lettered in back on a silver background

3512 **Operating Fireman and Ladder Car** 59-61
Unpainted red/white. Repro ladders available
Same ladders used on 494 Beacon Tower
1. Black ladder (2) **150**
2. Silver ladder (4) **225**

3545 **TV Car** 61,62 Black/white (4) **185**
Two men, yellow TV camera/blue base.

3545 Mock-up (See Vol. 5, p. 70) **5X**

6111/6121 Flat Car with Logs or Pipes 55-58
Steel-stamped car made in a number of
colors. HS lettering is either serif or non-serif,
the latter being harder to find. Add $5. Some
boxes stamped with different suffixes. NDV
1. Red/white (1) **25**
2. Yellow/black (1) **25**
3. Light, medium and dark gray/white (3) **40**

6151 **Range Patrol Truck** 58
White/black plastic *Range Patrol* truck
1. Orange/black (2) **100**
2. Light yellow/black (2) **100**
3. Dark yellow/black (2) **100**
4. Cream/black (4) **125**

6262 **Wheel Car** (8 pairs of wheels with axles) 56,57
1. Black/white, metal trucks (2) **75**
2. Red/white, metal trucks (5) **500▲**

6264 **Fork-Lift Car** 57-60 Red/white
Came with 264 Operating Fork Lift. Hard
to find in original box. Add $50
1. Plastic trucks (2) **75**
2. Metal trucks (2) **75**

6311 **Pipe Car** 55 Reddish brown/white (3) **65**

6343 **Barrel Ramp Car** 61,62 Red/white (2) **60**
6 stained barrels. Came in set 11222

6361 *See Log Car chapter*

6362 *See Special Load Car chapter*

6401-1 **Flat Car** 64 Gray no lettering (1) **5**
*Note: 6401-1 through 6406 are General-type flat
cars which came with a number of different loads.
All were unnumbered except 6404 and 6405.*

6402-25 **Flat Car** 64 Gray no lettering (2) **6**

6402 **Flat Car with Reels or Boat** 64,65,69
Gray plastic, *Timken* trucks, 1
operating and 1 non-operating coupler.
Known to come with the following loads
1. Blue and white boat (3) **100**
2. 2 Dark-orange cable reels (3) **75**
3. 2 Light-orange cable reels (3) **75**
   2 operating couplers

6404 **Auto** A60 Black/white/one auto
General-type flat car
1. Red auto/gray bumpers (2) **60**
2. Brown auto/gray bumpers (4) **400***

6405 **Flat with Trailer** 61 Maroon/yellow (3) **50**
Yellow van/no markings

6406 **Auto** U Tuscan or Gray Flat/no markings
1. Dark yellow auto/gray bumpers A61 (5) ***
2. Medium yellow auto/gray (4) **125**
   bumpers A61
3. Brown auto/gray bumpers U61-63 (4+) **400***
4. Green auto/gray bumpers U61-63 (4+) **400***

6407 *See Military and Space Chapter*

6409-25 **Flat Car with Pipes** 63 Red/white (2) **25**
No numbers

6411 **Flat Car** 48-50 Logs
1. Flat light gray/black (2) **30**
2. Glossy medium gray/black (4) **40**

6414 **Autoloader** 55-66
Flatcar (6511-2 mold) with black superstructure
added. Came with premium cars and cheapened
cars. The premium cars had bumpers,
windshields, axles and rubber tires. The
cheapened versions had no bumpers,
windshields, axles or tires.
1. Red/white, metal trucks, 6414 to (2) **125**
   right of *Lionel*. Red, white, blue
   and yellow premium cars.
2. Same with Timken trucks, 6414 (2) **125**
   to left of *Lionel*.
3. Same with 4 red premium cars, (4) **300**
   gray plastic bumpers
4. Same with 4 yellow premium cars, (4) **350**
   gray plastic bumpers
5. Same with 4 green premium cars, (5) **1800▼**
   gray plastic bumpers
6. Same with 4 brown premium cars, (5) **1800▼**
   gray plastic bumpers
7. 6414-85, 4 cheapened cars, 2 red (4) **750▼**
   2 yellow, 6414 on left
8. Decal on superstructure. 6414 (4) **500**
   on decal, not on flatcar. 4 red
   premium cars, gray plastic bumpers.
   Reproduction decals available.
9. Black/white **Fake**

6416 **Boatloader** 61-63 Red/white/black (4) **200**
*Note: Timken or Arch-bar trucks. NDV.
Car originally came with 4 boats. The boats
were made by Athearn and had a white
hull, blue top, and brown interior. Athearn
made the boat in a number of different
colors but only the blue/white boat came
with this car originally. In 1958, the same
boat (in red/white) was catalogued on the
HO gauge 0801 flatcar.*

6424 **2 Autos** 56-59 Two premium autos in a
number of the common colors. NDV
1. Black/white/plastic trucks (2) **60**
2. Red/white (5) **500***
3. Black/white/metal trucks (2) **60**

6430 **Piggy-Back Car** 56-58 Red/white
1. Metal trucks, 2 green 4-wheel vans, (3) **75**
   Lionel Trains plates
2. Same, 2 gray 4-wheel vans, (2) **75**
   Cooper Jarrett plates (aluminum
   background)
3. Same except white vans, black (2) **75**
   background on plates
4. Same except Timken trucks, 2 (5) **85**
   yellow 2-wheel vans, *Cooper Jarrett*
   plates (Aluminum background) and
   Fruehauf labels

6431 **Piggy-Back Car** 66 Red/white
Midge Toy Tractor and two white unmarked
vans. Some of the vans had holes on the
sides for a sign. Most didn't have holes.
1. Vans with holes for name plates (4+) **225**
2. Vans without holes (4) **175**
*Note: Midge Toy Tractor has been re-
issued by the Midge Toy Company*

6440 **Piggy-Back Van Car** 60-63 Red/white
1. 2 gray 2-wheel vans, no plates (2) **85**
   2 operating couplers
2. Same except 1 operating coupler (3) **85**
   1 non-operating coupler
3. Sears vans (Vol. 5, pg 59) **5P**

6467 **Miscellaneous Car** 56 Red/white/
black bulkheads stakes/metal trucks (2) **60**

6469 **Liquified Gas Car** 63 Red/white (4) **250**

6477 **Miscellaneous Car** 57,58 Red/white (2) **75**
Black bulkheads/5 plastic pipes

6500 **Bonanza Airplane Car** 62,63 Black/white
1. Airplane/red top/white bottom/ (4) **550▲**
   red wings
2. White top/red bottom/white wings (4+) **600▲**
*Note: Airplane reproductions exist.
Originals have Lionel Corp. in raised lettering*

6501 **Jet Boat Car** 62,63 Red/white (3) **150**
One white/brown boat

6502 **Girder Car** 62 Black/white (3) **60▼**
No number/light orange *Lionel* girder

6502-50 Girder Car A62 Blue/white (2) **50▼**
No lettering/dark orange *Lionel* girder

6502-75 Girder Car 64 Light blue/white (3) **60▼**
No lettering/dark orange *Lionel* girder

6511 Pipe Car 53-56
5 aluminum-colored plastic pipes
1. Red/white lettering (1) **35**
2. Brown/white lettering (3) **60**

6512 See Military and Space

6660 Boom Car 58 (3) **85**
Red/white, yellow boom on black metal base

6670 Derrick Car 59,60
1. *6670* to left of *Lionel* (3) **80**
2. *6670* to right of *Lionel* (4) **100**

6800 Airplane Car 57-60 Red/white
1. Airplane/black top/yellow bottom (4) **225**
2. Airplane/yellow top/black bottom (4+) **275**
Reproduction planes available

6801 Boat Car 57-60 Red/white
1. Boat – white hull/brown deck/6801 (3) **150**
2. Boat – yellow hull/wht deck/6801-50 (3) **150**
3. Boat – blue hull/white deck/6801-75 (3) **150**
Reproduction boats available

6802 US Steel Girder 58,59 Red/white (2) **65**
Black *US Steel* girders come
w/ and w/o 6418. NDV

6810 Piggy-Back Car 58 (3) **60**
Red/white, one 4-wheel white van,
Cooper Jarrett plates (black background)

6812 Track Maintenance Car 59-61 Red/white
Bases and tops are interchangeable.
Repro men available.
1. Dark yellow base and top (2) **100**
2. Black base, gray top (2) **100**
3. Gray base, black top (2) **100**
4. Cream base and top (4+) **250***
5. Light yellow base and top (4) **200***

6816 Allis Chalmers Bulldozer Car 59,60
1. Red/white
  a. Light orange bulldozer, *Allis* (4) **600**
    Chalmers in black
  b. Dark-orange bulldozer, *Allis* (4) **600**
    Chalmers in white
2. Black/white (5) **800▲**

6817 Allis Chalmers Scraper Car 59,60
1. Red/white, light orange scraper (4) **600**
2. Red/white, dark orange scraper, (4) **800▲**
   wire windshield, white *Allis Chalmers*
3. Black/white (5) **800▲**

6818 Transformer Car 58 (2) **75**
Red/white, black transformer

6821 Crate Car 59,60 (2) **40**
Red/white, tan crates

6825 Trestle Bridge Car 59-62 Red/white (2) **75**
Black trestle/same trestle came in gray

6826 Christmas Tree Car 59,60 Red/white (4) **200**
Price assumes original trees which were
kind of pitiful looking.

6827 P&H Steam Shovel (kit) 60-63 Black/white
1. Dark yellow steam shovel (4) **200**
2. Light yellow steam shovel (4) **200**

6828 P&H Crane (kit) 60-63, 66
1. Black/white flatcar (4) **250**
2. Red/white flatcar (4+) **800▲**
Crane came in both light yellow and
dark yellow. NDV
*Note: 6827 and 6828 came with booklet depicting
the history of P&H. Among the many fascinating
tidbits is the derivation of P&H. The P is for Alonzo
Pawling and the H is for Henry Harnischfeger.
Came with light or dark yellow crane. NDV*

Gondolas

1002 Lionel Scout 48-52
1. Blue/white (2) **20**
2. Black/white (1) **10**
3. Yellow/black, knuckle couplers (4) **400***
4. Silver/black, knuckle couplers (4) **400***
5. Red/white, knuckle couplers (4) **400***

2452 Pennsylvania 45-47 Black/white
Brakewheels, sometimes came with barrels
1. Regular wheels (1) **15**
2. Whirly wheels (4) **40**
3. Dished-out wheels (4) **40**
4. Stamped 6462 rather than 2452 **X**

2452X Pennsylvania 46,47 Black/white (1) **20**
2452X stamped on frame

4452 Pennsylvania *Electronic Set* 46-48 (4) **100**

6002 Gondola 50 Black/white (3) **15**

6012 Lionel 51-56 Black/white (1) **5**

6032 Lionel 52,53 (1) **5**

6042 Lionel U59-61
1. Black unpainted/white (1) **5**
2. Blue painted/white (1) **5**

6062 New York Central 59-64 Black/white (1) **10**

6062-50 New York Central 69 Black/white (2) **10**

6112 Lionel 56-58 Black/white 4 red cannisters
1. Black/white (1) **10**
2. Blue unpainted/white (1) **10**
3. White/black (4) **30**

6142 Lionel 61-66 Black/white (1) **5**

6162 NYC 61-63 Blue/white (1) **10**

6162-60 Alaska 59
1. Yellow/blue (3) **65**
2. Tan/blue **X**

6162-110 NYC 64-69 2 red cannisters
1. Blue/white (2) **10**
2. Red /white (4) **150▲**

6342 NYC 56-58,64-69 Red/white (3) **45**
Goes with Culvert Loader

6452 Pennsylvania 48,49 Black/white
1. 6462 on side, 48 (3) **35**
  6452 stamped on base
2. 6452 on side and base, 49 (2) **20**

6462-500 NYC Pink/blue Girl's Train (4) **175**

6462 New York Central 49-56
1. Black/white (1) **10**
2. Red/white (1) **10**
3. Green/white (2) **10**
4. Painted orange (Vol. 5, p. 95) **5X**
5. Painted gold **5X**
6. Gray/black **5X**
7. Gray/white **5X**
8. Gray/red **5X**
9. Glossy green/white **5X**
10. Blue/black **5X**

6562 NYC 56-58
1. Gray/maroon (2) **50**
2. Red/white (2) **50**
3. Black/white (2) **50**
4. Gray/red (3) **60**

Hoppers

2456 Lehigh Valley 48
1. Matte black/white (3) **75**
2. Glossy black/white (4) **90**

2856/2956 B&O 46,47 Black/white (4) **300**
*Note: This was the prewar 2956 which was cataloged in 46
and 47 in gray with postwar trucks and the number 2856.
2856 was never made but some black 2956 hoppers turn up
with postwar trucks. Whether Lionel or a service station or a
customer put the trucks on, no one knows. But it's a nice car
anyway.*

3456 Norfolk & Western 50-55 Black/white
Operating bottom hatches/came
with 456 Coal Ramp
1. Corner braces (2) **75**
2. No corner braces (3) **90**

6076 Lehigh Valley U63
1. Gray/black (1) **15**
2. Black/white (1) **15**
3. Red/white (1) **15**
4. Yellow/black (3) **20**

6076 AT&SF U63 Gray/black (1) **10**

6076 AT&SF TTOS Convention Car (4) **50**
(overstamped)

6176 Lehigh Valley 64-66, 69
1. Different shades of yellow with blk (1) **10**
  or blue lettering
2. Gray/black (1) **10**
3. Black/white (1) **10**
4. Black/gray (2) **10**

6176-100 Unpainted Olive drab/no lettering (4) **100**

6176-1967 TTOS Convention Car 67 (4) **65**

6346-56 Alcoa 56 Silver/blue
Quad/hatch covers/no center brace hole
1. Silver/blue HS (2) 85
2. Silver/red HS X
3. Silver/blue decal 5P

6436-1 Lehigh Valley 55 Black/white
1. No spreader bar holes (3) 75
2. Spreader bar and holes (2) 65

6436-25 Lehigh Valley 55-57 Maroon/white (2) 65
No covers/spreader bar

6436-110 Lehigh Valley 63-68 Red/white 63-66,68
1. *Built Date 3/5/63* (4) 100
2. No built date 63,64-66,68 (2) 50

6436-500 Lehigh Valley Girl's Set 57,58 (4) 400
Lilac/maroon/w or w/o spreader bar holes

6436-1969 TCA Convention Car U 69 Red/wht (4) 150
Spreader bar/no cover

6446-1 N&W Hopper Gray/black covered 54,55,57,63
1. 546446 on car, 1954 (2) 75
2. 6446-25 on car, 1955,57 (2) 75
3. 6446-25 on car/spreader bar/plastic (4) 150
AAR trucks, 1963

6446-25 N&W Black/white covered
1. 54-6446 on car (2) 75
2. 6446-25 on car (2) 75

6446-25 Norfolk & Western 55-57
Specials made for *N&W RR*
1. Gold/white 5P
2. Pink/black 5P
3. Light blue/white 5P
4. Silver/white 5P

6446-60 Lehigh Valley 63 Red/white covered (4) 350

6456 Lehigh Valley 48-55
1. Black/white 49-51 (1) 10
2. Maroon/white 51 (2) 20
3. Gray/maroon 54 (2) 20
4. Glossy red/yellow 55 (4) 200
5. Glossy red/white 55 (5) 700▲
6. Gray/white X

6476 Lehigh Valley 57-69
1. Unpainted red plastic/white 57 (1) 10
2. Unpainted black plastic/white 57 (2) 10
3. Unpainted gray plastic/black 57 (3) 15
Note: Made through 1969 in many different colors,
some with road names and some without, cataloged
and uncataloged. None are worth more than $20.

6476-1 TTOS 69 Convention Car (4) 60

6476-125 Lehigh Valley 64 Yellow/black (2) 15
Note: 6176 on car

6476-135 Lehigh Valley 68,69 (2) 10
Unpainted mustard yellow plastic/red

6536 Minneapolis & St. Louis 58,59,63
1. Red/white 58,59 (3) 85
2. Shinier Red/white 63 (3+) 95

6636 Alaska 59,60 Black/yellow (3+) 90

6736 Detroit & Mackinac 60-62
1. Red/white (3) 60
2. Red/white, *Mackinac Mac's* face (4) 75
filled in due to flaw in die

Log Cars

2411 Big Inch Flat Car 46-48 Light gray/black
Same frame as 2419 Work Caboose.
1. In 46 & 47 came with metal pipes. (4) 125
Original pipes have ridge inside. Reproductions are smooth inside
2. In 47 & 48 came with 3 wood logs, (2) 50
stained or unstained

3361-55 Log Dump 55-59 Gray/black (2) 50
Variations: different shades of gray;
different types of lettering. NDV
This car is a 6362 rail car with a dumping
mechanism added

3362 Helium Tank Unloading 61-63
Dark green/white/3 silver-painted wood tanks
1. White lettering (3) 70
2. No lettering or data (3) 70
Note: It is easy to remove the RS lettering
and leave no trace

3364 Operating Log Dump Car 65-69 (2) 60
Dark green/white with 3 dark stained logs
Note: Same car as 3362 but with logs. Catalog
showed picture of 3362 but listed 3364. In 1969,
box stamped 3362/3364; no number on car. NDV

3451 Log Dump 46,47 Black/white 5 unstained logs
1. Rubber-stamped (3) 60
2. Heat-stamped (2) 50

3461 Log Dump 49-55
1. Black/white RS & HS 49-54 (2) 50
2. Green/white/dark logs 54,55 (3) 80
Note: Logs stained dark for the first
time in 54

6361 Timber Transport Car 60,61, 64-69
Green/white
1. Black chains (3) 75
2. Gold chains (4) 125▲
Note: Gold chain version believed to come
from Madison Hardware

Merchandise Cars

3454 PRR Merchandise Car 46,47
1. Silver/blue (3) 150
2. Silver/red (5) 1000▲
Note: Baby Ruth on original cartons but
not on reproductions.

3854 Pennsylvania 46,47 Dark brown/white 11" long
1. Brown door 46 only (4+) 600
2. Black door 46,47 (4) 500

Refrigerator Cars
Operating

3462 Milk Car 47,48 Unpainted aluminum doors
1. Glossy wht/brass-base mechanism (4) 175▲
2. Dull white/later mechanism (2) 60

3472 Milk Car 49-53
1. Metal doors 49 only (3) 75
2. Plastic doors (2) 65

3482 Milk Car 54,55
1. 3472 lower right/early production (3) 100
2. 3482 lower right (2) 75

3662-1 Milk Car 55-60, 64-66 White/brown
1. Built date/55-60 (3) 90
2. No built date/64-66 (3+) 125

3672 Bosco 59,60 Yellow/Tuscan
1. Painted yellow (4) 350
2. Yellow plastic (3) 300

Non-Operating

6472 Milk Car 50-53 Dull white (2) 45

6482 Milk Car 57 White (4) 85

6572 Railway Express 58,59,U64
1. Dark green/metal trucks 58.59 (4) 125
2. Light green *Madison Hardware* U64 (2) 90
Plastic trucks

6672 Santa Fe 54-56 White/brown non-operating
1. Black lettering/L in circle (3+) 100
2. Same but no L in circle (3+) 100
3. Blue lettering/L in circle (3) 75
4. Blue/3 lines of data right of door (5) 500*
Note: Roof came in both a reddish and
chocolate shade of brown. NDV

Special Load Cars

6362-55 Railway Truck Car 55, 56 Orange/blk (2) 50
Load: 3 trucks only/no couplers

6428 US Mail 60, 61, 65, 66
Red/white/blue w/HS Black/white lettering
1. Lettering on both sides (3) 45
2. Lettering on one side (Fakes Made) (4) 75

6445 Fort Knox Car 61-63 Aluminum/black (3) 125

6475 Libby's Crushed Pineapple U63 (3) 100
Blue/white, 4 vats with silver labels
Red and blue lettering
Note: Car comes in different shades of blue. NDV

6475 Pickle Car 60-62 Tan/brown/green
1. Slats on pickle vats (2) 75
2. No slats on pickle vats (4) 150

6475 Heinz 57 Pickle Car X
Tan/brown/green

6519 Allis Chalmers Condenser Car 58-61
1. Light orange/blue/gray condenser (2) 75▲
2. Dark orange/blue/gray condenser (3) 100▲

| 6530 | Fire Safety Training Car 60, 61
Red/white | (3) | 75 |

Searchlight Cars

| 3520 | Lionel Lines 52,53 Gray/black | (2) | 75 |
| | Orange generator/gray searchlight/on-off switch/serif and non-serif lettering. NDV | | |

3530	Operating Generator Car 56-58		
	1. Orange generator	(3+)	200
	2. Gray generator	(5)	*
	Note: The base of pole came in black (common), blue (hard to find) and yellow (rare). Some fuel tanks are black and some are blue. On some cars the white stripe goes through the ladder (long stripe) and on others it does not (short stripe).		

3620	Lionel Lines 54-56 Gray/black		
	1. Searchlight gray plastic	(2)	50
	2. Searchlight orange plastic painted gray	(4)	100
	3. Searchlight orange plastic		X
	Note: Shown in 54 catalog, p. 20. Beware of painted gray version with the paint removed		

3650	Lionel Lines Extension Searchlight 56-59		
	1. Gray frame/black	(3)	85
	2. Dark gray frame/black	(4)	175

6520	Lionel Lines 49-51 Gray/black/gray housing		
	Same die-cast depressed-center frame as 2461		
	1. Green generator 49	(4)	350▲
	2. Orange generator	(2)	65
	3. Unpainted gray generator		*
	4. Unpainted maroon generator	(3)	75
	5. Tan generator	(5)	325*
	Note: Some cars may have faded orange generators and black housings. NDV		

6822	Lionel 61-69 Red/white		
	1. Gray searchlight housing	(2)	60
	2. Black searchlight housing	(3)	75

Stock Cars

3356	Operating Horse Car and Corral	(3)	175
	56-60, 64-66 Green/yellow		
	Car only	(2)	75

3366	Circus and 3356-150 Corral 59-62	(4)	325▲
	White/red		
	Car only	(3)	150

3656	Armour Stock Car 49-55 Orange		
	Includes cattle and corral		
	1. Black lettering/*Armour* sticker 49	(4)	225▲
	2. White lettering/*Armour* 49,50	(3)	100
	3. White lettering/no *Armour* 50-55	(2)	85

| 6356-1 | NYC 54,55 Yellow/black | (2) | 50 |

| 6376 | Lionel Lines Circus Car 56,57
White/red | (2+) | 85 |

| 6434 | Poultry 58,59 Red/white/gray doors | (3) | 75 |

| 6473 | See Action Cars | | |

| 6556 | Katy 58 Red/white
Set 2513W headed by 2329 Virginian | (4) | 275 |

| 6646 | Lionel Lines 57 Orange/black | (3) | 50 |

6656	Lionel Lines 50-55 Yellow/black		
	1. *Armour* sticker 50	(4)	100
	2. No *Armour* sticker 50-55	(2+)	30

Tank Cars

Early

| 2555 | Sunoco 46-48 Aluminum
Same car as the 2755 | (3) | 85 |

| 2755 | Sunoco 45 Aluminum
Prewar tank car with postwar trucks | (4) | 200 |

2855	Sunoco 46,47 Black		
	1. Gas-Oil in decal 46	(4)	250▲
	2. No Gas-Oil 47	(4+)	300▲

| 2855 | Sunoco 47 Gray No Gas-Oil in decal | (4+) | 300▲ |

| 6555 | Sunoco 49,50 Silver/black | (3) | 80 |

Two-Dome

2465	Sunoco 46-48 Silver		
	1. Black lettering/decal in center 46	(4)	300▲
	2. Same but decal off to one side 46	(1)	15
	3. Blue lettering 47	(2)	25
	4. Silk screening 48	(2)	25

| 6045 | Lionel Lines 58-63 | (1) | 20 |

| 6045 | Cities Service U60 Green/white
Non-operating couplers | (2) | 40 |

| 6463 | Rocket Fuel 62,63 White/red | (3) | 50 |

| 6465 | Sunoco 48-56 Silver | (1) | 15 |
| | *Note: Common car with lots of variations, none of which are worth more than $15.* | | |

6465	Gulf 58		
	1. Unpainted black plastic tank	(3)	100
	2. Painted black plastic tank	(3)	100
	3. Painted gray plastic tank	(3)	100

| 6465 | Lionel Lines 58,59
Gray, orange or black. NDV | (1) | 25 |

| 6465 | Cities Service 60-62 Green/white
Operating couplers | (3) | 50 |

| 6465-60 | Gulf 58 Gray/blue/black | (2) | 50 |

Three-Dome

| 6415 | Sunoco 53-55 Silver/black | (1) | 25 |

| 6425 | Gulf 56-58 Silver/blue | (2) | 45 |

Single-Dome

6315	Gulf 56-59,66-69		
	1. Glossy orange/black tank	(3)	60
	2. Flat orange/black tank	(3)	60
	3. Solid orange tank	(2)	50
	4. Solid orange tank with *6315 Chemical Tank Car* on ends	(2)	50

| 6315 | Lionel Lines 63-65 Orange/black
Plastic trucks | (2) | 50 |

6315-60	Lionel Lines 63,64		
	1. Unpainted orange plastic no built date	(3)	40
	2. Same as 1 with built date	(4)	60
	3. Painted orange	(4)	50

Scout Type

| 1005 | Sunoco 48-50 Gray tank
Single-dome | (1) | 10 |

| 6015 | Sunoco 54,55 | (1) | 12 |

| 6025 | Gulf 56,57 | (1) | 12 |

| 6035 | Sunoco 52,53 | (1) | 12 |

1965-1967 TCA Convention Cars

Note: Special 6464 cars with brass and aluminum doors made for the Train Collecters Association. Fakes have turned up. Check the doors. The inside of the doors on originals is aluminum, outside is brass. On fakes, the doors are all brass.

TCA 1965 Convention Cars

| 6464-1965 | TCA Pittsburgh | (5) | 300 |

| 6464-1965X | Pittsburgh | (5) | 350 |

TCA 1966 Convention Cars

| 6517-1966 | TCA Bay Window Caboose | (4) | 500 |

TCA 1967 Convention Cars

| 6464-250 | Western Pacific (159 made) | (5) | 350 |

| 6464-375 | Central of Georgia (100 made) | (5) | 350 |

| 6464-475 | Boston & Maine Decal version | | 5P |

| 6464-475 | Boston & Maine (3 made) | | 5X |

| 6464-525 | Minneapolis & St. Louis (7 made) | | 5X |

| 6464-650 | Denver & Rio Grande Western (137 made) | (5) | 350 |

| 6464-700 | A.T. & S.F. (92 made) | (5) | 350 |

| 6464-735 | New Haven (3 made) | | 5X |

| 6464-900 | New York Central (2 made) | | 5X |

Operating Accessories

30   **Water Tower** 47-50
1. Brown roof, black superstructure/   (4)   **195**
   doubled-walled tank, fill hole in roof,
   30 RS in black on base
2. Red roof, brown superstructure/   (3+)   **135**
   singled-walled tank, fill hole in roof,
   30 RS in black on base
3. Same as 2, gray roof   (3+)   **135**
   brown superstructure
4. Gray roof, brown superstructure   (3)   **125**
   single-walled tank, no fill hole, no RS number

38   **Water Tower** 46,47 Clear, plastic funnel
and packet of water coloring tablets
1. Red roof   (4)   **350▲**
2. Brown roof   (4+)   **375▲**

93   **Water Tower** 46-49   (3)   **45**
Aluminum/red base/black spout

97   **Coal Elevator** 46-50   (3)   **175**
Yellow bunker with red roof/black Bakelite
base/with controller/classic *Lionel* accessory

114   **Newsstand with Horn** 57-59   (3)   **200**
Yellow building/silver roof/brown base

118   **Newsstand with Whistle** 58   (3)   **100**
Yellow/silver/brown base

125   **Whistle Shack** 50-55 Similar to 145 Automatic
Gateman with whistle White sides/red roof
1. Light or dark gray base   (2)   **50**
2. Green base   (3)   **65**

128   **Animated Newsstand** 57-60   (3)   **165**
Green/red/tan base/came with newspaper
inserted in boy's hand/reissued by
Fundimensions in 82 as 2308

138   **Water Tower** 53-57 Brn tank& frame
Gray base/black operating spout
1. Gray roof/53 only   (4)   **125**
2. Orange roof/54-57   (3)   **100**

161   **Mail Pick-Up Set** 61-63   (4)   **100**
Tan base/red bag holder/gray painted bag
with magnet plus second magnet to be glued
to car. Price assumes second magnet

164   **Log Loader** 46-50 Green/yellow/red   (3)   **250**
with two-button controller. Classic

175   **Rocket Launcher** 58-60   (4)   **225**
Price assumes complete with 175-50 rocket,
counter, tower and crane. Repro rockets avail.

182   **Magnet Crane** 46-49   (4)   **225**
With 165C controller/black base/aluminum-
painted frame/2460 crane car

192   **Operating Control Tower** 59,60   (3)   **200**
Yellow tower/green frame/gray base/
beware of heat damage to roof/usually found
with top piece missing/reissued in 84 as 2316

193   **Industrial Water Tower** 53-55 Green shed/
gray base/silver top with red flashing light
1. Red superstructure   (2)   **100**
2. Black superstructure   (4)   **140**

197   **Rotating Radar Antenna** 58,59 Black plastic
gridwork/*Lionel* in orange letters
1. Gray platform   (3)   **100**
2. Orange platform   (3+)   **110**

199   **Microwave Relay Tower** 58,59   (3+)   **75**
Gray tower/white antenna/base inter-
changeable with 195 Floodlight Tower

264   **Operating Fork Lift Platform** 57-60   (4)   **275**
Black base/brown deck area/orange lift
truck with blue man/white crane/red 6264
with lumber. Excellent performer

282   **Gantry Crane** 54,55 Gray frame/black
superstructure/white lettering/3 lever
controller. 282C comes with both gray
glued-on smokestack and black
smokestack molded in plastic. NDV
1. Black magnet 54   (3)   **225**
2. Nickel plated magnet,   (4)   **250**
   molded black 6560 cab minus wire
   detailing on boom 55

282R   **Gantry Crane** 56,57 Same as 282   (3)   **225**
with modified motor and platform/282R on cab
with gray smokestack molded in plastic

299   **Code Transmitter Beacon Set** 61-63 (3)   **125**

334   **Operating Dispatching Board** 57-60 (3)   **225**
Green board/tan base/blue man

342   **Culvert Loader** 56-58   (4)   **250**
Black metal base/red/gray building/
operates with 345 and 6342 culvert car

345   **Culvert Unloading Station** 57-59   (4)   **325▲**
Black metal base/gray ramp/red-gray
tower/operates with 342 and 6342

346   **Culvert Unloader** U64,65 *Sears*   (4+)   **225**
Manual identical to 348/9836 set with
2347 C&O GP-7/hand operated with crank

347   **Cannon Firing Range Set** U64   (4+)   **550***
Olive drab/4 cannons/4 silver shells
9820 *Sears* Military Set

348   **Culvert Unloader** 66-69   (4)   **225**
Manual 348s are 346s with a piece of tape,
348 rubber-stamped on it placed over the
346 number on the box

350   **Engine Transfer Table** 57-60   (4)   **325**
Black metal base/yellow building/red light
on top/with 350-89 rail brackets

350-50   **Transfer Table Extension** 57-60   (4)   **200**
Black metal base/with 350-898 rail brackets

352   **Ice Depot** 55-57 White shed/red roof/blue
man with orange arms and paddle/with
6352-1 car
1. Brown base   (4+)   **250**
2. Red base   (4)   **225**

362   **Barrel Loader** 52-57 Gray base/yellow ramp
brown plastic fence/cream or blue man. NDV
1. Gray molded plastic base   (3)   **125**
2. Painted gray base   (3+)   **125**

364   **Conveyor Lumber Loader** 48-54
1. Painted gray (smooth)   (3)   **125**
2. Painted crackle gray   (3+)   **125**

375   **Turntable** 62-64 Battery operated   (4)   **225**

397   **Diesel Operating Coal Loader** 48-57
Gray metal base/red tray
1. Yellow motor cover/yard light   (5)   **400**
2. Blue motor cover/no yard light   (2)   **150**

413   **Countdown Control Panel** 62 Gray   (3)   **50**
Can be used to operate any operating car

415   **Diesel Fueling Station** 55-67   (3)   **175**
White/red/gray base/blue tank/white

419   **Heliport Control Tower** 62   (4)   **350▲**
Red tower/gray roof/spring mechanism/
yellow dish/yellow-black copter/one-piece prop

443   **Missile Launching Platform** 60-62   (3)   **65**
Blue launcher on tan base/with ammo dump

445   **Switch Tower** 52-57 Two blue men   (2)   **85**
White tower/green roof/maroon base

448   **Missile Firing Range Set** 61-63   (3)   **85**
Gray launcher/tan base/6448 Target car

455   **Oil Derrick** 50-54 Red base/green tower
1. Green top   (3)   **175**
2. Red top   (4)   **250▲**

456   **Coal Ramp** 50-55 with 3456 *N&W* Operating
Hopper/designed to operate with 397 Coal
Loader/red light/456C controller/red tray
1. Dark gray ramp   (3)   **190**
2. Light gray ramp   (2)   **190**

460   **Piggyback Transportation** 55-57
Came with 2 versions of lift trucks
1. White heat-stamped lettering   (3)   **125**
2. Black stick-on label/white lettering   (2)   **125**
Note: Must have lift truck driver.

460P   **Piggyback Platform** 55-57   (5)   **125**
460P on box

461   **Platform with Truck and Midge** U66 (4)   **150**
Gray base/white *Midge Toy* trailer

462   **Derrick Platform Set** 61,62   (4)   **225▲**
Tan base/yellow crane/3 black cranks

464   **Lumber Mill** 56-60 Gray base/red roof (2)   **125**
Reissued as 2301 in 1980/original has
464 in window

470   **Missile Launching Platform** 59-62   (2)   **85**
Tan base/blue launcher/6470 Target car

497   **Coaling Station** 53-58
1. Dark green roof/metal brace   (4)   **250**
2. Dark green roof/no brace   (3)   **200**
3. Light green roof/no brace   (3)   **200**

Trackside Accessories, Street Lamps, Light Towers

35	**Boulevard Lamp** 45-49		
	1. Aluminum	(2)	10
	2. Gray	(3)	15

45	**Gateman** 46-49 White/red/green base	(2)	45

45N	**Gateman** 45 White/red/green base	(2)	45

56	**Lamp Post** 46-49 2 Shades of green. NDV	(2)	40

58	**Goose Neck Lamp Post** 46-50 Ivory, diecast	(2)	40

65	**Highway Lamp Post** Green 45-49 diecast, uses L452W bulb. Make sure bulb lights	(3)	60

70	**Yard Lamp** 49,50 Black, swivel light/ round, Bakelite base/came with early versions of the 397 coal loader	(4)	65

71	**Lamp Post** 49-59 Gray, diecast	(2)	30

75	**Goose Neck Lamps** 61-73 Black. (2 in set box) Price for 2	(2)	45

76	**Boulevard Street Lamps** 55-66,68,69 Dark green, unpainted plastic/3 in set box. Price for 3	(1)	20

89	**Flagpole** 56-58 with *Lionel* pennant White pole/tan base/*American Flag*	(4)	65

140	**Automatic Banjo Signal** 54-56 Black with operating arm	(2)	50

145	**Automatic Gateman** 50-66 White/red or maroon roof/green metal base/ white, plastic crossbuck/red-gold *Lionelville* sticker above door/Gateman either unpainted blue plastic or painted with flesh-colored hands and face. NDV	(1)	50

148	**Dwarf Trackside Light** 57-60 Tan/blk (4) Requires 148C switch for operation/reissued in 1984 as 2115		90▼

150	**Telegraph Pole Set** 47-50 Set of 6 brown, plastic poles with track clips	(3)	45

151	**Semaphore** 47-69 Operating plastic blade/ painted yellow tip with red/green translucent plastic inserts		
	1. Black base/painted aluminum pole	(1)	50
	2. Blk base/unpainted aluminum pole	(3)	60
	3. Green base/painted aluminum pole	(2)	60

152	**Automatic Crossing Gate** 45-49 Red, diecast base with pedestrian gate	(1)	50

153	**Automatic Block Control** 45-69 Green Controls two trains on single loop	(1)	50
	1. Painted aluminum pole	(1)	40
	2. Unpainted aluminum pole	(2)	50

154	**Automatic Highway Signal** 45-59		
	1. Black base, diecast sign	(1)	50
	2. Orange base, diecast sign	(4)	100▲
	3. Black base with plastic sign	(1)	50

155	**Blinking Light Signal Bell** 55-57 (2) Black/white plastic base contains bell/ same lights as 154		40

163	**Single Target Block Signal** 61-69 Blk (2)		40

195	**Floodlight Tower** 57-66,69 (2) Tan base/gray tower/8 lights/8 light extension designed to be clipped to other side		75

195-75	**Eight-bulb Extension for 195**	(4)	25

252	**Automatic Crossing Gate** 50-62,63 (1) Black base/black-white gate		35

253	**Block Control Signal** 56-59 (3) Tan base/black control box/white pole		40

262	**Highway Crossing Gate** 62-66,69		
	1. Black/white gate	(1)	50
	2. Red/white gate	(4)	60

308	**Railroad Sign Set** 45-49 (1) Five die-cast signs		25

309	**Yard Sign Set** 50-59 (1) 12 plastic signs with diecast bases/orange box with blue letters		25

310	**Billboard Set** 50-68 with 3 different billboards		
	1. Green frame	(1)	5
	2. Yellow frame	(5)	50*
	3. Red frame	(5)	75*

353	**Trackside Control Signal** 60,61 (1) Tan/white/black		25

394	**Rotary Beacon** 49-53		
	1. Tower sheet metal painted red	(2)	50
	2. Same painted green	(3)	115
	3. Tower unpainted aluminum	(3)	75
	4. Tower sheet metal painted aluminum	(2)	50
	5. Aluminum/red base	(4)	100

395	**Floodlight Tower** 49,50,52-56		
	1. Green painted tower	(3)	85
	2. Yellow painted tower	(4)	150▲
	3. Silver painted tower	(2)	50
	4. Red painted tower	(3)	100
	5. Unpainted aluminum	(2)	50

410	**Billboard Blinker** 56-58 Black (2) Designed to go with 310 billboard		50

450	**Signal Bridge** 52-58 Spans 2 tracks (3) Gray base/black metal gridwork/2 lights		90

452	**Gantry Signal** 61-63 (4) Gray base/black metal gridwork		175▼

494	**Rotary Beacon** 54-66 Black base		
	1. Red tower	(3)	50
	2. Unpainted aluminum tower	(3)	50
	3. Painted aluminum tower	(3)	50

920	**Scenic Display Set** 57,58	(3)	100

920-2	**Tunnel Portals** 57	(3)	50

970	**Ticket Booth** 58-60	(3)	100

1045	**Operating Watchman** 46-50 (2) Red base/blue man with flesh-colored hands and face/aluminum pole/nickel or brass RR warning sign. NDV		50

1047	**Operating Switchman** 59-61 (4) Green metal base/blue switchman with red flag/blue or black fuel tank on base. NDV		200▼

Bridges

214	**Girder Plate Bridge** 53-69 (1) *LIONEL* on sides. Turns up with *US Steel* girders from 6418. NDV		15

313	**Bascule Bridge** 46-49 (3+) Green base/yellow/red shack/black alignment frame/aluminum bridge		500

314	**Plate Girder Bridge** 45-48,50 Gray (3) Sheet metal base/diecast sides		20

315	**Trestle Bridge** 46,47 Aluminum (3) Illuminated		100

316	**Trestle Bridge** Gray same as 315	(2)	40

317	**Trestle Bridge** 50-56 Gray same as 315	(3)	25

321	**Trestle Bridge** 58-64 Aluminum (2) Sheet metal base/gray plastic sides		15

332	**Arch Under Bridge** 59-66 (2) Black metal span/gray plastic sides		50

902	**Lionel Elevated Trestle Set** 59	(4)	65

Stations

115	**Lionel City Station** 46-49 Prewar (4) carry-over Cream/red/red base with auto train stop		350

132	**Passenger Station** 49-55 Illuminated (2) White/green/maroon base/auto train stop		70

133	**Passenger Station** 57,61,62,66 (2) White/green/maroon roof, Illuminated		70

156	**Station Platform** 46-49 Illuminated (3) Green base/red roof/diecast posts/picket fence with signs/also prewar 155, 39-42		95

157	**Station Platform** 58,59 Green roof/illuminated Black metal posts/signs		
	1. Maroon base	(3)	70
	2. Molded, red base	(4)	100

256	**Freight Station** 50-53 (2) Maroon/white/green, Picket fence with billboards		50

257	**Freight Station** 56,57 Diesel horn Same as 256 with battery-powered horn and control button		
	1. Maroon base	(2)	90
	2. Brown base	(4)	100

356	**Operating Freight Station** 52-57 Maroon/white Picket fence with signs/two blue baggage men with carts/green, orange, or red carts known to exist/some baggage loads lithographed. NDV		
	1. Dark green roof	(2)	90
	2. Light green roof	(4)	125▲
365	**Dispatch Station** 59	(3)	120
465	**Sound Dispatching Station** 56,57 Tan base/red room/gray roof/yellow dish/ with gray microphone	(2)	125

Replacement Accessories

Note: These were the smaller items, such as the cans for the operating milk car, that were often lost or broken. Lionel sold replacements, usually in a group, which came in their own boxes or other packages. Each box had its own catalog number. Most items are extremely hard to find. Values and rarity ratings are based on the items being in their original packaging.

L363	**Miniature Lamps**	(3)	15
L461	**Miniature Lamps**	(3)	15
SP	**Smoke Pellets** 48-69 (box of 12)	(4)	150
0209	**Six Small Barrels**	(1)	10
40	**Box of 8 Cable Reels**	(4)	100
44-80	**Four Missiles** (envelope) 59-60	(2)	15
47-73	**12-Volt Red Lamps** (box of 12)	(4)	25
55-150	**24 Ties for Tie-Jector** 59,60 (envelope)	(3)	15
64-15	**12-Volt Opal Lamps** (box of 12)	(4)	25
111-50	**Trestle Set**	(5)	250
111-100	**Two Trestle Tiers** (envelope) 60	(3)	7
122	**Lamp Assortment Kit**	(4)	65
123-60	**Lamp Assortment Kit**	(5)	25
152-33	**12-Volt Red Lamps** (box of 12)	(4)	25
153-23	**6-8-Volt Red Lamps** (box of 12)	(4)	25
160	**Unloading Bin** 52-55	(1)	5
164-64	**Five Logs** 52-58	(1)	15
165-53	**18-Volt Red Lamps** (box of 12)	(4)	25
175-50	**Rocket** (zip-lock plastic bag) 58-60	(4)	100
196	**Smoke Pellets** 46,47 Complete in display box	(5)	100
197-75	**Radar Head** 58-60	(4)	35
216	**Miniature Lamps**	(3)	15
264-150	**Twelve Boards for Forklift Platform** (envelope) 57-59	(3)	15

352-55	**Seven Ice Cubes for Icing Station** (envelope) 55-57	(4)	35
356-35	**Two Baggage Trucks** 52-56	(1)	35
362-78	**Six Barrels** 52-58	(1)	15
450L	**Signal Light Head** 52-58	(2)	25
460-150	**Two Piggyback Vans** 55-57 (either two white or two green vans)	(3)	45
464-150	**Six Boards for Lumber Mill** (envelope) 56-58	(3)	15
671-75	**Smoke Lamps**	(4)	75
703-10	**Smoke Lamp**	(5)	50
909	**Smoke Fluid** 58-69 (box of 4)	(2)	75
925	**Lubricant** 53-69 (with box)	(3)	35
1640-100	**1960 Presidential Special Kit** 60 To be attached to 2400 Series passenger cars	(3)	125
3330-100	**Operating Submarine Kit** 60	(3)	500
3356-100	**Nine Horses** 56-59	(2)	25
3356-150	**Horse Corral** 56,57	(4)	100
3357-27	**Components for Cop & Hobo Car**	(4)	25
3366-100	**Nine White Horses** 59,60	(3)	35
3424-100	**Two Tel-tale Poles** 56-58	(1)	25
3462P	**Milk Car Platform** 52-55	(2)	15
3462-70	**Seven Magnetic Milk Cans** 52-59	(1)	10
3530-50	**Telephone Pole,** searchlight 56,57	(3)	35
3656-34	**Nine Cattle** 52-58	(2)	15
3656-150	**Cattle Corral** 52-55	(4)	18
3662-79	**Seven Milk Cans** (envelope) 55-57,59	(1)	15
3672P	**Bosco Platform**	(4)	50
3672-79	**Seven Bosco Cans** 59,60	(4)	50
3927-75	**Track Cleaner** 56-69	(4)	35
6112-25	**Four Cannisters** 56-58 Came with either 4 red, 4 white, or 2 of each	(2)	10
6414-25	**Four Automobiles** 55-57	(4)	150
6454	**Replacement Car Bodies**	(4)	25
6511-24	**Five Pipes** 55-58	(3)	15
6650-80	**Missile** 59,60	(2)	10
6800-60	**Airplane** 57,58	(4)	175

6801-60	**Boat** 57,58	(3)	75
6816-100	**Bulldozer** 59,60	(4)	250
6817-100	**Earth Scraper** 59,60	(4)	350
6827-100	**Power Shovel** 60	(4)	125
6828-100	**Truck Crane** 60	(4)	125

Track

020X	**45 Degree Crossover** 46-59	(1)	10
020	**90 Degree Crossover** 45-61	(1)	15
022	**Remote Control Switches** 45-61 (pr)	(1)	90
022LH	**Remote Control Switch** 45-61	(1)	45
022RH	**Remote Control Switch** 45-61	(1)	45
042	**Manual Switches** (pair) 47-59	(3)	60
5/F	**Test Set**	(4)	2000▲
25	**Bumper** 46,47 Black O gauge	(3)	25
26	**Bumper** 48-50		
	1. Gray 48 only	(4)	50▲
	2. Red	(1)	25
110	**Trestle Set** 55-69 Packages of 22 or 24 trestles		
	1. Gray trestles	(2)	30
	2. Black trestles	(4)	35
111	**Trestle Set** 56-69 10 Trestles	(1)	15
112	**Super O Switches** (pair)	(3)	100
112LH	**Super O Switch** 62-66	(3)	50
112RH	**Super O Switch** 62-66	(3)	50
112-125	**Super O Switch** 57-61	(3)	50
112-150	**Super O Switch**	(3)	50
130	**60 Degree Crossing**	(3)	75
142	**Manual Super O Switches** (pr) 57-66	(3)	80
142-124	**LH Manual Super O Switch**	(3)	40
142-150	**RH Manual Super O Switch**	(3)	40
260	**Bumper** 51-69		
	1. Red diecast for regular O	(1)	25
	2. Black plastic for Super O	(5)	60
760	**Package of 16 Sections, 072 Track** 50, 54-57	(3)	60
1025	**Bumper** 46,47 027 gauge Black with lamp & one section of track	(2)	12

Note: See page 174 for Transformers

Lionel Cataloged Sets
1945-1969

The Ultimate Challenge

Collectors are always seeking a new frontier or the "next level." The next level for veteran train collectors is the acquisition of boxed sets in the best condition possible. This relatively new phenomenon is good for the hobby because it keeps the blood boiling and interest alive. As every collector knows, the joy of gazing pales next to the thrill of the chase.

Prices for individual items have been well documented in numerous price guides over the past 20-plus years. While fluctuations still occur, prices for the same items in similar condition are pretty much the same all over. Not so with sets. Because the demand for sets is relatively new, prices have not been established. A collector may find a huge price variance for the same set in similar condition at the same meet. As recently as the late 80s dealers would "break-up" sets believing they could get more selling the items individually. No longer. *Boxed-Sets* are the new train collecting buzzwords for the 90s.

As demand increases, prices increase. More items appear for sale, supply catches up with demand, and prices gradually fall. While this collecting cycle may apply to items where there is a supply – like Santa Fe F-3s – it will not apply to sets because there just aren't that many. Think about it. How many sets – given the eagerness of the recipient and the nature of people – survive for 30 to 40 years in excellent condition?

For the train collector, collecting boxed sets is the ultimate challenge.

How We Arrived At Prices

Our methods used to price individual items include observing prices at meets, noting prices in the club newsletters and magazines, and weighing the input of our network of consultants. Another ingredient added to the mix is our experience. We have been watching train prices since 1970 and have a firm grasp on the market. After weighing all the input, we take a consensus to arrive at the price we print in our guide.

For sets, a new method was needed. Lionel made over 400 cataloged sets in their postwar era. To wait until we had observed an asking price for each – there just aren't that many sets for sale – would have severely upset Edna Jones, our production person at Chilton Books, who keeps talking frantically about missed deadlines. So we devised a new method.

To arrive at the prices which appear in this set guide, we added the values – assuming *Excellent* condition – of the individual items without boxes, the individual boxes, and the set box. Since prices for individual boxes are also relatively uncharted (we authored the only other existing price guide for boxes), this method is a bit shaky but it is the best currently available and allows us to finish the book, which is calming to Edna.

In establishing prices for any new category, you have to start somewhere. This is our start. As always, we invite suggestions from our readers. As our research deepens and we observe more prices for sets and individual boxes, we will publish updates.

Condition

There are well established grading standards for individual items (see page 140), but none for sets. Until the collecting organizations establish condition standards for sets, we will establish our own, using the existing terms but applying new definitions appropriate for sets.

For a Postwar Lionel set to be in *Like New* condition, it must have the original set box, individual boxes (if appropriate), plus all incidentals – track, transformer, instruction sheets, and anything else (billboards, wire, lockons, smoke pellets, etc.), which originally came with the set. All items – boxes and hardware – must be in *Like New* condition. For a box to be *LN,* it must have all flaps, the cardboard crisp, no tears or bruises, no rust, etc.

We chose the next grade lower, *Excellent,* to be our standard for pricing. To be *Excellent,* a set must have the set box, all individual boxes, and all major incidentals but not the minor incidentals (wire, track, lockons, etc.). We consider major incidentals to be those items which only come in that particular set, like the Girl's Train white transformer or the stickers which came with the Campaign Special of 1960.

The boxes can be torn a little, maybe missing one or two flaps – but they must be fairly crisp with no major holes or tears.

We chose *Excellent* because it is unrealistic for a collector to ever find a wide assortment of postwar Lionel sets in *Like New* condition. For example, at the 1993 Train Collectors Association national convention in St. Paul, Minnesota, of the approximately 100 postwar sets offered for sale, only one or two could be considered *Like New.* The rest were *Excellent* or less.

What's A Set Box Worth?

Boxes for expensive sets like the Congressional are in big demand because they dramatically affect the selling price. A Congressional set with individual boxes but not the set box in *Excellent* condition will bring around $4000. With the box, the seller may get $5000 or more. Boxes for sets which contain rare items are also in demand, like the 1963 *Space Prober* set which contains the 6407 Flat Car with missile (Pencil Sharpener Car). Some sets defy pricing because they are never offered for sale. An example would be the *Father and Son* set featured on the cover of the 1960 catalog. We know of only three in existence and none have ever been offered for sale. What's that set worth? We say $9500 but who knows? Common starter sets are also in demand but prices are far lower.

When's A Set Not A Set?

A set is not right when the contents aren't right. Dealers often make up sets and either intentionally or unintentionally include the wrong cars. It is not difficult to do. Consider: In 1956 Lionel introduced the Central of Georgia and Great Northern 6464-boxcars. They were re-issued in 1966 with the same numbers but with different frames, trucks, body type, and couplers. If you are considering buying a 1956 set which included these cars, make sure they are the 1956 version, not the 1966.

Numbers

Sets are listed in numerical order with the set number which appears in the catalog. Set numbers did not appear in the 1955, 1956, and 1957 catalogs. The set numbers for those years appeared in dealer price supplements. Both three-digit and four-digit set numbers were printed. We used the four-digit numbers only.

Names

The sets are named even though Lionel seldom gave names to their sets. We arrived at the names by taking a phrase from the catalog copy. While this may be considered corny by some, we thought it was fun so we did it.

Rarity Rating

5 is rare, 1 is common. As with individual items, price does not always follow rarity. Some sets, like the *Girl's Train* and *Congressional Set*, are high priced but relatively common. In general, the older sets from the 40s and early 50s are the hardest to find.

When Buying

Approach every deal with a healthy skepticism. If the boxes are crisp, check the contents. Dealers often put *VG* hardware in boxes that are *LN* or *Excellent.* Check it out and be prepared to negotiate. Sellers usually price items expecting to come down 10 to 20 percent (or more). Most importantly, have fun.

Lionel Cataloged Sets

1945-1969

463W	**Lionel O Gauge Four Car, 45**	**(5)**	**650**
	Freight Set		
224	2-6-2 w/2466W Tender		
2458	Automobile Car		
2452	Pennsylvania Gondola Car		
2555	Sunoco Oil Car		
2457	Pennsylvania Caboose		
1000W	**027 3-Car Set, 55**	**(4)**	**225**
2016	2-6-4 w/6026W Tender		
6014	Baby Ruth Box Car, red		
6012	Lionel Gondola		
6017	Lionel Lines Caboose		
1001	**027 3-Car Set, 55**	**(3)**	**325**
610	Erie Diesel Switcher		
6012	Lionel Gondola		
6014	Baby Ruth Box Car, red		
6017	Lionel Lines Caboose		
1111	**Lionel Scout Set, 48**	**(2)**	**150**
1001	2-4-2 w/1001T Tender		
1002	Lionel Gondola, blue		
1005	Sunoco Oil Car		
1007	Lionel Lines Caboose		
1112	**Lionel Scout Set, 48**	**(4)**	**200**
1101	2-4-2 w/1001T Tender		
1002	Lionel Gondola, blue		
1004	Baby Ruth Box Car		
1005	Sunoco Oil Car		
1007	Lionel Lines Caboose		
1113	**Lionel Scout Train, 50**	**(3)**	**150**
1110	2-4-2 w/1001T Tender		
1002	Lionel Gondola, black		
1005	Sunoco Oil Car		
1007	Lionel Caboose		
1115	**Lionel Scout, 49**	**(4)**	**150**
1110	2-4-2 w/1001T Tender		
1002	Lionel Gondola, black		
1005	Sunoco Oil Car		
1007	Lionel Lines Caboose		
1117	**Lionel Scout, 49**	**(3)**	**150**
1110	2-4-2 w/1001T Tender		
1002	Lionel Gondola, black		
1005	Sunoco Oil Car		
1004	Baby Ruth Box Car		
1007	Lionel Lines Caboose		
1119	**Scout 3-Car Freight, 51, 52**	**(2)**	**150**
1110	2-4-2 w/1001T Tender		
1002	Lionel Gondola, black		
1004	Baby Ruth Box Car, side nick		
1007	Lionel Lines Caboose		
1400	**Lionel 027 Passenger Set, 46**	**(4)**	**675**
221	2-6-4 NYC w/221T Tender		
2430	Pullman, blue		
2430	Pullman, blue		
2431	Observation, blue		
1400W	**Lionel 027 Passenger Set, 46**	**(5)**	**800**
221	2-6-4 NYC w/221W Tender		
2430	Pullman, blue		
2430	Pullman, blue		
2431	Observation, blue		
1401	**Lionel 027 Freight Outfit, 46**	**(3)**	**150**
1654	2-4-2 w/1654T Tender		
2452	Pennsylvania Gondola		
2465	Sunoco Oil Car		
2472	Pennsylvania Caboose		

1401W	**Lionel 027 Freight Outfit, 46**	**(5)**	**250**
1654	2-4-2 w/1654W Tender		
2452	Pennsylvania Gondola		
2465	Sunoco Oil Car		
2472	Pennsylvania Caboose		
1402	**Lionel 027 Passenger Set, 46**	**(4)**	**500**
1666	2-6-2 w/2466T Tender		
2440	Pullman, green		
2440	Pullman, green		
2441	Observation, green		
1402W	**Lionel 027 Passenger Set, 46**	**(5)**	**600**
1666	2-6-2 w/2466W Tender		
2440	Pullman, green		
2440	Pullman, green		
2441	Pullman, green		
1403	**Lionel 027 Freight Train, 46**	**(4)**	**425**
221	2-6-4 NYC w/221T Tender		
2411	Lionel Lines Pipe Car		
2465	Sunoco Oil Car		
2472	Pennsylvania Caboose		
1403W	**Lionel 027 Freight Train, 46**	**(5)**	**525**
221	2-6-4 NYC w/221W Tender		
2411	Lionel Lines Pipe Car		
2465	Sunoco Oil Car		
2472	Pennsylvania Caboose		
1405	**Lionel 027 Freight Train, 46**	**(3)**	**175**
1666	2-6-2 w/2466T Tender		
2452	Pennsylvania Gondola		
2465	Sunoco Oil Car		
2472	Pennsylvania Caboose		
1405W	**Lionel 027 Freight Train, 46**	**(5)**	**250**
1666	2-6-2 w/2466W Tender		
2452	Pennsylvania Gondola		
2465	Sunoco Oil Car		
2472	Pennsylvania Caboose		
1407B	**Lionel 027 Switcher Bell Outfit, 46**	**(5)**	**900**
1665	0-4-0 w/2403B Tender		
2452X	Pennsylvania Gondola		
2560	Lionel Lines Crane		
2419	D L & W Wrecking Car		
1409	**Lionel 027 Freight Train, 46**	**(4)**	**400**
1666	2-6-2 w/2466T Tender		
3559	Coal Dump Car		
2465	Sunoco Oil Car		
3454	Operating Merchandise Car		
2472	Pennsylvania Caboose		
1409W	**Lionel 027 Freight Train, 46**	**(5)**	**500**
1666	2-6-2 w/2466W Tender		
3559	Coal Dump Car		
2465	Sunoco Oil Car		
3454	Operating Merchandise Car		
2472	Pennsylvania Caboose		
1411W	**Freight Outfit, 46**	**(4)**	**225**
1666	2-6-2 w/2466WX Tender		
2452X	Pennsylvania Gondola		
2465	Sunoco Oil Car		
2454	Baby Ruth Box Car		
2472	Pennsylvania Caboose		
1413WS	**Lionel 027 Freight Train, 46**	**(3)**	**350**
2020	Pennsy Turbine w/2466WX Tender		
2452X	Pennsylvania Gondola		
2465	Sunoco Oil Car		
2454	Baby Ruth Box Car		
2472	Pennsylvania Caboose		
1415WS	**Lionel 027 Freight Set, 46**	**(4)**	**550**
2020	Pennsy Turbine w/2020W Tender		
3459	Operating Dump Car		
3454	Operating Merchandise Car		
2465	Sunoco Oil Car		
2472	Pennsylvania Caboose		

1417WS	**Lionel 027 Freight Outfit, 46**	**(4)**	**500**
2020	Pennsy Turbine w/2020W Tender		
2465	Sunoco Oil Car		
3451	Automatic Unloading Lumber Car		
2560	Lionel Lines Crane Car		
2419	D L & W Wrecking Car		
1419WS	**Lionel 027 Freight Train, 46**	**(5)**	**900**
2020	Pennsy Turbine w/2020W Tender		
3459	Operating Dump Car		
97	Coal Elevator		
2452X	Pennsylvania Gondola		
2560	Lionel Lines Crane Car		
2419	D L & W Wrecking Car		
1421WS	**Lionel 027 Freight Train, 46**	**(5)**	**1000**
2020	Pennsy Turbine w/2020W Tender		
3451	Operating Lumber Car		
164	Log loader		
2465	Sunoco Oil Car		
3454	Operating Merchandise Car		
2472	Pennsylvania Caboose		
1423W	**Lionel 3-Car Freight Outfit, 48, 49**	**(3)**	**150**
1655	2-4-2 w/6654W Tender		
6452	Pennsylvania Gondola		
6465	Sunoco Oil Car		
6257	Lionel Caboose		
1425B	**Switcher Freight, 48, 49**	**(4)**	**850**
1656	0-4-0 w/6403B Tender		
6456	Lehigh Valley Hopper, black		
6465	Sunoco Oil Car		
6257X	Lionel Caboose, 48		
6257	Lionel Caboose, 49		
1426WS	**Lionel Passenger Set, 48, 49**	**(4)**	**600**
2026	2-6-2 w/6466WX Tender		
6440	Pullman, green		
6440	Pullman, green		
6441	Observation, green		
1427WS	**Lionel 3-Car Freight Set, 48**	**(3)**	**250**
2026	2-6-2 w/6466WX Tender		
6465	Sunoco Oil Car		
6454	Box Car		
6257	Lionel Caboose		
1429WS	**4-Car Freight Set, 48**	**(3)**	**225**
2026	2-6-2 w/6466WX Tender		
3451	Automatic Lumber Car		
6465	Sunoco Oil Car		
6454	Box Car		
6357	Lionel Caboose		
1430WS	**Passenger Train, 48, 49**	**(4)**	**800**
2025	2-6-2 w/6466WX Tender		
2400	Maplewood Pullman		
2402	Chatham Pullman		
2401	Hillside Observation		
1431	**Lionel Freight Train, 47**	**(4)**	**150**
1654	2-4-2 w/1654T Tender		
2452X	Pennsylvania Gondola		
2465	Sunoco Oil Car		
2472	Pennsylvania Caboose		
1431W	**Lionel Freight Train, 47**	**(4)**	**150**
1654	2-4-2 w/1654W Tender		
2452X	Pennsylvania Gondola		
2465	Sunoco Oil Car		
2472	Pennsylvania Caboose		
1432	**Lionel Passenger Set, 47**	**(4)**	**550**
221	2-6-4 NYC w/221T Tender		
2430	Pullman, blue		
2430	Pullman, blue		
2431	Observation, blue		
1432W	**Lionel Passenger Set, 47**	**(4)**	**600**
221	2-6-4 NYC w/221W Tender		
2430	Pullman, blue		
2430	Pullman, blue		
2431	Observation, blue		

1433	Lionel Freight Train, 47	(4)	300
221	2-6-4 NYC w/221T Tender		
2411	Flat Car With Pipes/Logs		
2465	Sunoco Oil Car		
2457	Pennsylvania Caboose		

1433W	Lionel Freight Train, 47	(4)	300
221	2-6-4 NYC w/221W Tender		
2411	Flat Car With Pipes/Logs		
2465	Sunoco Oil Car		
2457	Pennsylvania Caboose		

1434WS	Passenger Train, 47	(4)	400
2025	2-6-2 w/2466WX Tender		
2440	Pullman, green		
2440	Pullman, green		
2441	Observation, green		

1435WS	Lionel Freight Train, 47	(3)	250
2025	2-6-2 w/2466WX Tender		
2452X	Pennsylvania Gondola Car		
2454	Baby Ruth Box Car		
2457	Pennsylvania Caboose		

1437WS	Lionel Freight Set, 47	(3)	275
2025	2-6-2 w/2466WX Tender		
2452X	Pennsylvania Gondola Car		
2465	Sunoco Oil Car		
2454	Baby Ruth Box Car		
2472	Pennsylvania Caboose		

1439WS	Lionel Freight Outfit, 47	(4)	425
2025	2-6-2 w/2466WX Tender		
3559	Automatic Coal Dump Car		
2465	Sunoco Oil Car		
3454	Automatic Merchandise Car		
2457	Pennsylvania Caboose		

1441WS	Lionel De Luxe Work Outfit, 47	(4)	550
2020	Pennsy Turbine w/2020W Tender		
2461	Lionel Lines Transformer Car		
3451	Lionel Lines Lumber Car		
2560	Lionel Lines Crane Car		
2419	D L & W Wrecking Car		

1443WS	Lionel Freight Set, 47	(4)	425
2020	Pennsy Turbine w/2020W Tender		
3459	Automatic Dump Car		
3462	Milk Car and Platform		
2465	Sunoco Oil Car		
2457	Pennsylvania Caboose		

1445WS	Lionel Freight Train, 48	(4)	325
2025	2-6-2 w/6466WX Tender		
3559	Automatic Dump Car		
6465	Sunoco Oil Car		
6454	Box Car		
6357	Lionel Caboose		

1447WS	Lionel De Luxe Work Train, 48, 49	(4)	525
2020	Pennsy Turbine w/6020W Tender, 48, 49		
3451	Automatic Lumber Car, 48		
3461	Automatic Lumber Car, 49		
2461	Lionel Lines Transformer Car, 48		
6461	Lionel LInes Transformer Car, 49		
2460	Lionel Lines Crane Car, 48, 49		
6419	D L & W Wrecker-Caboose, 48, 49		

1449WS	Lionel 5-Car Freight Outfit, 48	(4)	450
2020	Pennsy Turbine w/6020W Tender		
3462	Automatic Milk Car with Platform		
6465	Sunoco Oil Car		
3459	Automatic Ore Dump Car		
6411	Lionel Lines Flat Car with Logs		
6357	Lionel Caboose		

1451WS	3-Car Freight, 49	(3)	275
2026	2-6-2 w/6466WX Tender		
6462	NYC Gondola with Barrels		
3464	Operating Box Car		
6257	Lionel Caboose		

1453WS	4-Car Freight Train, 49	(3)	325
2026	2-6-2 w/6466WX Tender		
3464	Operating Box Car		
6465	Sunoco Oil Car		
3461	Operating Lumber Car		
6357	Lionel Caboose		

1455WS	4-Car 027 Freight Set, 49	(3)	400
2025	2-6-2 w/6466WX Tender		
6462	NYC Gondola Car		
6465	Sunoco Oil Car		
3472	Operating Milk Car with Platform		
6357	Lionel Caboose		

1457B	Diesel Freight, 49, 50	(4)	625
6220	Lionel Diesel Switcher		
6462	NYC Gondola Car with Six Barrels		
3464	Operating Box Car		
6520	Operating Searchlight Car		
6419	D L & W Railroad Wrecker-Caboose		

1459WS	027 Gauge 5-Car Freight Outfit, 49	(4)	550
2020	Pennsy Turbine w/6020W Tender		
6411	Lionel Lines Flat Car with Logs		
3656	Operating Cattle Car Stock and Platform		
6465	Sunoco Oil Car		
3469	Operating Ore Dump Car		
6357	Lionel Caboose		

1461S	3-Car Freight With Smoke, 50	(2)	150
6110	2-4-2 w/6001T Tender		
6002	NYC Gondola Car		
6004	Baby Ruth Box Car		
6007	Lionel Caboose		

1463W	Lionel 027 3-Car Freight, 50	(2)	150
2036	2-6-4 w/6466W Tender		
6462	NYC Gondola Car		
6465	Sunoco Oil Car		
6257	Lionel Caboose		

1463WS	027 3-Car Freight, 51	(3)	200
2026	2-6-4 w/6466W Tender		
6462	NYC Gondola Car		
6465	Sunoco Oil Car		
6257	Lionel Caboose		

1464W	027 3-Car Pullman, 50	(4)	2000
2023	Union Pacific Twin Diesel Alcos, yellow		
2481	Plainfield Pullman		
2482	Westfield Pullman		
2483	Livingston Observation		

1464W	027 3-Car Pullman, 51	(4)	900
2023	Union Pacific Twin Diesel Alcos, silver		
2421	Maplewood Pullman, gray roof		
2422	Chatham Pullman, gray roof		
2423	Hillside Observation, gray roof		

1464W	3-Car Pullman, 52, 53	(4)	1000
2033	Union Pacific Twin Diesel Alcos, silver		
2421	Maplewood Pullman, silver roof		
2422	Chatham Pullman, silver roof		
2423	Hillside Observation, silver roof		

1465	3-Car Freight, 52	(2)	150
2034	2-4-2 w/6066T Tender		
6032	Lionel Gondola Car		
6035	Sunoco Oil Car		
6037	Lionel Lines Caboose		

1467W	027 Diesel 4-Car Freight Set, 50, 51	(3)	650
2023	Union Pacific Twin Diesel Alcos, yellow, 50		
2023	Union Pacific Twin Diesel Alcos, silver, 51		
6656	Stock Car		
6465	Sunoco Oil Car		
6456	Lehigh Valley Hopper		
6357	Lionel Caboose		

1467W	4-Car Freight, 52, 53	(4)	525
2032	Erie Twin Diesel Alcos		
6656	Stock Car		
6456	Lehigh Valley Hopper		
6465	Sunoco Oil Car		
6357	Lionel Caboose		

1469WS	Lionel 027 4-Car Freight, 50, 51	(2)	225
2035	2-6-4 w/6466W Tender		
6462	NYC Gondola Car		
6465	Sunoco Oil Car		
6456	Lehigh Valley Hopper, black, 50		
6456	Lehigh Valley Hopper, maroon, 51		
6257	Lionel Caboose		

1471WS	Lionel 5-Car Freight Set, 50, 51	(3)	350
2035	2-6-4 w/6466W Tender		
3469X	Operating Ore Dump Car		
6465	Sunoco Oil Car		
6454	Box Car		
3461X	Operating Lumber Car		
6357	Lionel Caboose		

1473WS	Lionel 4-Car Freight, 50	(3)	425
2046	4-6-4 w/2046W Tender		
3464	Operating Box Car		
6465	Sunoco Oil Car		
6520	Operating Searchlight Car		
6357	Lionel Caboose		

1475WS	Lionel 5-Car Freight Set, 50	(3)	525
2046	4-6-4 w/2046W Tender		
3656	Operating Cattle Car and Platform		
3461X	Operating Lumber Car		
6472	Refrigerated Car		
3469X	Operating Ore Dump Car		
6419	D L & W Wrecker-type Caboose		

1477S	027 3-Car Freight, 51, 52	(3)	200
2026	2-6-4 w/6466T Tender		
6012	Lionel Gondola Car		
6014	Baby Ruth Box Car, white, side nick		
6017	Lionel Lines Caboose		

1479WS	027 4-Car Freight, 52	(3)	425
2056	Berkshire w/2046W Tender		
6462	NYC Gondola Car		
6465	Sunoco Oil Car		
6456	Lehigh Valley Hopper		
6257	Lionel Caboose		

1481WS	5-Car Freight, 51	(3)	325
2035	2-6-4 w/6466W tender		
3464	Operating Box Car		
6465	Sunoco Oil Car		
3472	Operating Milk Car and Platform		
6462	NYC Gondola Car		
6357	Lionel Caboose		

1483WS	5-Car Freight, 52	(4)	625
2056	Berkshire w/2046W Tender		
3472	Operating Milk Car and Platform		
6462	NYC Gondola Car		
3474	Operating Box Car		
6465	Sunoco Oil Car		
6357	Lionel Caboose		

1484WS	4-Car Pullman, 52	(4)	1000
2056	Berkshire w/2046W Tender		
2421	Maplewood Pullman, silver roof		
2422	Chatham Pullman, silver roof		
2429	Livingston Pullman, silver roof		
2423	Hillside Observation, silver roof		

1485WS	027 3-Car Freight, 52	(3)	225
2025	2-6-4 w/6466W Tender		
6462	NYC Gondola Car		
6465	Sunoco Oil Car		
6257	Lionel Caboose		

1500	**027 3-Car Freight, 53, 54**	(1)	150
1130	2-4-2 w/6066T Tender		
6032	Lionel Gondola Car		
6034	Baby Ruth Box Car		
6037	Lionel Lines Caboose		

1501S	**027 3-Car Freight, 53**	(2)	150
2026	2-6-2 w/6066T Tender		
6032	Lionel Gondola Car		
6035	Sunoco Oil Car		
6037	Lionel Lines Caboose		

1502WS	**027 3-Car Pullman, 53**	(4)	750
2055	4-6-4 w/2046W Tender		
2421	Maplewood Pullman		
2422	Chatham Pullman		
2423	Hillside Observation		

1503WS	**027 4-Car Freight, 53**	(2)	325
2055	4-6-4 w/6026W Tender		
6462	NYC Gondola Car, black, 53		
6462	NYC Gondola Car, green, 54		
6465	Sunoco Oil Car		
6456	Lehigh Valley Hopper, black, 53		
6456	Lehigh Valley Hopper, green, 54		
6257	Lionel Caboose		

1505WS	**027 4-Car Freight, 53**	(3)	450
2046	4-6-4 w/2046W Tender		
6464-1	Western Pacific Box Car		
6462	NYC Gondola Car		
6415	Sunoco Oil Car		
6357	Lionel Caboose		

1507WS	**027 5-Car Freight, 53**	(3)	425
2046	4-6-4 w/2046W Tender		
3472	Operating Milk Car and Platform		
6415	Sunoco Oil Car		
6462	NYC Gondola Car		
6468	Automobile Car, blue		
6357	Lionel Caboose		

1509WS	**027 5-Car Freight, 53**	(2)	500
2046	4-6-4 w/2046W Tender		
3520	Operating Searchlight Car		
6456	Lehigh Valley Hopper		
3469	Operating Dump Car		
6460	Lionel Lines Crane Car		
6419	D L & W Work Caboose		

1511S	**027 4-Car Freight, 53**	(4)	300
2037	2-6-4 w/6066T Tender		
6032	Lionel Gondola Car		
3474	Operating Box Car		
6035	Sunoco Oil Car		
6037	Lionel Lines Caboose		

1513S	**027 4-Car Freight, 54, 55**	(1)	175
2037	2-6-4 w/6026T Tender		
6012	Lionel Gondola Car		
6014	Baby Ruth Box Car, washout red		
6015	Sunoco Oil Car		
6017	Lionel LInes Caboose		

1515WS	**027 5-Car Freight, 54**	(4)	500
2065	4-6-4 w/2046W Tender		
6415	Sunoco Oil Car		
6462	NYC Gondola Car		
6464-25	Great Northern Box Car		
6456	Lehigh Valley Hopper, gray		
6357	Lionel Caboose		

1516WS	**027 3-Car Passenger, 54**	(4)	750
2065	4-6-4 w/2046W Tender		
2434	Newark Pullman		
2432	Clifton Pullman		
2436	Summit Observation		

1517W	**027 4-Car Freight, 54**	(4)	1000
2245P/C	The Texas Special F-3, AB		
6464-225	Southern Pacific Box Car		
6561	Lionel Lines Cable Car		
6462	NYC Gondola Car, green		
6427	Lionel Lines Caboose		

1519WS	**027 5-Car Freight, 54**	(4)	550
2065	4-6-4 w/6026W Tender		
3461	Operating Lumber Car		
6462	NYC Gondola Car, red		
6356	NYC Stock Car		
3482	Operating Milk Car with Platform		
6427	Lionel Lines Caboose		

1520W	**The Flashing Star of the South West, 54**	(5)	2000
2245P/C	The Texas Special F-3, AB		
2432	Clifton Vista-Dome		
2435	Elizabeth Pullman		
2436	Summit Observation		

1521WS	**027 5-Car Freight, 54**	(4)	750
2065	4-6-4 w/2046W Tender		
3620	Operating Searchlight Car		
3562	Operating Barrel Car, black		
6561	Lionel Lines Cable Car		
6460	Lionel Lines Crane Car, black cab		
6419	D L & W Work Caboose		

1523	**Lionel Work Train, 54**	(4)	750
6250	Seaboard Diesel Switcher		
6511	Lionel Pipe Car		
6456	Lehigh Valley Hopper, gray		
6460	Lionel Lines Crane Car, red cab		
6419	D L & W Work Caboose		

1527	**027 3-Car Work Train, 55**	(4)	500
1615	0-4-0 w/1615T Tender		
6462	NYC Gondola		
6560	Lionel Lines Crane Car, gray cab		
6119	D L & W Work Caboose		

1529	**027 3-Car Freight, 55**	(5)	750
2028	Pennsylvania GP-7		
6311	Lionel Pipe Car		
6436	Lehigh Valley Hopper		
6257	Lionel Caboose		

1531W	**027 4-Car Freight, 55**	(4)	650
2328	Burlington GP-7		
6462	NYC Gondola, red		
6456	Lehigh Valley Hopper		
6465	Sunoco Oil Car		
6257	Lionel Cabooose		

1533WS	**027 Freight Hauler, 55**	(4)	450
2055	4-6-4 w/6026W Tender		
3562	Operating Barrel Car, yellow		
6436	Lehigh Valley Hopper		
6465	Sunoco Oil Car		
6357	Lionel Caboose		

1534W	**027 Passenger Train, 55**	(4)	1000
2328	Burlington GP-7		
2434	Newark Pullman		
2432	Clifton Vista-Dome		
2436	Summit Observation		

1536W	**Pride of the Katy and Frisco, 55**	(4)	2000
2245P/C	The Texas Special F-3, AB		
2432	Clifton Vista-Dome		
2432	Clifton Vista-Dome		
2436	Summit Observation		

1537WS	**027 4-Car Freight, 55**	(4)	575
2065	4-6-4 w/2046W Tender		
3562	Operating Barrel Car, yellow		
3469	Operating Dump Car		
6464-275	State of Maine Box Car		
6357	Lionel Caboose		

1538WS	**027 Passenger Train, 55**	(4)	900
2065	4-6-4 w/2046W Tender		
2435	Elizabeth Pullman		
2434	Newark Pullman		
2432	Clifton Vista-Dome		
2436	Summit Observation		

1539W	**027 5-Car Freight, 55**	(4)	900
2243P/C	Santa Fe F-3, AB		
3620	Operating Searchlight Car		
6446	N & W Covered Hopper		
6561	Lionel Lines Cable Car		
6560	Lionel Lines Crane Car		
6419	D L & W Work Caboose		

1541WS	**027 5-Car Freight, 55**	(4)	600
2065	4-6-4 w/2046W Tender		
3482	Operating Milk Car with Platform		
3461	Operating Lumber Car		
6415	Sunoco Oil Car		
3494	NYC Operating Box Car		
6427	Lionel Lines Caboose		

1542	**027 3-Car Freight, 56**	(3)	225
520	GE 80-Ton Electric		
6014	Baby Ruth Box Car, red		
6012	Lionel Gondola		
6017	Lionel Caboose		

1543	**027 3-Car Freight, 56**	(4)	250
627	Lehigh Valley GE 44-Ton Diesel		
6121	Lionel Pipe Car		
6112	Canister Gondola		
6017	Lionel Caboose		

1545	**027 4-Car Freight, 56**	(4)	325
628	Northern Pacific GE 44-Ton Diesel		
6424	Twin Auto Car		
6014	Baby Ruth Box Car, red		
6257	Lionel Caboose		

1547S	**027 Freight Hauler, 56**	(4)	175
2018	2-6-4 w/6026T Tender		
6121	Lionel Pipe Car		
6112	Canister Gondola		
6014	Baby Ruth Box Car, red		
6257	Lionel Caboose		

1549S	**027 3-Car Work Train, 56**	(4)	900
1615	0-4-0 w/1615T Tender		
6262	Wheel Car		
6560	Lionel Lines Crane Car		
6119	D L & W Work Caboose, orange		

1551S	**027 4-Car Freight, 56**	(4)	400
621	Jersey Central Switcher		
6362	Railway Truck Car		
6425	Gulf Oil Car		
6562	Canister Gondola		
6257	Lionel Caboose		

1552	**027 Passenger Train, 56**	(5)	1200
629	Burlington GE 44-Ton Diesel		
2434	Newark Pullman		
2432	Clifton Vista-Dome		
2436	Summit Observation		

1553W	**027 5-Car Freight, 56**	(4)	600
2338	Milwaukee GP-7		
6430	Cooper-Jarrett Van Car		
6462	NYC Gondola, red		
6464-425	New Haven Box Car		
6346	Alcoa Covered Hopper		
6257	Lionel Caboose		

1555WS	**027 Freight Hauler, 56**	(3)	400
2018	2-6-4 w/6026W Tender		
3361	Operating Lumber Car		
6464-400	B & O Box Car		
6462	NYC Gondola, red		
6257	Lionel Caboose		

164

1557W **027 5-Car Work Train, 56** (4) 525
621 Jersey Central Switcher
6436 Lehigh Valley Hopper
6511 Lionel Pipe Car
3620 Operating Searchlight Car
6560 Lionel Lines Crane Car
6119 D L & W Work Caboose

1559W **027 5-Car Freight Train, 56** (4) 750
2338 Milwaukee GP-7
6414 Evans Auto Loader
3562 Operating Barrel Car, yellow
6362 Railway Truck Car
3494-275 State of Maine Operating Box Car
6357 Lionel Caboose

1561WS **027 5-Car Freight Train, 56** (4) 600
2065 4-6-4 w/6026W Tender
6430 Cooper-Jarrett Van Car
3424 Wabash Operating Brakeman Box Car
6262 Wheel Car
6562 Canister Gondola
6257 Lionel Caboose

1562W **027 Passenger Train, 56** (4) 2000
2328 Burlington GP-7
2442 Clifton Vista-Dome
2442 Clifton Vista-Dome
2444 Newark Pullman
2446 Summit Observation

1563W **027 5-Car Freight, 56** (4) 1750
2240P/C Wabash F-3, AB
6467 Miscellaneous Car
3562 Operating Barrel Car, yellow
3620 Operating Searchlight Car
6414 Evans Auto Loader
6357 Lionel Caboose

1565W **027 5-Car Freight, 56** (4) 600
2065 4-6-4 w/6026W Tender
3662 Operating Milk Car with Platform
3650 Searchlight Extension Car
6414 Evans Auto Loader
6346 Alcoa Covered Hopper
6357 Lionel Caboose

1567W **The Pride of the Santa Fe, 56** (4) 1000
2243P/C Santa Fe F-3, AB
3356 Operating Horse Car with Corral
3424 Wabash Operating Brakeman Box Car
6672 Santa Fe Refrigerator Box Car
6430 Cooper-Jarrett Van Car
6357 Lionel Caboose

1569 **027 4-Car Freight, 57** (3) 300
202 Union Pacific Alco, A
6014 Frisco Box Car, white
6111 Lionel Log Car
6112 Lionel Canister Car
6017 Lionel Lines Caboose

1571 **027 5-Car Freight, 57** (4) 450
625 Lehigh Valley GE 44-Ton
6424 Twin Auto Car
6476 Lehigh Valley Hopper
6121 Lionel Pipe Car
6112 Lionel Canister Car
6017 Lionel Lines Caboose

1573 **027 5-Car Freight, 57** (4) 250
250LT Pennsy 2-4-2 w/250T Tender
6025 Gulf Oil Car
6112 Lionel Canister Car
6464-425 New Haven Box Car
6476 Lehigh Valley Hopper
6017 Lionel Lines Caboose

1575 **027 5-Car Freight, 57** (4) 400
205P/T Missouri Pacific Alcos, AA
6111 Lionel Log Car
6121 Lionel Pipe Car
6112 Lionel Canister Car
6560 Lionel Lines Crane Car
6119 D L & W Work Caboose

1577S **027 6-Car Freight, 57** (4) 250
2018 2-6-4 w/1130T Tender
6121 Lionel Pipe Car
6464-475 Boston & Maine Box Car
6111 Lionel Log Car
6014 Frisco Box Car, red
6112 Lionel Canister Car
6017 Lionel Lines Caboose

1578S **027 Passenger Train, 57** (5) 550
2018 2-6-4 w/1130T Tender
2434 Newark Pullman
2432 Clifton Vista-Dome
2436 Mooseheart Observation

1579S **027 7-Car Freight, 57** (4) 300
2037 2-6-4 w/1130T Tender
6111 Lionel Log Car
6025 Gulf Oil Car
6476 Lehigh Valley Hopper
6468 New Haven Automobile Car
6112 Lionel Canister Car
6121 Lionel Pipe Car
6017 Lionel Lines Caboose

1581 **027 7-Car Freight, 57** (4) 600
611 Jersey Central Switcher
6476 Lehigh Valley Hopper
6024 Nabisco Box Car
6424 Twin Auto Car
6464-650 Rio Grande Box Car
6025 Gulf Oil Car
6560 Lionel Lines Crane Car
6119 D L & W Work Caboose

1583WS **027 King of the High Iron, 57** (3) 250
2037 2-6-4 w/6026W Tender
6482 Refrigerator Car
6112 Canister Gondola
6646 Stock Car
6121 Lionel Pipe Car
6476 Lehigh Valley Hopper, black
6017 Lionel Lines Caboose

1585W **027 9-Car Freight Train, 57** (4) 425
602 Seaboard Switcher
6014 Frisco Box Car, white
6121 Lionel Pipe Car
6025 Gulf Oil Car
6464-525 Minneapolis & St. Louis Box Car
6112 Canister Gondola
6024 Nabisco Box Car
6476 Lehigh Valley Hopper, gray
6111 Lionel Log Car
6017 Lionel Lines Caboose

1586 **027 Passenger Train, 57** (4) 700
204P/T Santa Fe Alcos, AA
2432 Clifton Vista-Dome
2432 Clifton Vista-Come
2436 Mooseheart Observation

1587S **Lady Lionel Pastel Train Set, 57, 58** (4) 4000
2037-500 2-6-4 w/1130T-500 Tender
6462-500 NYC Gondola
6464-515 MKT Box Car
6436-500 Lehigh Valley Hopper
6464-510 NYC Box Car
6427-500 Pennsylvania Caboose

1589WS **027 King of the High Iron, 57** (4) 500
2037 2-6-4 w/6026W Tender
6464-450 Great Northern Box Car
6111 Lionel Log Car
6025 Gulf Oil Car, orange
6024 Nabisco Box Car
6424 Twin Auto Car
6112 Canister Gondola
6017 Lionel Lines Caboose

1590 **027 4-Car Steam Freight, 58** (3) 300
249 2-4-2 w/250T Tender
6014 Bosco Box Car, red
6151 Flat Car with Range Patrol Truck
6112 Gondola with Canisters
6017 Lionel Lines Caboose

1591 **U.S. Marine Land & Sea Limited, 58** (4) 1100
212 USMC Alco, A
6809 Flat Car with Military Units
6807 Flat Car with Military Units
6803 Flat Car with Military Units
6017-50 USMC Caboose

1593 **5-Car Diesel Work Train, 58** (4) 650
613 Union Pacific Switcher
6476 Lehigh Valley Hopper
6818 Flat Car with Transformer
6660 Boom Car
6112 Gondola with Canisters
6119 D L & W Work Caboose

1595 **027 Marine Battlefront Special, 58** (5) 1675
1625 0-4-0 w/1625T Tender
6804 Flat Car with Military Units
6808 Flat Car with Military Units
6806 Flat Car with Military Units
6017 Lionel Lines Caboose, gray

1597S **6-Car Coal King Smoking Freighter, 58** (4) 325
2018 2-6-4 w/1130T Tender
6014 Bosco or Frisco Box Car, orange
6818 Flat Car with Transformer
6476 Lehigh Valley Hopper, red
6025 Gulf Tank Car, black
6112 Gondola with Canisters, blue
6017 Lionel Lines Caboose

1599 **027 6-Car Freight, 58** (3) 450
210 The Texas Special Alco's, AA
6801-50 Flat Car with Boat, yellow hull
6014 Bosco, orange or Frisco, red Box Car
6424-60 Automobile Flat Car
6112-1 Gondola with Canisters, black
6465-60 Gulf Tank Car, gray
6017 Lionel Lines Caboose

1600 **027 3-Car Passenger Set, 58** (4) 900
216 Burlington Alco, A
6572 REA Reefer Car
2432 Clifton Vista-Dome
2436 Mosseheart Observation

1601W **027 5-Car Diesel Freight, 58** (4) 925
2337 Wabash GP-7
6800 Airplane Car
6464-425 New Haven Box Car
6801 Boat Car
6810 Flat Car with Van
6017 Lionel Lines Caboose

1603WS **Whistling Mountain Climber, 58** (4) 375
2037 2-6-4 w/6026W Tender
6424 Twin Auto Car
6014-60 Bosco Box Car, white
6818 Flat Car with Transformer
6112 Gondola with Canisters
6017 Lionel Lines Caboose

165

1605W	027 6-Car Diesel Freight, 58	(4)	825
208	Santa Fe Twin Diesel Alco's, AA		
6800	Airplane Car		
6464-425	New Haven Box Car		
6801	Boat Car		
6477	Flat Car with Pipes		
6802	Girder Car		
6017	Lionel Lines Caboose		

1607W	Trouble Shooter Work Set, 58	(4)	475
2037	2-6-4 w/6026W Tender		
6465	Gulf Tank Car		
6818	Flat Car with Transformer		
6464-425	New Haven Box Car		
6112	Gondola with Canisters		
6660	Boom Car		
6119	D L & W Work Caboose		

1608W	Merchants Limited Passenger Set, 58	(5)	1650
209P/T	New Haven Alco's, AA		
2434	Newark Pullman		
2432	Clifton Vista-Dome		
2432	Clifton Vista-Dome		
2436	Mooseheart Observation		

1609	027 3-Car Steam Freight, 59, 60	(2)	125
246	2-4-2 w/1130T Tender		
6162-25	Gondola with Canisters, blue		
6476	Lehigh Valley Hopper, red		
6057	Lionel Lines Caboose		

1611	027 4-Car Alaskan Freight, 59	(3)	650
614	Alaska Diesel Switcher		
6825	Flat Car with Arch Trestle Bridge		
6162-50	Alaska Gondola		
6465	Lionel Lines Tank Car, black		
6027	Alaska Caboose		

1612	The General Old-Timer Outfit, 59, 60	(1)	375
1862	4-4-0 General w/1862T Tender		
1866	General Mail-Baggage Car		
1865	General Passenger Car		

1613S	4-Car Baltimore & Ohio Steam Freight, 59	(4)	300
247	2-4-2 w/247T Tender		
6826	Flat Car with Christmas Trees		
6819	Flat Car with Helicopter		
6821	Flat Car with Crates		
6017	Lionel Lines Caboose		

1615	5-Car Boston & Maine Diesel Freight, 59	(4)	625
217P/C	Boston & Maine Alco's, AB		
6800	Airplane Car		
6464-475	Boston & Maine Box Car		
6812	Track Maintenance Car		
6825	Flat Car with Arch Trestle Bridge		
6017-100	Boston & Maine Caboose		

1617S	5-Car Busy Beaver Steam Work Train, 59	(4)	825
2018	2-6-4 w/1130T Tender		
6816	Flat Car with Allis Chalmers Tractor Dozer		
6536	Minneapolis & St. Louis Hopper		
6812	Track Maintenance Car		
6670	Derrick Car		
6119	D L & W Work Caboose		

1619W	5-Car Santa Fe Diesel Freight, 59	(3)	425
218P/T	Santa Fe Twin Diesel Alco's, AA		
6819	Flat Car with Helicopter		
6802	Flat Car with Two Girders		
6801	Flat Car with Boat		
6519	Allis Chalmers Car		
6017-185	A T & S F Caboose, gray		

1621WS	Construction Special Steam Freight, 59	(3)	325
2037	2-6-4 w/6026W Tender		
6825	Flat Car with Arch Trestle Bridge		
6519	Allis Chalmers Car		
6062	Gondola with Three Cable Reels		
6464-475	Boston & Maine Box Car		
6017	Lionel Lines Caboose		

1623W	5-Car Northern Pacific Diesel Freight, 59	(5)	950
2349	Northern Pacific GP-9		
3512	Operating Fireman-Ladder Car		
3435	Operating Aquarium Car		
6424	Flat Car with Two Autos		
6062	Gondola with Three Cable Reels		
6017	Lionel Lines Caboose		

1625WS	5-Car Action King Steam Freight, 59	(4)	400
2037	2-6-4 w/6026W Tender		
6636	Alaska Hopper		
3512	Operating Fireman-Ladder Car		
6470	Exploding Target Car		
6650	IRBM Missile Launching Car		
6017	Lionel Lines Caboose		

1626W	4-Car Santa Fe Diesel Passenger, 59	(4)	650
208P/T	Santa Fe Twin Diesel Alco's, AA		
3428	Operating U.S. Mail Car		
2412	Santa Fe Vista-Dome, blue stripe		
2412	Santa Fe Vista-Dome, blue stripe		
2416	Santa Fe Observation, blue stripe		

1627S	027 3-Car Steam Freight, 60	(1)	125
244	2-4-2 w/244T Tender		
6062	Gondola with Three Cable Reels		
6825	Flat Car with Arch Trestle Bridge		
6017	Lionel Lines Caboose		

1629	4-Car C & O Diesel Freight, 60	(1)	325
225	C & O Alco, A		
6650	Missile Launching Car		
6470	Exploding Target Car		
6819	Flat Car with Helicopter		
6219	C & O Caboose		

1631WS	4-Car Industrial Steam Freight, 60	(2)	325
243	2-4-2 w/243W Tender		
6519	Allis Chalmers Car		
6812	Track Maintenance Car		
6465	Cities Service Tank Car		
6017	Lionel Lines Caboose		

1633	Land-Sea-Air 2 Unit Diesel Freight, 60	(3)	750
224P/C	US Navy Alco, AB		
6544	Missile Firing Car		
6830	Submarine Car		
6820	Aerial Missile Transport Car		
6017-200	US Navy Caboose		

1635WS	Heavy-Duty Special Steam Freight, 60	(4)	450
2037	2-6-4 w/243W Tender		
6361	Timber Transport Car		
6826	Flat Car with Christmas Trees		
6636	Alaska Hopper		
6821	Flat Car with Crates		
6017	Lionel Lines Caboose		

1637W	5-Car Twin Unit Diesel Freight, 60	(4)	550
218P/T	Santa Fe Twin Alco's, AA		
6475	Pickle Car		
6175	Flat Car with Rocket		
6464-475	Boston & Maine Box Car		
6801	Flat Car with Boat		
6017-185	Santa Fe Caboose		

1639WS	Power House Special Steam Freight, 60	(5)	1750
2037	2-6-4 w/243W Tender		
6816	Flat Car with Allis Chalmers Tractor Dozer		
6817	Flat Car with Allis Chalmers Motor Scraper		
6812	Track Maintenance Car		
6530	Fire and Safety Training Car		
6560	Lionel Lines Crane Car		
6119	D L & W Work Caboose		

1640W	Presidential Campaign Special, 60	(3)	650
218P/T	Santa Fe Twin Alco's, AA		
3428	Operating US Mail Box Car		
2412	Santa Fe Vista-Dome, blue stripe		
2412	Santa Fe Vista-Dome, blue stripe		
2416	Santa Fe Observation, blue stripe		
1640-100	Kit For Presidential Special		

1641	3-Car Headliner Steam Freight, 61	(1)	125
246	2-4-2 w/244T Tender		
3362	Helium Tank Unloading Car		
6162	Gondola with Canisters		
6057	Lionel Lines Caboose		

1642	3-Car Circus Special Steam Freight, 61	(2)	175
244	2-4-2 w/1130T Tender		
3376	Operating Giraffe Car		
6405	Flat Car with Piggyback Van		
6119	D L & W Work Caboose		

1643	4-Car Sky-Scout Diesel Freight, 61	(2)	275
230	Chesapeake & Ohio Alco, A		
3509	Satellite Launching Car		
6050	Lionel Lines Savings Bank Box Car		
6175	Flat Car with Rocket		
6058	Chesapeake & Ohio Caboose		

1644	Frontier Special General Passenger, 61	(2)	475
1862	4-4-0 General w/1862T Tender		
3370	Animated Sheriff and Outlaw Car		
1866	General Mail-Baggage Car		
1865	General Passenger Car		

1645	027 4-Car Diesel Freight, 61	(3)	240
229	Minneapolis & St. Louis Alco, A		
3410	Helicopter Launching Car		
6465	Cities Service Tank Car		
6825	Flat Car with Trestle Bridge		
6059	Minneapolis & St. Louis Caboose		

1646	4-Car Utility Steam Freight, 61	(2)	225
233	2-4-2 w/233W Tender		
6162	Gondola with Canisters		
6343	Barrel Ramp Car		
6476	Lehigh Valley Hopper, red		
6017	Lionel Lines Caboose		

1647	Freedom Fighter Missile Launcher Outfit, 61	(4)	950
45	USMC Mobile Missile Launcher		
3665	Minuteman Missile Launching Car		
3519	Automatic Satellite Launching Car		
6830	Submarine Transport Car		
6448	Exploding Target Range Car		
6814	First Aid Medical Car		

1648	5-Car Supply Line Steam Freight, 61	(2)	275
2037	2-6-4 w/233W Tender		
6062	Gondola with Cable Reels		
6465	Cities Service Tank Car		
6519	Allis Chalmers Car		
6476	Lehigh Valley Hopper, red		
6017	Lionel Lines Caboose		

1649	027 5-Car Two Unit Diesel Freight, 61	(5)	525
218P/C	Santa Fe Alco, AB		
6343	Barrel Ramp Car		
6445	Fort Knox Gold Bullion Transport Car		
6475	Pickle Car		
6405	Flat Car with Piggyback Van		
6017	Lionel Lines Caboose		

1650	5-Car Guardian Steam Freight, 61	(4)	450
2037	2-6-4 w/233W Tender		
6544	Missile Firing Car		
6470	Exploding Target Car		
3330	Operating Submarine in Kit Form		
3419	Operating Helicopter Launching Car		
6017	Lionel Caboose		

1651	4-Car All Passenger Diesel, 61	(3)	650
218P/T	Santa Fe Twin Alco's, AA		
2414	Santa Fe Pullman, blue stripe		
2412	Santa Fe Vista-Dome, blue stripe		
2412	Santa Fe Vista-Dome, blue stripe		
2416	Santa Fe Observation, blue stripe		

1800	The General Frontier Pack, 59, 60	(2)	400
1862	4-4-0 General w/1862T Tender		
1877	Flat Car with Six Horses		
1866	General Mail-Baggage Car		
1865	General Passenger Car		
	General Story Book		

1805	Land-Sea-And Air Gift Pack, 60	(4)	1750
45	USMC Mobile Missile Launcher		
3429	USMC Operating Helicopter Launching Car		
3820	USMC Operating Submarine Car		
6640	USMC Missile Launching Car		
6824	USMC First Aid Medical Car		

1809	The Western Gift Pack, 61	(2)	300
244	2-4-2 w/1130 T Tender		
3370	Animated Sheriff and Outlaw Car		
3376	Operating Giraffe Car		
1877	Horse Transport Car		
6017	Lionel Lines Caboose		

1810	The Space Age Gift Pack, 61	(2)	450
231	Rock Island Alco, A		
3665	Minuteman Missile Launching Car		
3519	Satellite Launching Car		
3820	Operating Submarine Car		
6017	Lionel Lines Caboose		

2100	Lionel O Passenger Train, 46	(5)	550
224	2-6-2 w/2466T Tender		
2442	Pullman, brown		
2442	Pullman, brown		
2443	Observation, brown		

2100W	Lionel O Passenger Train, 46	(4)	500
224	2-6-2 w/2466W Tender		
2442	Pullman, brown		
2442	Pullman, brown		
2443	Observation, brown		

2101	Lionel O Gauge Freight Set, 46	(5)	400
224	2-6-2 w/2466T Tender		
2555	Sunoco Oil Car		
2452	Pennsylvania Gondola		
2457	Pennsylvania Caboose		

2101W	Lionel O Gauge Freight Set, 46	(4)	325
224	2-6-2 w/2466W Tender		
2555	Sunoco Oil Car		
2452	Pennsylvania Gondola		
2457	Pennsylvania Caboose		

2103W	Lionel O Gauge Freight Set, 46	(4)	425
224	2-6-2 w/2466W Tender		
2458	Pennsylvania Automobile Car		
3559	Operating Coal Dump Car		
2555	Sunoco Oil Car		
2457	Pennsylvania Caboose		

2105WS	Lionel Freight Outfit, 46	(4)	450
671	Pennsy Turbine w/2466W Tender		
2555	Sunoco Oil Car		
2454	Baby Ruth Box Car		
2457	Pennsylvania Caboose		

2110WS	Lionel Passenger Train, 46	(5)	1750
671	Pennsy Turbine w/2466W Tender		
2625	Irvington Pullman		
2625	Irvington Pullman		
2625	Irvington Pullman		

2111WS	Lionel Freight Train, 46	(5)	825
671	Pennsy Turbine w/2466W Tender		
3459	Operating Dump Car		
2411	Lionel Lines "Big Inch" Flat Car w/Metal Pipes		
2460	Lionel Lines Crane Car		
2420	D L & W Wrecking Car		

2113WS	Lionel O Gauge Freight Outfit, 46	(5)	2000
726	Berkshire w/2426W Tender		
2855	Sunoco Oil Car		
3854	Operating Merchandise Car		
2457	Pennsylvania Caboose		

2114WS	O Passenger Outfit, 46	(5)	2500
726	Berkshire w/2426W Tender		
2625	Irvington Pullman		
2625	Irvington Pullman		
2625	Irvington Pullman		

2115WS	O Gauge Work Train With Smoke, 46	(5)	1400
726	Berkshire w/2426W Tender		
2458	Automobile Car		
3451	Automatic Unloading Lumber Car		
2460	Lionel Lines Crane Car		
2420	D L & W Wrecking Car		

2120S	De Luxe Passenger, 47	(5)	500
675	2-6-2 w/2466T Tender		
2442	Pullman, brown		
2442	Pullman, brown		
2443	Observation, brown		

2120WS	De Luxe Passenger, 47	(4)	525
675	2-6-2 w/2466WX Tender		
2442	Pullman, brown		
2442	Pullman, brown		
2443	Observation, brown		

2121S	Lionel Freight Set, 47	(5)	375
675	2-6-2 w/2466T Tender		
2452	Pennsylvania Gondola		
2555	Sunoco Oil Car		
2457	Pennsylvania Caboose		

2121WS	Lionel Freight Set, 47	(4)	375
675	2-6-2 w/2466WX Tender		
2452	Pennsylvania Gondola		
2555	Sunoco Oil Car		
2457	Pennsylvania Caboose		

2123WS	Lionel Freight Set, 47	(4)	450
675	2-6-2 w/2466WX Tender		
2458	Pennsylvania Automobile Car		
3559	Automatic Dump Car		
2555	Sunoco Oil Car		
2457	Pennsylvania Caboose		

2124W	Lionel Passenger Set, 47	(4)	3300
2332	Pennsylvania GG-1		
2625	Irvington Pullman		
2625	Madison Pullman		
2625	Manhattan Pullman		

2125WS	Lionel Freight Train, 47	(4)	575
671	Pennsy Turbine w/671W Tender		
2411	Lionel Lines Flat Car with Pipes/Logs		
2454	Baby Ruth Box Car		
2452	Pennsylvania Gondola		
2457	Pennsylvania Caboose		

2126WS	Lionel Passenger Set, 47	(4)	1750
671	Pennsy Turbine w/671W Tender		
2625	Irvington Pullman		
2625	Madison Pullman		
2625	Manhattan Pullman		

2127WS	Lionel Work Train, 47	(4)	750
671	Pennsy Turbine w/671W Tender		
3459	Automatic Dump Car		
2461	Lionel Lines Transformer Car		
2460	Lionel Lines Crane Car		
2420	D L & W Wrecker-Caboose		

2129WS	Lionel Freight Set, 47	(4)	2000
726	Berkshire w/2426W Tender		
3854	Operating Merchandise Car		
2411	Lionel Lines Flat Car with Pipes/Logs		
2855	Sunoco Oil Car		
2457	Pennsylvania Caboose		

2131WS	De Luxe Work Train, 47	(4)	1100
726	Berkshire w/2426W Tender		
3462	Operating Milk Car with Platform		
3451	Automatic Lumber Car		
2460	Lionel Lines Crane Car		
2420	D L & W Wrecker-Caboose		

2133W	Twin Diesel O Gauge Freight Train, 48	(4)	1250
2333P/T	Santa Fe or New York Central F-3, AA		
2458	Automobile Car		
3459	Operating Ore Dump Car		
2555	Sunoco Oil Car		
2357	Lionel Caboose		

2135WS	Lionel Freight Train, 48, 49	(3)	350
675	2-6-2 w/2466WX Tender, 48		
675	2-6-2 w/6466WX Tender, 49		
2456	Lehigh Valley Hopper, 48		
6456	Lehigh Valley Hopper, 49		
2411	Lionel Lines Flat Car with Logs, 48		
6411	Lionel Lines Flat Car with Logs, 49		
2357	Lionel Caboose, 48		
6457	Lionel Caboose, 49		

2136WS	Passenger Train, 48, 49	(4)	600
675	2-6-2 w/2466WX Tender, 48		
675	2-6-2 w/6466WX Tender, 49		
2442	Pullman, brown, 48		
6442	Pullman, brown, 49		
2442	Pullman, brown, 48		
6442	Pullman, brown, 49		
2443	Observation, brown, 48		
6443	Observation, brown, 49		

2137WS	De Luxe Freight Train, 48	(3)	400
675	2-6-2 w/2466WX Tender		
2458	Automobile Car		
3459	Operating Ore Dump Car		
2456	Lehigh Valley Hopper		
2357	Lionel Caboose		

2139W	Lionel 4-Car Freight Set, 48	(3)	1250
2332	Pennsylvania GG-1		
3451	Operating Lumber Car		
2458	Automobile Car		
2456	Lehigh Valley Hopper		
2357	Lionel Caboose		

2139W	O Gauge 4-Car Freight Outfit, 49	(3)	1200
2332	Pennsylvania GG-1		
6456	Lehigh Valley Hopper		
3464	Operating Box Car		
3461	Operating Lumber Car		
6457	Lionel Caboose		

2140WS	De Luxe Passenger Set, 48, 49	(4)	900
671	Pennsy Turbine w/2671W Tender		
2400	Maplewood Pullman		
2402	Chatham Pullman		
2401	Hillside Observation		

2141WS	Four-Car Freight Train, 48, 49	(3)	500
671	Pennsy Turbine w/2671W Tender, 48, 49		
3451	Operating Lumber Car, 48		
3461	Operating Lumber Car, 49		
3462	Operating Milk Car with Platform, 48		
3472	Operating Milk Car with Platform, 49		
2456	Lehigh Valley Hopper, 48		
6456	Lehigh Valley Hopper, 49		
2357	Lionel Caboose, 48		
6457	Lionel Caboose, 49		

2143WS	De Luxe Work Train, 48	(4)	700
671	Pennsy Turbine w/2671W Tender		
3459	Operating Ore Dump Car		
2461	Lionel Lines Transformer Car		
2460	Lionel Lines Crane Car		
2420	D L & W Wrecker-Caboose		

2144W	**3-Car De Luxe Passenger Outfit, 48, 49**	**(4)**	**2500**
2332	Pennsylvania GG-1		
2625	Irvington Pullman		
2627	Madison Pullman		
2628	Manhattan Pullman		

2145WS	**4-Car Freight Set, 48**	**(4)**	**850**
726	Berkshire w/2426W Tender		
3462	Automatic Milk Car with Platform		
2411	Lionel Lines Flat Car with Logs		
2460	Lionel Lines Crane Car		
2357	Lionel Caboose		

2146WS	**Lionel Pullman Train, 48, 49**	**(5)**	**2300**
726	Berkshire w/2426W Tender		
2625	Irvington Pullman		
2627	Madison Pullman		
2628	Manhattan Pullman		

2147WS	**4-Car Freight Set, 49**	**(3)**	**400**
675	2-6-2 w/6466WX Tender		
3472	Operating Milk Car and Platform		
6465	Sunoco Oil Car		
3469	Operating Ore Dump Car		
6457	Lionel Caboose		

2148WS	**Lionel O Deluxe Pullman Set, 50**	**(5)**	**5000**
773	Hudson w/2426W Tender		
2625	Irvington Pullman		
2627	Madison Pullman		
2628	Manhattan Pullman		

2149B	**O Gauge 4-Car Diesel Work Train, 49**	**(4)**	**750**
622	Lionel Diesel Switcher		
6520	Operating Searchlight Car		
3469	Operating Ore Dump Car		
2460	Lionel Lines Crane Car		
6419	D L & W Railroad Wrecker-Caboose		

2150WS	**O Deluxe Passenger Set, 50**	**(4)**	**850**
681	Pennsy Turbine w/2671W Tender		
2421	Maplewood Pullman		
2422	Chatham Pullman		
2423	Hillside Observation		

2151W	**5-Car O Gauge Diesel Set, 49**	**(3)**	**1100**
2333P/T	Santa Fe or New York Central F-3, AA		
3464	Operating Box Car		
6555	Sunoco Oil Car		
3469	Operating Ore Dump Car		
6520	Operating Searchlight Car		
6457	Lionel Caboose		

2153WS	**4-Car De Luxe Work Train, 49**	**(4)**	**600**
671	Pennsy Turbine w/2671W Tender		
3469	Operating Ore Dump Car		
6520	Operating Searchlight Car		
2460	Lionel Lines Crane Car		
6419	D L & W Railroad Wrecker-Caboose		

2155WS	**4-Car Freight Train, 49**	**(4)**	**850**
726	Berkshire w/2426W Tender		
6411	Lionel Lines Flat Car with Logs		
3656	Operating Cattle Car, Stock and Platform		
2460	Lionel Lines Crane Car		
6457	Lionel Caboose		

2159W	**Lionel 5-Car Freight, 50**	**(5)**	**2000**
2330	Pennsylvania GG-1		
3464	Operating Box Car		
6462	NYC Gondola Car		
3461X	Operating Lumber Car		
6456	Lehigh Valley Hopper		
6457	Lionel Caboose		

2161W	**Twin Diesel Freight, 50**	**(3)**	**1250**
2343	Santa Fe Twin Diesel F-3's, AA		
3469X	Operating Ore Dump Car		
3464	Operating Box Car		
3461X	Operating Log Car		
6520	Operating Searchlight Car		
6457	Lionel Caboose		

2163WS	**4-Car Freight, 50, 51**	**(3)**	**575**
736	Berkshire w/2671WX Tender		
6472	Refrigerator Car		
6462	NYC Gondola Car		
6555	Sunoco Oil Car, 50		
6465	Sunoco Oil Car, 51		
6457	Lionel Caboose		

2165WS	**O 4-Car Freight Set, 50**	**(3)**	**650**
736	Berkshire w/2671WX Tender		
3472	Operating Milk Car and Platform		
6456	Lehigh Valley Hopper		
3461X	Operating Lumber Car		
6457	Lionel Caboose		

2167WS	**3-Car Freight, 50, 51**	**(3)**	**425**
681	Pennsy Turbine w/2671W Tender		
6462	NYC Gondola Car		
3464	Operating Box Car		
6457	Lionel Caboose		

2169WS	**5-Car Freight w/Smoke and Whistle, 50**	**(5)**	**2750**
773	Hudson w/2426W Tender		
3656	Operating Cattle Car and Platform		
6456	Lehigh Valley Hopper		
3469X	Operating Ore Dump Car		
6411	Lionel Lines Log Car		
6457	Lionel Caboose		

2171W	**Twin Diesel Freight, 50**	**(3)**	**1250**
2344	New York Central Twin Diesel F-3's, AA		
3469X	Operating Ore Dump Car		
3464	Operating Box Car		
3461X	Operating Log Car		
6520	Operating Searchlight Car		
6457	Lionel Caboose		

2173WS	**Lionel 4-Car Freight, 50, 51**	**(3)**	**550**
681	Pennsy Turbine w/2671W Tender		
3472	Operating Milk Car and Platform		
6555	Sunoco Oil Car, 50		
6465	Sunoco Oil Car, 51		
3469X	Operating Ore Dump Car		
6457	Lionel Caboose		

2175W	**Magnificent Twin Diesel Freights, 50, 51**	**(3)**	**1200**
2343	Santa Fe Twin Diesel F-3's, AA		
6456	Lehigh Valley Hopper, black, 50		
6456	Lehigh Valley Hopper, maroon, 51		
3464	Operating Box Car		
6555	Sunoco Oil Car, 50		
6465	Sunoco Oil Car, 51		
6462	NYC Gondola Car		
6457	Lionel Caboose		

2177WS	**3-Car Freight, 52**	**(4)**	**325**
675	2-6-2 w/2046W Tender		
6462	NYC Gondola Car		
6465	Sunoco Oil Car		
6457	Lionel Caboose		

2179WS	**4-Car Freight, 52**	**(3)**	**425**
671(rr)	Pennsy Turbine w/2046WX Tender		
3464	Operating Box Car		
6465	Sunoco Oil Car		
6462	NYC Gondola Car		
6457	Lionel Caboose		

2183WS	**4-Car Freight, 52**	**(2)**	**550**
726(rr)	Berkshire w/2046W Tender		
3464	Operating Box Car		
6462	NYC Gondola Car		
6465	Sunoco Oil Car		
6457	Lionel Caboose		

2185W	**Magnificent Twin Diesel Freights, 50, 51**	**(3)**	**1200**
2344	New York Central Twin Diesel F-3's, AA		
6456	Lehigh Valley Hopper, black, 50		
6456	Lehigh Valley Hopper, maroon, 51		
3464	Operating Box Car		
6555	Sunoco Oil Car, 50		
6465	Sunoco Oil Car, 51		
6462	NYC Gondola Car		
6457	Lionel Caboose		

2187WS	**5-Car Freight, 52**	**(4)**	**500**
671	Pennsy Turbine w/2046WX Tender		
6462	NYC Gondola Car		
3472	Operating Milk Car and Platform		
6456	Lehigh Valley Hopper, maroon		
3469	Operating Ore Dump Car		
6457	Lionel Caboose		

2189WS	**Transcontinental Fast Freight, 52**	**(4)**	**650**
726	Berkshire w/2046W Tender		
3520	Operating Searchlight Car		
3656	Operating Cattle Car and Platform		
6462	NYC Gondola Car		
3461	Operating Lumber Car		
6457	Lionel Caboose		

2190W	**Lionel Super Speedliner, 52, 53**	**(3)**	**2000**
2343	Santa Fe Twin Diesel F-3's, AA, 52		
2353	Santa Fe Twin Diesel F-3's, AA, 53		
2533	Silver Cloud Pullman		
2532	Silver Range Vista Dome		
2534	Silver Bluff Pullman		
2531	Silver Dawn Observation		

2191W	**4-Car Diesel Freights, 52**	**(3)**	**1500**
2343	Santa Fe Twin Diesel F-3's, AA		
2343C	Santa Fe B Unit		
6462	NYC Gondola Car		
6656	Stock Car		
6456	Lehigh Valley Hopper		
6457	Lionel Caboose		

2193W	**4-Car Diesel Freights, 52**	**(3)**	**1500**
2344	New York Central Twin Diesel F-3's, AA		
2344C	New York Central B Unit		
6462	NYC Gondola Car		
6656	Stock Car		
6456	Lehigh Valley Hopper		
6457	Lionel Caboose		

2201WS	**Highballing Freight, 53, 54**	**(3)**	**550**
685	4-6-4 w/6026W Tender, 53		
665	4-6-4 w/6026W Tender, 54		
6462	NYC Gondola Car		
6464-50	Minneapolis & St. Louis Box Car		
6465	Sunoco Oil Car		
6357	Llonel Caboose		

2203WS	**Highballing Freight, 53**	**(4)**	**550**
681	Pennsy Turbine w/2046WX Tender		
3520	Operating Searchlight Car		
6415	Sunoco Oil Car		
6464-25	Great Northern Box Car		
6417	Pennsylvania Caboose		

2205WS	**5-Car Freight, 53**	**(3)**	**600**
736	Berkshire w/2046W Tender		
3484	Pennsylvania Operating Box Car		
6415	Sunoco Oil Car		
6468	Automobile Car, blue		
6456	Lehigh Valley Hopper		
6417	Pennsylvania Caboose		

2207W	**Triple Diesel Freight, 53**	**(3)**	**1500**
2353	Santa Fe Twin Diesel F-3's, AA		
2343C	Santa Fe B Unit		
3484	Pennsylvania Operating Box Car		
6415	Sunoco Oil Car		
6462	NYC Gondola Car		
6417	Pennsylvania Caboose		

168

2209W **Triple Diesel Freight, 53** (3) 1500
2354 New York Central Twin Diesel F-3's, AA
2344C New York Central B Unit
3484 Pennsylvania Operating Box Car
6415 Sunoco Oil Car
6462 NYC Gondola Car
6417 Pennsylvania Caboose

2211WS **4-Car Freight, 53** (4) 550
681 Pennsy Turbine w/2046WX Tender
3656 Operating Cattle Car with Platform
3461 Operating Lumber Car
6464-75 Rock Island Box Car
6417 Pennsylvania Caboose

2213WS **5-Car Freight, 53** (3) 600
736 Berkshire w/2046W Tender
3461 Operating Lumber Car
3520 Operating Searchlight Car
3469 Operating Ore Car
6460 Lionel Lines Crane Car
6419 D L & W Work Caboose

2217WS **O Gauge 4-Car Freight, 54** (4) 1000
682 Pennsy Turbine w/2046WX Tender
3562 Operating Barrel Car, gray
6464-175 Rock Island Box Car
6356 NYC Stock Car
6417 Pennsylvania Caboose

2219W **Fairbanks-Morse Power Giant, 54** (4) 1250
2321 Lackawanna FM
6415 Sunoco Oil Car
6462 NYC Gondola Car, green
6464-50 Minneapolis & St. Louis Box Car
6456 Lehigh Valley Hopper, gray
6417 Pennsylvania Caboose

2221WS **O Gauge 5-Car Freight, 54** (3) 600
646 4-6-4 w/2046W Tender
3620 Operating Searchlight Car
3469 Operating Dump Car
6468 Automobile Car, blue
6456 Lehigh Vally Hopper, gray
6417 Lionel Lines Caboose

2222WS **Lionel O Gauge 3-Car Pullman Set, 54** (4) 1800
646 4-6-4 w/2046W Tender
2530 REA Baggage Car, large or small door version
2532 Silver Range Vista-Dome
2531 Silver Dawn Observation

2223W **O Gauge 5-Car Freight, 54** (5) 2500
2321 Lackawanna FM
3482 Operating Milk Car with Platform
3461 Operating Lumber Car
6464-100 Western Pacific Box Car
6462 NYC Gondola Car, red
6417 Lehigh Valley Caboose

2225WS **Lionel 5-Car Work Freight, 54** (4) 750
736 Berkshire w/2046W Tender
3461 Operating Lumber Car
3620 Operating Searchlight Car
3562 Operating Barrel Car, gray
6460 Lionel Lines Crane Car, black cab
6419 D L & W Work Caboose

2227W **O Gauge 5-Car Freight, 54** (3) 1500
2353 Santa Fe Twin Diesel F-3's, AA
3562 Operating Barrel Car, gray
6356 NYC Stock Car
6456 Lehigh Valley Hopper, red
6468 Automobile Car, blue
6417 Lionel Lines Caboose

2229W **O Gauge 5-Car Freight, 54** (4) 1500
2354 New York Central Twin Diesel F-3's, AA
3562 Operating Barrel Car, gray
6356 NYC Stock Car
6456 Lehigh Valley Hopper, red
6468 Automobile Car, blue
6417 Lionel Lines Caboose

2231W **O Gauge 5-Car Freight, 54** (4) 2500
2356 Southern Twin Diesel F-3's, AA
2356C Southern B Unit
6561 Lionel Lines Cable Car
6511 Lionel Pipe Car
3482 Operating Milk Car with Platform
6415 Sunoco Oil Car
6417 Lionel Lines Caboose

2234W **Super-Streamliner, 54** (3) 3000
2353 Santa Fe Twin Diesel F-3's, AA
2530 REA Baggage Car, small door
2532 Silver Range Vista-Dome
2533 Silver Cloud Pullman
2531 Silver Dawn Observation

2235W **O Gauge 4-Car Freight, 55** (3) 550
2338 Milwaukee Road GP-7
6436 Lehigh Valley Hopper
6362 Railway Truck Car
6560 Lionel Lines Crane Car, red
6419 D L & W Work Caboose

2237WS **O Gauge 3-Car Freight, 55** (3) 400
665 4-6-4 w/6026W Tender
3562 Operating Barrel Car, yellow
6415 Sunoco Oil Car
6417 Pennsylvania Caboose

2239W **O Gauge Streak-Liner, 55** (4) 2000
2363P/C Illinois Central F-3, AB
6672 Santa Fe Refrigerator Car
6464-125 NYC Box Car
6414 Evans Auto Loader
6517 Lionel Bay Window Caboose

2241WS **O Gauge Freight Snorter, 55** (4) 550
646 4-6-4 w/2046W Tender
3359 Operating Twin-Bin Dump Car
6446 N & E Covered Hopper
3620 Operating Searchlight Car
6417 Pennsylvania Caboose

2243W **The High and the Mighty, 55** (4) 1500
2321 Lackawanna FM
3662 Operating Milk Car with Platform
6511 Lionel Pipe Car
6462 NYC Gondola Car, red
6464-300 Rutland Box Car
6417 Lionel Lines Caboose

2244W **The Sweetest Sight on Rails, 55** (4) 2500
2367P/C Wabash F-3, AB
2530 REA Baggage Car
2533 Silver Cloud Pullman
2531 Silver Dawn Observation

2245WS **Whistles While She Works, 55** (4) 850
682 Pennsy Turbine w/2046W Tender
3562 Operating Barrel Car
6436 Lehigh Valley Hopper
6561 Lionel Lines Cable Car
6560 Lionel Lines Crane Car
6419 D L & W Work Caboose

2247W **O Gauge 5-Car Freight, 55** (4) 2500
2367P/C Wabash F-3, AB
6462 NYC Gondola Car, red
3662 Operating Milk Car with Platform
6464-150 Missouri Pacific Box Car
3361 Operating Log Car
6517 Lionel Lines Bay Window Caboose

2249WS **O Gauge 5-Car Freight, 55** (4) 900
736 Berkshire w/2046W Tender
3359 Operating Twin-Bin Dump Car
3562 Operating Barrel Car, yellow
6414 Evans Auto Loader
6464-275 State of Maine Box Car
6517 Lionel Lines Bay Window Caboose

2251W **The High and the Mighty, 55** (4) 2500
2331 Virginian FM
3359 Operating Twin-Bin Dump Car
3562 Operating Barrel Car, yellow
6414 Evans Auto Loader
6464-275 State of Maine Box Car
6517 Lionel Lines Bay Window Caboose

2253W **A Miracle of Modeling Accuracy, 55** (4) 2500
2340-25 Pennsylvania GG-1, green
3620 Operating Searchlight Car
6414 Evans Auto Loader
3361 Operating Log Car
6464-300 Rutland Box Car
6417 Pennsylvania Caboose

2254W **The Congressional, 55** (4) 5000
2340-1 Pennsylvania GG-1, tuscan red
2544 Molly Pitcher Pullman
2543 William Penn Pullman
2542 Betsy Ross Vista-Dome
2541 Alexander Hamilton Observation

2255W **O Gauge 4-Car Work Train, 56** (4) 600
601 Seaboard Switcher
3424 Wabash Operating Brakeman Box Car
6362 Railway Truck Car
6560 Lionel Lines Crane Car
6119 D L & W Work Caboose, orange

2257WS **O Gauge 5-Car Freight, 56** (3) 500
665 4-6-4 w/2046W Tender
3361 Operating Log Car
6346 Alcoa Covered Hopper
6467 Miscellaneous Car
6462 NYC Gondola Car, red
6427 Lionel Lines Caboose

2259W **O Gauge 5-Car Freight, 56** (3) 850
2350 New Haven Electric
6464-425 New Haven Box Car
6430 Cooper-Jarrett Van Car
3650 Searchlight Extension Car
6511 Lionel Pipe Car
6427 Lionel Lines Caboose

2261WS **O Gauge Freight Hauler, 56** (4) 650
646 4-6-4 w/2046W Tender
3562 Operating Barrel Car, yellow
6414 Evans Auto Loader
6436 Lehigh Valley Hopper
6376 Circus Car
6417 Pennsylvania Caboose

2263W **O Gauge 5-Car Freight, 56** (4) 1000
2350 New Haven Electric
3359 Operating Twin-Bin Dump Car
6468 New Haven Automobile Box Car
6414 Evans Auto Loader
3662 Operating Milk Car with Platform
6517 Lionel Lines Bay Window Caboose

2265SW **O Gauge 5-Car Freight, 56** (4) 750
736 Berkshire w/2046W Tender
3620 Operating Searchlight Car
6430 Cooper-Jarrett Van Car
3424 Wabash Operating Brakeman Box Car
6467 Miscellaneous Car
6517 Lionel Lines Bay Window Caboose

2267W	**Proud Giant of the Rails, 56**	(4)	1650
2331	Virginian FM		
3562	Operating Barrel Car, yellow		
3359	Operating Twin-Bin Dump Car		
3361	Operating Lumber Car		
6560	Lionel Lines Crane Car		
6419	D L & W Work Caboose		
2269W	**Majestic O Gauge Freight Set, 56**	(5)	3900
2368P/C	Baltimore & Ohio F-3, AB		
3356	Operating Horse Car with Corral		
6518	Transformer Car		
6315	Gulf Chemical Car		
3361	Operating Log Car		
6517	Lionel Lines Bay Window Caboose		
2270W	**Proud Giant of the Rails, 56**	(5)	5500
2341	Jersey Central FM		
2533	Silver Cloud Pullman		
2532	Silver Range Vista-Dome		
2531	Silver Dawn Observation		
2271W	**O Gauge 5-Car Freight Train, 56**	(4)	3000
2360-25	Pennsylvania GG-1, green		
3424	Wabash Operating Brakeman Box Car		
3662	Operating Milk Car with Platform		
6414	Evans Auto Loader		
6418	Machinery Car		
6417	Pennsylvania Caboose		
2373W	**From the Midwest to the East, 56**	(5)	4000
2378P/C	The Milwaukee Road F-3, AB		
342	Operating Culvert Loader		
6342	Culvert Car		
3562	Operating Barrel Car, yellow		
3662	Operating Milk Car with Platform		
3359	Operating Twin-Bin Dump Car		
6517	Lionel Lines Bay Window Caboose		
2274W	**The Great Congressional, 56**	(5)	5000
2360-1	Pennsylvania GG-1, Tuscan red		
2544	Molly Pitcher Pullman		
2543	William Penn Pullman		
2542	Betsy Ross Vista-Dome		
2541	Alexander Hamilton Observation		
2275W	**O Gauge 4-Car Freight, 57**	(3)	750
2339	Wabash GP-7		
3444	Animated Gondola		
6464-475	Boston & Maine Box Car		
6425	Gulf Oil Car		
6427	Lionel Lines Caboose		
2276W	**Budd RDC Commuter Set, 57**	(4)	2000
404	Baltimore & Ohio Budd Unit		
2559	Baltimore & Ohio Passenger Car		
2559	Baltimore & Ohio Passenger Car		
2277SW	**O Gauge 4-Car Work Train, 57**	(4)	550
665	4-6-4 w/2046W Tender		
3650	Extension Searchlight Car		
6446	N & W Covered Hopper		
6560	Lionel Lines Crane Car		
6119	D L & W Work Caboose		
2279W	**O Gauge 5-Car Freight, 57**	(3)	825
2350	New Haven Electric		
6464-425	New Haven Box Car		
6424	Twin Auto Car		
3424	Operating Brakeman Box Car		
6477	Flat Car with Pipes		
6427	Lionel Lines Caboose		
2281W	**O Gauge 5-Car Freight, 57**	(3)	1200
2243	Santa Fe F-3, AB		
3562	Operating Barrel Car, orange		
6464-150	Missouri Pacific Box Car		
3361	Operating Log Car		
6560	Lionel Lines Crane Car		
6119	D L & W Work Caboose		

2283WS	**O Gauge 5-Car Freight, 57**	(4)	625
646	4-6-4 w/2046W Tender		
3424	Operating Brakeman Box Car		
3361	Operating Log Car		
6464-525	Minneapolis & St. Louis Box Car		
6562	Gondola Car, black		
6357	Lionel Caboose		
2285W	**O Gauge 5-Car Freight, 57**	(4)	1750
2331	Virginian FM		
6418	Machinery Car		
6414	Evans Auto Loader		
3662	Operating Milk Car with Platform		
6425	Gulf Oil Car		
6517	Lionel Lines Bay Window Caboose		
2287W	**O Gauge 5-Car Freight, 57**	(5)	1800
2351	The Milwaukee Road Electric		
342	Operating Culvert Loader		
6342	NYC Culvert Car		
6464-500	Timken Box Car		
3650	Extension Searchlight Car		
6315	Gulf Oil Car		
6427	Lionel Lines Caboose		
2289WS	**Super O Freight Train, 57**	(4)	750
736	Berkshire w/2046W Tender		
3359	Operating Twin-Bin Dump Car		
3494-275	State of Maine Operating Box Car		
3361	Operating Log Car		
6430	Cooper-Jarrett Van Car		
6427	Lionel Lines Caboose		
2291W	**Dream-Liner of the Western Roads, 57**	(4)	2750
2379P/C	Rio Grande F-3, AB		
3562	Operating Barrel Car, orange		
3530	Operating Generator Car		
3444	Animated Gondola		
6464-525	Minneapolis & St. Louis Box Car		
6657	Rio Grande Caboose		
2292WS	**Crack Super O Luxury Liner, 57**	(4)	1500
646	4-6-4 w/2046W Tender		
2530	REA Baggage Car		
2533	Silver Cloud Pullman		
2532	Silver Range Vista-Dome		
2531	Silver Dawn Observation		
2293W	**Pride of the Eastern Lines, 57**	(5)	2750
2360	Pennsylvania GG-1, tuscan red		
3662	Operating Milk Car with Platform		
3650	Extension Searchlight Car		
6414	Evans Auto Loader		
6518	Transformer Car		
6417	Pennsylvania Caboose		
2295WS	**The Grand Daddy of all Steamers, 57**	(5)	3000
746	Norfolk and Western w/746W Tender		
342	Operating Culvert Loader		
6342	NYC Culvert Car		
3530	Operating Generator Car		
3361	Operating Log Car		
6560	Lionel Lines Crane Car		
6419-100	N & W Work Caboose (576419 on car)		
2296W	**Crack Super O Luxury Liner, 57**	(4)	5000
2373P/T	Canadian Pacific Twin Diesel F-3's, AA		
2552	Skyline 500 Vista-Dome		
2552	Skyline 500 Vista-Dome		
2552	Skyline 500 Vista-Dome		
2551	Banff Park Observation		
2297SW	**The 16 Wheeler Class J, 57**	(5)	3250
746	Norfolk and Western w/746W Tender		
264	Operating Fork Lift		
6264	Lumber Car		
3356	Operating Horse Car with Corral		
345	Operating Culvert Unloader		
6342	NYC Culvert Car		
3662	Operating Milk Car with Platform		
6517	Lionel Lines Bay Window Caboose		

2501W	**Super O Work Train, 58**	(4)	825
2348	Minneapolis & St. Louis GP-9		
6464-525	Minneapolis & St. Louis Box Car		
6802	Flat Car with Girders		
6560	Lionel Lines Crane Car		
6119	D L & W Work Caboose		
2502W	**Super O Rail-Diesel Commuter, 58**	(5)	1900
400	B & O RDC Passenger Motor Unit		
2559	B & O Commuter Passenger Car		
2550	B & O Baggage-Mail Car		
2503WS	**Timberland Special Freight, 58**	(4)	600
665	4-6-4 w/2046W Tender		
3361	Operating Lumber Car		
6434	Illuminated Poultry Car		
6801	Boat Car		
6536	Minneapolis & St. Louis Hopper		
6357	Lionel Caboose		
2505W	**5-Car Super O Freight, 58**	(4)	1550
2329	Virginian Rectifier Electric		
6805	Atomic Energy Disposal Car		
6519	Allis Chalmers Car		
6800	Airplane Car		
6464-500	Timken Box Car		
6357	Lionel Caboose		
2507W	**5-Car Super O Diesel Freight, 58**	(5)	2000
2242P/C	New Haven F-3, AB		
3444	Animated Gondola Car		
6464-425	New Haven Box Car		
6424	Twin Auto Car		
6468-25	New Haven Automobile Car		
6357	Lionel Caboose		
2509WS	**The Owl 5-Car Freight, 58**	(4)	700
665	4-6-4 w/2046W Tender		
6414	Auto Transport Car		
3650	Extension Searchlight Car		
6464-475	Boston & Maine Box Car		
6805	Atomic Energy Disposal Car		
6357	Lionel Caboose		
2511W	**Super O Electric Work Train, 58**	(4)	1150
2352	Pennsylvania Electric		
3562	Operating Barrel Car, orange		
3424	Operating Brakeman Box Car		
3361	Operating Lumber Car		
6560	Lionel Lines Crane Car		
6119	D L & W Work Caboose		
2513W	**6-Car Super O Freight Train, 58**	(5)	2000
2329	Virginian Rectifier Electric		
6556	Katy Stock Car		
6425	Gulf Tank Car		
6414	Auto Transport Car		
6434	Illuminated Poultry Car		
3359	Twin-Dump Car		
6427-60	Virginian Caboose		
2515WS	**5-Car Mainliner Steam Freight, 58**	(4)	825
646	4-6-4 w/2046W Tender		
3662	Operating Milk Car with Platform		
6424	Twin Auto Car		
3444	Animated Gondola Car		
6800	Airplane Car		
6427	Lionel Lines Caboose		
2517W	**5-Car Super O Diesel Freight, 58**	(5)	2500
2379	Rio Grande F-3, AB		
6519	Allis Chalmers Car		
6805	Atomic Energy Disposal Car		
6434	Illuminated Poultry Car		
6800	Airplane Car		
6657	Rio Grande Caboose		
2518W	**Super O Passenger Train, 58**	(5)	1650
2352	Pennsylvania Electric		
2533	Silver Cloud Pullman		
2534	Silver Bluff Pullman		
2531	Silver Dawn Observation		

2519W — 6-Car Super O Diesel Freight, 58 (4) 1900
2331	Virginian FM
6434	Illuminated Poultry Car
3530	Operating GM Generator Car
6801	Boat Car
6414	Auto Transport Car
6464-275	State of Maine Box Car
6557	Illuminated Smoking Caboose

2521WS — 6-Car Super O Freight Train, 58 (5) 2350
746	Norfolk & Western w/746W Tender
6805	Atomic Energy Disposal Car
3361	Operating Lumber Car
6430	Flat Car with 2 Cooper-Jarrett Vans
3356	Operating Horse Car with Corral
6557	Illuminated Smoking Caboose

2523W — Super O Super Chief Freight, 58 (5) 1900
2383	Santa Fe Twin Diesel F-3's, AA
264	Operating Fork Lift Platform Set
6264	Lumber Car
6434	Illuminated Poultry Car
6800	Airplane Car
3662	Operating Milk Car with Platform
6517	Lionel Lines Bay Window Caboose

2525WS — 6-Car Super O Work Train, 58 (5) 3000
746	Norfolk & Western w/746W Tender
345	Culvert Unloading Station and Car
342	Culvert Loader and Car
6519	Allis Chalmers Car
6518	Transformer Car
6560	Lionel Lines Crane Car
6419-100	N & W Work Caboose

2526W — Super Chief Passenger, 58 (4) 2000
2383P/T	Santa Fe Twin Diesel F-3's, AA
2530	REA Baggage Car
2532	Silver Range Vista-Dome
2532	Silver Range Vista-Dome
2531	Silver Dawn Observation

2527 — Super O Missile Launcher Outfit, 59, 60 (3) 725
44	US Army Mobile Missile Launcher
3419	Operating Helicopter Launching Car
6844	Missile Carrying Car
6823	Flat Car with IRBM Missiles
6814	First Aid Medical Car
943	Exploding Ammo Dump

2528WS — 5-Star Frontier Special Outfit, 59-61 (2) 750
1872	4-4-0 General w/1872T Tender
1877	Flat Car with Six Horses
1876	General Mail-Baggage Car
1875W	General Passenger Car with Whistle

2529W — 5-Car Virginian Rectifier Work Train, 59 (4) 1275
2329	Virginian Rectifier Electric
3512	Operating Fireman-Ladder Car
6819	Flat Car with Helicopter
6812	Track Maintenance Car
6560	Crane Car
6119	D L & W Work Caboose

2531WS — Super O 5-Car Steam Freight, 59 (5) 1250
637	2-6-4 w/Whistle Tender
3435	Operating Aquarium Car
6817	Flat Car with Allis Chalmers Motor Scraper
6636	Alaska Hopper
6825	Flat Car with Arch Trestle Bridge
6119	D L & W Work Caboose

2533W — 5-Car Great Northern, 59 (5) 1850
Electric Freight
2358	Great Northern Electric
6650	IRBM Missile Launching Car
6414	Auto Transport Car
3444	Animated Gondola Car
6470	Exploding Target Car
6357	Lionel Caboose

2535WS — Super O 5-Car Hudson, 59 (4) 1000
Steam Freight
665	4-6-4 w/2046W Tender
3434	Operating Chicken Car with Sweeper
6823	Flat Car with IRBM Missiles
3672	Operating Bosco Car
6812	Track Maintenance Car
6357	Lionel Caboose

2537W — 5-Car New Haven Diesel Freight, 59 (5) 2500
2242P/C	New Haven F-3, AB
3435	Operating Aquarium Car
3650	Searchlight Extension Car
6464-275	State of Maine Box Car
6819	Flat Car with Helicopter
6427	Lionel Lines Caboose

2539WS — 5-Car Hudson Steam Freight, 59 (5) 1500
665	4-6-4 w/2046W Tender
3361	Operating Lumber Car
464	Operating Lumber Mill
6464-825	Alaska Box Car
3512	Operating Fireman-Ladder Car
6812	Track Maintenance Car
6357	Lionel Caboose

2541W — 5-Car Super Chief Freight, 59 (5) 2350
2383P/T	Santa Fe Twin Diesel F-3's, AA
3356	Operating Horse Car with Corral
3512	Operating Fireman-Ladder Car
6519	Allis Chalmers Car
6816	Flat Car with Allis Chalmers Tractor Dozer
6427	Lionel Lines Caboose

2543WS — 6-Car Berkshire Steam Freight, 59 (5) 1500
736	Berkshire w/2046W Tender
264	Operating Fork Lift Platform Set
6264	Lumber Car
3435	Operating Aquarium Car
6823	Flat Car with IRBM Missiles
6434	Illuminated Poultry Car
6812	Track Maintenance Car
6557	Smoking Caboose

2544W — 4-Car Super Chief Streamliner, 59, 60 (4) 3250
2383P/T	Santa Fe Twin Diesel F-3's, AA
2530	REA Baggage Car
2563	Indian Falls Pullman, red stripe
2562	Regal Pass Vista-Dome, red stripe
2561	Vista Valley Observation, red stripe

2545WS — 6-Car N & W Space-Freight, 59 (5) 3000
746	Norfolk & Western w/746W Tender
175	Rocket Launcher
6175	Flat Car with Rocket
6470	Exploding Target Car
3419	Operating Helicopter Car
6650	IRBM Missile Launching Car
3540	Operating Radar Scanning Scope Car
6517	Lionel Lines Bay Window Caboose

2547WS — 4-Car Variety Special Steam Freight, 60 (4) 650
637	2-6-4 w/2046W Tender
3330	Operating Submarine in Kit Form
6475	Pickle Car
6361	Timber Transport Car
6357	Lionel Caboose

2549W — A Mighty Military Diesel Outfit, 60 (2) 1200
2349	Northern Pacific GP-9
3540	Operating Radar Scanning Scope Car
6470	Exploding Target Car
6819	Flat Car with Helicopter
6650	Missile Launching Car
3535	Operating Security Car with Rotating Searchlight

2551W — 6-Car Great Northern Diesel Freight, 60 (5) 2250
2358	Great Northern Electric
6828	Harnischfeger Mobile Construction Crane Car
3512	Operating Fireman-Ladder Car
6827	Harnischfeger Power Shovel Car
6736	Detroit & Mackinac Hopper
6812	Track Maintenance Car
6427	Lionel Lines Caboose

2553WS — The Majestic Berkshire 5-Car Freight, 60 (4) 1300
736	Berkshire w/2046W Tender
3830	Operating Submarine Car
3435	Operating Aquarium Car
3419	Operating Helicopter Car
3672	Operating Bosco Car with Matching Platform
6357	Lionel Caboose

2555W — Over & Under Twin Railroad Empire, 60 (5+) 9500
2383P/T	Santa Fe Twin Diesel F-3's, AA
3434	Operating Chicken Car with Sweeper
3366	Operating Circus Car with Matching Corral
6414	Auto Transport Car
6464-900	NYC Box Car
6357-50	Santa Fe Caboose
110-85	Trestle Set
———	Matching Set of Lionel HO Trains

2570 — 5-Car Husky Diesel Freight, 61 (4) 625
616	Santa Fe Switcher
6822	Night Crew Searchlight Car
6828	Harnischfeger Truck Crane Car
6812	Track Maintenance Car
6736	Detroit & Mackinac Hopper
6130	Sante Fe Work Caboose

2571 — Fort Knox Special Steam Freight, 61 (4) 450
637	2-6-4 w/736W Tender
3419	Operating Helicopter Launching Car
6445	Fort Knox Gold Bullion Transport Car
6361	Timber Transport Car
6119	D L & W Work Caboose

2572 — 5-Car Space Age Diesel Freighter, 61 (3) 850
2359	Boston & Maine GP-9
6544	Missile Firing Car
3830	Operating Submarine Car
6448	Exploding Target Range Car
3519	Automatic Satellite Launching Car
3535	Security Car with Rotating Searchlight

2573 — 5-Car TV Special Steam Freight, 61 (4) 1250
736	Berkshire w/736W Tender
3545	Operating TV Monitor Car
6416	Boat Transport Car
6475	Pickle Car
6440	Twin Piggyback Van Transport Car
6357	Lionel Caboose

2574 — 5-Car Defender Diesel Freight, 61 (4) 1750
2383P/T	Santa Fe Twin Diesel F-3's, AA
3665	Minuteman Missile Launching Car
3419	Operating Helicopter Launching Car
448	Missile Firing Range Set
6448	Exploding Target Car
3830	Operating Submarine Car
6437	Lionel Lines Caboose

2575 — 7-Car Dynamo Electric Freight, 61 (5) 3000
2360	Pennsylvania GG-1, single stripe
6530	Fire and Safety Training Car
6828	Harnischfeger Truck Crane Car
6464-900	NYC Box Car
6827	Harnischfeger Power Shovel Car
6560	Lionel Lines Crane Car
6437	Pennsylvania Caboose

2576 — 4-Car Super Chief Streamline, 61 (4) 3000
2383P/T	Santa Fe Twin Diesel F-3's, AA
2563	Indian Falls Pullman
2562	Regal Pass Vista-Dome
2562	Regal Pass Vista-Dome
2561	Vista Valley Observation

4109WS — Lionel Electronic Control Set, 46, 47 (4) 1000
671R	Pennsy Turbine w/4671W Tender
4452	Gondola Car
4454	Box Car
5459	Automatic Dump Car
4457	Caboose

4110WS **Lionel Electronic Railroad, 48, 49** **(5)** **2000**
671R   Pennsy Turbine w/4671W Tender
4452   Gondola Car
4454   Box Car
5459   Operating Ore Dump Car
4357   Caboose
97   Operating Coal Elevator
151   Automatic Semaphore

11201 **Fast Starter Steam Freight, 62** **(1)** **150**
242   2-4-2 w/1060T Tender
6042-75   Gondola with Cable Reels
6502   Steel Girder Transport Car
6047   Lionel Lines Caboose

11212 **4-Unit Cyclone Diesel Freight, 62** **(2)** **250**
633   Santa Fe Diesel Switcher
3349   Turbo Missile Firing Car
6825   Flat Car with Arch Trestle Bridge
6057   Lionel Lines Caboose

11222 **5-Unit Vagabond Steam Freight, 62** **(2)** **150**
236   2-4-2 w/1050T Tender
3357   Cop and Hobo Car
6343   Barrel Ramp Car
6119   D L & W Work Caboose

11232 **027 5-Unit Diesel Freight, 62** **(4)** **325**
232   New Haven Alco, A
3410   Helicopter Launching Car
6062   Gondola with Cable Reels
6413   Mercury Capsule Carrying Car
6057-50   Lionel Lines Caboose, orange

11242 **Trail Blazer Steam Freight, 62** **(2)** **125**
233   2-4-2 w/233W Tender
6465   Cities Service Tank Car
6476   Lehigh Valley Hopper, red
6162   Gondola with Canisters
6017   Lionel Lines Caboose

11252 **027 7-Unit Diesel Freight, 62** **(4)** **425**
211   The Texas Special Twin Alco's, AA
3509   Satellite Launching Car
6448   Exploding Target Range Car
3349   Turbo Missile Firing Car
6463   Rocket Fuel Tank Car
6057   Lionel Lines Caboose

11268 **027 6-Unit Diesel Freight, 62** **(3)** **1000**
2365   Chesapeake & Ohio GP-7
3619   Reconnaissance Copter Car
3470   Aerial Target Launching Car
3349   Turbo Missile Firing Car
6501   Jet Motor Boat Transport Car
6017   Lionel Lines Caboose

11278 **7-Unit Plainsman Steam Freight, 62** **(3)** **250**
2037   2-6-4 w/233W Tender
6473   Rodeo Car
6162   Gondola with Canisters
6050-110   Swifts Savings Bank Car
6825   Flat Car with Arch Trestle Bridge
6017   Lionel Lines Caboose

11288 **7-Unit Orbitor Diesel Freight, 62** **(4)** **750**
229P/C   Minneapolis & St. Louis Alco, AB
3413   Mercury Capsule Launching Car
6512   Cherry Picker Car
6413   Mercury Capsule Carrying Car
6463   Rocket Fuel Tank Car
6059   Minneapolis & St. Louis Caboose

11298 **7-Unit Vigilant Steam Freight, 62** **(4)** **450**
2037   2-6-4 w/233W Tender
3419   Operating Helicopter Launching Car
6544   Missile Firing Car
6448   Exploding Target Range Car
3330   Operating Submarine in Kit Form
6017   Lionel Lines Caboose

11308 **027 6-Unit Diesel Passenger, 62** **(3)** **650**
218P/T   Santa Fe Twin Diesel Alco's, AA
2414   Santa Fe Pullman, blue stripe
2412   Santa Fe Vista-Dome, blue stripe
2412   Santa Fe Vista-Dome, blue stripe
2416   Santa Fe Observation, blue stripe

11311 **Value Packed Steam Freighter, 63** **(2)** **100**
1062   0-4-0 w/1061T Tender
6409-25   Flat Car with Pipes
6076-100   Hopper Car
6167   Caboose

11321 **027 5 Unit Diesel Freighter, 63** **(2)** **250**
221   Rio Grande Alco, A
3309   Turbo Missile Launching Car
6076-75   Lehigh Valley Hopper Car
6042-75   Gondola with Cable Reels
6167-50   Caboose, yellow

11331 **Outdoorsman Steam Freight, 63** **(2)** **150**
242   2-4-2 w/1060T Tender
6473   Rodeo Car
6476-25   Lehigh Valley Hopper
6142   Gondola with Canisters
6059-50   Minneapolis & St. Louis Caboose

11341 **Space-Prober Diesel Freight, 63** **(4)** **1100**
634   Santa Fe Diesel Switcher
3410   Helicopter Launching Car
6407   Flat Car with Missile
6014-335   Frisco Box Car, white, with or without coin slot
6463   Rocket Fuel Tank Car
6059-50   Minneapolis & St. Louis Caboose

11351 **Land Rover Steam Freight, 63** **(2)** **225**
237   2-4-2 w/1060T Tender
6050-100   Swift Box Car
6465-100   Lionel Lines Tank Car
6408   Flat Car with Pipes
6162   Gondola with Canisters
6119-100   D L & W Work Caboose

11361 **Shooting Star Diesel Freight, 63** **(4)** **750**
211P/T   The Texas Special Twin Alco's, AA
3665-100   Minuteman Missile Launching Car
3413-150   Mercury Capsule Launching Car
6470   Exploding Target Car
6413   Mercury Capsule Carrying Car
6257-100   Lionel Lines Caboose

11375 **Cargomaster Steam Freight, 63** **(4)** **700**
238   2-4-2 w/234W Tender
6822-50   Night Crew Searchlight Car
6414-150   Auto Transport Car
6465-150   Tank Car
6476-75   Lehigh Valley Hopper
6162   Gondola with Canisters
6257-100   Lionel LInes Caboose

11385 **Space Conqueror Diesel Freight, 63** **(5)** **2000**
223P/218C   Santa Fe Alco, AB
3619-100   Reconnaissance Copter Car
3470-100   Aerial Target Launching Car
3349-100   Turbo Missile Launching Car
6407   Flat Car with Missile
6257-100   Lionel Lines Caboose

11395 **Muscleman Steam Freight, 63** **(4)** **600**
2037   2-6-4 w/234W Tender
6464-725   New Haven Box Car
6469-50   Liquefied Gas Tank Car
6536   Minneapolis & St. Louis Hopper
6440-50   Twin Piggy-Back Van Car
6560-50   Crane Car
6119-100   D L & W Work Caboose

11405 **027 6-Unit Diesel Passenger, 63** **(3)** **725**
218   Santa Fe Twin Diesel Alco's, AA
2414   Santa Fe Pullman, blue stripe
2412   Santa Fe Vista-Dome, blue stripe
2412   Santa Fe Vista-Dome, blue stripe
2416   Santa Fe Observation, blue stripe

11420 **4-Unit Steam Freight, 64** **(2)** **100**
1061   0-4-0 w/1061T Tender
6042-250   Gondola
6167-25   Caboose

11430 **5-Unit Steam Freight, 64** **(2)** **125**
1062   0-4-0 w/1061T Tender
6176   Hopper Car
6142   Gondola
6167-125   Caboose

11440 **5-Unit Diesel Freight, 64** **(2)** **225**
221   Rio Grande Alco, A
3309   Turbo Missile Launching Car
6176-150   Lehigh Valley Hopper, black
6142-125   Lionel Gondola, blue
6167-100   Lionel Lines Caboose, red

11450 **6-Unit Steam Freight, 64** **(2)** **150**
242   2-4-2 w/1060T Tender
6473   Rodeo Car
6142-75   Gondola with Canisters, green
6176-50   Lehigh Valley Hopper, black
6059-50   Minneapolis & St. Louis Caboose

11460 **7-Unit Steam Freight, 64** **(3)** **150**
238   2-4-2 w/234W Tender
6014-335   Frisco Box Car, white
6465-150   Lionel Lines Tank Car, orange
6142-100   Gondola with Canisters, blue
6176-75   Lehigh Valley Hopper, yellow
6119-100   D L & W Work Caboose

11470 **7-Unit Steam Freight, 64** **(4)** **225**
237   2-4-2 w/1060T Tender
6014-335   Frisco Box Car, white
6465-150   Lionel Lines Tank Car, orange
6142-100   Gondola with Canisters, blue
6176-50   Lehigh Valley Hopper, yellow
6119-100   D L & W Work Caboose

11480 **7-Unit Diesel Freight, 64** **(4)** **500**
213P/T   Minneapolis & St. Louis Twin Alco's, AA
6473   Rodeo Car
6176-50   Lehigh Valley Hopper, black
6142-150   Gondola with Cable Reels
6014-335   Frisco Box Car, white
6257-100   Lionel Lines Caboose

11490 **5-Unit Diesel Passenger, 64, 65** **(3)** **650**
212P/T   Santa Fe Twin Alco's, AA
2404   Santa Fe Vista-Dome
2405   Santa Fe Pullman
2406   Santa Fe Observation

11500 **7-Unit Steam Freight, 64, 65, 66** **(3)** **250**
2029   2-6-4 w/234W Tender
6465-150   Lionel Lines Tank Car, orange
6402-50   Flat Car with Cable Reels
6176-75   Lehigh Valley Hopper, yellow, 64, 66
6176   Lehigh Valley Hopper, black, 65
6014-335   Frisco Box Car, white
6257-100   Lionel Lines Caboose, 64
6059   Minneapolis & St. Louis Caboose, 65, 66

11510 **7-Unit Steam Freight, 64** **(4)** **275**
2029   2-6-4 w/1060T Tender
6465-150   Lionel Lines Tank Car, orange
6402-50   Flat Car with Cable Reels
6176-75   Lehigh Valley Hopper, yellow
6014-335   Frisco Box Car, white
6257-100   Lionel Lines Caboose

11520 **6-Unit Steam Freight, 65, 66** **(2)** **150**
242   2-4-2 w/1062T Tender
6176   Lehigh Valley Hopper
3364   Operating Log Car
6142   Gondola with Canisters
6059   Minneapolis & St. Louis Caboose

11530	**5-Unit Diesel Freight, 65, 66**	**(2)**	**200**
634	Santa Fe Diesel Switcher		
6014-335	Frisco Box Car, white		
6142	Gondola with Canisters		
6402	Flat Car with Cable Reels		
6130	Santa Fe Work Caboose		

11540	**6-Unit Steam Freight, 65, 66**	**(4)**	**225**
239	2-4-2 w/242T Tender		
6473	Rodeo Car		
6465	Lionel Lines Tank Car		
6176	Lehigh Valley Hopper		
6119	D L & W Work Caboose		

11550	**6-Unit Steam Freight, 65, 66**	**(3)**	**225**
239	2-4-2 w/234W Tender		
6473	Rodeo Car		
6465	Lionel Lines Tank Car		
6176	Lehigh Valley Hopper		
6119	D L & W Work Caboose		

11560	**7-Unit Diesel Freight, 65, 66**	**(2)**	**250**
211P/T	The Texas Special Twin Alco's, AA		
6473	Rodeo Car		
6176	Lehigh Valley Hopper		
6142	Gondola with Canisters		
6465	Lionel Lines Tank Car		
6059	Minneapolis & St. Louis Caboose		

11590	**5-Unit Illuminated Passenger Set, 66**	**(3)**	**750**
212P/T	Santa Fe Twin Alco's, AA		
2408	Sante Fe Vista-Dome		
2409	Sante Fe Pullman		
2410	Sante Fe Observation		

11600	**7-Unit Steam Freight Set, 68**	**(3)**	**800**
2029	2-6-4 w/234W Tender		
6014-335	Frisco Box Car, white		
6476	Lehigh Valley Hopper, yellow		
6315	Lionel Lines Tank Car		
6560	Lionel Lines Crane Car		
6130	Santa Fe Work Caboose		

11710	**Value Packed Steam Freighter, 69**	**(3)**	**150**
1061	2-4-2 w/1062T Tender		
6402	Flat Car with Cable Reels		
6142	Gondola with Canisters		
6059	Minneapolis & St. Louis Caboose		

11720	**5-Unit Diesel Freighter, 69**	**(4)**	**250**
2024	Chesapeake & Ohio Alco, A		
6142	Gondola with Canisters		
6402	Flat Car with Cable Reels		
6176	Lehigh Valley Hopper, yellow		
6057	Caboose, brown		

11730	**6-Unit Diesel Freight, 69**	**(3)**	**325**
645	Union Pacific Diesel Switcher		
6402	Flat Car with Boat		
6014-85	Frisco Box Car, orange		
6142	Gondola with Canisters		
6176	Lehigh Valley Hopper, black		
6167	Union Pacific Caboose		

11740	**7-Unit Diesel Freight, 69**	**(4)**	**350**
2041	Rock Island Twin Diesel Alco's, AA		
6315	Lionel Lines Tank Car		
6142	Gondola with Canisters		
6014-410	Frisco Box Car, white		
6476	Lehigh Valley Hopper, yellow		
6057	Caboose, brown		

11750	**7-Unit Steam Freight, 69**	**(5)**	**500**
2029	2-6-4 w/234T Pennsylvania Tender		
6014-85	Frisco Box Car, orange		
6476	Lehigh Valley Hopper, black		
6473	Rodeo Car		
6315	Gulf Tank Car		
6130	Santa Fe Work Caboose		

11760	**7-Unit Steam Freight, 69**	**(3)**	**300**
2029	2-6-4 w/234W Tender		
6014-410	Frisco Box Car, white		
6315	Lionel Lines Tank Car		
6476	Lehigh Valley Hopper, black		
3376	Giraffe Car		
6119	Santa Fe Work Caboose		

12502	**Prairie-Rider Gift Pack, 62**	**(4)**	**600**
1862	General 4-4-0 W/1862T Tender		
3376	Operating Giraffe Car		
1877	General Horse Car		
1866	General Mail Baggage Car		
1865	General Passenger Car		

12512	**Enforcer Gift Pack, 62**	**(4)**	**950**
45	USMC Mobile Missile Launcher		
3413	Mercury Capsule Launching Car		
3619	Reconnaissance Copter Car		
3470	Aerial Target Launching Car		
3349	Turbo Missile Firing Car		
6017	Lionel Lines Caboose		

12700	**7-Unit Steam Freight, 64**	**(4)**	**1000**
12710	**7-Unit Steam Freight, 64-66**	**(4)**	**1000**
736	Berkshire w/736W Tender		
6464-725	New Haven Box Car		
6162-100	Gondola with Canisters, blue		
6414-75	Auto Transport Car, 64		
6414	Auto Transport Car, 65, 66		
6476-135	Lehigh Valley Hopper, yellow		
6437	Pennsylvania Caboose		

12720	**7-Unit Diesel Freight, 64**	**(4)**	**1500**
12730	**7-Unit Diesel Freight, 64-66**	**(4)**	**1500**
2383P/T	Santa Fe Twin Diesel F-3's, AA		
6464-725	New Haven Box Car		
6162-100	Gondola with Canisters, blue		
6414-75	Auto Transport Car, 64		
6414	Auto Transport Car, 65, 66		
6476-135	Lehigh Valley Hopper, yellow		
6437	Pennsylvania Caboose		

12740	**9-Unit Diesel Freight, 64**	**(5)**	**1500**
12750	**9-Unit Diesel Freight, 64**	**(5)**	**1500**
2383P/T	Santa Fe Twin Diesel F-3's, AA		
3662	Operating Milk Car with Platform		
6822	Night Crew Searchlight Car		
6361	Timber Car		
6464-525	Minneapolis & St. Louis Box Car		
6436-110	Lehigh Valley Hopper		
6315-60	Lionel Lines Tank Car		
6437	Pennsylvania Caboose		

12760	**9-Unit Steam Freight, 64**	**(4)**	**1500**
12770	**9-Unit Steam Freight, 64**	**(5)**	**1500**
736	Berkshire w/736W Tender		
3662	Operating Milk Car with Platform		
6822	Night Crew Searchlight Car		
6361	Timber Car		
6464-525	Minneapolis & St. Louis Box Car		
6436-110	Lehigh Valley Hopper		
6315-60	Lionel Lines Tank Car		
6437	Pennsylvania Caboose		

12780	**6-Unit Diesel Passenger, 64-66**	**(4)**	**2500**
2383P/T	Santa Fe Twin Diesel F-3's, AA		
2523	President Garfield Pullman		
2522	President Harrison Vista-Dome		
2523	President Garfield Pullman		
2521	President McKinley Observation		

12800	**6-Unit Diesel Freight, 65, 66**	**(2)**	**650**
2346	Boston & Maine GP-9		
6428	U.S. Mail Car		
6436-110	Lehigh Valley Hopper		
6464-475	Boston & Maine Box Car		
6415	Sunoco Tank Car		
6017	Boston & Maine Caboose		

12820	**8-Unit Diesel Freight, 65**	**(4)**	**1500**
2322	Virginian FM		
3662	Operating Milk Car with Platform		
6822	Night Crew Searchlight Car		
6361	Timber Car		
6464-725	New Haven Box Car		
6436-110	Lehigh Valley Hopper		
6315	Lionel Lines Caboose		
6437	Pennsylvania Caboose		

12840	**Back by Popular Demand, 66**	**(4)**	**1000**
665	4-6-4 w/736W Tender		
6464-375	Central of Georgia Box Car		
6464-450	Great Northern Box Car		
6431	Piggyback Car w/Trailers & Tractor		
6415	Sunoco Tank Car		
6437	Pennsylvania Caboose		

12850	**8-Unit Diesel Freight, 66**	**(4)**	**1500**
2322	Virginian FM		
3662	Operating Milk Car with Platform		
6822	Night Crew Searchlight Car		
6361	Timber Car		
6464-725	New Haven Box Car		
6436-110	Lehigh Valley Hopper		
6315	Lionel Lines Tank Car		
6437	Pennsylvania Caboose		

13008	**6-Unit Champion Steam Freight, 62**	**(4)**	**350**
637	2-6-4 w/736W Tender		
3349	Turbo Missile Firing Car		
6448	Exploding Target Range Car		
6501	Jet Motor Boat Transport Car		
6119	D L & W Work Caboose		

13018	**6-Unit Starfire Diesel Freight, 62**	**(5)**	**1250**
616	Santa Fe Diesel Switcher		
6500	Beechcraft Bonanza Transport Car		
6650	Missile Launching Car		
3519	Satellite Launching Car		
6448	Exploding Target Range Car		
6017-235	Santa Fe Caboose		

13028	**6-Unit Defender Diesel Freight, 62**	**(2)**	**857**
2359	Boston & Maine GP-9		
3665	Minuteman Missile Launching Car		
3349	Turbo Missile Firing Car		
3820	USMC Operating Submarine Car		
3470	Aerial Target Launching Car		
6017-100	Boston & Maine Caboose		

13036	**6-Unit Plainsman Steam Outfit, 62**	**(4)**	**950**
1872	General 4-4-0 w/1872T Tender		
6445	Fort Knox Gold Bullion Car		
3370	Animated Sheriff and Outlaw Car		
1876	General Mail Baggage Car		
1875W	General Passenger Car with Whistle		

13048	**7-Unit Super O Steam Freight, 62**	**(3)**	**850**
736	Berkshire w/736W Tender		
6822	Night Crew Searchlight Car		
6414	Auto Transport Car		
3362	Helium Tank Unloading Car		
6440	Twin Piggyback Van Transport Car		
6437	Lionel Lines Caboose		

13058	**7-Unit Vanguard Diesel Freight, 62**	**(3)**	**1650**
2383P/T	Santa Fe Twin Diesel F-3's, AA		
3619	Reconnaissance Copter Car		
3413	Mercury Capsule Launching Car		
6512	Cherry Picker Car		
470	Missile Launching Platform		
6470	Exploding Target Car		
6437	Lionel Lines Caboose		

13068 **8-Unit Goliath Electric Freight, 62** (5) 3000
2360 Pennsylvania GG-1, single stripe
6464-725 New Haven Box Car
6828 Harnischfeger Truck Crane Car
6416 Boat Transport Car
6827 Harnischfeger Power Shovel Car
6530 Fire and Safety Training Car
6475 Pickle Car
6437 Pennsylvania Caboose

13078 **5-Unit Presidential Passenger, 62** (5) 3500
2360 Pennsylvania GG-1, single stripe
2523 President Garfield Pullman
2522 President Harrison Vista-Dome
2522 President Harrison Vista-Dome
2521 President McKinley Observation

13088 **6-Unit Presidential Passenger, 62** (4) 2600
2383P/T Santa Fe Twin Diesel F-3's, AA
2523 President Garfield Pullman
2522 President Harrison Vista-Dome
2522 President Harrison Vista-Dome
2521 President McKinley Observation

13098 **Goliath Steam Freight, 63** (5) 2000
637 2-6-4 w/736W Tender
6469 Liquefied-Gas Tank Car
6464-900 New York Central Box Car
6414 Auto Transport Car
6446 N & W Covered Hopper
6447 Pennsylvania Caboose

13108 **7-Unit Super O Diesel Freight, 63** (4) 1050
617 Santa Fe Diesel Switcher
3665 Minuteman Missile Launching Car
3419 Helicopter Launching Car
6448 Exploding Target Range Car
3830 Operating Submarine Car
3470 Aerial Target Launching Car
6119-100 D L & W Work Caboose

13118 **8-Unit Super O Steam Freight, 63** (4) 1500
736 Berkshire w/736W Tender
6446-60 Lehigh Valley Covered Hopper
6827 Harnischfeger Power Shovel Car
3362 Helium Tank Unloading Car
6315-60 Lionel Lines Tank Car
6560 Lionel Lines Crane Car
6429 D L & W Work Caboose

13128 **7-Unit Super O Diesel Freight, 63** (4) 1825
2383P/T Santa Fe Twin Diesel F-3's, AA
3619 Reconnaissance Copter Car
3413 Mercury Capsule Launching Car
6512 Cherry Picker Car
448 Missile Firing Range Set
6448 Exploding Target Range Car
6437 Pennsylvania Caboose

13138 **Majestic Electric Freight, 63** (5) 3000
2360 Pennsylvania GG-1, single stripe
6464-725 New Haven Box Car
6828 Harnischfeger Truck Crane Car
6416 Boat Transport Car
6827 Harnischfeger Power Shovel Car
6315-60 Lionel Lines Tank Car
6436-110 Lehigh Valley Hopper
6437 Pennsylvania Caboose

13148 **Super Chief Passenger, 63** (4) 2600
2383 Santa Fe Twin Diesel F-3's, AA
2523 President Garfield Pullman
2523 President Garfield Pullman
2522 President Harrison Vista-Dome
2521 President McKinley Observation

13150 **9-Unit Super O Steam Freight, 64-66** (5) 3000
773 Hudson w/773W Tender
3434 Operating Chicken Car with Sweeper
6361 Timber Car
3662 Operating Milk Car with Platform
6415 Sunoco Tank Car
3356 Operating Horse Car with Corral
6436-110 Lehigh Valley Hopper
6437 Pennsylvania Caboose

A Sampling of Uncataloged Sets

Sears Halloween Set 1960 (4) 2000
1882 General black/orange and 1882T
tender, 1885 blue, unlighted, 1887, 1866

Sears 9694 (5) 4000
746, 746W (long stripe), 3419, 3540,
3330, 6544, 3535

Sears 9836 1965 (5) 5000
2347 C&O GP-7, 3662, 6342, 6315,
6464-725, 6414 with 4 red autos with
gray bumpers, 6437 and 346 manually
operated culvert loader, 5 310 billboards,
plus switches and track. Packed in large
white carton with *Allstate* markings

Sears Military Set (5) 1200
221 *USMC* or *Santa Fe* Alco and four olive drab,
unlettered freight cars: 6076, 6112, 3349, 6824

Sears 5958 1951 (4) 750
2023AA, 6656, 6465, 6456, 6357

Sears 9671 1954 (4) 900
2245AB, 6462, 6464-225, 6561, 6427

Sears 9652 1960 (4) 900
225P, 6361, 6817, 6812, 6670, 6119-100

Sears 9820 1964 (4) 2200
240, 3666, flat car with tank, 6470,
6814, 347 with soldiers

JC Penney X924-0690 1964 (4) 500
221 *Santa Fe*, 6176-100, 6142, 3349, 6824

JC Penney X924-3700 1965 (4) 1000
2322, 3662, 6822, 6315, 6361, 6436,
6464-725, 6437

705 1956 (4) 550
629, 2432, 2434, 2436

Libby's 19263 1963 (3) 350
1062, *SP* tender, 6050 *Libby's*, 6076,
6475 *Libby's*, 6167

Transformers

Note: *Usually sought by operators, not collectors. Transformers not listed are worth less than $30.*

ECU-1	Train Control Unit, Electronic set	(4)	150
KW	50-65 190 Watts	(3)	175
SW	61-66 130 Watts	(3)	75
TW	53-60 175 Watts	(2)	125
V	46,47 150 Watts	(3)	80
VW	48,49 150 Watts	(2)	135
Z	45-47 250 Watts	(2)	125
ZW	48,49 250 Watts	(3)	175
ZW	50-66 275 Watts	(2)	250▲
1043	**Girls Train** (Ivory case)	(4)	300▲

Lionel Postwar Boxes

Introduction

The emergence of box collecting, like sets, is a natural outgrowth of collectors wanting to upgrade.

The hobby's first box guide appeared in the fall, 1992 issue of our *Toy Train Revue Journal.* The publishing of that guide generated comments and new information (which we have included in this guide), but boxes remain a relatively new area of collecting and prices are still unsettled and largely undetermined.

How This Guide Works

Boxes are listed in numerical order. We list the asking price for a box in *LN* condition. To be *LN* a box must be complete with box liner, inserts, instruction sheets (if applicable), and the ends and inner flaps may not be torn.

Only boxes valued at $20 or higher are listed. If you don't see a box listed, either we unintentionally omitted it or it is worth less than $20.

The prices are a result of a much smaller-than-normal sampling as few prople have made a serious study of box prices. As more collectors buy and sell boxes, more accurate prices will be established.

Rarity Rating

5 is rare. 1 is common. We use plus and minus signs to fine tune the rating.

Why Are Boxes Hot?

Boxes are hot because they add value to an item. A *LN* 2242 New Haven without the box is $1700. With the box, it's $2500. Also, collectors are constantly upgrading and the original box is the next logical step after acquiring an item in *LN* condition without the box. Another reason is the high prices of the hardware. Unable to afford the contents, many collectors are content to just go after the box. There's the challenge angle, too. It was the function of the box to protect the item. Over the years, the box took the abuse while the item rested safely inside. The argument could be made it is more challenging to find the box for the item in good shape than it is to find the item.

For whatever reason, boxes are hot.

Types of Boxes – A Quick History and Legend

    1945-1958, blue & orange, (B&O)
    1959,1960, orange perforated box, (OPerf)
    1961-1965, orange picture box, (OPix)
    1962, orange perforated picture box, (OPP)
    1962-1969, plain white box, (PWB)
    1966, window box, (WB)
    1968, 1969, Hagerstown checkerboard, (C)
    1969, Hillside checkerboard, (C)

Buyer Beware

With the increase in demand, comes an increase in scams. A *LN* or *Mint* box doesn't mean the item inside is in a similar condition. Some dealers are buying *LN* or *Mint* boxes, putting hardware rated at *VG* or *Ex* inside, and selling the entire package as boxed-mint. Before buying, take the item out of the box and examine it carefully.

This practice of creating boxed-mint items can lead to another problem. The wrong box can be put with the item or, in the case of boxed sets, the wrong items with the wrong boxes. Just because the number on the item matches the number on the box, doesn't mean it's the right box for the item.

We Need Your Help

Determing prices is an evolving work which can be aided immensely by our readers. Tell us about boxes we missed or prices you believe are inaccurate.

Postwar Boxes

No.	Item	Rarity	Value
ECU-1	Electronic Control Unit	(4)	30
ZW	Transformer	(2)	20
30	Water Tower	(3)	35
38	Water Tower	(4+)	75
41	US Army Switcher	(2)	25
42	Picatinny Arsenal Switcher	(4)	60
44	US Army Mobile Missile Launcher	(3)	40
45	USMC Mobile Missile Launcher	(3+)	50
50	Gang Car (O&B)	(3)	20
51	Navy Yard Switcher	(2+)	35
52	Fire Fighting Car	(3)	45
53	Rio Grande Snow Plow	(3)	50
54	Ballast Tamper	(3)	40
55	Tie-Jector	(3+)	45
56	Minn. & St. Louis Min Loco	(4)	85
57	AEC Switcher	(4+)	150
58	Great Northern Rotary Snowplow	(4)	125
59	Minuteman Switcher	(4+)	150
60	Trolley	(2)	25
65	Motorized Handcar	(3+)	50
68	Executive Inspection Car	(3)	45
69	Motorized Maintenance Car	(3+)	45
89	Flagpole	(4)	20
97	Coal Elevator	(3)	35
110-85	Trestle Set	(5)	150
114	Newsstand with Horn	(3)	35
115	Lionel City Station	(3+)	45
118	Newsstand with Whistle	(3)	30
128	Animated Newsstand	(2)	25
132	Passenger Station	(3)	20
133	Passenger Station	(2)	20
138	Water Tower	(3)	30
150	Telegraph Pole Set	(2)	20
164	Log Loader	(3)	40
175	Rocket Launcher	(3)	45
182	Magnetic Crane	(3)	45
192	Operating Control Tower	(4)	45
193	Industrial Water Tower	(3)	25
197	Rotating Radar Antenna	(3+)	20
202	Union Pacific A	(3+)	40
204P	Santa Fe Alco Powered A Unit	(3)	45
204P	Santa Fe Alco Dummy A Unit	(3)	45

205P	Missouri Pacific Alco Powered A Unit	(4)	50
205T	Missouri Pacific Alco Dummy A Unit	(4)	50
208P	Santa Fe Alco Powered A Unit	(3)	40
208T	Santa Fe Alco Dummy A Unit	(3)	40
209P	New Haven Alco Powered A Unit	(4+)	85
209T	New Haven Alco Dummy A Unit	(4+)	85
210P	Texas Special Alco Powered A Unit	(2)	35
210T	Texas Special Alco Dummy A Unit	(2)	35
211P	Texas Special Alco Powered A Unit	(3)	25
211T	Texas Special Alco Dummy A Unit	(3)	25
212	USMC Alco Powered A Unit	(3)	50
212T	USMC Alco Dummy A Unit	(5)	400
212P	Santa Fe Alco Powered A Unit	(4)	40
212T	Santa Fe Alco Dummy A Unit	(4)	40
213P	Minn. & St. Louis Alco Powered A Unit	(4)	45
213T	Minn. & St. Louis Alco Dummy A Unit	(4)	45
215	Santa Fe Alco Powered A Unit	(?)	?
216P	Burlington Alco Powered A Unit	(4+)	75
216	Minn & St. Louis Alco Powered A Unit	(?)	?
217P	Boston & Maine Alco Powered A Unit	(3+)	45
217C	Boston & Maine Alco Dummy B Unit	(3+)	45
218P	Santa Fe Alco Powered A Unit	(2)	30
218C	Santa Fe Alco Dummy B Unit	(3+)	40

218T	Santa Fe Alco Dummy A Unit	(3)	35
219	Missouri Pacific Alco AA	(?)	?
220P	Santa Fe Alco Powered A Unit	(4)	45
221	Rio Grande Alco Powered A Unit		NOB
221	Santa Fe Powered A Unit		NOB
221	USMC Powered A Unit		NOB
221	2-6-4 Steam	(3+)	45
221T	Tender	(3+)	35
221W	Tender	(3+)	40
222	Rio Grande Alco Powered A Unit		NOB
223P	Santa Fe Alco Powered A Unit	(4)	55
224P	Navy Alco Powered A Unit	(4)	60
224C	Navy Alco Dummy B Unit	(4)	60
224	2-6-2 Steam	(3)	35
225	C&O Alco Powered A Unit	(?)	?
226	Boston & Maine Alco AB	(?)	?
227	Canadian National Alco Powered A Unit		NOB
228	Canadian National Alco Powered A Unit	(3)	35
229P	Minn. & St. Louis Alco Powered A Unit	(3+)	45
229C	Minn. & St. Louis Alco Dummy B Unit	(3+)	45
230	C&O Alco Powered A Unit	(?)	?
231	Rock Island Powered A Unit	(?)	?
232	New Haven Alco A	(?)	?
233	2-4-2 Steam	(3)	30
233W	Tender	(3)	25
235	2-4-2 Steam		NOB
236	2-4-2 Steam	(2)	25
237	2-4-2 Steam	(3)	25
238	2-4-2 Steam	(3)	30
239	2-4-2 Steam	(3)	25

240	2-4-2 Steam		NOB
241	2-4-2 Steam		NOB
242	2-4-2 Steam	(?)	?
242T	Tender	(3)	25
243	2-4-2 Steam	(3)	40
243W	Tender	(3)	25
244	2-4-2 Steam	(3)	30
244T	Tender	(4)	30
245	2-4-2 Steam	(4)	35
247	2-4-2 Steam	(3)	35
247T	Tender	(3)	20
248	2-4-2 Steam	(3)	25
249	2-4-2 Steam	(3)	35
250	2-4-2 Steam	(3)	35
250T	Tender	(3)	25
251	2-4-2 Steam		NOB
256	Freight Station	(2)	20
257	Freight Station W/Horn	(4)	40
264	Operating Forklift Platform	(3)	45
282	Gantry Crane	(3)	45
282R	Gantry Crane	(3+)	55
299	Code Transmitter Beacon Set	(2)	20
313	Bascule Bridge	(3+)	100
334	Operating Dispatching Board	(3)	40
342	Operating Culvert Loader	(2)	45
345	Operating Culvert Unloader	(3)	50
346	Manual Culvert Unloader	(4+)	65
347	Cannon Firing Range		NOB
348	Manual Culvert Unloader	(4)	50
350	Transfer Table	(4)	35
350-50	Transfer Table Extension	(4+)	50
352	Ice Depot	(2)	35
362	Barrel Loader	(2)	20
364	Lumber Loader	(3)	20

No.	Description	Grade	Price
365	Dispatch Station	(2)	30
375	Turntable	(2)	35
397	Diesel Operating Coal Loader	(2)	30
400	B&O Budd Car	(3)	65
404	B&O Budd Car	(3+)	75
415	Diesel Fueling Station	(3)	35
419	Heliport Control Tower	(4+)	85
443	Missile Launching Platform	(3)	25
445	Switch Tower	(2+)	20
448	Missile Firing Range Set	(3)	20
452	Gantry Signal	(3+)	35
455	Oil Derrick	(2+)	40
456	Coal Ramp	(2)	30
460	Piggyback Transportation	(2)	25
460P	Piggyback Platform	(5)	100
461	Platform w/Truck and Trailer	(4)	60
462	Derrick Platform Set	(4)	75
464	Lumber Mill	(2)	35
465	Sound Dispatching Station	(2+)	30
470	Missile Launching Platform	(2)	25
497	Coaling Station	(3+)	45
520	Box Cab Electric	(?)	?
600	MKT GM Switcher	(3)	45
601	Seaboard GM Switcher	(2+)	40
602	Seaboard GM Switcher	(2+)	40
610	Erie GM Switcher	(3)	45
611	Jersey Central	(3)	40
613	Union Pacific GM Switcher	(4)	85
614	Alaska GM Switchers	(4)	75
616	Santa Fe GM Switcher	(3+)	60
617	Santa Fe GM Switcher	(4)	65
621	Jersey Central GM Switcher	(3)	40
622	Santa Fe GM Switcher	(3)	50
623	Santa Fe GM Switcher	(2+)	45
624	C & O GM Switcher	(3)	40
625	Lehigh Valley GE 44-Ton	(3+)	40
626	Baltimore & Ohio GE 44-Ton	(4)	65
627	Lehigh Valley GE 44-Ton	(3)	40
628	Northern Pacific GE 44-Ton	(3)	40
629	Burlington GE 44-Ton	(4)	75
633	Santa Fe GM Switcher	(4)	40
634	Santa Fe GM Switcher	(4)	40
635	Union Pacific GM Switcher	(?)	?
637	2-6-4 Steam	(3+)	35
645	Union Pacific GM Switcher	(?)	?
646	4-6-4 Steam	(3)	45
665	4-6-4 Steam	(2+)	45
671	6-8-6 Steam	(2+)	45
671R	6-8-6 Steam	(4)	75
671W	Tender	(3+)	35
675	2-6-2 Steam	(3)	35
681	6-8-6 Steam	(3)	40
682	6-8-6 Steam	(3+)	65
685	4-6-4 Steam	(2+)	40
726	2-8-4 Steam	(3)	60
726RR	2-8-4 Steam	(3)	45
736	2-8-4 Steam	(2+)	50
736W	Tender	(4)	45
746	4-8-4 Norfolk & Western	(4)	100
746W	Tender (Short Stripe)	(3+)	75
746WX	Tender (Long Stripe)	(4+)	125
773	4-6-4 Hudson Steam (1950)	(4)	175
773	4-6-4 Hudson Steam (1964)	(4)	125
773W	Tender	(4+)	95
920	Scenic Display Set	(2)	20
958	Vehicle Set (White Box Only)	(4+)	25
963-100	Frontier Set	(4)	100
970	Ticket Booth	(2)	20
986	Farm Set	(4)	25
987	Town Set	(4+)	25
988	Railroad Structure Set	(4+)	25
1047	Operating Switchman	(4)	25
1050	0-4-0 Steam		NOB
1050T	Tender		NOB
1055	Texas Special Alco Powered A Unit		NOB
1065	Union Pacific Alco Powered A Unit		NOB
1066	Union Pacific Alco Powered A Unit		NOB
1130T	Tender	(3)	20
1130T-500	Tender (Girls Train)	(5-)	150
1615	0-4-0 Steam	(2+)	45
1615T	Tender	(3)	35
1625	0-4-0 Steam	(4)	75
1625T	Tender	(4)	50
1640-100	Presidential Kit	(3)	50
1656	0-4-0 Steam	(3+)	65
1665	0-4-0 Steam	(4)	75
1666	2-6-2 Steam	(3)	35
1862	4-4-0 Steam	(4)	50
1862T	Tender	(4)	50
1865	W & A passenger car	(3)	40
1866	W & A passenger car	(3)	35
1872	4-4-0 Steam	(4)	60
1872T	Tender	(4)	40
1875	W & A passenger car	(5)	100
1875W	W & A passenger car	(3)	45
1876	W & A passenger car	(3)	30
1877	Flat W/Horses and Fences	(2)	30
1882	4-4-0, 1882T		NOB
1885	W & A passenger car		NOB
1887	Flat W/Horses and Fences		NOB
2016	2-6-4 Steam	(3)	30

2018	2-6-4 Steam	(2)	30
2020	6-8-6 Steam	(2+)	40
2020W	Tender	(3)	35
2023	(MC) Union Pacific Alco AA	(3)	85
2024	C&O Alco A	(?)	?
2025	2-6-2 Steam	(2)	30
2026	2-6-2 Steam	(2)	30
2026X	2-6-2 Steam	(?)	?
2028	Pennsylvania GP-7	(3)	65
2029	2-6-4 Steam	(2+)	35
2031	(MC) Rock Island Alco AA	(3)	75
2032	(MC) Erie Alco AA	(3)	75
2033	(MC) Union Pacific Alco AA	(4)	85
2034	2-4-2 Steam	(2)	30
2035	2-6-4 Steam	(2)	30
2036	2-6-4 Steam	(3)	30
2037	2-6-4 Steam	(2)	30
2037-500	2-6-4 Steam (Girls Train)	(4+)	150
2041	Rock Island Alco AA	(?)	?
2046	4-6-4 Steam	(2+)	45
2046W	Tender	(2)	35
2046WX	Tender	(4)	45
2046WPRR	Tender	(4)	45
2055	4-6-4 Steam	(3)	40
2056	4-6-4 Steam	(3)	45
2065	4-6-4 Steam	(2)	45
2240P	Wabash F-3 Powered A Unit	(3)	150
2240C	Wabash F-3 Dummy B Unit	(3+)	150
2242P	New Haven F-3 Powered A Unit	(4)	175
2242C	New Haven F-3 Dummy B Unit	(4)	175
2243P	Santa Fe F-3 Powered A Unit	(2+)	65
2243C	Santa Fe F-3 Dummy B Unit	(3)	65

2245P	Texas Special F-3 Powered A Unit	(3)	125
2245C	Texas Special F-3 Dummy B Unit	(3+)	125
2321	Lackawanna FM	(3)	125
2322	Virginian FM	(3)	100
2328	Burlington GP-7	(2+)	70
2329	Virginian Electric	(4)	150
2330	GG-I	(4+)	250
2331	Virginian FM	(3)	150
2332	GG-I	(3)	95
2333P	Santa Fe F-3 Powered A Unit	(2+)	65
2333T	Santa Fe F-3 Dummy A Unit	(3)	65
2333P	NYC F-3 Powered A Unit	(3)	75
2333T	NYC F-3 Dummy A Unit	(3+)	75
2337	Wabash GP-7	(4)	75
2338	Milwaukee Road GP-7	(2)	65
2339	Wabash GP-7	(3+)	75
2340-1	GG-1/Tuscan 5 gold stripes	(4)	250
2340-25	GG-1/Green 5 gold stripes	(4)	250
2341	Jersey Central FM	(4+)	500
2343P	Santa Fe F-3 Powered A Unit	(2)	65
2343T	Santa Fe F-3 Dummy A Unit	(3)	65
2343C	Santa Fe F-3 Dummy B Unit	(2+)	75
2344P	NYC F-3 Powered A Unit	(3)	70
2344T	NYC Dummy A Unit	(3+)	70
2344C	NYC Dummy B Unit	(3)	80
2345P	Western Pacific F-3 Powered A Unit	(3+)	175
2345T	Western Pacific F-3 Dummy A Unit	(4)	175
2346	Boston & Maine GP-7	(4)	85
2347	C&O GP-7	(5)	300
2348	Minn & St. Louis GP-9	(3+)	95

2349	Northern Pacific GP-9	(3)	95
2350	New Haven EP-5	(2+)	85
2351	Milwaukee Road EP-5	(3+)	125
2352	Pennsylvania EP-5	(3+)	150
2353P	Santa Fe F-3 Powered A Unit	(2)	75
2353T	Santa Fe F-3 Dummy A Unit	(3)	75
2354P	NYC F-3 Powered A Unit	(3)	85
2354T	NYC F-3 Dummy A Unit	(3+)	85
2355P	Western Pacific F-3 Powered A Unit	(3+)	175
2355T	Western Pacific F-3 Dummy A Unit	(4)	175
2356P	Southern F-3 Powered A Unit	(3)	150
2356T	Southern F-3 Dummy A Unit	(3+)	150
2356C	Southern F-3 Dummy B Unit	(3+)	175
2358	Great Northern EP-5	(4+)	250
2359	Boston & Maine GP-9	(3)	85
2360-1	GG-1	(4)	250
2360-25	GG-1 Brunswick green	(4)	275
2363P	Illinois Central F-3 Powered A Unit	(3)	150
2363C	Illinois Central F-3 Dummy B Unit	(3+)	150
2365	Chesapeake & Ohio GP-7	(3+)	95
2367P	Wabash F-3 Powered A Unit	(3)	135
2367C	Wabash F-3 Dummy B Unit	(3+)	135
2368P	Baltimore & Ohio F-3 Powered A Unit	(4)	275
2368C	Baltimore & Ohio F-3 Dummy B Unit	(4)	275
2373P	Canadian Pacific F-3 Powered A Unit	(4)	250
2373T	Canadian Pacific F-3 Dummy A Unit	(4)	250
2378P	Milwaukee Road F-3 Powered A Unit	(4)	275

No.	Description	Grade	Price
2378C	Milwaukee Road F-3 Dummy B Unit	(4)	275
2379P	Rio Grande F-3 Powered A Unit	(3)	165
2379C	Rio Grande F-3 Dummy B Unit	(3+)	165
2383P	Santa Fe F-3 Powered A Unit	(3)	65
2383T	Santa Fe F-3 Dummy A Unit	(2)	65
2400	Maplewood Pullman	(4)	45
2401	Hillside Observation	(4)	40
2402	Chatham Pullman	(4)	45
2403B	Tender	(4)	45
2404	Santa Fe Vista Dome	(3+)	30
2405	Santa Fe Pullman	(3+)	35
2406	Santa Fe Observation	(3+)	30
2408	Santa Vista Dome	(4)	30
2409	Santa Fe Pullman	(4)	35
2410	Santa Fe Observation	(4)	30
2412	Santa Fe Vista Dome	(3)	35
2414	Santa Fe Pullman	(3)	35
2416	Santa Fe Observation	(3)	30
2419	DL&W Work Caboose	(3)	25
2420	DL&W Work Caboose	(3)	25
2421	Maplewood Pullman	(2)	25
2422	Chatham Pullman	(2)	25
2423	Hillside Observation	(2)	20
2429	Livingston Pullman	(3)	35
2430	Pullman	(3+)	30
2431	Observation	(3+)	25
2432	Clifton Vista Dome	(2+)	25
2434	Newark Pullman	(2+)	25
2435	Elizabeth Pullman	(2+)	25
2436	Mooseheart Observation	(3)	35
2440	Observation	(3)	25
2441	Observation	(3)	25
2442	Pullman	(3)	25
2442	Clifton Vista Dome	(4)	45
2443	Observation	(3)	25
2444	Newark Pullman	(4)	55
2445	Elizabeth Pullman	(5-)	100
2446	Summit Observation	(4)	40
2454	Pennsylvania Boxcar	(4)	50
2460	Bucyrus Erie Crane Car	(3+)	45
2461	Transformer Car	(3)	30
2466T	Tender	(3)	30
2466W	Tender	(3)	30
2466WX	Tender	(4)	35
2481	Plainfield Pullman	(4+)	125
2482	Westfield Pullman	(4+)	125
2483	Livingston Observation	(4+)	125
2521	President McKinley Obsv	(3+)	85
2522	President Harrison Vista Dome	(3+)	85
2523	President Garfield Pullman	(3+)	95
2530	Baggage Car (B & O)	(2+)	60
2530	Baggage Car (OPerf)	(5)	150
2531	Silver Dawn Observation	(2)	35
2532	Silver Range Vista Dome	(2)	40
2533	Silver Cloud Pullman	(2+)	40
2534	Silver Bluff Pullman	(2+)	40
2541	Alexander Hamilton Observation	(3)	95
2542	Betsy Ross Vista Dome	(3+)	95
2543	William Penn Pullman	(3+)	95
2544	Molly Pitcher Pullman	(3+)	95
2550	Baltimore & Ohio Budd	(4)	100
2551	Banff Park Observation	(4)	100
2552	Skyline 500 Vista Dome	(4)	100
2553	Blair Manor Pullman	(4+)	175
2554	Craig Manor	(4+)	175
2555	Sunoco Tank Car	(3+)	25
2559	Baltimore & Ohio Budd	(3+)	85
2560	Lionel Lines Crane	(4)	35
2561	Vista Valley Observation	(4)	100
2562	Regal Pass Vista Dome	(4)	115
2563	Indian Falls Pullman	(4)	115
2625	Irvington (1946-1949)	(3)	65
2625	Irvington (1950)	(4+)	100
2625	Madison (1947)	(3)	65
2625	Manhattan (1947)	(3)	65
2627	Madison (1948,1949)	(3)	65
2627	Madison (1950)	(4+)	100
2628	Manhattan (1948, 1949)	(3)	65
2628	Manhattan (1950)	(4+)	100
2671W	Tender	(3)	35
2671WX	Tender	(4)	45
2755	Sunoco Tank Car aluminum	(3)	25
2758	Pennsylvania Automobile Boxcar	(2)	20
2855	Sunoco Tank Car	(4)	65
3330	Flat Car w/Operating Sub Kit	(3)	50
3330-100	Operating Submarine Kit	(4)	125
3349	Turbo Launching Car	(3)	20
3356	Operating Horse Car w/Corral	(2)	35
3356-2	Operating Horse Car	(4)	25
3356-150	Operating Horse Car Corral	(5)	125
3357	Cop and Hobo Car	(2)	25
3359-55	Lionel Lines Twin Dump Car	(3)	30
3360	Burro Crane	(3)	45
3366	Operating Circus Car w/ Corral	(3+)	75
3370	Sheriff & Outlaw Car	(3+)	35
3376	Operating Giraffe Car	(2)	25
3376-160	Operating Giraffe Car	(4)	35
3386	Operating Giraffe Car		NOB
3409	Operating Helicopter Car		NOB

3410	Operating Helicopter Car		NOB
3413	Mercury Capsule Car	(3)	35
3419	Operating Helicopter Car	(2+)	25
3424	Wabash Brakeman Car	(2)	20
3428	US Mail Car	(3+)	30
3429	USMC Helicopter Launch Car		NOB
3434	Operating Chicken Car	(3)	30
3435	Aquarium Car	(3)	60
3444	Erie Animated Gondola	(3)	40
3454	PRR Merchandise Car	(3+)	30
3460	Flatcar W/Trailors	(3)	25
3470	Aerial Target Launching Car	(3)	25
3474	Western Pacific Operating Boxcar	(3)	25
3484	PRR Operating Box Car	(3)	20
3484-25	Santa Fe Operating Boxcar	(3)	20
3494-1	NYC Operating Boxcar	(3)	25
3494-150	Missouri Pacific Operating Boxcar	(3+)	35
3494-275	State Of Maine Operating Boxcar	(2+)	30
3494-550	Monon Operating Boxcar	(4)	85
3494-625	Soo Operating Boxcar	(4)	85
3509	Satellite Car		NOB
3510	Satellite Car		NOB
3512	Operating Fireman and Ladder Car	(3)	35
3519	Operating Satellite Car	(3)	25
3530	Operating Generator Car	(3)	30
3535	AEC Security Car	(3)	25
3540	Operating Radar Car	(4)	40
3545	Operating TV Monitor Car	(4)	40
3562-1	Operating Barrel Car	(3)	25
3562-25	Operating Barrel Car	(2)	20
3562-50	Operating Barrel Car	(2)	20
3562-75	Operating Barrel Car	(3)	25

3619	Helicopter Reconnaissance Car	(3+)	40
3665	Minuteman Missile Launching Car	(3)	30
3666	Cannon Box Car		NOB
3672	Operating Bosco Milk Car	(3+)	75
3820	Operating Submarine Car		NOB
3830	Operating Submarine Car	(3)	30
3854	Pennsylvania Merchandise Car	(4)	85
3927	Track Cleaning Car	(2)	20
4357	SP Caboose	(4)	45
4452	Pennsylvania Gondola	(4)	45
4454	Baby Ruth Box Car	(4)	45
4457	Pennsylvania Caboose	(4)	40
5459	Operating Dump Car	(4)	45
6014	Chun King Box Car	(?)	?
6014-60	Bosco Box Car	(4)	35
6014-100	Airex Box Car	(3)	25
6014-150	Wix Box Car	(4+)	75
6014-410	Frisco Box Car	(4)	15
6017-50	USMC Caboose	(3)	35
6017-85	Lionel Lines Caboose	(4)	45
6017-100	Boston & Maine Caboose	(3+)	25
6017-200	US Navy Caboose	(4+)	50
6020W	Tender	(3)	25
6024-60	RCA Whirlpool Box Car	(4)	35
6026T	Tender	(3)	20
6026W	Tender	(3)	25
6027	Alaska Caboose	(4)	35
6044-1X	McCall/Nestle's Boxcar	(5)	200
6050	Libby's Tomato Juice Boxcar		NOB
6119	DL&W Work Caboose	(2+)	20
6119-25	DL&W Work Caboose	(3)	20
6119-50	DL&W Work Caboose	(3)	20
6119-100	DL&W Work Caboose	(3)	20
6119-125	Lionel Rescue Unit		NOB

6151	Flat Car With Range Patrol Truck	(3)	30
6162-60	Alaska Gondola	(3)	40
6162-110	NYC Blue Gondola	(3)	20
6162-110	NYC Red Gondola (Paste-On-Label)	(4+)	35
6175	Flat Car W/Rocket	(3)	25
6220	Santa Fe GM Switcher	(3)	60
6250	Seaboard GM Switcher	(3)	60
6257X	SP Caboose	(4)	50
6262	Wheel Car	(3)	25
6264	Lumber Car	(4+)	65
6311	Flat Car With Pipes	(?)	?
6315	Gulf Tank Car	(2)	25
6343	Barrel Ramp Car	(3)	20
6346-56	Alcoa Covered Hopper	(3)	30
6352-25	Ice Car	(5)	75
6356	NYC Stock Car	(2+)	20
6357-50	AT&SF	(4+)	125
6362	Railway Truck Car	(3+)	30
6376	Circus Car	(3)	25
6401	Flat Car	(5)	100
6403B	Tender	(3+)	45
6405	Flat W/Trailer	(4)	35
6406	Flat Car With Single Auto		NOB
6407	Flat Car With Missile	(5-)	125
6408	Flat Car With Pipes		NOB
6409-25	Flat Car With Pipes		NOB
6413	Mercury Capsule Car	(3+)	35
6414	Automobile Car (B&O)	(2+)	25
6414	Automobile Transport Car (OPerf)	(4)	45
6414	Automobile Transport Car (OPix)	(3)	30
6414	RS 6414 on end flap (WB)	(4)	75
6414-25	Four Autos	(4)	65
6414-85	Automobile Transport Car	(5-)	100

180

Number	Description		Value
6416	Boat Loader	(3+)	50
6417	NYC Porthole Caboose	(2)	20
6417-50	Lehigh Valley Caboose	(3)	35
6418	Machinery Car	(3+)	35
6419-100	DL&W Work Caboose	(3)	20
6420	DL&W Work Caboose	(3)	35
6424-110	Flat Car With Two Autos	(2+)	25
6427-60	Virginian	(4)	85
6427-500	Pennsylvania Caboose	(4+)	100
6429	DL&W	(4+)	150
6430	Flat Car W/Trailers	(3)	25
6431	Piggy-Back Car w/Midge Toy Tractor	(3+)	75
6434	Poultry Car	(3)	30
6436	Lehigh Valley Hopper	(2+)	20
6436-25	Lehigh Valley Hopper	(2+)	20
6436-110	Lehigh Valley Hopper	(3)	25
6436-500	Lehigh Valley Hopper	(4+)	100
6440	Pullman	(3)	30
6441	Observation	(3)	30
6442	Pullman	(3)	30
6443	Observation	(3)	30
6445	Fort Knox Gold Bullion Car	(3+)	35
6446	N&W Covered Hopper (B&O)	(2+)	20
6446	Cement Car (OPR)	(4+)	35
6446-25	N&W Covered Hopper	(2+)	20
6446-60	Lehigh Valley Covered Hopper	(5-)	85
6447	Pennsylvania Caboose	(5-)	125
6448	Exploding Box Car	(2+)	20
6454	Baby Ruth Boxcar	(4)	75
6460	Bucyrus Erie Crane Car	(2)	25
6461	Transformer Car	(3+)	25
6462-500	NYC Gondola (Girls Train)	(4+)	100
6463	Rocket Fuel Tank Car	(3+)	35
6464-1	Western Pacific Boxcar	(2)	30
646-25	Great Northern Boxcar	(2)	25
6464-50	Minn. & St. Louis Boxcar	(2)	25
6464-75	Rock Island Boxcar	(3)	25
6464-100	Western Pacific Boxcar (Yellow Feather)	(3)	35
6464-125	New York Central Boxcar	(3)	35
6464-150	Missouri Pacific Boxcar	(3)	40
6464-175	Rock Island Boxcar (50, Silver, Overstamp)	(3+)	30
6464-175	Rock Island Boxcar (175 Stamped on Box)	(4+)	65
6464-175	Rock Island Boxcar (C)	(3)	20
6464-200	Pennsylvania Boxcar (B&O)	(3+)	40
6464-200	Pennsylvania Boxcar (C)	(3)	30
6464-225	Southern Pacific Boxcar	(2+)	30
6464-250	Western Pacific Boxcar (B&O)	(5)	175
6464-250	Western Pacific Boxcar (WB)	(3)	40
6464-275	State of Maine Boxcar	(3)	35
6464-300	Rutland Boxcar	(3)	40
6464-325	Sentinel Boxcar	(4)	85
6464-350	MKT Boxcar	(4)	75
6464-375	Central of Georgia Boxcar (B&O)	(3)	30
6464-375	Central of Georgia Boxcar (WB)	(2)	25
6464-400	Baltimore & Ohio Boxcar (B&O)	(3)	30
6464-400	Baltimore & Ohio Boxcar (C)	(3)	25
6464-425	New Haven Boxcar	(2)	20
6464-450	Great Northern Boxcar (B&O)	(3)	30
6464-450	Great Northern Boxcar (WB)	(2)	25
6464-475	Boston & Maine Boxcar	(3)	20
6464-475	Boston & Maine Boxcar (OPerf)	(4+)	35
6464-500	Timken Boxcar (B&O)	(3)	30
6464-500	Timken Boxcar (C)	(3)	25
6464-510	NYC Pacmaker Boxcar (Girls Train)	(4+)	150
6464-515	Katy Boxcar Type	(4+)	150
6464-525	Minn. & St. Louis Boxcar	(3)	20
6464-650	Rio Grande Boxcar (B&O)	(3)	40
6464-650	Rio Grande Boxcar (WB)	(3)	35
6464-700	Santa Fe Boxcar (OPI)	(3+)	35
6464-700	Santa Fe Boxcar (WB)	(3)	30
6464-725	New Haven Boxcar (OPix)(735 on box)	(2+)	20
6464-725	New Haven Boxcar (WB)(735 on box)	(3+)	25
6464-725	New Haven Boxcar (C)(425 on box)	(4)	40
6464-825	Alaska Boxcar	(4)	75
6464-900	NYC Boxcar	(3)	25
6464-1965	TCA Pittsburgh Boxcar	(4)	45
6466W	Tender	(3)	20
6466WX	Tender	(4)	35
6467	Miscellaneous Car	(3)	20
6468	Baltimore & Ohio Boxcar	(2)	20
6468X	Baltimore & Ohio Boxcar	(5-)	95
6469	Liquified Gas Car	(4)	35
6475	Pickle Car	(2)	20
6475	Libbys Pickle Car		NOB
6475	Heinz Pickle Car		XXX
6477	Miscellaneous Car w/ Pipes	(3)	20
6480	Exploding Boxcar		NOB
6500	Beechcraft Bonanza Transport Car (OPix)	(4+)	85
6500	Beechcraft Bonanza Transport Car(OPP)	(5-)	85
6501	Jet Boat Car	(3+)	35
6502	Girder Car/Black/White		NOB
6502-50	Girder Car/Blue/White		NOB
6502-75	Girder Car/Light Blue/White		NOB
6511	Flatcar w/Pipes	(3)	20

6512	Cherry Picker Car	(3+)	35	6657	Rio Grande Caboose	(3+)	45	6816	Flatcar w/Bulldozer	(4)	65
6517	Lionel Lines Bay Window Caboose	(2)	25	6660	Boom Car	(4)	25	6816-100	Bulldozer (B&O)	(5-)	NRS
6517-75	Erie Bay Window Caboose	(4)	100	6670	Derrick Car	(4)	25	6816-100	Bulldozer (Photo Box*)	(5)	NRS
6517-1966	TCA 1966 Conv. Car	(4)	35	6672	Refrigerator Car	(3)	25	6817	Flatcar w/Scraper	(4)	65
6518	Transformer Car	(3+)	35	6736	Detroit & Mackinac Hopper	(3+)	30	6817-100	Scraper (PWB)	(5-)	NRS
6519	Allis Chalmers Car	(3+)	25	6800	Airplane Car (B&O)	(3)	35	6817-100	Scraper (Photo Box)	(5)	NRS
6520	Searchlight Car	(3)	20	6800	Airplane Car (OPix)	(4+)	50	6819	Flat Car With Helicopter	(3+)	30
6530	Fire And Safety Training Car	(3+)	35	6800-60	Airplane	(4)	65	6820	Missile Transport Car	(4)	60
6544	Missile Launching Car	(3)	25	6801	Flat Car With Boat	(3)	25	6821	Flat Car With Crates	(3+)	25
6556	Katy Stock Car	(4)	55	6801-50	Flat Car With Boat	(3+)	30	6822	Nightcrew Searchlight Car	(3)	20
6557	Lionel Smoking Caboose	(3)	40	6801-75	Flat Car With Boat	(3)	25	6823	Flat Car With Missiles	(3)	25
6560	Bucyrus Erie Crane Car	(2)	20	6802	Flat Car With Girders	(4)	20	6824	USMC First Aid Medical Car		NOB
6560-25	Bucyrus Erie Crane Car	(3)	20	6803	Flat Car With Military Units	(3+)	45	6824-50	First Aid Medical Car		NOB
6561	Cable Car	(3)	25	6804	Flat Car With Military Units	(3+)	45	6825	Flat Car With Trestle	(3)	20
6572	Railway Express Car (B&O)	(3+)	35	6805	Radioactive Waste	(3+)	35	6826	Flat Car w/Christmas Trees	(3+)	30
6572	Railway Express Car (OPix)	(3)	30	6806	Flat Car With Military Units	(3+)	45	6827	Flat Car With P&H Steam Shovel	(3)	45
6630	Missile Launcher		NOB	6807	Flat Car With Military Unit	(3)	35	6827	Power Shovel	(3)	35
6640	USMC Missile Launcher		NOB	6808	Flat Car With Military Units	(3+)	45	6828	Flat Car With P&H Crane	(3)	45
6650	Missile Launching Flat Car	(3)	25	6809	Flat Car With Military Units	(3+)	45	6828	Truck Crane	(3)	35
6651	USMC Cannon Car		NOB	6810	Flat Car With Van	(3)	25	6830	Flat Car With Submarine	(3+)	35
				6812	Track Maintenance Car	(3)	25	6844	Flat Car With Missiles	(3)	25
				6814	First Aid Medical Car	(3)	30				

Note:

? Indicates not sure if box exists.

* Refers to box with photograph of item on the end flap.

RS Indicates rubber-stamped lettering.

MC Indicates master carton.

Sources

Auctions

Christie's
219 East 67th Street
New York, New York 10021
212-606-0543

Ted Mauer
1931 North Charlotte Street
Pottstown, Pa. 19464

Lloyd Ralston Gallery
173 Post Road
Fairfield, Ct. 06430
203-255-1233

Sotheby's
1334 York Ave.
New York, New York 10021
212-6067424

Books and Magazines

Carstens Publications
PO Box 700
Newton, New Jersey 07860
201-383-3355

Chilton Book Co.
201 King of Prussia Road
Radnor, Pa. 19089

Garden Railways
PO Box 61461
Denver, Co. 80206
1-303-733-4779

Kalmbach Publishing
PO Box 1612
Waukesha, Wis. 53187

O Gauge Railroading
PO Box 239
Nazareth, Pa. 18064

S-Gaugian
Heimberger Publishing Co.
7236 West Madison Street
Forest Park, Ill. 60130

TM Books and Video
Box 279
New Buffalo, Mi. 49117
1-800-892-2822

Trainmaster
PO Box 1499
Gainesville, Fla. 32602

Electronics

Dallee Electronics
10 Witmer Road
Lancaster, Pa. 17602

Depotronics
PO Box 2093
Warrendale, Pa. 15086
412-776-4061

QSI Industries Inc.
2575 Kathryn St. #25
Hillsboro, Oregon 97124
503-591-5786

Ott Machine Services
118 East Ash Street
Lombard, Ill. 60148

Layout Construction

Don Cardiff
St Charles, Ill.

Create-A-Pike
Barillaro Trains
19 Sillmanville Road
Colchester, Ct. 06415

Clark Dunham
Stonebridge Road
Pottersville, New York 12860
518-494-3688

Don Danuser
Box 62
Hood, Va. 22723
703-948-4279

Layouts Unlimited, Inc.
PO Box 926
Valley Stream, New York 11580
516-593-1580

Manufacturers

Aristo-Craft
346 Bergen Ave.
Jersey City, New Jersey 07304

Bachmann Industries
1400 East Erie Ave.
Philadelphia, Pa. 19124
215-533-1600

Bowser Manufacturing
21 Howard Street
Montoursville, Pa. 17754

K-Line Electric Trains
PO Box 2831
Chapel Hill, North Carolina 27515
800-866-9986

LGB of America
6444 Nancy Ridge Drive
San Diego, Ca. 92121

Lionel Trains, Inc.
50625 Richard W Blvd.
Chesterfield, Michigan 48051
313-949-4100

Marketing Corp. of America
Box 225
Birmingham, Michigan 48012
313-288-5155

Marklin Inc.
PO Box 51319
New Berlin, Wis. 53151

Marx Trains
c/o Jim Flynn
209 East Butterfield Road
Suite 228
Elmhurst, Ill. 60126
708-941-3843

McCoy Manufacturing
PO Box 444
Kent, Washington 98032
206-852-5595

MTH Electric Trains
9693 Gerwig Lane
Columbia, Md. 21046

Pride Lines
651 West Hoffman Ave.
Lindenhurst, New York 11757
516-225-0033

Putt Trains
PO Box 463
Orwell, Ohio 44076

Red Caboose
PO Box 2490
Longmont, Co. 80502
303-772-8813

Right-of-Way Industries
1145 Highbrook Street
Akron, Ohio 44301
216-535-9200

Charles Ro Supply Co.
347 Pleasant Street
Malden, Ma. 02148

Third Rail
138 West Cambell Ave.
Cambell, Ca. 95008
408-866-1727

Toy Train Historical Foundation
20700 Ventura Blvd.
Suite 205
Woodland Hills, Ca. 91364

Train Express
4365 West 96th Street
Indianapolis, Indiana 46268
317-879-9300

Weaver Models
177 Wheatley Ave.
Northumberland, Pa. 17857

Williams Electric Trains
8835 F-Columbia Parkway
Columbia, Md. 21045
410-997-7766

Charles C. Wood
PO Box 179
Hartford, Ohio 44424
216-772-5177

Mobil Displays

Great Train Shows, Inc.
PO Box 126
Cochranton, Pa. 16314
814-425-3696

Operating Layouts

All Aboard S-Gauge Railroad
1952 Landis Valley Road
Lancaster, Pa. 17601
717-393-0850

Carnegie Science Center
Pittsburgh, Pa. 15212
412-237-3337

Children's Museum
Indianapolis, Indiana

Choo Choo Barn
Rt. 741
Strasburg, Pa. 17575

Entertrainment
Mall of America
Bloomington, Minn. 55425
612-851-9211

Lionel Visitors Center
Chesterfield, Michigan
313-949-4100

Lionel Railroad Club
10236 West Fond du Lac Ave.
Milwaukee, Wis. 53223
414-353-8840

Lionel Railroad Club
c/o Gary Muller
9212 Dana Dale Ct.
St. Louis, Mo. 63123
314-631-0233

Lionel Railroad Club
c/o Tom Wilburn
739 Linden Court
San Bruno, Ca. 94066
415-588-5535

Train Collectors Museum
Paradise Lane
Strasburg, Pa. 17575

Museum of Science & Industry
Chicago, Ill.

Roadside America
Roadside Drive
Shartlesville, Pa. 19554
215-488-6241

Trainland USA
Colfax, Iowa 50054
515-674-3813

Valley Junction Train Station & Museum
401 Railroad Place
West Des Moines, Iowa 50625
515-274-4424

Train Clubs

American Flyer Collectors Club
PO Box 13269
Pittsburgh, Pa. 15243

Lionel Operating Train Society
Box 62240
Cincinnati, Ohio 45241

Lionel Collectors Club of America
PO Box 479
La Salle, Ill. 61301

National Association of S Gaugers
c/o Mike Ferraro
280 Gordon Road
Matawan, New Jersey 07747

National Model Railroad Assoc.
4121 Cromwell Road
Chattonooga, Tn. 37421
615-892-2846

Toy Train Operating Society
25 West Walnut Street
Suite 308
Pasadena, Ca. 91103
1-818-578-0673

Train Collectors Association
PO Box 248
Strasburg, Pa. 17579

Train Shows

Great American Train Show
PO Box 1745
Lombard, Ill. 60148
708-834-0652

Greenberg Shows, Inc.
7566 Main Street
Sykesville, Md. 21784
410-795-7447

Northern Jersey Train-O-Rama
c/o Donald Brill
39 6th Street
Dover, New Jersey 07801

St. Vincent DePaul's Train Show
1510 DePaul Street
Elmont, Long Island,
New York 11003
516-352-2127

The Westchester Toy & Train Assoc., Inc.
217-36 50th Ave.
Bayside, New York 11364
1-718-228-6282

York Train Show
c/o Jules Ermel
65 Arbor Road
Cinnaminson, New Jersey 08077
609-829-4222

Vehicles, Structures & Figures

Arttista Accessories
1616 South Franklin Street
Philadelphia, Pa. 19148

Buildings Unlimited
PO Box 239
Nazareth, Pa. 18064

Chapman Creations
3379 Route 46
Intervale Gardens Apt. 10B
Parsippany, NJ. 07054
201-299-8611

Design Preservations
Box 280
Crestone, Co. 81131

Eastwood Automobilia
580 Lancaster Ave.
Malvern, Pa. 19355
215-640-1450

Pioneer Valley Models
PO Box 4928
Holyoke, Ma. 01041

Steam-Era Structures Co.
PO Box 54285
Cincinnati, Ohio 45254

Triple Diamond Replicas Inc.
2211 South Mt. Prospect
Des Plaines, Ill. 60018

Brasilia Press
PO Box 2023
Elkhart, Indiana 46515

Videos

Encore Entertainment
626 South Main
Frankenmuth, Mi. 48734
517-652-8881

Pentrex
2652 East Walnut Street
Pasadena, Ca. 91107
818-793-3400

The Train Station
12 Romaine Road
Mountain Lakes, New Jersey 07046
201-263-1979

TM Books & Video
Box 279
New Buffalo, Michigan 49117
219-879-2822

Video Rails
5076 Santa Fe
San Diego, Ca. 92109
619-581-0303

Additional Information

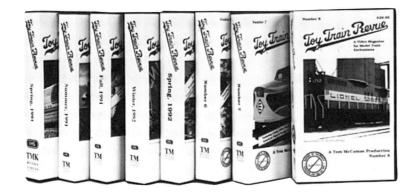

The *Toy Train Revue* video magazine is devoted to every aspect of toy trains. Each show is a snappy 60 minutes of lay-outs, collections, interviews, product reviews, operating tips, and factory tours – a great mix of toy train action, how-tos, and commentary.

Produced by well known toy train video producer, Tom McComas. The *Toy Train Revue* video magazine is both entertaining and informative. It may be purchased by subscription or individually, as each issue is released.
To order, call 1-800-892-2822

The *Toy Train Revue Journal* is a market report, tip sheet, and price guide all rolled into one quarterly magazine – the essential companion for the toy train collector and operator.

Our hobby has changed dramatically over the past few years and not all the changes have been for the good. Unscrupulous practices like selling fakes and re-productions as originals are costing innocent collectors thousands of dollars. The *Toy Train Revue Journal* addresses these issues and others which are crucial to the growth of the hobby.

The *TTRJ* also contains articles on collecting and operating toy trains, what's hot and what's not, and price guide updates. It is current, relevant, and necessary, ideal for both the beginner and seasoned collector.
To order, call 1-800-892-2822.

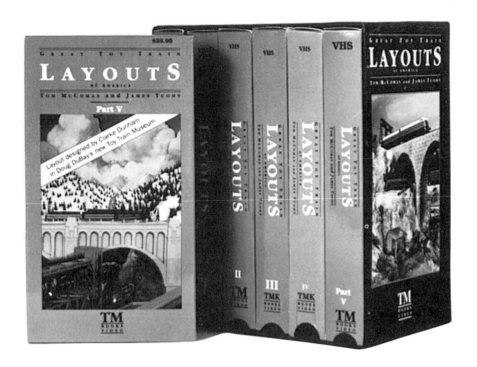

This six-part video series is an in-depth study of the most elaborate model train layouts in America. Almost six hours of action plus interviews with the layout builders. Trains and accessories of every era and almost every manufacturer. Each 45 to 55 minute show is filled with tips and hints and insights on how the experts build layouts.

Part two was chosen by *People Magazine* as one of the ten best videos of the year. If you are thinking about building a layout, or just enjoy good stories about toy trains and the people who love them, this series is a must. **To order call 1-800-892-2822.**

A delightful and innovative video. Thirty minutes of toy trains, real trains, real animals, kids singing, rockets to the moon, fireworks – even a brief appeal for environmental awareness. Fast-paced action that will keep your kids (and older kids, too) enchanted time and time again.

This video is a marvelous way to introduce your kids to the fun and excitement of toy trains. They will laugh, they will learn and they will want to watch it again.

I Love Toy Trains replaced *Thomas The Tank* as my kids favorite video. Best babysitter in town." Michael Salnick, Palm Beach, Fla. **To order, call 1-800-892-2822**

For free TM catalog, call:
1-800-892-2822